Becoming Human Again

Becoming Human Again
The Theological Life of Gustaf Wingren

Bengt Kristensson Uggla

Translated by Daniel M. Olson

CASCADE Books • Eugene, Oregon

BECOMING HUMAN AGAIN
The Theological Life of Gustaf Wingren

Copyright © 2016 Bengt Kristensson Uggla. All rights reserved. Except for brief quotations in critical publications or reviews, no part of this book may be reproduced in any manner without prior written permission from the publisher. Write: Permissions, Wipf and Stock Publishers, 199 W. 8th Ave., Suite 3, Eugene, OR 97401.

Cascade Books
An Imprint of Wipf and Stock Publishers
199 W. 8th Ave., Suite 3
Eugene, OR 97401

www.wipfandstock.com

PAPERBACK ISBN: 978-1-62032-283-3
HARDCOVER ISBN: 978-1-4982-8867-5
EBOOK ISBN: 978-1-5326-0369-3

Cataloguing-in-Publication data:

Names: Uggla, Bengt Kristensson. | Olson, Daniel M., translator.

Title: Becoming human again : the theological life of Gustaf Wingren / Bengt Kristensson Uggla ; translated by Daniel M. Olson. | Gustaf Wingren : människan och teologin. English.

Description: Eugene, OR : Cascade Books, 2016 | Includes bibliographical references and index.

Identifiers: ISBN 978-1-62032-283-3 (paperback) | ISBN 978-1-4982-8867-5 (hardcover) | ISBN 978-1-5326-0369-3 (ebook)

Subjects: LSCH: Wingren, Gustaf, 1910–2000. | Theologians—Sweden—Biography.

Classification: BX8080.W554 U45 2016 (paperback) | BX8080.W554 U45 (ebook)

Manufactured in the U.S.A.   07/07/16

Contents

1 **Entering Wingren's Theological Life** | 1
   Our Personal Beginnings | 2
   Narratives and Confrontations | 7
   Contextualization | 18
   Engaging with Wingren's Works | 25

2 **The First Confrontation** | 33
   The Battle for the Professorial Chair | 33
   The Apostasy | 48
   Attack! | 52
   "The Operation Was a Success, but the Patient Died" | 60

3 **Sources** | 70
   Nygren's Grand Narrative of Pure Christian Love | 72
   Cracks in the Historical Foundations | 79
   Sleepless in Basel | 96
   Berlin 1938 | 106

4 **The Practical Turn** | 116
   Science versus Science | 119
   Hermeneutics as Practical Philosophy | 131
   A Concrete Systematic Theology | 145
   Grain-of-Wheat Eschatology | 153

5 Metamorphosis and Recontextualization | 167
A Stranger in 1968 | 170
A New Colleague Enters the Scene: Greta Hofsten | 181
Hermeneutical Mediations: Continuity through Change | 195
Is There a University in Valdemarsvik? | 209

6 The Final Academic Battlefield | 214
Echoes from 1949 | 215
Quarreling Professors | 231
Confusions: Lack of Social Contextualization | 241
The Romantic Narrative: Continental Thinking | 247

7 Systematic Theology Turned Critique of Civilization | 255
"If a Baptized Person Runs a Hot Dog Stand . . ." | 260
Critique of the Ideology of Growth | 266
Creation Theology Becomes Ecological Theology | 282
Shifting Theological Metaphors | 290

8 "This Plague of Egocentricity" | 297
Complicated Relationships with the Church | 302
"Turn Your Face towards the Storm and Sing Heave-Ho!" | 325
A Church without the Middle Ages? | 342
Being for Others | 360

Acknowledgments | 367
Postscript to the English Edition | 371
Literature and Other Sources | 373
Index | 387

1

Entering Wingren's Theological Life

THIS BOOK DEALS WITH Gustaf Wingren (1910–2000), one of the most influential and creative Swedish theologians of the twentieth century. I became acquainted with him around 1980, after he had retired. I had known about Wingren before then, and attended several of his many public lectures during the latter half of the 1970s. At that time in Sweden, Wingren's name was on the lips of many, and at several of the public events at which he lectured I was given the opportunity to speak to him briefly. It was, however, not until I had left Gothenburg, where I had started my academic studies, and moved to Lund in January 1982 that I embarked on a more personal relationship with him.

My years in Lund came to have far-reaching effects on my worldview. The most important influence on my intellectual development during that period was not, however, the formal academic coursework. The opportunities for informal education and personal cultivation, which were still so much a part of the culture of that city and its university, had a far greater impact on me. I truly enjoyed the way that unexpected learning adventures could occur at almost any time or place in the ancient, spired city of Lund. I knew that I shared this experience with many others, but did not realize that even Wingren had once been overwhelmed by the same dizzying excitement for learning. Fifty-five years earlier, in 1927, at the tender age of sixteen, he had arrived in Lund on the night train one warm summer morning. He would remain there, in what he considered to be the spiritual capital of Sweden, for the rest of his life. As for me, I left after less than five years.

Our Personal Beginnings

I do not remember exactly when it was, but sometime in January 1982, during my first few weeks in Lund, I was invited to the home of Gustaf Wingren and his second wife, Greta Hofsten (1927–96). Over time, their intellectual collaboration developed to such a degree that they were almost inseparable. The professor, who had retired five years earlier, wanted to discuss theology with me. He said it with an eagerness that should have piqued my curiosity about what awaited me, but I was a novice at the time. Nonetheless, I did prepare for our meeting by reading several of his most important works. I rode my bicycle through the cobblestoned streets of central Lund to the high-rise building at Warholms väg 6B, and climbed the narrow staircase to the second floor. Gustaf, in his characteristic knitted sweater, was already waiting at the top of the stairs. The apartment door stood ajar on the left side of the hallway behind him, as it would always be whenever I came to visit during my years in Lund. On this particular occasion, however, I entered a completely new and unknown environment for the first time.

As I entered the apartment, I was struck by the spartan furnishing and sparse decor. To the left of the main hallway were two bedrooms, where the Hofsten-Wingrens each had their own little cubbyhole, furnished in the same way with a narrow single bed, a bedside table, and, I believe, some sort of wardrobe. Greta's room also contained a small desk. Straight on down the hallway was the living room, where a pair of old beds had been made into a rather uncomfortable sitting area. Apart from that, the room was dominated by two substantial armchairs, both placed with their backs to the balcony windows to make use of the light for reading. On several tables, piles of books lay stacked one upon the other. Later I learned that the books were ordered in a sequence and that the order in which they lay would change according to the couple's shifting intellectual priorities and how their discussions had progressed. As soon as the books landed on their tables they were quickly devoured by the two voracious readers. It struck me that there was no television in the apartment; that probably guaranteed them the time for so much reading. The gracious warmth with which they received me made me feel welcome at once. However, in this cerebral home there was hardly any time for respite or rest.

Beyond the living room, at the back of the apartment, was another good-sized room, which served as Gustaf's study and library. His collection of books had been decimated six years earlier in the divorce settlement with his first wife, Signhild. The kitchen was equally as spartan, but blue doors on the cabinets gave some color to the room, and the small table under the window seemed to invite guests to meals and conversation. During my nearly five years in Lund, I partook in numerous lunch and dinner discussions at that little kitchen table. These were never large or elaborate parties. I cannot remember that we were ever more than four people seated around that table, although when I look back at my journals from those years, I realize that there were exceptions. The meal always began with Gustaf saying grace in Latin. The food was simple and in traditional Swedish style, and was washed down with *aquavit*.

On the day in January 1982 when I was first invited to the Wingren home, I looked forward eagerly to the opportunity to discuss theology with the world-famous theologian. I remember how Gustaf told a number of animated stories to help explain what he meant. In order to follow his reasoning, you had to pay careful attention to the tiny details as well as to the drastic leaps in the string of stories that carried his presentation forward. I can still see the excitement in his eyes and hear the engagement in his voice from this first private meeting. Most of all, I remember the level of energy in our discussion.

As we talked, Gustaf gradually became quite agitated, even furious. For the life of me, I could not understand why my questions, simple objections, and opinions brought out such a remarkable mixture of anger and amusement in him. The longer we spoke, the more our discussion developed into what seemed a magnificent quarrel. Evening fell, the apartment darkened, and finally, our discussion came to an end. Gustaf's wife, Greta, said a few friendly words to me as I departed, but the entire escapade left me rather crestfallen. I left Warholms väg with the definite feeling that our new friendship had already reached its end.

Several days later, Gustaf telephoned me. To my great surprise, he told me that he was eager to see me again. He sounded enthusiastic. "We must continue our talk," he declared. He said that he had found our discussion especially refreshing. When could I come back? Perplexed, I stood in my dormitory hallway with the telephone receiver in my hand. Slowly, I began to realize what sort of person I was dealing with. Gustaf Wingren was the sort who found odd enjoyment in confrontation. If there were not yet any burning conflicts in which he could become involved, he would create them on his own. And when the confrontations were over, he wove dramatic stories about them. His rhetoric was peppered with anecdotes that were as entertaining as they were pertinent, and he presented them carefully and painstakingly, one after the other. He seemed to use his stories as critical barbs to provoke and tease, in the hope of luring people into the arena of discourse. His use of narrative and his seeming desire to ridicule were inseparable. Through his fantastic tales about people and ideas in confrontation, Gustaf (and Greta, who after his retirement came to be his most important colleague, although she held no academic position) opened up a vast intellectual world for me—a world that in reality became my most important university during my years in Lund.[1]

I soon realized that the Gustaf Wingren with whom I had begun to socialize was in many respects a completely different person from the one earlier generations of Lund students and teachers had encountered as a professor, advisor, and colleague. Those who had attended the University in the 1960s always referred to their old teacher simply as "Wingren." When I met former students who had attended in the decades prior to the 1960s (and who were not much younger than their former advisor; several of them had by then become bishops in the Church of Sweden), they spoke of Professor Wingren. With few exceptions, members of both of these groups looked quite surprised when my contemporaries and I spoke about, and even addressed, their old professor simply as Gustaf. I now understand that I did not fully recognize the profound transformation the professor had undergone, personally as well as theologically. In the mid-1970s he shed his impeccable dark suit and carefully knotted

---

1. My confusing first encounter with the conflict-loving Wingren, including his surprising desire for continued contact after that, was not unique. Many others had similar experiences with him. Bengt Hallgren, one of his doctoral students who later became a bishop, relates a journal entry that he made on 30 April 1954: "I presented my essay on Luther and church discipline in the ethics seminar. Wingren said, 'Within Luther research, there is a lacuna, and it is church discipline. I know of no one who has been able to do research in this area, nor do present-day writers seem able to, either.' Discouraged, I went home to the traditional Walpurgis celebration at the Kalmar student association house." Yet, Hallgren then relates that three weeks later, he was summoned to Professor Wingren, who now wanted him to begin his dissertation work. Hallgren, "Käre Gustaf!," 101. In a similar way, former Archbishop of Sweden Bertil Werkström, who had also been one of Wingren's doctoral students, tells of how he once was invited together with a group of former doctoral students to meet with their old teacher. During the lively debate that took place that evening, Werkström took a rather passive role, and listened with interest to what the others had to say. The next morning, the group met for breakfast at the hotel. Wingren went straight to Werkström and said, "Bertil, you are a man without passion!" Werkström, "Minnesbilder," 106.

necktie for an outdoor hiking jacket, a knitted sweater, and practical, soft-soled shoes. In this new uniform, he bounded through the city on protest marches and other progressive events, which often had a strong presence of young people. Professor Wingren had undergone a metamorphosis and become Gustaf. This afforded me the opportunity to come into closer contact with him, but at the same time, I believe this also obscured my perception of him, so that I was not really aware of the discontinuities in his life and the complications that were characteristic of his earlier personal history. As a result, I underestimated the importance of the transformation his theology had undergone from the 1970s onward, when he had recontextualized the entirety of his theological system and transformed it into a critique of society. An innovative hermeneutical approach allowed him to recycle the theological sources and concepts that he had developed in an *academic* context by reconfiguring them according to a *social* frame of reference. Thus he generated an entire new series of books. This hermeneutical transformation is the focal point of this biography.

How did this happen? What were his personal and intellectual resources that made this transformation possible? The prerequisites for change may have lain dormant as a potential resource and seem to have intensified over a long period of time. Today, with the historical distance gained from a half-century of theoretical considerations, it is easier for us to realize that the changes that occurred in Wingren's theological agenda in the late 1940s were in fact integral parts of a more general *turn toward practical wisdom*, a scientific reorientation that also characterized the changes that occured in other disciplines within the humanities and social sciences during that period. For this study, I have taken my point of departure in an understanding of hermeneutics as a practical philosophy, inspired by Hans-Georg Gadamer (1900–2002), where interpretation is defined not as a pure theoretical method, but as *always already application* in concrete situations. This frame of reference makes it possible to place the practical turn that occurred in Wingren's theological agenda around 1950, and that was first made evident in his composite and challenging book *The Living Word: A Theological Study of Preaching and the Church* (1949/1960), into a broader philosophical context. In this work, he elaborated on not only a *theological hermeneutics* (that is, an interpretation theory for theology) but also a *hermeneutical theology* (a hermeneutically conveyed and contextually anchored comprehension of the phenomenon we refer to as Christianity).[2] I hold that it is in this particular book that we may identify the roots of two paradoxical lines of thought that were of profound importance for Wingren's interpretation of Christianity. These were the driving forces behind his extensive process of theological recontextualization during the 1970s and 1980s. First, he gained the insight that the continuity of the Christian faith can only be maintained through change (a theological hermeneutics); and second, the idea that the distinct character of this faith is inextricably bound to the capacity to manifest its radical openness toward creation (a hermeneutic theology). For this reason, it is no coincidence that the very concepts of *change* and *continuity*, together with the concepts of *openness* and *distinctness*, served as fundamental themes in the two books in which he manifested his process of theological recontextualization.[3] Moreover, this was not a matter of a compromise or a balancing act, but instead we are confronted with a radically dialectic figure of thought: the continuity of what we refer to as Christian faith can only be maintained *by* change, and the distinctness of this faith can only be maintained *through* openness.

Among the unique and essential sources of inspiration behind Wingren's theological path, there is one in particular that has been entirely overlooked in all of the literature about him. The fact is that the major inspiration for his theology of social critique that he started to develop from the age of sixty, and which became the theological program of the remaining decades of his life, emanated from a source outside of both academia and theology, namely, Greta Hofsten, his new life partner. Long before anyone else, she recognized the latent potential for social criticism embedded in Wingren's hermeneutically informed creation theology. Consequently, she also recognized the possibility of taking the theological texts he had originally developed within the academic sphere and rewriting them so that they could be applied in a new context, that of society.

I have thus chosen to structure this presentation from the perspective of how an *academic* frame of reference, which was the primary context of Wingren's theological work until the 1960s, was gradually replaced by a theology in which *social* contextualization became the primary

---

2. I use these concepts as they are presented by Jeanrond in *Theological Hermeneutics*.

3. Cf. the Swedish titles of Wingren's books *Continuity and Change* (*Växling och kontinuitet*, 1972) and *Creation and Gospel* (*Öppenhet och egenart*, 1979/1979, which means "Openness and Distinctness").

defining factor of his work. The question then follows as to how the third public sphere of theology, namely, that of the church, features in this description.[4] According to the conventional understanding of Wingren's theology, it might be considered somewhat provocative that I have left the issue of the church until last. However, against this prevalent view, I maintain that it is a misconception to characterize Wingren as a man of the church, whose primary and sole ambition was to deliver edification to communities of pious believers. In order to develop a comprehensive view of Wingren, we need to define him according to a broader intellectual view. Only if we recognize Wingren as a theologian who felt completely at home initially in an academic public sphere, and later in a social public sphere, will we be able to recognize the important contribution he made to a church that for long periods of his life he found it difficult to embrace. This is what I hope to make clear in chapter 8 of this book. Thus, not until the last chapter will I pose the critical question, what was Wingren's relationship to the church? Those with the patience to read that far will find an answer.

Narratives and Confrontations

Gustaf Wingren often stated, "For every situation in life, there is a story"—after which he would immediately begin to tell one. His intention with all of these stories was to cast new and unexpected light on particular contemporary situations. Throughout his life he delighted in tall stories, yarns, and academic anecdotes that combined the comic and burlesque with the deeply serious. Yet storytelling held a value that for him went far beyond entertainment or the purely didactical. Narrative was not a neutral medium filled with an already fixed and predetermined content, or a mere illustration of something already recognized. Instead, he was convinced that the stories themselves generate their own message. In narratives, the form and the content are inextricably bound together. Quite simply, there are things that are expressed best, or perhaps only, through storytelling. The philosopher Paul Ricoeur (1913–2005) argued convincingly that there is a basic ontological relationship between human identity and narrative: "Time becomes human time to the extent that it is organized after the manner of a narrative; narrative, in turn, is meaningful

---

4. In my presentation, I elaborate on the three publics of theology (society, academy, church), in accordance with Tracy, *The Analogical Imagination*.

to the extent that it portrays the features of temporal experience."[5] As human beings we would probably not be able to communicate, or even recognize who we are, without stories. The fundamental importance of narrative in Wingren's theology stretches from the meaning he ascribed to the parables of the *gospels* to the grand story of salvation history, which on a macro level configured his view of the Christian creed as well as the biblical canon. I would assert that Wingren was grounded in the firm and fundamental conviction that we cannot comprehend or talk about the Christian faith without telling stories.

During my years of intense conversations with Wingren, I heard many stories from his lips, but I also experienced the rise of a number of new stories *about* him as well as *by* him. I have included many of these stories in this book, not first and foremost because they are entertaining, but rather because I am convinced that they are of extraordinary importance if we want to understand the hermeneutical creation theology that Wingren developed, as well as his own intellectual temperament.

Wingren had a good sense of humor. Humor was, in fact, an integral part of his theology.[6] With delight he would quote Karl Barth (1886–1968), who once discovered that in a new, well-received book, Bishop John T. A. Robinson had actually copied the works of several German theologians. Thus, Barth stated crassly, "Here comes a man who scrapes the foam off three glasses of beer, splashes the drops into a fourth glass, and then sells it as the water of life."[7] When Wingren recounted this story, he relished each and every word: "three glasses of beer," of course, represent three important German theologians, "foam" emphasizes the superficiality of Robinson's analysis, "the water of life" is a double entendre, hinting both at its strong theological overtones and the cosmetic superficiality inherent in these false claims, and so on. Wingren recited such formulations with obvious delight. He enjoyed the force of each twist and turn in the story. Not even his fundamental theological disagreement with Barth (whom he so often mentioned in extraordinarily critical ways) obscured the admiration he felt for anyone who could achieve such a precise and subtle narrative configuration.

Once, on a train to Stockholm together with three colleagues from the Faculty of Theology at Lund University, Wingren and an older

5. Ricoeur, *Time and Narrative*, 1, 3.

6. Cf. Karlsson's discussion of the significance of humor in the theology of Wingren in *Predikans samtal*, 158–63.

7. Wingren, *Mina fem universitet* (1991), 88.

colleague spent a long time regaling each other with amusing stories about various faculty members. Finally, Wingren leaned toward his two younger travel companions and said, "No one will ever tell any funny stories about you two." The two younger colleagues proceeded to refute this insult to their perceived honor with long-winded accounts of all of the important tasks and duties they were managing: ". . . and while you've been out fooling around, we have been at our desks, taking care of our work!" Wingren sat quietly, listening, until they finished speaking. When they were finally silent, he leaned forward again and said, "*Now* I have got another funny story to tell!"

Whether or not this story is true, it demonstrates the narrative culture that Wingren propagated, as well as the quick wit (bordering on spitefulness) that often accompanied it and which he enjoyed. It must also be noted that he avoided administrative duties like the plague and tried to unload them onto his department colleagues. When his department's rotational duties nonetheless forced him to serve as chair of the department and faculty, the secretary had to work extremely hard to keep his administrative tasks under control. Nevertheless, in this anecdote about the train ride to Stockholm, he used a story to ensnare his colleagues, and then he incorporated multiple stories into one another like Russian *matryoshka* dolls: an event in which his colleagues are involved in telling stories becomes the starting point for a new story, which in turn becomes part of the story he is telling at the moment.

Understanding the point of such stories requires the listener to pay attention to the intrigue and the details subtly incorporated into the drama, and the listener must also be familiar with the cast of characters. Despite his humble background, knowing who the public characters were was something that had captivated Wingren's interest from his early boyhood. In his family home in the small town of Valdemarsvik, there had been no books, but there was a daily newspaper and yearly almanacs, to which he devoted great attention. "Already as a teenager, I could name all of the members of the Swedish parliament and their various political parties, all the members of the Swedish Academy and the Royal Academy of Science, all county governors, members of the Cabinet, and bishops."[8] Through dedicated study of personnel listings, the young reader of almanacs soon learned the intricate patterns of the most wide-ranging networks and root systems in the church as well as the academic world. This

---

8. Wingren, "Bredden gick förlorad" (1991), 123.

also provided him with the rare ability to predict imminent collisions between different agendas and positions. I remember how thrilled he was in a particular situation, when he had put two family trees, both of which he was quite familiar with, into juxtaposition, and suddenly realized that the person in question must be a direct descendant of Charles Darwin![9]

There is a close connection between Wingren's culture of narration and his pronounced appetite for intrigues in the broadest sense of the word. This interest was frequently focused on the complex interplay associated with various academic appointments. He took careful note of how the "players" moved and positioned themselves as the "game" proceeded. Like a football coach, he registered carefully all changes in the game and made observations from the field in his notebooks. His interest in the drama of the academic playing field is evident in these notebooks. For example, in the mid-1960s, he noted, "Ebeling has accepted Tübingen . . . Trilhaas has refused Munich . . . Possible that Gärtner would rather have . . . the Oslo faculty sought by . . . area experts . . ."[10] His great interest in strategic and tactical operations, evidenced by these sorts of notes, must be taken seriously in the reading of his publications and his actions as well. Nothing he said or wrote seems to have been done on a whim. Everything seems to have been consciously positioned in a dramatic context.

Wingren had a well-developed ability to interpret what was happening on the playing field, and his interest in the intrigue, which sustains the narrative function of stories, was melded together with what he himself described as an almost fanatical interest in the drama of real football matches. In his memoirs, he relates visiting the Grundtvig Højskole, a community college (*folkhøjskole*) in Hillerød, Denmark, to present a lecture. During his visit he snuck away from his host, Rector and Professor Ole Jensen, to the student lounge to enjoy a World Cup football match on television. He explained his actions in this way: "I take

---

9. The person in question was Lars Haikola, assistant professor of philosophy of religion at Lund University, later an academic leader at several institutions of higher learning, and University Chancellor in Sweden from 2010 to 2014. Haikola himself has confirmed that Wingren's conclusion was in fact true, with one modification. Haikola's maternal grandfather, Charles Earnest Overton, who also had Darwin as one of his Christian names, and Lars Haikola are in fact related to the more famous Charles Darwin, but through his "maternal grandfather's paternal grandfather's cousin—more or less."

10. Personal notebooks from the mid-1960s preserved in Gustaf Wingren's uncatalogued personal archives in the Lund University Library.

an almost pathological interest in such things."[11] In another section of his memoirs, he systematically employs football metaphors to describe the logic in academic interplay. He likens the appointments of university professors to "league finals" and speaks of "matches" that can be won or lost. When the "final whistle" has been blown on the "playing field," the "spectators" voice their reactions, sometimes even uttering accusations of "referee error." He even used these metaphors to describe his own experience and career. Unable to hide his disappointment, he states, "For a footballer to have to hear such a dressing-down about a victorious final play again and again, the gold medal—that is, the professorship—can be a bit heavy to wear."[12] His particular choice of football as metaphor is not by coincidence. More than once, Wingren bought a copy of the newspaper *Aftonbladet* (Evening News), flipped immediately to the sports pages, cut out the scores for the Swedish football league *Allsvenskan*—and then threw away the newspaper. Besides theology, football was the only thing of interest to him. Hence, for him, theology was like football—but without a ball. Wingren, of course, shared this great interest in football with many others, including many intellectuals. In his later years, philosopher and Nobel Prize–winning author Albert Camus (1913–60) is said to have surprised his intellectual friends by telling them he was grateful to football for teaching him the most about the difficult questions of life: battle, coincidence, and interaction on the field.[13]

Wingren's attraction to drama and narrative was also tied to his lifelong work with issues of exegetics and biblical theology. In particular, inspiration gained from biblical scholar Karl Ludwig Schmidt (1891–1956) and the form-critical school of exegesis helped him place the parables of the *gospels* at the heart of his interest in exegesis. Like a string of pearls, these short stories repeatedly show how Jesus acted, with comments added to explain the meaning. Often, these parables contain a critical moment of surprise in which Jesus suddenly turns the listener's expectations upside down. However, the narrative basis of Wingren's theological

11. Wingren, *Mina fem universitet* (1991), 153. In his private notebooks from his later years, Wingren departed from his otherwise strict focus on work-related notes and took it upon himself to write more about everyday diversions. When he did so, it was in particular his crazy interest in football that often was recorded, as for example during the World Cup matches of 1990, when he noted evening after evening: "TV night at ANNA's place (Scotland vs. Sweden in Genoa) . . . TV night at ANNA's (Costa Rica vs. Sweden in Genoa) . . . We visited Anna (TV, Cameroon vs. England) . . ."

12. Wingren, *Mina fem universitet* (1991), 25ff.

13. Eklund, "Bokkrönikan."

reflections, with its focus on drama and symbolism, also associated him with another theologian, Gustaf Aulén (1879-1977), by whom he had been strongly influenced but to whom he seldom referred, and against whom he never directed any serious criticism.[14]

Wingren's interest in narrative, drama, intrigue, and confrontation has also influenced his own written depictions of himself. In works such as *Creation and Gospel: The New Situation in European Theology* (1979/1979) and *My Five Universities: Memories* (1991), the narrative voice is evident when he presents his own theological position. Yet it must be kept in mind that in these autobiographical depictions Wingren's presentation is marked by a strong need to configure the story in his own particular way. Thus, anyone who attempts to write about Wingren faces the challenge of capturing Wingren together with the act of his storytelling—without being captured by his own story.

Wingren's interest in narrative and dramatic structure was also present in the particular way he wrote his books. First, he devoted considerable time to thinking through the overarching structure. When this was completed, he pinned the outline to the door of his office, where it thereafter served as a strategic map of the operations he was planning. He would then alternately think and write, chapter after chapter, following his outline to the letter, even down to the exact number of pages he had indicated for each section of the book. In the text that emerged, written by hand in his characteristic style (which resulted from his deformed right hand), he would add only those corrections that would fit on the pages of the manuscript, or on notes pasted onto the edges of the pages; then, finally, he would send it off to a secretary to have it typed.[15] As

---

14. In addition to Gustaf Aulén, there is evidence of noteworthy ties to other theologians, which Wingren himself mentioned only seldom, and then only fleetingly, such as Arvid Runestam and Torsten Bohlin. Göran Bexell has illustrated these ties in his *Teologisk etik i Sverige sedan 1920-talet*, 173-77.

15. Wingren never used a typewriter, and due to his difficult-to-read handwriting, he was dependent on help from others. During most of his marriage to his first wife, Signhild, she seems to have rewritten all of his manuscripts, in any case, during the years from 1942 to 1960. Toward the end of the 1960s, however, this task seems to have been transferred to the departmental secretaries, and the thanks that he made to them in the acknowledgment sections of his books were almost an art in themselves. In one book from 1968 we can read the following words: "Finally, the willing staff of the Theologicum: Mrs. Ylva Norrman, Mrs. Karin Wernant and Miss Ingrid Bengtsson—typed the final version of my manuscript. To them, I now say thank you." Wingren, *Einar Billing* (1968), 6, not included in the English translation. These formulations sound nonetheless subdued compared to the praises he directed toward Miss

a result, Wingren's books are usually very well organized. I would even posit that a good deal of their content and message is to be found in the very structure of the tables of contents. Yet anyone who develops a close familiarity with any of Wingren's works soon realizes that various sections often seem to have been placed under the wrong headings. Brilliant formulations, sometimes of an aphoristic nature, as well as analysis, along with summaries of central themes, seem to lie strewn arbitrarily throughout the text without any relation to the basic order of the book. In contrast to the table of contents, the actual content of the different sections of the book is not ordered in a particularly systematic way. It is as if the contents had been gathered together like a series of arguments, aphorisms, and narratives, and then placed arbitrarily, relatively independent of the overall order, in a way that in fact may resemble the manner in which the parables are ordered, and which vary considerably in the four gospels.

When Wingren attempted to defend himself in the debate that followed his book *The Silent Interpreter: What Theology Is and What It Ought to Be* (1981), he candidly confessed that his work certainly contained repetitions and unclear points, but then frenetically referred to the table of contents and the index as the most important keys for readers seeking to understand what he was trying to convey: "It took me days of work to assemble this index . . . Along with the table of contents, it is one of the book's most important sections."[16] The care that Wingren invested in the indexes of his books is indicative of the strategic attention with which he conceived them. Nothing mentioned in the indexes is there by chance. Moreover, from the 1940s onward all of his books, with very few

---

Bengtsson, who had now become Mrs. Lilliehöök, in, for example a book from 1972: "Among my assistants, Mrs. Ingrid Lilliehöök is in a class by herself. She is attention to detail personified, an invaluable resource for someone who must deliver a useable book manuscript and who himself writes only by hand. My thanks go to all involved, but especially to her." Wingren, *Växling och kontinuitet* (1972), 10. Two years later he wrote the following in a foreword: "And finally, as usual, Mrs. Lilliehöök. She typed up my final manuscript, and she always sees through and understands my corrections to my own text—often one correction on top of another, sometimes a third on top of the previous two. I do not know how she does it but I want her to know how much I appreciate her and her work." Wingren, *Credo* (1974/1981), 15.

16. Wingren, "Pensionärer och avlidna" (1982), 5. His personal journal shows that for two entire weeks (June 19–July 2), he worked with the index of *The Silent Interpreter* (1981), but there is also a note that this time it was Greta Hofsten who typed up the final index on July 6–7, and then the entire manuscript was sent to the publisher in Stockholm the following day.

exceptions, have three indexes: one index for names, another for subjects, and a third a register of Bible quotations cited in the text. It is there, at the end of his books, that the reader finds the list of characters, the plot, and the sources of the drama Wingren places on the stage.

The second major characteristic of Wingren's intellectual style is his focus on conflict. It is no exaggeration to claim that he loved confrontations and found much of his intellectual nourishment and inspiration in these confrontations. The many conflicts that peppered his academic career are almost unequalled on the Swedish university scene, and it is in and through these battles that Wingren's own position becomes evident. To use an idea posited by Associate Professor Edgar Almén, it is as if Wingren, by staging such confrontations, was trying to hunt down the basic precepts of thought present in various arguments.[17]

During my time in Lund, I witnessed firsthand a number of Wingren's unusually vehement confrontations, which often revolved around the issue of women's right to serve as ordained ministers in the Church of Sweden. When he once challenged Bishop Bertil Gärtner to a debate in the Petersgården Church in Lund on ordination of women as ministers, the two clerics shouted indignantly at one another, faces bright red, until those of us in attendance truly feared they would come to blows. Seldom have I seen such aggression in a debate. On another occasion, 13 May 1982, I was visiting Uppsala and found myself at a gathering where the entire group of Uppsala's theology professors were to debate Wingren on the theme of "Science, Interpretation, Proclamation." This proved to be a marathon debate that began at 7:15 p.m. and continued until 10:40 that evening. Author Lars Andersson was also there. Many years later he remembered the smoldering atmosphere of the event in this way:

> That evening I went to the University. In Room 10, Gustaf Wingren was raging against Uppsala and everything that it stood for. Exegete Lars Hartman, dogmatician Anders Jeffner, and practical theologian Åke Andrén sat with him, all at the same podium. One after the other they rose, made their case, were flayed alive by Wingren as they stood, and then sank back into their chairs, on Wingren's left and right.[18]

Swedish theology has not witnessed a similarly spectacular event (which, I should add, was not an isolated one) since Wingren's departure from the

---

17. Almén, "Wingrens teologiska argument," 15.
18. Andersson, "Kväll i maj," 53–54.

scene. In some ways this may be a relief, but there may well be many who, like me, miss the kind of intensity and sense of engagement that Wingren brought to our theological discourse.

Without a doubt, one of the major characteristics of Wingren's intellectual method was that he developed his theological ideas through confrontation and conflict. He himself hinted that he had been something of a troublemaker during his youth in the town of Valdemarsvik. Similarly, as a professor of theology, he was drawn to conflict. His expressions of appreciation for those who chose to confront him must be understood in light of this background. He regarded it almost as a form of dueling, which became obvious to all—in the early 1980s, for example, he wrote in a letter, "I am very happy that at least Jeffner chooses the path of confrontation. He and I will meet at the Theological Society in Lund on February 3, 1982."[19]

There are stories from faculty meetings at which his suggestions evoked no discussion, since they were met with general approval, and were quickly voted into effect. In such situations, Wingren could quickly lose his composure and become visibly disappointed. Many who did not know him well underappreciated his predisposition for conflict, and furthermore, did not understand that he in fact *wanted* to be met with resistance. Professor Carl-Gustaf Andrén, a longtime colleague, later president of the University and national university chancellor in Sweden, tells of a faculty meeting at which his colleague Wingren was especially unpleasant. As the meeting broke up, Andrén brutally grabbed Wingren in the doorway and gave him a sound scolding before dismissing him with the words, "Now you may leave!" It became clear that Wingren appreciated and respected this sort of heavy-handed treatment, for at the next faculty meeting he was in a wonderful mood, and to the great surprise of his colleagues offered to take on a number of tasks.[20] It seems to me that he actually respected those who confronted him. It was as if he sought mutual recognition through these conflicts: they served as a way for him to discover other people's positions on issues and allowed him to calibrate his arguments. However, as Associate Professor Lars-Olle Armgard, Wingren's former doctoral student, commented, "You never quite knew whether he wanted *everyone* to think the way he did, or *no one*."[21]

19. Wingren to Per Erik Persson, 28 September 1981.
20. Interview with Carl-Gustaf Andrén, 21 January 2010.
21. Interview with Lars-Olle Armgard, 18 January 2010.

Author Tim Adams describes a similar mindset in his book about the tennis player John McEnroe. In a long series of matches against his archrival, Björn Borg, McEnroe reached the heightened feeling of euphoria that he needed in order to play at the top of his game and that, in an odd way, made him whole. Great tennis players, like great chess players or great boxers, cannot exist in isolation: they require a rivalry, an equal, to allow them to discover what they really might be capable of.[22]

In his love of conflict, Wingren's intellectual style resembled that of another author to whom he devoted many years of detailed study, the reformer Martin Luther. With the exception of his two catechisms, Luther was almost incapable of writing systematic texts. Luther's work consists mostly of polemic, even in the instances when he wrote Bible commentaries. Wingren also shared Luther's enjoyment of everyday things such as food and drink, earthy discussions, and a humor that was equally as uplifting as it was burlesque.[23]

Confrontation was also vital to Wingren's understanding of the Christian faith itself. Conflict served a decisive theological function for him, since he believed that the phenomenon to which we refer as Christianity (a word that does not exist in biblical vocabulary) does not become evident until it is confronted by something that threatens to negate this belief. In keeping with the theological importance he ascribed to stories, he maintained that without taking these conflicts seriously, it was not possible to understand what Christianity is. Not until Christian faith is confronted by something that threatens it does it become necessary to articulate what otherwise remains embedded in the life of faith as tacit knowledge. In his book *Change and Continuity: Theological Criteria* (1972), Wingren expounded his most systematic presentation of the "analysis of confrontation" that was so vital to his methodology. Here he stresses, "*Confrontations* play an extraordinary role in the unbiased, objective analysis of continuity and change throughout the history of Christianity."[24] In Wingren's hermeneutics, this analysis of confrontation determines the criteria for judging how change and continuity relate to one another in every contextual interpretation of Christian faith. This basic perspective is also found in the work of a Swedish professor of an

---

22. Adams, *On Being John McEnroe*.

23. Cf. Kedidjan: "But if, like him, one has read through Luther's collected texts in black-letter type, and found significant pleasure and enjoyment in it, perhaps one cannot avoid becoming a little like Luther in his ways." "Griftetal" [eulogy], 3.

24. Wingren, *Växling och kontinuitet* (1972), 8.

earlier generation, Einar Billing (1871-1939), who strongly influenced Wingren. In one instance, Wingren demonstrated how the universal elements in Billing's work were to be found as "silent prerequisites" for his reasoning: "Only when these universal elements were *threatened* did Billing try to articulate these presuppositions, which up to that time he had assumed as self-evident."[25]

It is easy to recognize the potential strengths and advantages of this conflictual methodology, particularly in regard to the development of Wingren's own theological work. Through it he was able to bring together productively a number of conflicts that moved his thinking forward in a way that otherwise might not have been possible. As with storytelling, confrontations served as a way for him to define and cultivate his own position. In general, there seems to be a close connection between creativity and the occurrence of conflict. New and unexpected ideas often originate from collisions between differing, extant phenomena.

Yet, this approach also has a darker side, and carries risks. As a matter of fact, the incessant confrontations often created an unhealthy work environment at Lund University. The greatest conflict in Wingren's life was with his own predecessor, Anders Nygren. This conflict (which will be revisited many times throughout this study) came more or less as a complete surprise to Wingren's contemporaries. Furthermore, over time, it became increasingly passionate and irreconcilable. Some of the risks inherent in a perspective based on conflict include the difficulty of maintaining an open, inquisitive attitude toward complex issues and the loss of nuance in debate, as well as loss of openness toward the convictions and arguments of others. Confrontation can also significantly deteriorate to the extent that it short-circuits academic dialogue and transforms discussion into a violent and destructive battleground. In an individual who may be already too categorical, a lack of willingness to negotiate and compromise may make it difficult to take responsibility for, or manage, an institution or organization. In environments in which people are already fearful of conflict, such inflexibility also risks destroying personal relationships. During an anniversary conference held in honor of the then eighty-five-year-old Wingren, his one-time Associate Professor Gunnar Hillerdal pointed out that Wingren's refusal to compromise and his constant provocations and attacks created an unbearable atmosphere among the faculty, which also affected his students:

25. Wingren, *Exodus Theology* (1968/1969), 156.

> You made it difficult for us students sometimes, and perhaps even more difficult for yourself, by refusing to compromise. Today, almost half a century later, I really think the climate in Lund after 1950 could have been a little better if you had listened and reasoned more concerning various possibilities. Differing viewpoints can in fact complement one another.[26]

It seems that others became inadvertently caught up in these battles and also suffered from them. Clearly, the man who crafted one of the most important and creative achievements of twentieth-century Swedish theology was not without his shortcomings. Yet, what appears to be a person's greatest weakness can often, if used creatively, become his greatest strength. Gaining an understanding of Wingren's theology requires us to take his particular intellectual style seriously: the mixture of humor and earnestness, warmth and provocation, which characterized his narrative way of thinking and his many conflicts. His use of stories and confrontations brought both advantages and disadvantages. This was probably also rooted in Wingren's working-class background, and was itself a phenomenon of the folk culture in which he grew up. As he mingled with the cultured sons of the state church clergy in the halls of Lund, this tanner's boy from the small town of Valdemarsvik never truly felt at ease.

Wingren enjoyed and had a great interest in people. There are many who witnessed his capacity to recognize and receive the most widely varied personalities with genuine curiosity, graciousness, and warmth. Yet he also felt that he needed to "pinpoint" people, as he put it, by telling a story or coaxing forth something controversial from them, which might serve as a point of departure for discussion. In order to approach the soul of Wingren as constructive theologian, then, it is necessary to focus not only on storytelling but also on his many confrontations—without becoming involved and transformed into a combatant in the trench warfare of his many academic battles. To do so successfully requires that we not only read the text carefully but also understand the context.

Contextualization

This book is comprised of a series of contextualizations that I have employed, partly to place the theology of Gustaf Wingren into a historical context for the purpose of making it accessible, and partly to show

---

26. Hillerdal, "Det teologiska klimatet i Lund omkring 1950," 38.

how his capacity to decontextualize and recontextualize his theological sources may be considered one of the great innovations in his theological project.

When presented in terms of simple biographical data, most people's lives may seem somewhat trivial, or in the worst case, so repetitive that they become lost in obscurity. Yet, life is in reality lived in the spaces between the fixed coordinates, and what we find there is what makes a difference. Thus, in order to understand our lives in a comprehensive way, narration is a necessity. Only when narrated will the meaning of our lives be disclosed.

Gustaf Fredrik Wingren was born on 29 November 1910, in the journeyman's cottage at the tannery at Tryserum, in Kalmar County, on the border between the provinces of Småland and Östergötland, on the Swedish east coast. For most of his childhood he lived in the small town of Valdemarsvik. His parents had recently moved to the area and upon their arrival the previous year they lost their firstborn child. Gustaf's father originated from Laholm, in the province of Halland, and his mother from the Roslagen district north of Stockholm. Aside from a short stay in the village of Floda, outside of Gothenburg, in 1914–15, and half a year spent in Gälevad, outside of Örnsköldsvik in Norrland, Gustaf spent his first seventeen years in Valdemarsvik. Later, he also spent many summers and shorter visits there, and in fact even served as pastor there in 1940. His mother, Engla Theresia (née Sundman), gave birth to five children who survived, in 1910, 1912, 1914, 1916, and 1919. The last birth was a difficult one from which she never fully recovered. The following year she was admitted to the hospital in Söderby, and in March 1921 she died at the young age of thirty-four, when her youngest child was only two and a half years old. The tragic loss of their mother plunged the then ten-year-old Gustaf and his younger siblings into a chaotic home life. In this critical situation, the family was rescued by Engla Theresia's sisters; both were Methodists. Many years later, in 1971, Gustaf Wingren wrote a few words in an obituary for his aunt Signe, the saving angel:

> When her sister Teresia Wingren died in 1921, leaving five young children—of whom I was one—she entered our home and managed it until we all had left the nest. For a quarter-century, from 1922 to 1947, we lived in a place which today shines with light—the workers' quarters at the Norrbacka leather factory in Valdemarsvik.[27]

27. Wingren, "Signe Sundman. In Memoriam," *Norrköpings Tidningar*, 30 December 1971.

The children's father, Gustaf Fabian, was a tanner who changed jobs often in pursuit of independence, driven by dreams of establishing his own enterprise. He eventually settled down as a foreman at Karl Lundberg's tannery in Valdemarsvik. A child who grew up in such a working-class environment was expected to learn an "honest" trade so that he would be able to "walk through the gates of the factory, become a worker, and be paid wages like a real man."[28] To his father's sorrow, this was not to be the case with Gustaf, who was born with a congenital defect. His right hand was deformed, and he had only three and a half fingers. It seems that Gustaf's own greatest regret about his disability was that it limited his abilities as a football goalkeeper. However, it also meant that he would be the only one of the five children permitted to pursue an education, and he exhibited a remarkable gift for studies.

It is clear that the experience of having a physical disability had a great impact on Gustaf's perception of himself, as well as on his intellectual project. Later in life, when he had started his own family, he never spoke of his hand. When photographs were taken, he always hid it in his pocket, under a coat, or behind his back. His attempts to hide his deformed hand meant, paradoxically, that those closest to him were all the more aware of it. In his youth, Gustaf had abruptly ended a romantic relationship after being told that "people like him" were not allowed to marry and have children. In my investigations, I have found only one instance when he deliberately showed his right hand in public. When his name had been mentioned as a possible candidate for a bishopric in the diocese of Växjö, a senior master from Kalmar publicly argued that according to biblical tradition, a person with a *corpus defectus* could not be considered for the position. Wingren was at that moment already a professor in Lund and had no desire to become a bishop, yet his reaction to this statement was outrage. In the heat of the discussion, Wingren is said to have raised his right hand, shaking with anger.

German philosopher and social thinker Jürgen Habermas (b. 1929) also lives with a disability. Late in life, he related how the theory based upon the rationally motivated agreement of communicative action that he developed into a major theory of the communicative conditions inherent to democracy was inspired by his own early experiences as a schoolboy. Due to the congenital defect of a cleft palate, his speech was nasal and distorted. His classmates had difficulty understanding him,

---

28. Wingren, *Mina fem universitet* (1991), 25.

and even avoided him. It was this particular experience of not being taken seriously due to a disability that later served as inspiration for his lifelong investigation of the conditions and possibilities of communication.[29] It is worthwhile, therefore, to consider the importance Wingren's deformed right hand, which limited his ability to perform manual labor, may have had for his theological work, if we recognize its basis in the conviction that a human being is a living body, and the recognition of the ordinary vocational life as a gift from God. It cannot be a coincidence that a person who was himself unable to perform physical work chose to write his doctoral dissertation on Martin Luther's understanding of everyday labor as a calling ordained by God, yet God remains hidden as if concealed by a mask. It is also of significance that if it had not been for his hand, Wingren would rather have become a goalkeeper for the Åtvidaberg Football Club. He did all that he could to hide his deformed right hand, yet anyone who shook hands with him immediately became aware of it. In Valdemarsvik, his hand relegated him to the role of a cripple—yet it also provided him with the opportunity for further education and a research career. In the academic life at Lund University, Wingren's right hand served as a constant reminder of his roots, while at the same time it forever separated him from what would have been his natural community and career in Valdemarsvik.

Even as a young boy attending the Swedish Lutheran Church in his hometown, Gustaf nourished ideas of studying theology and becoming a pastor. In his memoirs he claims that his life's adventure did not really begin until he arrived in Lund on 10 July 1927. Even after his graduation from a private upper secondary school in Lund (the Spyken School), he still exhibited signs of debilitating homesickness. However, in the autumn term of 1929 he entered Lund University, and from that moment Lund was to become the fixed point around which his life would revolve for the rest of his days. It is generally known that educational institutions can take on a particularly important role in the lives of those who have not grown up in a tradition of higher learning, and for Wingren, entering Lund University was indeed a sort of homecoming.

After Wingren had fulfilled the basic requirements and was ready to select a specialization, it was far from clear which theological discipline he would choose. The newly appointed professor in New Testament exegetics, Hugo Odeberg (1898-1973) befriended Wingren. Odeberg

---

29. Habermas, *Between Naturalism and Religion*, 13-17.

recognized his student's great talent for research and saw in him a future professor. Despite this, by the middle of the 1930s, Wingren was drawn to another newly appointed professor, Ragnar Bring (1895–1988), who occupied the chair in systematic theology, with responsibility for instruction and examination in Christian dogmatics and symbolism. Bring had studied at Uppsala, and after several years at Åbo Akademi University (1931–34) had come to Lund as Aulén's successor and would remain there for the rest of his life. Bring, too, had great hopes for the young student and encouraged Wingren to focus his primary research on the early church fathers. If he had not been brutally interrupted by the outbreak of World War II in 1939, he might have maintained his focus on that subject. Sadly, the realities of the war closed off all possibility of visiting archives and major research establishments on the Continent. Initially, Wingren seems to have planned for *Irenaeus and Marcion: Studies on the Concept of Creation* (1939) to be a project for a complete book. In the end, it resulted only in an unpublished licentiate thesis, produced by the simplest means possible, but which nonetheless gained Wingren the highest academic grade. The same autumn that the war broke out, Wingren decided to enroll in the practical theological course in order to pursue ordination in the Church of Sweden. Yet the gigantic confrontation between good and evil that came to be a dominant grand narrative of the twentieth century dramatically changed the fundamental working conditions for Wingren. He was forced to make other plans and radically redirect his research interests. Instead of the early church fathers, he began to study a subject almost one and a half millennia younger than his previous area of interest, and with which he was quite unfamiliar at that time: Martin Luther and the theology of the Reformation. Thus, during the years that followed, he alternated research and study with service as an ordained pastor in the Church of Sweden, and in 1942, during one of the darkest periods of the war, he defended his dissertation, *Luther on Vocation* (1942/1957).

Nine years later, in 1951, he assumed a professorship in systematic theology, with responsibility for instruction and examination in theological ethics. Thus, at the age of forty-one, he began what would prove to be a long and extraordinarily successful career as a professor at Lund University. Despite a number of offers of professorships at leading international universities, including Basel, Göttingen, and Tübingen, and rather regularly being named as a candidate for bishoprics in various Swedish dioceses, he remained in Lund and was faithful to his professorship through the years. For the next twenty-six years, he would be almost completely consumed by academic activities.

His private life during these years seems to have followed a rather normal course of events without any dramatic changes. In 1943 he married Signhild Carlsson (1913–2000). With Signhild, whose father was a marine engineer at the Svea Shipping Company in Valdemarsvik and who had herself been trained as a nurse in the tradition of the Swedish Sophia Sisters in Stockholm, Gustaf had two children: Anna, born in 1946, and Anders, born in 1949. The family lived at several addresses in Lund— first on Studentgatan, then on Pålsjövägen, and then in an apartment at Vintergatan 2E. Some years later, they moved into a larger apartment at 2C in the same building. Despite the seemingly comfortable details of his family life, Wingren was interested in little other than theology. In many respects, he lived and worked on another plane of existence. He was often absent from the home but was nonetheless extremely interested in his children and their friends, and could be lively, pleasant, and funny. Nils-Gunnar Nilsson, a well-known culture editor for the newspaper *Sydsvenska Dagbladet*, who worked with Wingren for many years, relates that the first time he ascended the spiral staircase to the office in the professor's home, he was surprised to see that not only were the walls of the room filled with books from floor to ceiling, but the entire floor was covered by his son's extensive model train track.[30] Nevertheless, the University, with which he had a somewhat grudging love-hate relationship, was the real focal point of his existence. Signhild Wingren often defended her husband and sought to justify his absence from home and his long working hours by saying, "Gustaf works for humanity." One of his early doctoral students, Harry Aronson, later associate professor and then school administrator, relates one of his first encounters with his teacher:

> It is the early 1950s, and I am walking toward Lund Cathedral, and suddenly realize that I am on a collision course with Gustaf Wingren. His somewhat heavy frame moves onward toward Sandgatan [where the Faculty of Theology was located]. He is middle-aged, a relatively new professor, and carries a thin briefcase under his arm. His gaze is directed upward through round eyeglasses which had been out of fashion for quite a while, toward the steeples surrounding Lundagård Park. As a new licentiate student, I am unsure of myself at this unexpected meeting with the world of ideas, for I understand that this is

30. Interview with Nils-Gunnar Nilsson, 26 May 2010.

not just a person I am meeting, but a person who inhabits a theological universe, with which he assumes I, too, am familiar. The professor, of course, is privileged to speak first, and I can be expected to engage in a theological discourse . . . How can I manage a reply that will not sound too crazy . . . Finally, we are face to face. As expected, he immediately utters a statement about the current theological situation: "Barth is the most important theological thinker of our day—who thinks wrongly!" How should one reply to something like that?[31]

Wingren's work as a theologian consumed him. When young Harry Aronson met the professor on the street, he was well aware that he was meeting not only a person but a living, walking world of ideas, "a person who inhabits a theological universe." Wingren was a well-known public figure in Sweden at that time, and his work took him on many long journeys abroad. Indeed, his most important academic contacts were in the international arena. He seems to have kept his home life in Lund private, although his students and their families were regularly invited to gatherings and receptions in the Wingren home. Signhild Wingren often showered affection upon his doctoral students, as if they were a group of adopted sons.

The biographical data shows that by the mid-1970s winds of change had begun to whirl into the professor's life. In 1974 he suddenly withdrew his ordination as pastor in the Church of Sweden. Two years later he divorced his wife and married Greta Hofsten. He retired in 1977. As will be seen, these dramatic changes in his personal situation played a decisive role in his *turn toward society*, which appeared in his theological work from the 1970s and onward.

Gustaf Wingren died on 1 November 2000, less than one month before his ninetieth birthday. Probably he felt some measure of relief at having avoided the hypocrisy he associated with celebrations and speeches given on landmark birthdays. He often recalled an event that occurred early in his career during a celebration for a colleague. After having poured superlatives over the celebrant, the speaker of the day positioned himself at the back of the crowd, and exclaimed loudly, "It just makes me want to throw up!" Although Gustaf Wingren reveled in polemics and conflict, he hated this sort of hypocrisy (feeling that it was more honest to engage in open battle), which probably helped maintain the relative social isolation he already experienced at the University due to

---

31. Aronson, "Minnesbilder," 95.

the experiences he underwent when he migrated from the journeyman's cottage to academe. He kept his love of academic conflict and infighting alive until the end. In his very last interview, which he gave on 17 June 2000, he burst out, "When I served as a professor and was scolded every day—that was a wonderful time!"[32]

Engaging with Wingren's Works

The author is dead, but his many texts remain and endure, open for all to read. How should we today read and interpret these texts? As of his eighty-fifth birthday, Gustaf Wingren's bibliography encompassed over 750 publications.[33] However, he also wrote a number of articles after that, and his books continue to be released in new editions and translations even after his death. In addition, he also penned innumerable small articles, essays, and commentaries for newspapers and magazines. Altogether, the list of publications is impressive. In my presentation, I have limited myself to Wingren's major works, those that may be considered landmarks and "game pieces" that he constructed and used in his strategic operations on the theological playing field. Articles and individual chapters from books have been added only in those instances where they provide something new and different. Moreover, archive materials and other unpublished sources, as well as interviews, have been of significant importance for my investigations. First and foremost, however, Wingren constructed his theological system and his self-understanding through his major books, which, in chronological order, may be listed as follows:

1942/1957   *Luthers lära om kallelsen / Luther on Vocation*

1947/1959   *Människan och inkarnationen enligt Irenaeus / Man and the Incarnation: A Study in the Biblical Theology of Irenaeus*

1949/1960   *Predikan: En principiell studie / The Living Word: A Theological Study of Preaching and the Church*

1954/1958   *Teologiens metodfråga / Theology in Conflict: Nygren, Barth, Bultmann*

1958/1961   *Skapelsen och lagen / Creation and Law*

---

32. Wingren in Gierdi, "Tolken som ikke tier," 7.
33. Ledin et al., "Gustaf Wingrens tryckta skrifter, 1933–1995."

1960/1964 *Evangeliet och kyrkan / Gospel and Church*

1968/1969 *Einar Billing: En studie i svensk teologi före 1920 / An Exodus Theology: Einar Billing and the Development of Modern Swedish Theology*

1972 *Växling och kontinuitet: Teologiska kriterier / Change and Continuity: Theological Criteria**

1974/1981 *Credo: Den kristna tros- och livsåskådningen / Credo: The Christian View of Faith and Life*

1979/1979 *Öppenhet och egenart: Evangeliet i världen / Creation and Gospel: The New Situation in European Theology*

1981 *Tolken som tiger: Vad teologin är och vad den borde vara / The Silent Interpreter: What Theology Is and What It Ought to Be**

1983 *En liten katekes / A Small Catechism** (coauthored with Greta Hofsten)

1983 *Människa och kristen: En bok om Irenaeus / Man and Christian: A Book on Irenaeus**

1985 *Gamla vägar framåt: Kyrkans uppgift i Sverige / Going Forth on Ancient Roads: The Mission of the Church in Sweden**

1989 *Texten talar: Trettio predikningar / The Text Is Speaking: Thirteen Sermons**

1991 *Tyngd och nåd i svensk skönlitteratur / Gravity and Grace in Swedish Literature**

1991 *Mina fem universitet: Minnen / My Five Universities: Memories**

(Titles marked with an asterisk [*] have not been published in English.)

This lengthy list of titles may seem daunting to the uninitiated. How can we engage with, read, understand, order, and contextualize this authorship? One way is to sort Wingren's books into different categories. From this perspective, we may first identify a group of books that disclose the historical sources of Wingren's theological thinking: *Luther on Vocation*

(1942/1957), *Man and Incarnation* (1947/1959), *An Exodus Theology* (1968/1969), *A Small Catechism* (1983), *Human and Christian* (1983), and *Gravity and Grace in Swedish Literature* (1991).

The second group consists of those books in which Wingren deals with issues of theological methodology, with a special focus on the problems of hermeneutics: *Theology in Conflict* (1954/1958), *Change and Continuity* (1972), and *The Silent Interpreter* (1981).

A third grouping is comprised of the books in which Wingren presents his attempts at a systematic presentation of the major components of the Christian faith: *Creation and Law* (1958/1961), *Gospel and Church* (1960/1964), and *Credo* (1974/1981).

Fourth and final are the two books that deal with and are directed more specifically toward the church: *Going Forth on Ancient Roads* (1985) and *The Text Is Speaking* (1989). It is notable that both of these books were published after Wingren's retirement. Today, however, after the publication of the Swedish edition of this book, we may add the posthumous *Homilies: Gustaf Wingren Preaches* (only in Swedish: *Postilla: Gustaf Wingren predikar*, 2010).

In addition, there are two books in which Wingren sought to tell his own story, providing an overview of his own authorship and placing it in context. Both of these books he also wrote after his retirement: *Creation and Gospel* (1979/1979) and his intellectual autobiography, *My Five Universities* (1991).

Lastly, over and above these groupings, we have to deal with a book that seems to defy classification: *The Living Word* (1949/1960). This is Wingren's most controversial book, and it has been the object of the most widely varied judgments. It was dismissed at its initial publication as nothing more than a piece of proclamatory preaching and has been declared unscholarly, bizarre, and rubbish. This did not stop the author himself from giving it his highest praise; in his later years, he spoke of it as "the best work I have ever written."[34] Indeed, the book is really remarkable, an almost volcanic book that was controversial from its first publication and has remained so ever since. I maintain that judgments passed on it by critics and enthusiasts, as well as the author himself, are rife with confusion, which must be dealt with by anyone wishing to gain an understanding of Wingren's theology.

---

34. Wingren, *Mina fem universitet* (1991), 118.

At first glance, it may appear that the books that Wingren published during the 1970s, 1980s, and 1990s were mere repeats of his early publications. However, a closer examination reveals that his works from those later decades actually were the result of a new theological direction he had begun to pursue. One of the basic assumptions I have made in this intellectual biography is that Wingren's thinking underwent a dramatic change from the 1970s onward, during a period of time in which he staged a personal metamorphosis and recontextualized his entire system of theology. After having worked primarily in the *academic* sphere, he redirected his theological path toward a critique of civilization by placing his theological reflection mainly in a *social* context. Wingren's works may thus be clearly divided into two major periods, and according to this periodization his second wave of books may be recognized as creative revisitations and recontextualizations of the theological system he had actually completed already by 1960. In effect, *Luther on Vocation* (1942/1957) is recast as social criticism in *A Small Catechism* (1983, written in collaboration with Greta Hofsten according to a model that the pair would use for several books in which their respective contributions were interspersed with one another). He reconsidered Irenaeus in *Man and Incarnation* (1947/1959) in a social context and offered an ideologically critical twist in *Human and Christian* (1983). He revisited the battles he waged in his 1954/1958 *Theology in Conflict*, and in a new guise focused on the social role of theology in *The Silent Interpreter* (1981). In the same way, his first systematic theological presentation of the Christian faith that had been released as two books due to the limitations of the original publisher, *Creation and Law* (1958/1961) and *Gospel and Church* (1960/1964), were reconfigured using the same basic structure, but with the aim of achieving a social recontextualization in *Credo* (1974/1981). However, as mentioned above, Wingren's book *The Living Word* (1949/1960) stands on its own outside any groupings of his other works, and is difficult to place. I ascribe to this book a unique, decisive role in Wingren's authorship, but I do so for reasons other than those the author himself indicated. In particular, some historical distance from the subject makes it easier to see that *The Living Word* can in fact be considered as the vital component in his *turn toward practical wisdom*.[35]

35. Bexell has previously argued that it is possible to identify three periods in the authorship of Wingren. Bexell, *Teologisk etik i Sverige sedan 1920-talet*, 144ff. To a large extent, I concur with this statement, even though my interpretation of these periods looks somewhat different. In addition, it has been my ambition to understand the inner logic of this developmental process.

Finally, before the story begins, we may ask the following question: Why publish a book about Wingren today? I am convinced that there are a number of good reasons for doing so. The very fact that Wingren has, in recent years, become a more or less unknown figure in the public theological discourse in Sweden and that today, only a decade after his death, hardly any of his texts are being used in current Swedish theological instruction provides a strong reason to call attention to his work. From having been a household name among theologians for nearly half a century, Wingren and his works are suddenly almost forgotten, even among those with a high degree of theological education. In this respect, he is only one of a number of theological giants who have been forgotten all too quickly, and this has resulted in the need for contemporary theologians to reinvent the wheel time and time again, or to be unnecessarily taken aback by challenges that could have been dealt with in a more constructive way had there been greater knowledge of the theological resources available.

It should be remembered that Sweden was a significant contributor to the international field of systematic theology during the middle decades of the previous century.[36] With no disrespect for the value of the initiatives being undertaken by contemporary Swedish theologians, it must be stated that no current systematic theologian in Sweden today measures up to the renown held by half a dozen theologians during the "golden age," from Nathan Söderblom and Gustaf Aulén to Anders Nygren and Gustaf Wingren. The silence is all the more remarkable because of these perspectives. By no means do I wish for unexamined acceptance, but I claim that twentieth-century Swedish theology truly deserves to be taken seriously and honored academically in the best way through the most stringent criticism and examination possible. Constructive reinterpretations of the works of these theologians must also by necessity be critical interpretations. However, to make this possible at all, we must revitalize this tradition and immerse ourselves anew in the works and thoughts of these theologians.

A second reason for writing a book about Wingren is that the year 2010 marked the one hundredth anniversary of his birth, which was celebrated by conferences at Lund University and other places. The world

---

36. Of course, Swedish researchers in other areas of theology also found international acceptance. For example, in the field of New Testament exegesis, Swedish names such as Anton Friedrichsen, Harald Riesenfeld, Krister Stendahl, and others are well known.

that he entered on 29 November 1910 was very different compared to the world we experience today. This was before the two world wars that left Europe and many other parts of the world in ruins, and also before the Cold War, which would leave its mark on the later decades of the twentieth century. The Swedish welfare state had not yet been created, and automobiles had not yet provided easy mobility for ordinary people. The Church of Sweden and the Swedish state were still firmly intertwined with one another at the top of a more or less authoritarian social order, in which the actions taken by local pastors and their bishops were regarded as affairs of the state. Sweden was in fact not yet a democracy in the modern sense of the word, and had scarcely begun the remarkably rapid process of industrialization and modernization that would eventually give the country one of the highest standards of living in the world. In 1910, the everyday reality for the vast majority of the Swedish people was that of an impoverished and largely rural society. For the family of Fabian Wingren, the tanner, as for most other Swedish families of the day, higher education was not an option. Only one of the Wingren children had the opportunity to pursue advanced studies: Gustaf. The other children—Maj, Lage, Harry, and Valborg—were dedicated to work that did not require higher education. When sixteen-year-old Gustaf arrived in Lund on 10 July 1927, he had never made a telephone call or used a flush toilet.

To write about the career of this gifted young man is also to tell part of the history of the twentieth century. When the story begins, Sweden was entering a process of industrialization, and when it ends, the halcyon days of Swedish industry were already over. It seems to me that this transformation of Swedish society must have influenced Wingren's theological endeavors. In a corresponding manner, the social transformation that we are experiencing today will bring dramatic changes in living conditions and contribute to the rise of new philosophical interpretations of the human condition. Given such a situation, a theology that allows itself to be transformed by the dynamic forces of a changing context, and which has, at the same time, actively embraced the possibilities it offers, has undoubtedly an important contribution to make. With Gustaf Wingren, this extraordinary capacity for recontextualization is grounded in a grain-of-wheat theology, a concept that we shall return to later on, and which implies that we can only effect change when we ourselves are prepared to be changed and that it is only by losing ourselves that we can find ourselves.

A further reason for writing this book is the theological implications of Gustaf Wingren's relationship with his second wife, Greta Hofsten. It is a matter of fact that as a leading theologian in Sweden, Wingren counted among his most important sources of inspiration a person who with time became his wife and life partner, but whose main institutional basis and competence was neither academic nor theological. At the time of their most intensive collaboration, Greta Hofsten was working as a postman. It is remarkable that, in all previous literature on Wingren, her influence on his theological thinking has been neglected. I myself maintain that it is not possible to gain an understanding of Wingren's theology in its entirety if we ignore the vital role Hofsten played in the second half of Wingren's authorship. An intellectual biographical presentation is required in order to capture the voices and personalities of this dynamic partnership. Otherwise, Hofsten will be neither seen nor heard—and one of the most important inspirations for Wingren's theology will remain invisible.

The collaboration between Greta Hofsten and Gustaf Wingren brought together two widely divergent networks that otherwise had few connections. Two worlds met in a conversation, the results of which stretch across important portions of twentieth-century Swedish intellectual history. In order to do justice to this more comprehensive picture, I have considered it a necessity to transcend the borders separating standard disciplines and break with traditional academic prose. It is my hope that a theological biography may give voice to the broader context that is necessary in order to understand Wingren's texts. Hence, it is obvious that a book about the life and work of Gustaf Wingren must also be in part a book about Greta Hofsten.

For me, the process of writing this book has also been a profound personal experience. During several formative years of my life I became acquainted with and was befriended by Gustaf Wingren and Greta Hofsten. However, for a long period of time I did not believe that I had sufficient distance for a critical and constructive awareness of his theological project. Only now have I been able to remove myself from the story that Wingren himself crafted so carefully, and thus been able to discover my own path through his writings as well as my own variant of the story of his life.

The final and most important reason for writing about Wingren is, of course, his theology. I am convinced that the hermeneutical theology of creation Wingren developed can make significant contributions today.

There are good reasons for putting this theology into effect in the current world, not as a nostalgic memorialization or as an attempt to defend some immovable conviction but as a creative new interpretation of Wingren's thinking, with the aim of inscribing his writings into the postliberal context that is ours today. In Wingren's work we face a theological endeavor full of themes highly pertinent to society, academia, and the church, as well as resources for theological thinking in the contemporary world. Late in his life, Wingren himself presented several attempts to explain the cohesion of his theology, but these attempts to put everything in the right order in the story of his life and his theology have not made things easier for anyone wishing to write about him. As a biographer, it has been necessary to be on my guard to avoid merely repeating his formulations and stories—and confrontations.[37] More than anything else, what has helped me create the necessary distance in order to discover new perspectives is the course of time itself.

---

37. To a great degree, this can be said to be the case with the studies that make a collective presentation of Wingren's theological project, such as Vander Goot, "The Fundamentality of Creation in the Theology of Gustaf Wingren" (1976); Øjestad, *Studie i Gustaf Wingrens teologi med særlig henblikk på hans forståelse av evangeliet og sosialetiken* (1975); Reilly, *Law and Gospel in the Theology of Gustaf Wingren* (1974); and Petrén, *Skapelse och frihet* (1995). The monumental (and failed) dissertation *Tigern som tolkar* (2004) by Stefánsson is in general difficult to approach. To a lesser degree, it could be said that this characterizes the presentations in which the theology of Wingren is part of a larger examination and the perspectives taken are more independently original, as is the case with Bexell, *Teologisk etik i Sverige sedan 1920-talet* (1981); Sigurdson, *Karl Barth som den andre* (1996); Sandahl, *Folk och kyrka* (1986); Anderson, *Gustaf Wingren and the Swedish Lutheran Renaissance* (2006); and the closing chapter of my own dissertation, *Kommunikation på bristningsgränsen* (1994). I would like to point out Karlsson, *Predikans samtal* (2000), and Håkansson, *Vardagens kyrka* (2001), as the most important contributions to research in this area, as they apply independent thinking regarding materials and perspectives.

2

The First Confrontation

WHERE DOES THE STORY of Gustaf Wingren begin? As with the telling of any history, there are many possible ways to begin, and almost as many ways to continue and conclude. The narrator's first step has its own implications; the starting point determines very much how the story will proceed. I have chosen to begin my own story about Wingren in a way that focuses on his ideas, contextualized though they may be, and at the same time in a way that from the very beginning emphasizes Wingren's obvious affinity with the academic context and public.

However, the fact that there are many possible ways to tell a story cannot be taken as license to tell it in a haphazard manner. When writing a narrative, a historian attempts to present something that has actually occurred. Historians must support their narrative through the use of traces and firsthand accounts, documents and archives, and they must always remain open to the entire spectrum of possible explanations that could lead to a different understanding of events that have occurred. In a sense, the historian always strives towards a more sound interpretation than can be found in other kinds of stories. From a scientific perspective, it seems equally as odd to designate a historian's narrative as a simple attempt to present yet another story among other stories as it is to lay claim to telling the final and only true story.

The Battle for the Professorial Chair

Let us enter Gustaf Wingren's world precisely in the middle of the previous century. The city of Lund had at that time about thirty-four thousand inhabitants and its university, which was one of only two major universities in Sweden, had around three thousand students. A significant number of these students—several hundred, in fact—were enrolled in the Faculty of Theology. The year is 1951, and forty-year-old Gustaf Wingren stands at the threshold of what will be a twenty-six-year career as university professor in systematic theology, with departmental responsibilities for instruction and examination in theological ethics. He had already served in this position as an interim faculty member for four weeks in 1946, and again for four and a half months in 1948. By the time Professor Anders Nygren left his university chair in 1949 to become bishop of Lund, Wingren had served as acting professor for so long that many of his students had begun to take for granted that he was already a full faculty member. He had even spent time as an acting professor at the universities in Tübingen and Göttingen, West Germany, as well as at Åbo Akademi University in Turku, Finland. Nonetheless, it was far from given that he would become the permanent appointee to the prestigious chair as professor in Lund. In fact, it was quite a surprise when Wingren defeated his own teacher, Associate Professor Herbert Olsson (1899–1969), who had built up admirable expertise on theologians from Thomas Aquinas to Martin Luther and John Calvin and had established himself as somewhat of an institution of culture and learning within the Faculty of Theology. It is telling that in the foreword to his doctoral dissertation, Wingren extended special thanks to then-Associate Professor Olsson, whose "unselfish nature is even greater than his reputation," for "constructive suggestions" and "helpful advice regarding the sources."[1] Along with Professor Ragnar Bring, Olsson had been an irreplaceable advisor when complicated wartime realities forced Wingren to hastily redirect the entire focus of his research from the early church fathers to the Reformation. As a doctoral student during the spring and autumn term of 1941, Wingren had followed Olsson's course lectures on the concept of law with great interest. In them, he found direct relevance to his dissertation, and later he described himself as "strongly influenced" by his teacher.[2] His attainment of the professorship was a sensitive subject on which he did not comment until much later, when he confessed that at

---

1. Wingren, *Luthers lära om kallelsen* (1942), vii–viii. It is of particular interest to note that these special thanks to Herbert Olsson, as well as to Anders Nygren and Ragnar Bring, were not included by Wingren in the English edition that was published fifteen years later.

2. Wingren, *Mina fem universitet* (1992), 73.

the time, he had carried the painful awareness that "Herbert Olsson is a much more cultivated man than I."[3]

When Wingren defended his doctoral dissertation *Luther on Vocation* in December 1942, Olsson, his teacher and an expert on Luther, served as the dissertation committee's faculty opponent. For no less than six hours, Associate Professor Olsson grilled the candidate with all manner of critical questions. Certainly, both Olsson and Wingren themselves, as well as the audience gathered in Carolina Hall, must have foreseen that both would be future candidates for the professorship—and so it came to be. At the end of the 1940s, Anders Nygren's choice to leave the university in favor of the church initiated a dramatic, drawn-out appointment process.

The application period for the position ended on 3 March 1949, and supporting documents were to be submitted by 1 June. Along with academic articles, resumes of previous service, and sample lectures, the evaluation process would place greatest weight upon the major books that each of the two most likely candidates had submitted. In addition to his dissertation, *The Fundamental Problem in Luther's Social Ethics*, vol. 1 (*Grundproblemet i Luthers socialetik*, 1, 1939; 219 pp.), Herbert Olsson had submitted *Calvin and the Theology of the Reformation* (*Calvin och Reformationens teologi*, 1934; 600 pp.), as well as a comprehensive manuscript for an even larger work: *Creation, Reason and Law in Luther's Theology* (*Skapelse, förnuft och lag i Luthers teologi*, 804 manuscript pages). Gustaf Wingren had submitted two historical investigations, *Luther on Vocation* (1942/1957; 272 pp.) and *Man and the Incarnation: A Study in the Biblical Theology of Irenaeus* (1947/1959; 263 pp.). In addition, only fourteen days before the final date for submission of materials, Wingren had completed a new book, which in form and content differed distinctly from all other works submitted by any of the applicants: *The Living Word: A Theological Study of Preaching and the Church* (1949/1960, 319 pp.). Much of the drama to come would center around the evaluation of this book. Was it of merit or demerit to its author? Measured quantitatively, Wingren's total production equaled less than two thirds of Olsson's. If Wingren's most recent book was disregarded, and only his historical works were considered, Olsson's total production was nearly twice that of Wingren's.[4]

3. Ibid.

4. It is true, as I have mentioned previously, that Wingren acknowledges in his autobiography (1991) that Herbert Olsson possessed greater learning than he himself

There were originally six applicants in all, one of whom withdrew, leaving only five. The others were Associate Professor Gösta Hök, Associate Professor Ruben Josefson, and Assistant Professor Henning Lindström, all of whom consistently rated as strong candidates. It soon became clear, however, that the real battle would be waged between Herbert Olsson and Gustaf Wingren, who were the oldest and the youngest applicants.

Two of those called on to serve as area experts on the evaluation committee, Professor Sigfrid von Engeström of Uppsala and Professor K. E. Skyddsgaard of Copenhagen, declined the task. This postponed the start of the evaluation process from 9 March until 17 September. Of the four final area experts on the committee, two were from Sweden and two from Denmark. The drama began early, with each of the two Swedish experts promoting a different candidate. Professor Ragnar Bring, also dean of the Faculty of Theology at Lund University and previously Wingren's academic advisor, wrote in his declaration that while Olsson was admittedly superior in regard to broader learning, he saw Wingren as clearly superior in terms of modern theology.[5] He reached the conclusion that it was unavoidable that the latter candidate should be appointed: "As a systematic theologian, he possesses *uncommonly* distinguishing qualifications," Bring wrote, adding that "he has exhibited great skill in primary historical research as well as discussion of the sources."[6] Bring placed Wingren as his first choice and Olsson as a good second choice. Bring's declaration emphasized Wingren as unusually skilled in systematic

---

did. Yet, in the same book, it also seems as if he is trying to hide the fact that Olsson's literary production was also quantitatively more extensive than his own. For this reason, it is somewhat misleading when Wingren recounts what he perceives as the general perception regarding the competition for the professorship: "Yes, when Wingren has read the source materials, he writes a book about the topic. When Olsson has plowed his way through a group of source materials, he then throws himself over another set of materials, and begins reading them instead." Ibid., 72. It is also quite clear that Olsson's influence was of vital importance for Wingren when he began to develop his own theology regarding creation and the law.

5. Bring, in Appendix 28A, protocol of the Faculty of Theology, meeting on 24 October 1950, 98.

6. Ibid., 102. However, Bring's appreciation of Wingren's competitor is also obvious. Immediately following his final decision, he adds, "But I cannot allow a younger researcher to go before Olsson, for whose learnedness I have the highest admiration, without expressing the opinion that it ought to be in the interest of the University to make it possible for him to continue his important program of research by arranging a permanent position for him, too." Ibid., 102.

theology, modern in his style; he considered him a breath of fresh international air in the Swedish theological milieu. Yet, according to Bring, while Wingren had "in an excellent way" and true to the tradition of Lund "provided a strictly historical viewpoint" in his first two works on Luther and Irenaeus, his more recent book, *The Living Word*, was more free and existential.[7] Regarding *The Living Word*, Bring expressed some doubts concerning Wingren's methods, his manner of argumentation, and portions of the book's polemics (which in fact partly were directed against Bring), and pointed out that it is "not entirely easy to comprehend *at once*." However, he then glossed over these problems with a flood of superlatives: the book was written with energy, humor, and focus. He viewed Wingren's remarkable "discernment and capacity for combining ideas" as the fruits of "a very unusually high level of theological knowledge." He felt that his book might in fact "represent the future development of scholarly methods in the field of theology more than (those of) other Swedish theologians."[8] Bring's declaration continued in this manner. Furthermore, he anticipated and refuted possible objections to the book, such as that it was better suited to churchly discussions. Thus, Bring seemed to be prepared in advance for critical reactions against this book. In fact, he may even have been in prior contact with the other Swedish member of the committee, Hjalmar Lindroth (1883–1979), professor of dogmatics at Uppsala University, regarding the book.

After pointing out weaknesses in Wingren's works on Luther and Irenaeus, Lindroth devoted the majority of his declaration to a blunt, negative criticism of *The Living Word*. Lindroth felt that with this book, Wingren had diverged from the mainstream of Swedish theology, and therefore its theses were completely useless.[9] He repeatedly complained that the book was mostly proclamatory preaching. Lindroth was convinced that Wingren, due to the presumed inspiration of Karl Barth, allowed theology and preaching to merge in *The Living Word*. Yet Lindroth also strongly criticized Wingren's criticism of Barth. Lindroth's opinion was clear: in *The Living Word*, Wingren showed scholarly shortcomings, and should thus be considered to be more of a preacher than a serious theologian.[10] In contrast to Wingren, Olsson is described as an analytical

7. Ibid., 88.
8. Ibid., 81, 87.
9. Lindroth, in Appendix 28B, protocol of the Faculty of Theology, meeting on 24 October 1950, 83.
10. Ibid., 85. Lindroth asserted, "His sentences gain not one bit more

researcher whose work is characterized by great learnedness and accuracy, who stands out as an author with "significant systematic theological strengths and consciousness."[11] Thus, Lindroth placed Olsson as his first choice, since he "decidedly surpassed his fellow applicants in knowledge, minute attention to his treatment of materials, analytical focus, originality and independence."[12] He maintained that Wingren ought to be placed last among the assistant professors who had applied, in other words, in fourth place, after Josefson and Hök, due to missgivings in respect to methodology.[13]

In the wake of Bring's and Lindroth's declarations, the two major candidates did not come out even: Olsson had a clear advantage. This made the opinions of the two Danish committee members even more important. As it would transpire, they would continue these opposing viewpoints in even sharper terms, further defining the disagreement that thus far had only been hinted at. According to the Danish members of the evaluation committee, this was a contest between Olsson the historian and Wingren the systematician.

Niels Hansen Søe (1895–1978), professor of ethics at Copenhagen University, stated in his declaration that Olsson was clearly "more robustly equipped with his completely superior knowledge of the Luther literature," but at the same time he felt that "Luther's theological thought is brought to life in a completely different way in Wingren's work."[14] The book *The Living Word* played into the positive remarks that Søe, who was strongly influenced by Barth, gave Wingren. Even though Søe disagreed with Wingren on many points, the book clearly showed that Wingren had the greatest systematic skill of all the applicants. Nonetheless he confessed that it was "painfully difficult" to make a choice between the two main candidates.[15] He added a few words that would become a point of controversy, stating that if the position to be filled had been in historical theology, he would possibly—"although not without doubts"—have

---

scientific-theological carrying capacity, because they are presented in the form of prophetic preaching." Ibid., 151.

11. Ibid., 71.

12. Ibid., 87.

13. Ibid., 86.

14. Søe, in Appendix 28C, protocol of the Faculty of Theology, meeting on 24 October 1950, 28ff.

15. Ibid., 36.

placed Olsson first, but as this was a matter of an appointment in systematic theology, he placed Wingren first.[16]

In his comprehensive statement, the professor from Aarhus University, Regin Prenter (1907-90), followed the same line as his fellow Dane. In the introduction to his declaration, he explicitly stated that the history of ideas could not be considered a major discipline within systematic theology.[17] He stated further that because qualifications in the major discipline warranted the heaviest consideration, the applicants' merits in systematic studies took precedence over those in history. Given this, and despite the criticisms leveled against it for a monotonous image of Barth, *The Living Word* was of decisive importance for Prenter's high evaluation of Wingren. Prenter maintained that the book was the only true systematic theological work submitted by any of the applicants.[18] Because Olsson had dealt only with history, and because his studies were also of an incomplete nature, Prenter recommended that he be placed in position two in the ranking, and clearly after Wingren, whom Prenter ranked as the first choice.

On 24 October 1950, the Faculty of Theology at Lund University gathered for their final decision-making meeting, at which all of the faculty's professors would consider the findings of the evaluation committee, and then express their own opinions regarding the appointment. Following the declarations of the committee, the score was 3 to 1 in Wingren's favor. However, while the committee members who favored Wingren had placed Olsson as a clear second choice, the member who favored Olsson had placed Wingren in *fourth* place. The decision was far from final, and both sides sought to mobilize support for their candidate. The meeting of the full Faculty of Theology was attended by six professors—but the final result of the meeting was a vote of 4 to 3 in favor of Wingren. In other words, there were seven votes. How could that be?

In a letter dated 20 September 1950, a little over one month before the faculty meeting, Dean Ragnar Bring wrote to the Chancellor of Universities in Sweden regarding Professor Sven Kjöllerström, who was on an academic leave of absence to pursue research during the very term in which the appointment to the professorship in systematic theology was to be decided. Professor Kjöllerström had neglected to request only

16. Ibid., 36.

17. Prenter, in Appendix 28D, protocol of the Faculty of Theology, meeting on 24 October 1950, 2.

18. Ibid., 17.

a partial leave of absence because he "had mistakenly been led to believe that he would have the right to participate in [faculty] duties such as a professorial appointment process, even though he had not specifically requested [partial leave] in his application for a leave of absence." Bring explained that now that a decision was to be made regarding the vacant chair in systematic theology, it was of vital importance that all members of the faculty be present to decide the matter. He continued:

> And since Kjöllerström has declared that he has no objections to participating in the considerations on this question, the faculty hereby respectfully requests that the Chancellor grant him permission to participate in the deliberations on the above-mentioned matter of the faculty appointment, without being prevented from doing so by his leave of absence.[19]

The request was granted, with far-reaching consequences. Here, it is obvious that Bring had taken on the role of kingmaker, mobilizing and coordinating support for Wingren.[20] Yet, the members of the faculty who supported Olsson were also well prepared and presented an organized attack during the meeting. Harald Eklund, professor of the philosophy of religion, stated that the Swedish and Danish committee members had made their recommendations based upon completely different principles. He objected strongly to the way in which the Danes prioritized systematic merits over the history of ideas, and that they had reduced history of ideas to, in Prenter's words, a "minor discipline." Eklund joined the Swedish members of the committee, both of whom claimed to consider historical and systematic merits as equal in value. And because all members of the committee had praised Olsson's systematic skills and had deemed him to be the strongest candidate in regard to historical studies, the position should logically go to Olsson. Eklund described Wingren as a simplicist in his systematic works as well as in his historical ones, and felt that his research was confessionalist.[21] The evaluation of *The Living Word* was especially important to Eklund, and he did not mince words

---

19. Bring, in Appendix 20, protocol of the Faculty of Theology, meeting on 24 October 1950.

20. A number of things imply that Bring was the driving force behind the appointment process: he had taken upon himself the task of serving as one of the area experts, and he also made the effort to write to the university chancellor in order to get the permission so that Kjöllerström would be allowed to participate and vote.

21. Eklund, in Appendix 28E, protocol of the Faculty of Theology, meeting on 24 October 1950, 10.

when he emphasized the theoretical difficulties, absurdities, and missteps that he felt characterized its presentation, due to Wingren's failure to observe the difference between objectivity and subjectivity. Eklund wrote that the committee members' support for Wingren—support that he was quick to point out came from researchers with a very close relationship to Wingren—was "exaggerated," and they also exaggerated Wingren's familiarity with the international theological scene. Eklund presented Olsson, in contrast to Wingren, as "a systematician more firmly rooted in reality, with deeper scholarly sincerity and greater independence in the treatment of the source materials from a systematic viewpoint."[22] Not surprisingly, he therefore concluded that Olsson, with his research in the history of ideas, was "far superior to all of his fellow candidates."[23]

Professor of church history Hilding Pleijel began his evaluation by underscoring how difficult he personally found it to make a decision between "these two excellent practitioners of scholarship."[24] Even though Wingren stood out as the most elegant stylist with the most flexible intellect, this had to be measured against the methodological difficulties inherent in the free and existential form of his most recent work, *The Living Word*. For this reason, he preferred Olsson's broader learning and detailed systematic analysis. This, in addition to Olsson's methodological reliability, motivated Pleijel to place Olsson in first place, before Wingren.

The next faculty declaration came from Wingren's former teacher of New Testament exegesis, Professor Hugo Odeberg. As a student in the mid-1930s, Wingren had suddenly forsaken Odeberg to follow Bring, which had turned him into an enemy. In his declaration, Odeberg followed the same course as Eklund and Pleijel. He, too, criticized *The Living Word*, which "cannot be meted high value in regard to this professorship," since from his own understanding of the fundamentally historical nature of Christianity, he emphasized the decisive value of studies in the history of ideas. The conclusion was thus obvious for him, "that *Associate Professor Olsson* holds in all respects a distinct advantage over all of the other applicants, and that he stands in a class by himself as a researcher."[25]

22. Ibid., 10.

23. Ibid., 16. To this he adds that Olsson's systematic competency has been underappreciated: "According to my understanding, Olsson is far superior to Wingren on general systematic viewpoints, as well." Ibid., 17.

24. Pleijel, in Appendix 28I, protocol of the Faculty of Theology, meeting on 24 October 1950, 1.

25. Odeberg, in Appendix 28J, protocol of the Faculty of Theology, meeting on 24 October 1950, 1.

The faculty members who supported Wingren's candidacy gave an impression of being equally as well organized (probably through the efforts of Professor Bring). However, one faculty member in favor of Wingren, Erland Ehnmark, a professor of the history of religion and psychology of religion, did not show any measure of involvement in the process. He touched upon several complications introduced by the evaluation committee, including the "Danish" view that the history of ideas was only a minor discipline. Given the strong Swedish theological tradition in the study of the history of ideas, it is not surprising that the Swedes found this viewpoint quite remarkable. However, Ehnmark supported Wingren and went on to make a rather remarkable statement:

> Since Prof. Bring has given Wingren a clear recommendation, and since I cannot judge the production of the applicants in an independent way, I find it most suitable to observe the reduced majority presented by the committee, and rank the applicants in the following order: 1. Wingren 2. Olsson . . .[26]

Gillis Gerleman, professor of exegetical theology, showed far more conviction and engagement. He took a tactical approach in his statement; rather than issuing a detailed judgment on the applicants' writings, he instead attacked the committee member who had attacked Wingren, that is, Lindroth. He refuted the basic assumptions Lindroth had made in his critical reading of Wingren's *The Living Word*. Gerleman argued that as professor of Old Testament exegesis, his own disciplinary speciality authorized him to pass judgment on a work on the early church fathers, namely, Wingren's book on Irenaeus, *Man and the Incarnation*. Gerleman suggested that Lindroth's committee statement made use of odd references. To prove that Lindroth's statement did not measure up, Gerleman quoted lengthy excerpts from *The Living Word* and sought to show Lindroth's one-sided treatment of the book. He pointed out that Lindroth failed to see that Wingren ascribed positive value to historical work, and that he had not blindly followed Barth at all but in fact systematically criticized Barth. As a result, Lindroth also did not recognize that Wingren in fact diverged from Barth's view on the *kerygma* when he criticized Barth's attempts to obliterate the border between theology and the sermon. Gerleman maintained that Lindroth had not only made an obvious misinterpretation, but he also lacked intimate knowledge of the

---

26. Ehnmark, in Appendix 28F, protocol of the Faculty of Theology, meeting on 24 October 1950, 3.

material with which he was dealing.²⁷ Gerleman's declaration, directed as it was toward refuting one of the committee members more than judging the applicants, put Olsson, "whose great knowledge, thoroughness, minute attention to detail, and analytical acumen has been given unreserved recognition by all of the committee members," in second place, while recommending Wingren for the position on the basis of his greater breadth and versatility. With a hinted reference to Søe's declaration, he reported that Wingren had the greatest talent for systematics.²⁸

The last member of Bring's camp was Sven Kjöllerström, who despite Bring's efforts was nonetheless unable to attend the meeting. Instead, Kjöllerström had sent his declaration and vote in a letter, where he summarized the situation and stated that the committee had presented a consistent evaluation of the applicants. The single dissenter was Lindroth, who Kjöllerström felt had been far too limited and misleading in his judgement of Wingren. Kjöllerström argued that by ranking Wingren in fourth place, Lindroth had avoided making a proper comparison between the two major candidates. However, the main purpose of Kjöllerström's declaration was to deal with the evaluation of Wingren's *The Living Word*, which he described as a stimulating work.²⁹ Although the book did not fall under his subject area (and despite the fact that it did not belong to the field of homiletics), Kjöllerström exploited the reference to the sermon in the Swedish title of the book (*Predikan*, "The Sermon") when he mustered all of his prestige as a professor of practical theology to demonstrate that it was "a scholarly achievement of significant measure."³⁰

The dramatic meeting of the Faculty of Theology ended with a final vote of four to three in Wingren's favor. Wingren's small lead was, however, due solely to the mobilization of Kjöllerström. Despite Odeberg's minor reservations, Wingren had avoided being relegated to fourth place at this stage.³¹ The appointment process had stirred up considerable emo-

---

27. Gerleman, in Appendix 28G, protocol of the Faculty of Theology, meeting on 24 October 1950, 4.

28. Ibid., 7.

29. Kjöllerström, in Appendix 28K, protocol of the Faculty of Theology, meeting on 24 October 1950, not paginated.

30. Ibid., not paginated.

31. Cf. the faculty protocol: "Assistant Professor Wingren was ranked in first place by four members (Professors Bring, Kjöllerström, Gerleman and Ehnmark), and in second place by two members (Professors Peijel and Eklund). Associate Professors

tions, and the University was about to experience a general conflict over views on the scientific nature of theology.

The appointment had a ripple effect that spread out all over the city, far beyond the Faculty of Theology. Karl Olivecrona, professor of jurisprudence at Lund University, wrote and published a tract regarding the appointment process, explaining that the issue was not only of great general public interest, but that for the academic community, it had "implications [that extend] far beyond this appointment."[32] On 5 December, only eleven days before the University Council was scheduled to discuss the matter, Olivecrona's tract *The Deciding Factor for a Professorship: Science or Proclamation of Faith?* (*Vetenskap eller trosförkunnelse som merit för professur?*) was released. In his publication, Olivecrona emphasized two major and related issues: how the discipline of systematic theology should be understood, and how the contents of Wingren's book *The Living Word* should be judged from an academic point of view. In regard to the first question, Olivecrona stated that the primary merits for the professor chair must be determined by research in the history of ideas, since Swedish systematic theology has received its completely scientific nature solely through historical studies. It is interesting to note that Olivecrona, grounded in the perspective of legal positivism, argued that a scientific view "prevails throughout our nation," and despite some variation from one country to another was nonetheless obligatory.[33] According to Olivecrona, it was important to evaluate the controversial book *The Living Word*, which had become the deciding factor in the

---

Josefson and Wingren were ranked as more or less equal, and in second place by one member (Professor Odeberg). Associate Professor Olsson was ranked in first place by three members (Professors Odeberg, Pleijel and Ehnmark), and in second place by four members (Professors Odeberg, Kjöllerström, Gerleman and Ehnmark). Associate Professor Josefson was ranked second and more or less equal to Wingren by one member (Professor Odeberg), and in third place by six members (Professors Bring, Pleijel, Kjöllerström, Gerleman, Ehnmark and Eklund)." Protocol of the Faculty of Theology, meeting on 24 October 1950, par. 28.

32. Olivecrona, *Vetenskap eller trosförkunnelse som merit för professur?*, 3, 19.

33. Olivecrona rejects the point of departure taken by the Danish area experts, for the following reason: "It is thus in complete conflict with the prevailing Swedish understanding to grant [the discipline of] the history of ideas the nature of a supporting science in systematic theology. Both of the Danish area experts have based their proceedings on an understanding which prevails in their own country, and to which the Swedish understanding does not correspond." Ibid., 14. This argumentation is in line with the author's understanding of the basis of the judicial law in power, according to the legal-positivistism which Olivecrona had developed, inspired by Axel Hägerström.

appointment process, against this background. For this reason, Olivecrona found it important to inform the general public about the contents of this book—for example, that it describes the sermon as "a divine act of battle in God's combat against Satan," and that the author in fact "asserts certain *dogmas* . . . he claims to proclaim the *correct* biblical faith."[34] For Olivecrona, it was absolutely clear that Olsson should be appointed to the position and that Wingren's theology did not measure up academically: "This is not a disputation over religious faith. Yet it must be upheld with the greatest firmness that in the determination of the merits for a professorship at a Swedish university proclamations of faith not be confused with scientific scholarship."[35]

Finally, on 16 December 1950, the contentious matter of the professorship in systematic theology came up for discussion and final decision at Lund University's Greater Academic Council. At this meeting, the University's president and vice president (*rektor* and *prorektor*), all of the University deans, and two representatives (professors) from each of the University's faculties would all have opportunity to state their position regarding the appointment. Once again, there were many who held strong opinions on the matter, and the lines of argumentation followed those that already had been established by the evaluation committee and the Faculty of Theology. Most of the members of the Greater Academic Council lacked expertise in theology and had to rely on the statements already made by the committee and the faculty. Professor of philosophy Gunnar Aspelin and other council members argued against appointing Wingren, citing criticisms brought by Lindroth of the evaluation committee (and again by Eklund of the Faculty of Theology), including Wingren's methodological shortcomings and the misgiving that Wingren would be unable to discern between academic theology and churchly preaching, or between the lecture podium and the pulpit. At the same time, these arguments were weakened by the fact that Wingren had won the majority of votes of both the evaluation committee and the faculty, and that confidence in Lindroth's evaluation had been undermined. Furthermore, Lindroth's placement of Wingren to a distant fourth place was questionable: "On that, no member of the faculty agrees with him" (Professor of History Sten Carlsson).[36] Yet, when the council finally voted, Olsson won

34. Ibid., 19, 16.
35. Ibid., 19.
36. Carlsson, in Appendix 101 N of Större akademiska konsistoriets i Lund protokoll den 16 December 1950, par. 101.

12 to 10 over Wingren. Given the powerful forces that had been set in motion, the numbers could well have been even higher.[37] However, the formal process within Lund University was now concluded, and it was time to await the final decision on the appointment from the Swedish government authorities. There would be respective decisions from the Chancellor of Universities and then from the Minister of Education. Three months later, on 13 March 1951, the Swedish Chancellor of Universities, Thore Engströmer, announced his decision: he recommended Olsson.[38]

The competition had been remarkably even. The weight of the discussions had shifted back and forth between the two main candidates throughout the various phases of the process. The result of the more than five hundred pages produced by the evaluation committee was a vote of 3 to 1 in Wingren's favor (with the exception of the humiliating fourth place vote he had received from Lindroth). Wingren also held the lead among the members of the Faculty of Theology by a vote of 4 to 3. In Lund's Greater Academic Council, however, Olsson gained the advantage with a "score" of 12 to 10. The national Chancellor of Universities favored

---

37. Even though it is not clear whether Bring may be regarded as a truthful witness on this issue, a letter he wrote to Wingren much later shows that he was also involved in the process that followed, including the decision of the Greater Academic Council—and that Lindroth and others also worked to see that the outcome thus could have favored Olsson even more: "During the competition in Lund in 1951, Lindroth argued strongly for Herbert Olsson, and sought by all means possible to direct me away from ranking you in first place. He indicated he had discovered that the academic council in Lund would completely disregard the Danish area experts if only he and I were in agreement. But as you know, I voted against the majority in the council, favoring you in first place, although the council was very stern, and might easily have been unanimously for Olsson." Ragnar Bring to Wingren, 4 April 1985 (writing errors corrected).

38. The Chancellor's report to the King in Council follows the same lines of argumentation as before, and takes support for its formulation from Lindroth, Eklund, and Aspelin. He concludes his report by stating that "the criticism that has been directed toward the controversial work *The Living Word* elicits great doubt regarding whether Associate Professor Wingren, due to his contributions in the fundamental systematic area, ought to be favored over Associate Professor Olsson. [Olsson's] progress in the history of ideas is obvious; he has also achieved prominent general admiration in systematic theology, and has been declared a scholar of great learning and skill. Despite the acumen, learning and talents that clearly distinguish Wingren as a scholar, I must declare due to the reasons I have indicated that Associate Professor Olsson should be named as the holder of the professorship in question." Universitetskanslerns för rikets universitet utlåtande till Konungen ang. återbesättande av professuren i systematisk teologi med undervisnings- och examinationsskyldighet i teologisk etik vid universitetet i Lund, den 13 mars 1951, 207/49.

Olsson as well. Even though the outcome was far from certain, in the last two instances, Olsson had taken the clear lead in the competition. Uncertainty over what the final outcome would be was further heightened by significant political turbulence in Sweden five years after the end of World War II. The final decision regarding the appointment was to be made by Sweden's Minister of Education, yet during the period in which the appointment proceedings took place, the holder of this post changed several times due to the shifting winds of national politics. In less than one year, no fewer than three individuals assumed the office. In 1951, Hildur Nygren, a counselor from the Swedish National Board of Health and Welfare, succeeded Josef Weijne after his sudden death. Minister Nygren made the final decision on the appointment, on 20 April—in Wingren's favor! Yet in the autumn of that year, she was replaced by Ivar Persson from Skabersjö, when a coalition government was formed between the Social Democratic Party and the Farmers Union Party. The way in which the government ministers had been replaced in such rapid succession only served to heighten the drama surrounding Lund's pending faculty appointment. It was no secret that Anders Nygren as bishop and former professor had taken advantage of his considerable network of influence and worked energetically in order to guarantee that Wingren would succeed him (in Sweden at that time, the Minister of Education was also responsible for ecclesiastical affairs; the actual title was Minister of Ecclesiastical Affairs). When the final decision was announced, the student newspaper *Lundagård* ran a joke announcement in the form of a birth notice playing on the fact that the departing professor and the Minister of Education happened to have the same last name:

> Born
>
> To Hildur and Anders Nygren:
>
> A professor.

Finally, when the department met on 4 May 1951, the faculty dean's first item on the agenda (paragraph 116) was to wish "Professor Wingren welcome as a member of the faculty."

Later on, Wingren often repeated that his book *The Living Word* almost cost him his professorship. The passing of the years has shown that this was nowhere near the truth.[39] Instead, it seems to have been this particular book that finally convinced three members of the evaluation

---

39. Bexell, *Teologisk etik i Sverige sedan 1920-talet*, 145 n. 4.

committee that he had the skills and knowledge to compete at all with Olsson for the chair.⁴⁰ The book was actually decisive for his career in more ways than one. Later, we shall discuss its contents, theoretical status, and importance from a broader philosophical perspective, and also examine how it may serve as a key when coping with the understanding of Wingren's theological project in its entirety.

The Apostasy

Later that same year, specifically on 3 November 1951, nine years after defending his doctoral dissertation, Gustaf Wingren stood ready at the podium in the assembly hall of the University to deliver his inauguration lecture. It was a grand academic celebration. The academic procession had just passed through the hall, accompanied by the tones of Johan Sebastian Bach's *Installation March*. The assembly included Wingren's father, dressed in a tailcoat for the first and last time in his life, along with three bishops (Edvard Rodhe, Gustaf Aulén and Anders Nygren), and many of the leading representatives of the theological establishment of Sweden. University President Bergendahl, who had also voted for Wingren in the Greater Academic Council, led the ceremonies, and Ragnar Norman and Bengt Hägglund, whom both later would become professors at the faculty, served as marshals. The event was to be followed by a dinner and numerous speeches at the historic Dalby Inn, just outside Lund.

Wingren used his inaugural adress to present his upcoming program as a newly-installed professor. At the very end of his lecture, he launched into his conclusion by stating that he faced "the unavoidable task of examining the expository work which has been carried out in the field of systematic theology between the years 1918 and 1923." Even those with only a basic familiarity with Swedish theology understood that one of the theologians who had published his expository works during the latter part of that period, and who was about to be subjected to Wingren's

---

40. The thank you letter sent by Gustaf Aulén, at that time bishop of Strängnäs, to Wingren in December 1949 for sending him *The Living Word* also speaks to this point. Aulén cannot find words to express his great appreciation for the book and its rhetorical strength, and ties its qualities directly to the ongoing competition for the professorial appointment: "Had I been one of the area experts on the appointment to the now-vacant professorship, I would not have hesitated for a single moment about who should be ranked in first place. It is my keen hope that those now entrusted with this task might understand where their pleasure lies." Gustaf Aulén to Wingren, 11 December 1949.

"retrospective theological examination" was his own predecessor, Anders Nygren.[41] Wingren made his point perfectly clear: in order to understand contemporary theology and cope with its problems, it was necessary to look back thirty years to the era of 1920 and perform a critical analysis of the writings of Anders Nygren and Karl Barth.

Given its controversial message and grand ambitions, the title of Wingren's inauguration lecture was rather unassuming: "Some Characteristic Features of Modern Theology." The basic structure of Wingren's presentation was a comparison between what he perceived as the two most important main types of systematic theology of the day: the dialectical theology (represented primarily by Karl Barth, but also by Rudolf Bultmann), and the Lundensian school of motif research (represented by Anders Nygren). He described both dialectical theology and Lundensian motif research as polemic reactions—in fact, excessively polemic reactions—against a previously dominant liberal theology.

It is important to note that already at this early stage, Wingren granted a key role to biblical exegesis in order to come to grips with the problems of theology. This was a view he would continue to maintain. However, it was not the Lundensian tradition of the history of religion, but rather, the form-critical school in exegetics, which Wingren utilized in order to demonstrate that the prevailing image of Jesus as an educated European was actually "an erroneous historical construction."[42] In a way, Wingren thus placed himself in the dialectical camp, without necessarily being a follower of Barth.[43] Instead, he had gained the insight from Karl Ludwig Schmidt that no matter how deeply a researcher immerses him-

---

41. Wingren, "Några karaktäristiska drag i modern teologi" (1951), 247. Nygren's early writings on philosophy of religion fall into the later portion of this period: *Religiöst apriori* (1921), *Dogmatikens vetenskapliga grundläggning* (1922), and *Filosofisk och kristen etik* (1923); and the following year he assumed his professorship. The works to which Wingren refers in the earlier portion of the indicated period are likely books such as Karl Barth's The Epistle to the Romans (1918/1922/1968).

42. Wingren, "Några karaktäristiska drag i modern teologi" (1951), 241. Wingren had gotten to know Karl Ludwig Schmidt in Basel during his four-month stint as a substitute for Barth in 1947. It is worth noting that Schmidt, who we shall have reason to revisit later in this book, stands out as perhaps the most important theoretical reference to whom Wingren made unreserved connections in his inaugural lecture.

43. The position Wingren takes in his inaugural adress falls chronologically and also theoretically somewhere in between *The Living Word* (1949/1960) and *Theology in Conflict* (1954/1958), in the sense that he ties into the kerygmatic moment, with an emphasis on the living word as found in Barth, but simultaneously also in the theological basis that Bultmann found in Heidegger's existential analytic of Being.

self in the historical material, in order to identify some sort of original data, he finds nothing static, no uniform or unequivocal message—other than a sermon about Christ, a *kerygma*, minor literary works about the parables, the contents of which obviously varied widely in time and space when addressing the practical needs of concrete situations in the early church. This point of departure in something contextual, dynamic and changeable stands in sharp contrast to Lundensian motif research, in which Nygren hoped to determine the unchangeable and pure nature of Christianity based on historical descriptions. Wingren sourly stated that the form of address used in the Bible and its connection to the normal human situation "makes an indistinct impression in comparison to the exact definitions employed by Swedish theology." In doing so, he was not merely making a quick reference to existential philosophy—he was also making an ice-cold, ironic comment on the unequivocal concepts and high scholarly ambitions of Lundensian motif research.[44]

Just before he closed his lecture by declaring his intention to administer a critical test of this type of theology, Wingren craftily pulled the rug out from under Nygren's theological project by stating that although there had been skepticism toward Nygren's foundational philosophical work since the early 1920s, Swedish theological scholars had continued, in the spirit of Nygren, to analyze given viewpoints from the past using his methodology for the history of ideas. Wingren completed his strategic pincer maneuver with the following scathing conclusion: "Using Nygren's philosophy, it may be possible to call this systematic theology, but this foundation has been eliminated."[45]

None of the people in the audience who listened to this concluding remark could possibly have misunderstood that Wingren was making a direct attack on his internationally renowned predecessor, the man who had paved the way for Wingren and done everything he could to guarantee that Wingren would be granted his new position. Even more incredible was that Nygren was personally in attendance. Not only was Nygren the most important theologian in Lund, he was bishop of Lund. Now, Nygren's successor was declaring that while philosophy and history support one another within Nygren's theology, neither of them hold up. It would have been scandalous enough to simply attack one's predecessor at any other time, but Wingren did so in his very inaugural address.

44. Wingren, "Några karaktäristiska drag i modern teologi" (1951), 146.
45. Ibid., 147.

Furthermore, the attack was aimed at one of the world's leading researchers in the field, who was now the bishop in the same city, in an era when the state Church of Sweden was still intact. The new professor of theology was actually disallowing the bishop. We can only imagine the flurry of uneasy thoughts in the minds of the attendees as they recessed from the hall to the tones of von Düben's *Narva March*. Wingren's personal journal entry for the day shows the conscious nature of his action: "Immediately submitted my manuscript to the *Swedish Theological Quarterly* (*Svensk Teologisk Kvartalskrift*)." The student newspaper *Lundagård* again struck the nail on the head with this comment: "Once he sat at the Bishop's feet; now he tramples on them."

Up to this point in his life, Wingren could probably have considered an alternative career in the church. In his memoirs, he indicates that had he lost this competition for the professorship, influential individuals would have seen to it that he would have been made the dean of Uppsala Cathedral.[46] But now, as a new professor in the year 1951, he took up a prominent position in the academic world, where he stayed until he retired. Over the years, he was asked quite regularly, nearly every other year, whether he would consider becoming a candidate for bishop in various dioceses. Each time he declined, using explanations that began with statements such as "the responsibilities of my professorship in Lund," "bound to my professorship," and "cannot leave my responsibilities at Lund University."[47]

It seems to have been in accordance with Wingren's intellectual profile to make his entrance into the highest level of the academic world in the context of a confrontation. As the successor to Nygren, he had in many ways seemed to be a classic Lundensian theologian. With one great exception, he had until now closely followed the traditions of Lundensian theology, from his strict immanent descriptive-historical method to his concrete choice of materials for study (Luther and Irenaeus). His peers must certainly have wondered what was going on. Wingren's methods as well as his sources followed the spirit of Nygren. What was the basis of the conflict?

Wingren's falling out with Nygren and Lundensian theology in November 1951 was met with silence. The newspapers did not report anything unusual, only the conventional proceedings. Had people

---

46. Wingren, *Mina fem universitet* (1991), 184.
47. Wingren's personal journals.

understood what Wingren said? Did anyone dare even say what they were thinking? Nothing notable occurred immediately after Wingren's installation, but three years later he would direct an attack in the form of a book, followed by a public debate that took place in 1956. Thus began what might best be described as an intellectual state of war. First, however, let us take a look at Wingren's book on theological method, *Theology in Conflict* (1954/1958), in which he further developed his ideas. This book, which he had in fact foreshadowed in *The Living Word* (1949/1960), makes it possible to broaden the perspective somewhat and sketch the wider intellectual context surrounding the conflict between Nygren and Wingren.

Attack!

When relating himself to the theology of Anders Nygren in his 1951 inaugural lecture, Gustaf Wingren only hinted at his critical remarks and objections. Three years later, the new professor developed his critique fully in his study *Theology in Conflict: Nygren, Barth, Bultmann*. Although the Swedish title, *Teologiens metodfråga* (*The Methodological Question of Theology*), seems incredibly formal, with this book he directed a systematic attack on the three most important theologians of the day: Anders Nygren, Karl Barth, and Rudolf Bultmann. He wrote the book between 10 September 1953 and 10 March 1954. A third of it was written during a stay in Aarhus, Denmark, where Wingren lectured and led seminars based on his new book project. By 17 December the book was on bookstore shelves. With this publication, he had completed the task he had set himself in 1949 on the last page of *The Living Word*, and which foreshadowed his inaugural lecture.[48] Characteristically, Wingren configured his new book as a confrontation, or critical investigation; he stated his own position indirectly.

Anders Nygren's program of motif research can be considered as a variant of the history of ideas, informed by a very special interpretation: after removing legal piety (*nomos*, in other words Judaism) from the equation, Nygren placed egocentricity (*eros*, in other words Catholicism) and theocentricity (*agape*, in other words Lutheranism) in contrast to one another as two overarching concepts. For Nygren, the central task of

---

48. Wingren, "Några karaktäristiska drag i modern teologi" (1951), 247. Cf. *Living Word* (1949/1960), 215 (note 2) and 309.

theology was to describe and identify *agape*, the basic and fundamental motif of Christianity, living faith as pure and distinctly Christian love. The two other basic motifs stand in juxtaposition against this unconditional love: *nomos* (the law), which represents the legal piety of Judaism, and *eros* (desire), which represents the metaphysical longing and striving characteristic of Hellenism and later Catholicism.[49]

In his 1954 book, Wingren leveled two critical objections against his predecessor's ideas. The first was that Nygren's focus on a purely historical description of the basic motif of Christianity (*agape*), as the answer to a purely formal, philosophically determined basic question, cuts off the gospel's relationship to the issue of guilt. Wingren stated laconically that "such questions are unknown in the biblical scriptures,"[50] because the gospel is part of a story of redemption in which humanity is determined by the acts of God, and it posits the questions of sin and bondage. According to Wingren, the gospel cannot be understood in an ethical vacuum, because then it cannot serve as an answer to the question of guilt. In his second objection, Wingren seizes hold of the significant roles that Marcion and Irenaeus play in Nygren's story as representatives of *agape*, since the necessity of the law is absent in both of them. As mentioned, the *nomos* motif soon disappears from Nygren's grand narrative. The dramatic triangle is thus transformed into a duel between *agape* and *eros*. Here Wingren, armed to the teeth with arguments from his own doctoral dissertation, argues that if Luther, according to Nygren, represents the purest and clearest expression of the concept of *agape*, then it is nonetheless remarkable that the works of Luther are rife with contexts in which *nomos*, *eros*, and *agape* intertwine and are actually closely associated with one another. Wingren's conclusion is clear: "If Nygren's analysis of Marcion is correct—and it is—we must give up and reject the combination of a philosophical question and an historical material, which is the very center of his system."[51] Furthermore, he also turned against Nygren's interpretation of the Christian faith as something timeless and unchanging.

---

49. Aulén's break dealt more or less primarily with *nomos*, in that it was his ambition to cleanse away all legalistic characteristics in his presentation of the concept of atonement. This motif, however, disappears early in Nygren's narrative, in which the history of *agape* instead became a matter of a struggle against *eros*, which constantly tends to pollute the unique nature of *agape*. Here, Nygren has been influenced, among other things, by Billing's focus on the contrast between Christianity and Hellenism, which figures as the major opposition in Nygren's great story of pure love.

50. Wingren, *Theology in Conflict* (1954/1958), 21.

51. Ibid., 101.

In contrast, Wingren understood the law to be in constant change and need of reinterpretation in order for it to function as an answer to the contemporary human situation, in the same way that the gospel by its nature is always time-bound.[52]

The very structure of this critical examination is vital to an understanding of both the substantive content of Wingren's critique and the constructive position it implied. Here he focuses on the methodological approach that he had already mentioned in *The Living Word* (1949/1960) as a "double phenomenological approach." This implies a dual structure. First, theology is a matter of *anthropology* inasmuch as all theology presupposes something about the human condition, and second, a matter of *hermeneutics* inasmuch as every theology presupposes something about how the New Testament should be interpreted. This presentation is thus organized around the inner, organic relationship between anthropology (focused upon actual demands) and hermeneutics (focused upon the factual sermon). Together they form the basis of a critique of the three authors, in effect using their own principles.[53]

In *Theology in Conflict* (1954/1958), Wingren stated more explicitly and elaborately what previously could only have been tacitly understood regarding Nygren's theological project. Now there was no longer any question about Wingren's opinion: motif research results in a falsification of the biblical message. This falsehood recurs in Nygren's philosophical foundation and cannot be rectified within the framework of Nygren's system. The entire construction must be demolished: "This hindrance cannot be removed within Nygren's theology. It is his very method of approach to the historical material that makes a correct interpretation of it impossible."[54] This is evident in a purely concrete way, when considering the shortcomings characterizing Nygren's anthropological assumptions. The law, as a constant ethical requirement in the everyday life of

---

52. Ibid., 141ff.

53. Ibid., 66, 68 (n. 69), and 202-6. In a letter to Jan Bengtsson dated 20 September 1986, Wingren explains the historical context of the growth of this double phenomenological approach in the following way: "I find myself in disagreement with Karl Barth, who began his dogmatics in 1927 in connection with Heidegger, and who thereafter discarded his own start, and began anew in 1932 with a rejection of Heidegger. In my critique of Barth, I return to the presentation from 1927, which Barth discards in 1932 (see 202ff. in particular). This implies a partial connection to Heidegger and not to Barth, neither in 1927 nor in 1932. The dual approach is something which I myself espouse, relatively alone in the field of modern theology."

54. Wingren, *Theology in Conflict* (1954/1958), 17.

all human beings, is in Nygren's story granted no role in determining the nature of the Christian faith. In effect, Nygren disconnects the gospel from the issue of guilt, thereby reducing it to an answer to a formal philosophical question.

In Wingren's assessment, Anders Nygren gets into trouble, and Karl Barth is met with even harsher treatment. Wingren takes his point of departure from how Barth based his theology on the separation between God and humanity. Because of the absence of the concept of a devil, that is, an active, tyrannical power of sin, Barth's theology is characterized by a divine war against humanity.[55] In the same way, Barth has merely turned liberal theology upside down: instead of using humanity as the point of departure for his study, he focuses exclusively on God. Nevertheless, since according to Barth's theology humanity's problem is not connected to guilt, he attributes human distress to a lack of knowledge. Revelation brings not liberation or forgiveness, but rather offers the requested knowledge. Wingren issues harsh judgment on Barth's theology, which not even its worldwide reputation can mitigate: "The removal of the fundamental mistake would mean the destruction of his theology."[56]

The theologian who fares best in Wingren's examination is Rudolf Bultmann (1884-1976). Wingren is not only more conciliatory in his judgment of Bultmann, he may also be recognized as a source of inspiration for Wingren's own theological conception—and one that scholars of Wingren's work may have underappreciated. Bultmann's influence on Wingren was evident early on in *The Living Word* (1949/1960) and in his inaugural lecture (1951), and became more important over time. Bultmann was also a representative of the form-critical school within exegetics, which was so vital for Wingren's own theological development. Wingren often lamented Bultmann's insignificant influence on Swedish

---

55. Here we can see an obvious influence from Bring, *Dualismen hos Luther*.

56. Wingren, *Theology in Conflict* (1954/1958), 28. Here, it is certainly questionable as to how correct Wingren was in his criticism, and in fact, this question has been raised by others. For example, see Ola Sigurdson's dissertation, in which he maintains that Wingren took over an interpretive tradition that had been initiated by Torsten Bohlin, who conceived of Barth's thinking in this way: "in his theology, the difference between God and human becomes a difference between two given abstract greatnesses that compete with one another, a qualitative difference." Sigurdson, *Karl Barth som den andre*, 66, 121ff. Ola Sigurdson also questions the basis for Wingren's critique in the texts of Karl Barth that he refers to, and criticizes Wingren for overlooking the social and political context and carrying his refinement of the positions too far. Furthermore, he maintains that both Barth and Wingren represent perspectives that are internal to the Christian faith. Ibid., 85-134.

New Testament scholarship and theology, but he could be considered an important inspiration behind Wingren's conceptualization of his 1954 book, as shown by the following quote: "Rudolf Bultmann combines anthropology and hermeneutics so intimately that it is impossible to discuss the anthropological problem itself."[57] Wingren's critique of Bultmann deals instead with the problems inherent in his strong connection to the philosophy of Martin Heidegger, which Wingren (inspired by Karl Jaspers) mentions as Bultmann's strange "preoccupation with the book of a single philosopher" who makes death an integral part of human nature, rather than a foreign enemy.[58] Bultmann's existential reduction of everything to a *here and now*, resulting in a gospel that contains only my own actuality, reduces guilt to a problem associated with a lack of self-realization, with the result that salvation is no longer comprehended as a victory over guilt and death, but rather as self-realization. Wingren concludes,

> Man is conceived of as guilty and as recognizing his guilt. This insight is very important in our time when most theological mistakes occur because of the failure to recognize guilt. Theology is guided by a common view of the world which is characterized by moral relativism. The result is that the Bible is read as a book of norms, rather than as a book of gospel.[59]

In summarizing the first portion of the book, which deals with anthropological presuppositions, Wingren presents some vital arguments that clarify what he understands as the pervasive problem in Nygren and Barth as well as Bultmann: that the law is missing. The Bible is being transformed into a book of norms instead of gospel. The effect of anthropological relativism is a moralistic understanding of the Bible. With Nygren, the law has been replaced by a formal philosophical question. With Barth, the law is absent due to the way in which the concept of revelation is instead focused on knowledge. Bultmann is in fact the only one of the three who assumes that humans have a relationship with law and guilt, even when they are not aware of the gospel's message. However, Bultmann's existential interpretation of the heart of the *kerygma*, the death and resurrection of Christ, is nonetheless ultimately problematic to Wingren, although to a lesser degree than with Nygren and Barth,

---

57. Wingren, *Theology in Conflict* (1954/1958), 45.
58. Ibid., 61.
59. Ibid., 59.

because his nihilism defends an interpretation of the gospel as the answer to an existential problem that for the individual is disconnected from the actual demands of community life.[60] Following this critical examination of three of the leading theologians of the day, Wingren states his position as follows:

> In conclusion we remind ourselves of the anthropological starting point. The gospel answers the question of guilt and bondage. When a different conception of man's situation is adopted, and such an idea, for instance, as man's lack of knowledge of God becomes an essential characteristic, the understanding of scripture necessarily becomes imprisoned in a false, rationalistic frame of reference.[61]

The second portion of Wingren's examination focuses on the hermeneutical presuppositions of theology, and here it is no coincidence that Nygren fares the worst under his examination. Nygren's theology is determined by a schedule in which timeless (philosophical) questions are answered by descriptions of historical material, to uncover unequivocal motifs of the same timeless nature. Against this idea, Wingren posits the necessity of change. In the same way that the law must be reinterpreted if it is to correspond to people's contemporary situations, "change becomes the necessary mark of the correct interpretation of the biblical word."[62] Thus, Wingren's focus on the significance of context and change stands in contrast to Nygren's idea of timeless unchangeableness: "All good interpretation of the Bible is contemporary. If it were not so, it would not be good. In that case the gospel would not encounter the actual, enslaving law."[63]

Because of the centrality of interpretation in dialectical theology, Wingren's analysis of Barth is somewhat different. Here, his criticism deals primarily with the dominance of the concept of the Revelation of Christ, which causes Christmas to (wrongly) dominate his theology, to the detriment of Easter. Once again, Wingren maintains that the problems associated with the dominance of the issue of knowledge rather than the occurrence of struggle, death, resurrection, and action are all

---

60. Ibid., 81.
61. Ibid., 80–81.
62. Ibid., 105.
63. Ibid., 154. Cf. "Any presentation which is capable of doing right by the biblical message is by its nature time-bound." Ibid., 142.

connected to the existence of a devil.[64] As before, in regard to Bultmann, his criticism deals with the spiritualization of the concept of guilt, resulting from the existential interpretation of death and resurrection. This makes the gospel primarily a question of *my own* death and *my own* resurrection, which also causes the unique occurrence of resurrection in the historical person of Jesus Christ to disappear altogether. But if the historical fact is lost, then, according to Wingren, the actual gift is also lost. In other words, spiritualization of the law has devastating consequences: "Guilt is separated from the relationship to the neighbor and is given an egocentric character: I have not realized my own existence. At the same time the gospel becomes egocentric; it gives me my existence, my life as 'an ability to become' (*Seinkönnen*)."[65] Yet Bultmann is the theologian least scathed by Wingren's criticism. Moreover, I once again want to state that Bultmann is, in general, an underappreciated source for Wingren's theological project.

Obviously, there may be varying opinions about how correct Wingren was in his criticism of the three foremost theologians of his day, but it is quite clear that what is at stake in his discussion on methodology and "theology in conflict" is far more than just a footnote.[66] What is at stake is the very question, what is Christian faith? In his own constructive systematic theology from the late 1950s, which he was later to elaborate, Wingren would cope with this question and more explicitly articulate the position implied in his criticism of and unequivocal disregard for the foremost theologians of the day.

In his combative 1954 book, *Theology in Conflict*, Wingren moved from mere disagreement with Nygren to an actual attack on him, although he flatteringly placed Nygren in the company of the theological giants of the day. By doing so, he also indicates a broader theological discussion when considering the possibilities and risks inherent in a postliberal theological situation.[67] The history of modern theology, like the develop-

---

64. Cf. how Wingren characterizes Barth's position: "There is no enemy, no struggle, no death and resurrection. Rather, a God appears, reveals himself, makes himself known to beings to whom he was previously unknown." Ibid., 115.

65. Ibid., 147.

66. For a discussion of the tenability of Wingren's interpretation of Barth, I again refer the reader to Sigurdson, *Karl Barth som den andre*, 85–134.

67. The term *postliberal* is used in a freer way associated with more general tendencies, and is not to be confused with, or limited to, a later established school of thought in theology referred to by the same name, and represented by theologians such as George Lindbeck, Hans Frei, and others.

ment of modern philosophy, is characterized by a pendulum-like swing between a subjective and an objective pole: on one side, a turn toward the subject, which in philosophy was manifested by Descartes and Kant, and which was transformed into a religious virtue by the Pietist movement, then developed into an anthropocentric program of Protestant culture within the dominant liberal theology of the nineteenth century; and on the other side, the fierce criticism it elicited from the generation of theologians of the early twentieth century, who, inspired by Kierkegaard's and Nietzsche's de-centered subject, sought instead to qualify the distinctly Christian as a radical *No* in relation to a seemingly unconditional acceptance of what may be recognized as universally human. It is clear that Wingren took a critical stance against the latter, which he himself labeled "a curious antiliberal mania" that characterized contemporary theology, and to some extent he partially defended liberal theology. In the 1930s and 1940s, any theologian who attempted to take the human seriously and discuss the historical background of the Bible texts was stamped as "liberal." Yet later, when Wingren was able to look back on these matters, he stated acerbically, "This cooperation between the very sophisticated Barthianism and really stupid fundamentalism, sometimes merely hypocritical, was the most fatal development of everything that started around 1920."[68]

In other words, Wingren argued that the antiliberal theological movement had thrown out the baby with the bathwater, or that they had quite simply turned the model of liberal theology upside down. When he criticized Nygren, Barth, and Bultmann for merely negating human possibilities, as did the spiritual revivalists of the nineteenth century, this did not mean that he thereby unconditionally affirmed liberal theology's uncritical belief in human reason that resulted in a theology without eschatology, which he later characterized as "an optimistic Creation faith which left the Liberal embarrassed about the Bible's own view of sin and death."[69] Due to strong connections to their own philosophies, both Nygren and Bultmann were subjected to Wingren's criticism for their tendency to obscure the problems of concrete guilt that are connected to their respective philosophical presuppositions. Barth, too, was subjected to criticism because of his focus on the knowledge of God, which Wingren associated with Barth's concept of revelation. Wingren also lev-

68. Wingren, *Exodus Theology* (1968/1969), 165.
69. Wingren, *Creation and Gospel* (1979/1979), 71.

eled criticism against the naïve conceptualization of the reconstructive biography of Jesus within liberal theology that focused on "the simple teachings of Jesus" (Adolf von Harnack).

According to Wingren, none of these theological attempts were able to do justice to the biblical material, which instead presupposes a theological interpretation of creation and the world. The gospel is directed not toward a lack of insight and knowledge, but rather is focused on guilt, which awaits forgiveness. Through the general belief in the Fatherhood of God and his Son, liberal theology became blinded to the fact that the four gospels do not offer the prerequisites needed to assemble a biography of Jesus. The conflict inherent in the idea of an active power of evil is foreign to the romantic, harmonious idyll inherent in the perspective of liberal theology. As a result, death is given only marginal attention, and religion gains a status that makes the tribulations of everyday life trivial and theologically irrelevant. Wingren distanced himself from the anthropocentrism of liberal theology, but also from Barth's anthropoclasm and rejection of human achievement. In theological terms, the gift of creation means primarily a de-centering of the subject. However, in keeping with Lutheran ethics, this de-centering instead places *the other* at the center of our interest, and the factual demands that the other directs toward us also bring a re-centering of the subject. The result is a phenomenological ethics that in the words of Emmanuel Lévinas may be described as a "humanism of the other," something that Wingren regards as a necessary, integrated part of any qualified determination of the Christian faith.[70] Later on, we shall return to this idea in greater detail.

"The Operation Was a Success, but the Patient Died"

The rapidly evolving and increased tensions in the relationship between Anders Nygren and Gustaf Wingren during the first half of the 1950s would soon be revealed in the public arena. In February 1956, almost two years after *Theology in Conflict* had been issued, the big debate that all had been waiting for finally took place. In full public glare, the two—Bishop of Lund Anders Nygren, who resided in the great bishop's mansion below the University Library, and Professor of Theology Gustaf

---

70. Cf. Lévinas, *Humanism of the Other*, as well as my own discussion of philosophical and theological anthropology in Kristensson Uggla, *Kommunikation på bristningsgränsen*, 510–38.

Wingren, who occupied an office in the newly renovated Theologicum, a red brick building in the very heart of the university district on the edge of Lundagård Park—clashed. At the time of their confrontation, the relationship between the bishop and the professor in small-town Lund had already been strained and frosty for half a decade. When the battle was over, their relationship was even worse than before. It seemed as if all communication between them had ceased.

Late in the autumn of 1955, the prelude to the debate included several landmark events in the personal lives of both men. On 15 November, Wingren participated in the faculty's official celebration of Nygren's sixty-fifth birthday, which must have been a special day of complexity for both of them. Eleven days later, Wingren rushed home to Valdemarsvik—his father was dying. On 29 November, he wrote in his private journal, "Father died today, on my forty-fifth birthday. *Church of Sweden Hymnal,* no. 94." About two months after this, on 7 February 1956, the local Theological Society in Lund arranged a debate between Nygren and Wingren on the issue of the methodology of theology, moderated by Berndt Gustafsson, who later became professor of the sociology of religion in the Faculty of Theology. Many of those in attendance that evening witnessed the intensity of the debate that went on from 7:30 p.m. to 12:30 a.m.

However, an extended discussion between Nygren and Wingren was published in the leading Swedish theological journal of the day, *Swedish Theological Quarterly* (STK). After the publication of both men's introductory articles, the journal was dominated by their rebuttals throughout the rest of 1956.

In his opening article, Nygren began by referring to Wingren's criticism, and then expressed relief that Wingren himself had called his own book "an occasional text," since this made it possible to separate it from Wingren's other "very valuable" works.[71] Nygren felt that the book in question was a "house of cards, which does not even rest upon the sand." He found ideas "which I myself consider quite foolhardy, at times even ridiculous."[72] In these introductory remarks, Nygren dismissed Wingren's criticism as a sheer, analogous false conclusion in which "his concepts run like a roller coaster." He questioned why the various basic motifs had to exclude one another.[73] Neither did he understand why Wingren

71. Nygren, "Till teologiens metodfråga," 21.

72. Ibid., 21ff.

73. Against the background of Nygren's strong argument that there should be no differences between them, it seems rather contradictory that he simultaneously writes,

took such opposition to the expression "religious statements," which he perceived as a neutral philosophical term, and why he put it in contrast to the address of the *kerygma*. Nygren maintained that his presentation of *agape* in Luther did indeed include the law as a necessary background, while emphasizing the importance of distinguishing between the law and *nomos* (legalism or obedience to the law).[74] Yet, he could not conceal his irritation over Wingren's tone and lack of clear distinctions: "The tendentious attitude spoils everything."[75]

Wingren replied to Nygren in a well-structured, almost didactic article, which he began by an attempt to establish "what this debate is not about": this was not a debate over the legitimacy of philosophy as an independent discipline, nor about the legitimacy of historical research within systematic theology. He rather maintained that motif research failed on the purely historical level. At the very outset of Nygren's story, his presentation of Marcion as a representative of the motif of *agape* should have raised suspicions, and, Wingren posited, the situation was further worsened by Nygren's views on the New Testament and Luther. On these points, it became clear that the concept of basic motifs did not work for purely historical reasons, since the philosophical issues wreaked havoc with the historical material. In other words, Wingren seemed to want to shift the debate to the "very method of approach to the historical material that makes a correct interpretation of it impossible."[76]

In the second number of the journal that year, Wingren completed this line of argumentation by recapitulating Nygren's image of the modified *agape* motif in John the Apostle, Marcion, and Irenaeus—as opposed to the purified version of *agape* only found in Luther. Wingren sought responses from Nygren that *nomos* in his argument really did serve as something more than just a contrasting background material against which *agape* stands in obvious distinction. The role oppointed to Marcion in Nygren's story made the universal claim of motif research a scientific disaster,[77] according to Wingren, who writes,

"Has it completely escaped him that the person who has been reached by the gospel is the very one who is deep in sin, the person who is against God and who stands under God's judgment?" Ibid., 21ff. This statement stands in stark contrast to the way in which Wingren ties together the law and sin with a fundamental perspective of creation theology.

74. Ibid., 30ff.
75. Ibid., 35.
76. Wingren, *Theology in Conflict* (1954/1958), 17.
77. Wingren, "Nomos och agape hos biskop Nygren" (1956), 124.

That Marcion is at all included in the presentation as a renewer of basic Christian elements is Bishop Nygren's mistake, which is tied to the fact that *agape* as an isolated idea is in general a mistake; namely, in its use as a complete description of the characteristics of Christianity.[78]

How could this problem be managed? Wingren complained about the attitude of infallibility that characterized Lundensian motif research, and which since the 1930s had made it indisputable that research in systematic theology must by necessity be reduced to historical research. This was certainly not the case outside of Sweden! He concluded his reply by urging the bishop not to engage in avoidances or remarks of formal logic—for with such things "Bishop Nygren will impress only the unaware"—but rather to keep to the issue at hand: is there really a *necessary* connection between *nomos* and *agape* in Nygren's analysis of the historical material?[79]

In the same number of the journal, Nygren issued a reply to the effect that Wingren's accusations were false. He complained about the lack of objectivity in "Wingren's illusionistic treatment" and the difficulties of carrying on a meaningful conversation with a "scholarly dictator":[80] "All or nothing—that is Wingren's slogan, and in this spirit he hopes to triumph."[81] After a litany on the lack of new scientific ideas in Wingren's rhetoric, Nygren refutes having said that Marcion's view was permeated by a stream of original Christianity. He then presents a series of tables in which he compares, point by point, "Wingren's Ideal" with "What Wingren Really Said" and "What I Have Actually Said." He then goes on the attack against his successor, thus concluding,

> It is a prerequisite for any meaningful debate that both parties equally respect the rules of the game which are part of the logic accepted by all cultured persons . . . It is a prerequisite for any meaningful debate that the factuality of the evidence presented may be relied upon.[82]

This paragraph reveals more than just Nygren's indignation over rules of order; his reference to "cultured persons" introduces what could be

---

78. Ibid., 125.
79. Ibid., 131.
80. Nygren, "Ytterligare till teologiens metodfråga," 133–34.
81. Ibid., 137.
82. Ibid., 142.

considered a class dimension into the debate, implying that Wingren, the social climber from Valdemarsvik, could be incapable of behaving properly in the hallowed halls of the great University. In his concluding sections, Nygren returns to the issue at hand, and presents a detailed explanation of his own position:

> My thesis is this: that *agape, the sin-forgiving love of God, is the basic motif of Christianity*. This means that God's sin-forgiving love is the very heart and center of the Christian message. Take away this, and the Christian message loses its power and meaning . . . It is this, my thesis, which Gustaf Wingren has attacked. Against it, he posits his thesis: that *agape, the sin-forgiving love of God, is not the basic motif of Christianity*. We cannot identify *agape* alone as the central issue of the Christian message. In other words, it is not possible to say *sola agape*. Only by adding *something more* to *agape*, namely, the law or *nomos*, may we achieve a true description of the contents of the gospel. In order to bring out the essence of Christianity, we must combine the motif of *agape* with the motif of *nomos*. Yet (for Wingren) this very combination of two competing basic motifs shows that we must give up the very concept of "basic motifs."[83]

Nygren concludes by emphasizing that he himself embraces the New Testament concept of *agape*, while his successor obviously embraces the Marcionite (or empty) concept of *agape*.

In his reply, which would be his last contribution to the debate, Wingren began with an almost exaggerated tone of indignation: "Unfortunately, I must make this second rebuttal in writing, as the conversation between Bishop Nygren and me has been broken off. Although Bishop Nygren speaks with the readers of this journal, he is not speaking with me."[84]

At this point in the debate, it becomes absolutely clear that Nygren and Wingren were no longer listening to one another. Instead, they seem to represent two incompatible intellectual paradigms. The onetime favorite disciple seems to be noticeably hurt by Nygren's derogatory tone. We can almost imagine Wingren waving his arms in defense as he declared that he had most certainly not presented any false facts about his own production. On the contrary, he claimed that the concept of a basic motif in Christianity had been proven wrong through his own

83. Ibid.
84. Wingren, "Filosofi och teologi hos biskop Nygren" (1956), 285.

historical examinations of the theology of the early church fathers and the Reformation. In addition, it was through his historical examinations that Nygren's grand narrative of pure Christian love had begun to deteriorate.[85] He maintained that Nygren had presented nothing more than "quotations out of context," "unilateralism," and "distortion," and that philosophy had led Nygren astray. Quite simply, the philosophical foundation of Nygren's work had determined the results of his research in the history of ideas. The general law through which God works in the everyday life of all people, regardless of their faith, and which Wingren claimed to have identified and put forward in his historical examinations, simply could not be included as a part of the context of *agape*, without derailing the entire schema.[86]

In his corrections to Nygren's comparative tables, Wingren disclosed something of a secret when he came to the matter of his student essay on Marcion. This essay had been published in the *Swedish Theological Quarterly* (STK) in 1936, thanks to the efforts of Ragnar Bring. However, it seems to have contained treachery within its very structure: at first, the essay obediently follows Nygren's rehabilitation of Marcion by identifying him as a representative of *agape*. Yet, in the final sentences, Wingren seems to have smuggled in a reservation. He questions whether it is really possible that the idea of *agape* in this grouping is capable of retaining its uniqueness, and then immediately replies, "A renewed examination of the issue will certainly show that the opposite is true."[87] Today, one wonders whether Nygren had even read that far in Wingren's essay, or whether he had not understood that one of his doctoral students—the very student who would become his successor at Lund—was undermining the historical foundations of his grand narrative of the essence of Christianity. One may also wonder whether Wingren, despite what he later claimed, was actually practicing a sort of academic shadowboxing for tactical reasons, and was not quite as honest about his disagreement with the renowned Lundensian theologian as he later wanted it to seem. This is a question to which we shall return several times later in this book.

---

85. Ibid., 285.

86. Ibid., 286. In this context, Wingren then continues, first arguing against Nygren that he indeed uses *nomos* and the law as synonymous concepts, and then clarifies his point: "There is a conflict between the law and the gospel, but both are the work of God." Ibid., 290, 293.

87. Ibid. 297, cf. Wingren, "Marcions kristendomstolkning" (1936), 332.

For now, however, let us return to the conclusion of Wingren's article from 1956. He further sharpens the discussion by asking the rhetorical question of how it could be that *agape*, which according to the universal claim of Lundensian theology is completely fundamental to and characteristic of Christianity, cannot accommodate the actual contents of either the Apostles or the Nicene Creed.[88] The strict uniformity characterizing Nygren's refined basic motif of Christianity is based upon principles that, according to Wingren, are in poor agreement with the Trinitarian structure of the Creed as well as the duality of law and gospel, making it impossible to find a uniform principle behind Luther's theology. The only reasonable alternative, therefore, would be to remove the concept of basic motifs of Christianity that Nygren had pulled like "a straightjacket over Lundensian theology."[89] Although it might seem hardly possible to heighten the tension of the debate any further, Wingren concluded with a sarcastic judgment on what had happened to the historical material following Nygren's attempts to maintain his philosophical basis: "The operation was a success, but the patient died."[90]

One may wonder if it is at all possible to say anything more after this barrage of attacks. In any case, Nygren had the last word, and in this instance, he made it a brief one. He stated that nearly everything had already been explained in his previous articles, but as a last appeal for reconciliation, he wondered whether his former student could simply "take his point of departure in *the complete concept of agape found in the New Testament*. We could then come to a deeper agreement."[91] Realizing that this hope was in vain, Nygren closed the door on the possibility of further exchange with a violent slam:

> Prof. Wingren imagined and wished that our discussion would proceed differently. He wanted to posit the questions, and wanted me to address them and treat them based on historical material, and thus "move our theological work forward in a positive way." Things have turned out otherwise.[92]

The rest is silence. All communication had ceased. Although this fact was probably very obvious to the readers, the bottom of the last page

---

88. Wingren, "Filosofi och teologi hos biskop Nygren" (1956), 299.
89. Ibid., 302, 310.
90. Ibid., 312.
91. Nygren, "Slutreplik angående teologiens metodfråga" (1956), 316.
92. Ibid., 322.

of Nygren's article bore the message "The discussion between Professor Wingren and Bishop Nygren is hereby ended. —Editor." The battle was over, but the smoke lay heavily upon the battlefield. The confrontation had shown just how vehement an academic disagreement could be and revealed the dark side of Wingren's model of confrontation in respect to interpersonal relationships. From time to time in the decades that followed, the bitterness that resulted from this debate would well up again, after having lain dormant for years.

What actually happened in this debate between the master, now bishop, and his protégé, the new professor? One can conclude that the debate was an academic one, and in a way entirely internal to the Lundensian context. In the debate Wingren demonstrated his pronounced theological style of conflict. The academic community was already aware that Wingren was prone to conflict, but from this time forward, it became the dominant pattern of his theological style. We also need to remind ourselves that he had attacked one of the most well-known theological works in the world, *Agape and Eros*, which to this day remains the most important Swedish contribution to international Christian theology. Its author, Anders Nygren, was recognized as one of the most prominent theologians in the world. In retrospect, it seems almost mysterious that Nygren himself did not realize what sort of a student he had at his side. Is it really possible that Wingren had concealed his critical opinions so completely that his inaugural address came as a complete surprise? Years later, Wingren declared that while working toward his bachelor's degree, and even as a graduate student, he had used some less-than-refined tricks to carefully avoid Nygren. For example, he took his exams in Nygren's courses only when Nygren himself was on leave for special tasks. He also related how, as a young student, he nearly "boiled with rage" when he read Nygren's writings, and even that he hated Nygren's way of linking philosophy and theology. Moreover, he claimed that he had not attempted to keep these aversions hidden from Nygren, Aulén, or Bring in any way. He even claimed that he talked about his objections in detail, and that in fact it was Nygren who tried to conceal their conflict and that this wrongfully made Wingren's behavior appear treacherous.[93]

93. Wingren, *Mina fem universitet* (1991), 58, and *Creation and Gospel* (1979/1979), 18. A number of things speak against this interpretation, such as, for example, Wingren's warm thanks to Nygren in the foreword to his doctoral dissertation, in which he presents Nygren as "a ground-breaking researcher, whose authorship since his early years as a student has been of fundamental importance for my entire theological

At the same time, it is also important to remember the strong ties that existed between Wingren and Nygren, even on the personal level. For example, Nygren was often present at various celebrations in the Wingren home. On 4 April 1946, Professor and Mrs. Nygren, along with Professor and Mrs. Bring, were special guests at the baptism of Gustaf and Signhild's daughter, Anna, and the organist for the occasion was the Nygren's son, Gotthard Nygren. Three years later, on 22 September 1949, Nygren, then a bishop, baptized the Wingren's second child in Lund Cathedral. It seems no coincidence that this baby boy, born in that eventful year of 1949, was given the name Anders! Wingren's journal for the period surrounding his professorial appointment process shows that just five days after the statements from the evaluation committee became public, on 21 August 1950, the family gathered together, with Anders and Irmgard Nygren visiting. It is not difficult to imagine the topic of conversation on that evening ... We may also wonder how we are to interpret the closing words of an article Wingren published in a 1950 Festschrift dedicated to Nygren, regarding how the hermeneutical problem ultimately culminates in "the old problem of the relationship between philosophy and theology." Wingren wrote, "No one in contemporary religious studies has demonstrated this problem with more clarity than Anders Nygren."[94] Was this sentence a tribute? Or a Trojan horse? None of this makes it any easier to understand Wingren's attack on his predecessor, but an examination of the sources does provide some elucidation. In the next chapter, these sources will be examined from a broader historical perspective.

The harsh tone of his debate with Anders Nygren did not prevent Gustaf Wingren from describing Nygren as the most important and influential theologian in Sweden. Even in 1988, after several decades of repeated attacks on his old teacher, he was able to write, "Nygren has given Swedish theology a recognizable face."[95] Yet, the 1950s debate over the methodology of theology was by no means marginal; it raised one of the most fundamental questions of theology: What is Christianity? The debate commenced when Wingren, after decades of undermining the historical foundations of Lundensian theology, raised his explicit objections to the validity of Nygren's wonderful story of the essence of Christianity. In doing so, he questioned the wisdom of an approach that sought

---

education." Wingren, *Luthers lära om kallelsen* (1942), vii. This statement is, however, not included in the English edition of the book, *Luther on Vocation* (1957).

94. Wingren, "Utläggningens problematik" (1950), 412.

95. Wingren, "Anders Nygren och svensk teologi idag" (1988), 11.

to identify the historically absolute, as well as a theology that attempted to isolate the distinctly Christian. With this in mind, and an awareness of how much was to be at stake in this debate, we can see that there may be in fact good reason for the intensity of the exchange.

3

Sources

BEHIND EVERY STORY THERE is always another hidden story. Every memory contains an excess of forgetfulness. Thus, in order to recall something from the past it is necessary to suppress even more than we recount. When we remind ourselves about something from the past, it means, necessarily, that we must exclude so much more. To tell a story means inevitably to remove the largest part. Each memory that we retrieve requires simultaneously a great deal of forgetting. Therefore, there is always already another story waiting to be told before each story begins. Every history has its own history. One of the enigmatic conditions intrinsic to writing history is that it deals with something that does *not* exist—or more correctly, something that *no longer* exists. History is something that remains to be written, and this requires at least two basic operations: *selection* and *narration*. The historian is forced to make drastic choices, and then organize the resulting, severely reduced material into a meaningful context with the help of some kind of narrative activity. This also means that it is always possible to tell yet another story about what has happened. In a similar way to every written history being doomed to operate according to the conditions of selection, so too must forgetting be perceived as an integral part of human memory. When almost everything has been pared down, we can then create, with the help of narratives, meaning from the material that remains. All too often, we fail to recognize the staggering consequences of this reasoning: in fact, we often have considerably more freedom in our relationship with the past than freedom to affect the future.

This also means that history can have neither a clear beginning nor a definitive ending. When leafing through our own personal journals, it becomes obvious to us that topics and ideas believed to be recent developments frequently have a long pre-history. For a discipline as steeped in tradition as theology, in which "the most important thing" has in a way always already occurred (and, it must be added, has also yet to be realized), and for which *anamnesis* and the treatment of memory are categories that are absolutely vital in order to think truly new and surprising thoughts, this is not such a strange thing. Yet, it is also generally accepted that even the freest and most creative thinking needs sources that can give life and provide content to the flight of thought. Thus, we are always already situated in tradition, even when we are not conscious of it. Furthermore, in order to break with one tradition, it is necessary to first re-enact another tradition.

In many ways, Gustaf Wingren seems to be an archetypal representative of Lundensian theology. Not only had his education and basic views been formed by this particular theological tradition, but also he would come to complete vital components of it. Nevertheless, in time he would go his own way. Late in life, when he was over eighty years of age, he expressed himself in the following way: "Considering the historical aspect, I am and will remain a true disciple of Anders Nygren. One might indeed dare to claim that I among all Swedish theologians am the most typical successor to Aulén and Nygren, although I am so in my own personal way."[1]

Against this background, one may ask the question, what brought about his disagreement with Nygren and the subsequent falling out and attack on his mentor? Many times, Wingren himself recalled that the decisive impulse for his breakaway came as a result of the "detour" that he made in 1947, when he was forced to confront an academic milieu radically different from the one in which he had been formed in Lund. When World War II ended and national borders were once again opened, Wingren was eager to use the opportunity to travel in strife-torn Europe. In those first years, immediately after the end of the war, he also found positions as a guest professor at several universities abroad. The greatest impact came when he served as a substitute teacher for Karl Barth in Basel, at a Continental university where theology was pursued in a way that was radically different from the way he was accustomed to and which he had fully mastered in isolation, at home in Lund, during the war. These life-changing experiences gave him considerable cause for thought, which in turn led him to revisit some of his own experiences and the

---

1. Wingren, *Mina fem universitet* (1991), 65.

early sources of his theological thinking. Thus, processes were brought into motion that led his thinking onto new pathways. This chapter takes us several steps backward in time, which will help us consider Wingren's new orientation from the perspective of the sources that he used for his theological reflection and confrontations.

Nygren's Grand Narrative of Pure Christian Love

Gustaf Wingren's attack on Anders Nygren did not simply arise out of nowhere. There was a previous history to this history, and in this particular case, it was literally a matter of history. The issue at hand was how to understand the story that defines the Christian faith and how to deal with the historical sources, which formed the support for this story. To understand this cohesion, it is helpful to consider the wider scene of systematic theology in Sweden during the twentieth century.

Hardly any other theoretical movement within Swedish theology that gained international attention and prestige can compete with the tradition known as Lundensian theology. Despite its reputation, it is, however, far from clear exactly what is meant by the term. This ambiguity can be explained by the fact that even one of its founding fathers, Gustaf Aulén, preferred not to speak of a Lund school of thought.[2] In many ways, Aulén is a giant among theologians in his own rights. However, he was also of vital importance to what came to be known as Lundensian theology, even though his own ties to Lund were somewhat tenuous. Aulén was not originally from Lund but came from the city of Kalmar. He did not receive his PhD from Lund, but from Uppsala, where he also served as associate professor. In 1933 he left Lund after two decades when he relinquished academic life to become bishop of Strängnäs in the Church of Sweden. Yet, through his work as a professor at Lund, Aulén, later in cooperation with Ragnar Bring, became an important link to the theology of Einar Billing and Nathan Söderblom, and the philosophy of Axel Hägerström, at Uppsala University.[3] By way of his professorship in Lund,

---

2. In his autobiography, *Från mina nittiosex år*, Aulén denotes this point with all the clarity he can muster. He describes both "Uppsala theology" (Söderblom and Billing) and "Lundensian theology" (Nygren, Aulén, and Bring) as "co-operating contrasts." Ibid., 91.

3. In Uppsala, Aulén had been part of the circle of theologians surrounding Einar Billing and Nathan Söderblom, from whom he had found inspiration for a theological project of his own. However, earlier on, he had also taken private lessons from Axel

which also included the academic discipline of history of doctrine, Aulén was also primarily responsible for the historical schedule, the perspective and the source material of which Nygren would later make use.

Inspiration from the works of Immanuel Kant and Friedrich Schleiermacher united Nygren with Aulén in their resistance towards intellectualism. Thus, Christianity was first and foremost not associated with dogma, but was rather a matter of faith; the manner of doctrinal expression that this faith took was of secondary importance. Before becoming his colleague, Nygren had been one of Aulén's students. During the early 1920s, before he assumed his professorship in 1924, Nygren worked on the philosophical foundations of systematic theology, dogmatics, and ethics. The aim of the three books he published in rapid succession in 1921, 1922, and 1923 was to develop a scientific defense for theology as an academic discipline. This was, however, achieved using philosophical principles other than those in favor at Uppsala University.[4] Using the background of Kant's transcendental deduction and Schleiermacher's concept of religion, Nygren developed a theory of the universality and necessity of religion, based on the idea of four independent areas of experience: the theoretical, the ethical, the esthetic, and the religious. While these experiences certainly cannot be considered to be sciences in themselves, they are all expressed in cultural items, each of which in and

---

Hägerström when the philosopher was still an unknown associate professor at Uppsala. Before he moved to Lund and assumed his professorship in systematic theology at the age of thirty-four, Aulén was able to witness Hägerström's early years as a professor. Without in any way becoming a student of Hägerström, he was deeply influenced by Hägerström's thesis that metaphysics and science could not be reconciled. Aulén took a critical stance against metaphysics, subjectivism, and idealism, and emphasized religion as a special area of experience, the principles of which may be deduced via transcendental reduction. This must all be comprehended against the background of Hägerström's, and also Phalén's, view of life influenced by natural science which, together with a rationalism that regarded reality as a logical system, contributed to the creation of a value-nihilistic cultural climate. That the Lundensian theologians affirmed many of the ideas of the new times was connected to the need for agreement on another front: that of church conservatism. The theologies of Billing and Söderblom, which wholeheartedly affirmed modern biblical criticism, had rendered Aulén immune to the mixture of old Lutheran orthodoxy and Pietism that risked transforming an uncritical symbiosis of exegetics and dogmatics into a dangerous amalgam of apologetic orthodoxy.

4. As mentioned earlier, Nygren presented his religious-philosophical foundation for systematic theology in his three books *Religiöst apriori* (1921), *Dogmatikens vetenskapliga grundläggning* (1922) and *Filosofisk och kristen etik* (1923). None of these books have been translated into English.

of itself can be observed and studied, and may thus become the object of scientific description. *The Scientific Foundation of Dogmatics* (*Dogmatikens vetenskapliga grundläggning*, 1922) builds upon the idea of the transcendental necessity of religion and that all true religion must be realized as something positive and historical. Thus it is possible to determine its essence. Nygren established a strict division of labor, in which philosophy was to lay the foundation of theology by establishing its *basic motifs*, that is, historically given theological answers to categorical questions of philosophy. Theology itself was to be responsible for the description of the historically posited belief. To state it simply, according to Nygren, it could be said that theology consists of philosophical questions and historical answers.

At the heart of Wingren's confrontation with Nygren we find the issue of how to understand the historical sources. Both of these men shared methodology to a large degree, but their respective studies had produced widely varying results. With regard to the selection of sources and method, Wingren seems in many ways to be a model disciple of Nygren. However, as will be seen, there were both advantages and disadvantages to focusing strictly on the careful studies in the history of ideas, as was the case in Lundensian theology. In fact, the conflict was based on precisely those areas associated with Nygren's favorite sources, Luther and Irenaeus, together with Marcion. In other words, the battlefield, as we saw in the previous chapter, consisted of Wingren's as well as Nygren's primary historical sources for their theological reflection. It was when Wingren investigated deeper into Nygren's own favorites, using the strict historical method that Nygren himself had originated, that Wingren found something different, something that Nygren had overlooked, and which in the long run would take the form of what Wingren himself describes as a death blow to his teacher's grand narrative of Christian faith.

Nygren's three major philosophical publications in the first half of the 1920s gained him a professor's chair in 1924, but they found no international recognition and were never translated. Lundensian theology first came into being in 1930, when Nygren took the step from the *philosophical* basis to more distinctly *theological* undertakings. This year saw the publication of two defining books by Aulén and Nygren, both of which became world famous and were vital to the establishment of the concept of Lundensian theology. Since 1913, Aulén had been a professor of systematic theology, with teaching and examination duties in dogmatics and symbolism. When he published *Christus Victor* (*Den kristna försoningstanken* [The Christian Idea of Atonement], 1930/1931), he was able to reap the benefits of his long-term work in the history of Christian doctrine.[5] The same year, Nygren published the first volume of *A History of the Christian Idea of Love: Eros and Agape* (*Den kristna kärlekstanken genom tiderna: Eros och Agape*, vol. 1, 1930/1932), which, together with the second and final volume of this work published six years later (1936–39), is better known internationally and published in one volume as *Agape and Eros* (1953). It is not coincidental that both of these works were mainly historical. Aulén had acquired a historical orientation from Billing and Söderblom in Uppsala. Nygren, who had received this orientation from his former teacher, arranged the historical materials according to new principles.

When Aulén, in *Christus Victor*, describes the story of how a classic dualistic-dramatic motif of atonement is being reshaped and manifested in the works of Irenaeus—"the Schleiermacher of the second century"— and then becomes obscured for a lengthy period during the Latin tradition, to finally be "renewed and deepened" as a result of Luther, it is impossible to deny that Aulén's story strongly echoes international precursors, such as Adolf von Harnack's *History of Dogma* (*Lehrbuch der Dogmengeschichte*, 1886–90), a work that was so well received that it gave rise to the academic discipline history of doctrine (*Dogmengeschichte*). We may also note that Bring's dissertation, *Dualism in Luther* (*Dualismen hos Luther*, 1929), also played an important role.

Both founding fathers of the Lundensian school of theology, Aulén and Nygren, were united in their desire to promote a distinctly Christian position, based on a premise of christology, where the line moved downward from above, from God in heaven to mankind on earth. However, while Aulén was focused on the idea of atonement, Nygren was occupied with the idea of love. Both of their books may be considered among the most important and widely read works of modern theology in general and Swedish theology in particular. However, just three years after the concept of a Lundensian theology came into more general acceptance, Aulén left Lund to become bishop. Thus, he had already left the scene when Nygren, in the second volume of his *Agape and Eros* (1936/1939), presented his grand narrative of pure Christian love. When Nygren,

5. In 1913, when Aulén assumed his professorship in systematic theology, with special responsibilities for dogmatics and symbolism, at Lund University, he immediately began to immerse himself thoroughly in the history of doctrine, which resulted in the textbook *Dogmhistoria* (*The History of Doctrine*), published in 1917.

approximately twelve years later, also became a bishop, the most important representatives of the Lundensian school of theology were no longer part of the academic world. Only Aulén's successor, Ragnar Bring, remained at Lund, along with an established theological research program—and a grand narrative.[6] Nygren's own successor, Wingren, made no serious attempts to attack Aulén, but mounted a frontal attack against Nygren's philosophical basis and the historical foundation of his grand narrative explaining the true Christian faith.[7] However, the main focus of Wingren's critique of Nygren's philosophical foundations, which he initially delivered publicly as part of his inaugural lecture in 1951, had been preceded by twelve years of historical studies during which Wingren had systematically undermined the historical foundations of the grand narrative of the Christian faith that Nygren had presented in *Agape and Eros*.

The premise for Nygren's narrative is that pure *agape* love, which characterizes the Christian faith, cannot actually exist outside Christianity. According to Nygren, *agape* is exclusively tied to a christological perspective that in turn implies an equally exclusive ecclesiological perspective. In accordance with Nygren's grand narrative of Christian love, *agape* and *eros* (as well as *nomos*, which disappears early in his narrative) have nothing to do with one another; they are to be considered as completely separate basic or fundamental motifs. Agape, God's path to humankind in the revelation, is theocentric and is mainly manifested at only one single point in history—in Christ. *Eros*, man's path to God through mysticism, is recognized as egocentric and manifested at many different points in history. However, over the course of history, these two basic motifs have come to be intermingled with one another, at times to the point of being unrecognizable. Nygren uses the term "synthesis," or more specifically "the *caritas*-synthesis," to denote the tendency throughout history to adapt Christianity to its surroundings, while "reformation"

---

6. In 1963, Ragnar Bring was succeeded by Per Erik Persson, who was not in any way a disciple of Nygren. Rather, he combined what seems to have been a basic inspiration from Aulén and Wingren with an ambition to make further contributions through influence from international perspectives. In hindsight, it is evident that Persson has been especially influential in Swedish theology, not least of all through his many doctoral students, a point that has previoulsy been underappreciated.

7. By linking Aulén to his background in Uppsala, Wingren tries to show his strong ties to Billing and thus demarcates his initial distance from Nygren. With time, Aulén was influenced by Nygren's program to such a degree (even more so than was Bring) that Billing's influence in Lund was severely limited. Wingren, *Exodus Theology* (1968/1969), 122–27.

denotes the tendency to refine Christianity. "The history of Christian ideas proceeds in a definite rhythm, alternating between two tendencies that we may call synthesis and reformation."[8] This is where Nygren's text—and the problems—begins.

In the first part of his history of the Christian idea of love, Nygren presents the historical context of the three basic motifs in conflict, in which *nomos* is derived from the Old Testament, the apostolic fathers, and the apologists (and the influence of Judaism); *eros* from Gnosticism and Alexandrian theology (influenced by Hellenism); while the original context for *agape* is Jesus and Paul in the New Testament. As a result of the decline of *agape* in association with the apostolic fathers, Marcion also plays an important role in the early church for the rediscovery of the idea of *agape* as something absolutely new entering the world with Christ. Three early church fathers each represent the positions of the three basic motifs: Tertullian is said to represent *nomos*, while Origen represents *eros* and Irenaeus represents *agape*.

Of principal significance for this account, and the critique that Wingren would later direct against Nygren's construction, is the prominent and surprising role ascribed to Marcion as a representative of the *agape* motif. Nygren did concede the Old Testament importance for *agape*, but mostly because it is only with the help of the Old Testament that the deepest meaning of *agape* can be gained and that Jesus may be understood. However, the *nomos* motif is only required as a *contrasting* background to clarify the gravity and depth of *agape*.[9] Despite the limitations associated with Marcion's view of creation, that is, incarnation and the resurrection of the flesh, Nygren could not escape from the fact that Marcion had the desire to make love the center of Christianity and that God in this view is recognized as unconditional love, that is, *agape*. He also stated appreciatively that, compared to the apologists and the Gnostics, Marcion was at least someone who had understood how absolutely new the Christian message is as an astounding revelation from above. However, because Marcion was excommunicated and rejected as

---

8. Nygren, *Agape and Eros*, 240.

9. Ibid., 245-446: "I. The preparation of the synthesis." Nygren attributes the breakthrough and return of the concept of *agape*, after the New Testament concept of love had been polluted and thinned out by the apostolic fathers until it was unrecognizable, to one man, whom the church in fact considered the greatest of heretics, namely, Marcion. This must be viewed in light of Adolf von Harnack's attempt to rehabilitate Marcion when he presented him as the most important theologian between Paul the Apostle and Augustine.

a heretic, and the *agape* motif became a heresy as well, Irenaeus instead became the main representative of *agape* directly connected to the primitive Christian faith. Based on his idea of incarnation and the words of the Apostles' Creed regarding the resurrection of the flesh, Irenaeus effectively distanced himself from all attempts to separate the Creator God from the Savior God. The only real complication Nygren recognizes in Irenaeus (besides the question whether his criticism really touches the deepest intentions of Marcion) is the limitation associated with his ideas regarding the natural immortality of the soul and the idea of deification—factors that in the end gave Luther priority over Irenaeus when Nygren decided who would be the great hero in the staged drama. In any case, the first act of his drama ends with the compromise of the third century between *eros* (Origen) and *agape* (Irenaeus).

In the first chapter of the second part of his history of the Christian idea of love, Nygren presents the *caritas*-synthesis, which had been introduced by Augustine when he moved from compromise to synthesis, and allowed Neo-Platonism and Christianity to meet and meld together into a spiritual unity. In the chapters that follow, Nygren traces the continuation of the historical process in which the original motif of *agape* was gradually corrupted and when the *eros* motif passes to the Middle Ages and the medieval doctrine of love.[10] Nygren shows how, after these centuries of decay, the true hero, Luther, takes the stage and breaks with Augustine. After "The Destruction of the Synthesis,"[11] the entire drama is resolved in and through "The Renewal of the Idea of Agape in the Reformation."[12] Nygren describes Luther, in opposition to the Catholic egocentric attitude of love, as *"the reformer of the Christian idea of love"* who through a Copernican turn returned theocentric love to the center of theology.[13] Because Luther, according to Nygren, so clearly described Christ through the use of the story of how God's love has paved a new way down to lost humankind, *"where the stream of love must be directed downwards"*[14]—and did not, like Irenaeus, labor with some sort of "deification"—it is through him that *agape* shines most brightly in Nygren's entire story. Here the distinct nature of Christian love becomes evident

---

10. Ibid., chapter 2 (449–562), chapter 3 (563–608), and chapter 4 (609–64).
11. Ibid., Part III (665–80).
12. Ibid., chapter 6 (681–737).
13. Ibid., 683.
14. Ibid., 735.

as something spontaneously given. It is neither upwardly rising, as with *eros*, nor legalistic, as with *nomos*. Agape is the pure love that is exclusive to the Christian faith and that does not require some outside impulse for its initiation. This love is always the same, regardless of what object it is directed towards, and beyond all estimation. Could it be any better? Who could be against such a wonderful idea of love?

Cracks in the Historical Foundations

In retrospect, it may seem remarkable that the typological method employed in Lundensian motif research could claim to be a positivistic science without any presuppositions. Today, we easily recognize that this story reflects the spirit of an era far different from ours. It is difficult for us today to imagine that Luther could ever have been granted hero status during the period 1920–1960, and be highlighted as a progressive historical figure who stood out as a critic of the establishment. However, it must be remembered that every age, including ours, tends to be blind to its own assumptions and prejudices. Science is a historical construct and a constantly changing institution, and the stances it has taken have varied over time. One day in the future our current scientific thinking will also be subjected to unkind critical examinations, ironical comments, and radical re-evaluations. For this reason, it may be wise to be careful when passing judgment and to avoid transforming, out of critical eagerness, the reality of the past into a series of anachronisms.

Anders Nygren is certainly connected with Nathan Söderblom and Einar Billing in his disassociation with an older theological paradigm, and together with his recognition of modern critical science, he may even appear as a quite radical figure of his day. However, with a little historical distance, it is not difficult to see in what way his theology, which claimed to be a science free of assumptions employing purely historical descriptions, was in fact determined by certain presuppositions. Yet, the very fact that only Lutheranism was allowed to represent a theocentric theology, while Catholicism was made to represent an egocentric theology, reveals how strongly the confessional determination of his presentation was with regard to its form and content. This pure historical science was in reality far from being as pure as it had grandly been declared.

Wingren's criticism of this school of thought came, however, from an unexpected direction—namely, from within. In his final article in the debate he waged with his predecessor in the journal *Swedish Theological Quarterly* (*STK*) in 1956, he wrote, almost in an apologetic way,

> I am nothing other than a pupil in this school, but a pupil who has sat down and read the two great authors who represent the *agape* motif, and who has emerged from this study in the possession of more knowledge of Irenaeus and Luther than before, but who along the way has been forced to renounce the entire apparatus of motif research, *because it is not suited to the historical material.*[15]

If these lines are to be taken seriously, Wingren came to terms with his teacher by closely following his path; in other words, by keeping to descriptions of historical material. He had thus focused on the two heroes in Nygren's grand narrative of pure Christian love: Irenaeus and Luther. However, upon closer examination of the sources, Wingren found something that differed from that which Nygren had highlighted in these texts. The results of his research would undermine the entire structure Nygren had built, so that the narrative at last fractured. But let us begin at the beginning.

Originally, it was Bring who proposed the subject for Wingren's doctoral dissertation. It was Bring's suggestion that Wingren should write his dissertation on the Gnostic heretic Marcion of Sinope (85–160), using the source materials that Adolf von Harnack had assembled a few years earlier.[16] As mentioned previously, Wingren had written his first essay on Marcion as an undergraduate, and it had been published in *Swedish Theological Quarterly* in 1936.[17] This essay was the first in a long series of publications reflecting this line of research. Three years later he pre-

---

15. Wingren, "Filosofi och teologi hos biskop Nygren" (1956), 296. Later on, in his memoirs, Wingren describes himself as "a true disciple of Anders Nygren"—but only in regard to sources and methods, that is, "the art of producing pure historical material from old sources." Wingren, *Mina fem universitet* (1991), 59.

16. Because Marcion was excommunicated and rejected as a heretic, his writings were destroyed. The only knowledge that we have regarding the contents of Marcion's theology comes from the texts written by the church fathers who campaigned against him and sought to refute him. In addition to his proposed rehabilitation of this early church figure, Adolf von Harnack also opened the field for further research on Marcion by presenting a reconstruction of his writings, which are collected in the appendix in *Marcion: Das Evangelium vom fremden Gott* (1924). It is primarily this material, plus the research milieu in which he achieved this reconstruction, that made Wingren's Marcion research possible.

17. Wingren, "Marcions kristendomstolkning" (1936), 316–38.

sented his licentiate thesis, *Irenaeus and Marcion—Studies on the Idea of Creation* (*Irenaeus och Marcion—studier över skapelsetanken*, 1939), and after the war he published the book *Man and the Incarnation: A Study in the Biblical Theology of Irenaeus* (1947/1959).[18]

In his unpublished licentiate thesis on Irenaeus and Marcion, Wingren began his presentation by placing his research on the early church fathers within a contemporary theological context.[19] He stated that the anti-liberal theological one-sided focus on the distinctly Christian had resulted in a situation where creation and law were being "noticed only to a small degree."[20] The reservation that Wingren had included, in a concealed manner, at the end of his earlier essay from 1936, he now stated explicitly, as when he explained the basis for his study:

> The examination of Marcion leads to the question of whether his dismissal of creation and law has also had consequences in regard to the concepts of salvation and revelation; or expressed another way, whether precisely the Christian idea of salvation presupposes a particular, positive thinking in regard to creation and law, so that a disregard of these ideas brings the destruction of the very idea of salvation.[21]

18. Thirty-five years later, in the wake of the great recontextualization of the 1970s, Wingren published *Human and Christian: A Book about Irenaeus* (1983), but that is another story, and I have chosen to deal with that book at a later point in my presentation (chs. 5–8).

19. This information comes from the notebook that Wingren kept during his period of study in Berlin in 1938, and in which he continued to write after his return home in 1939. It is now part of the unorganized papers of Gustaf Wingren in the Lund University Library. For the sake of simplicity, I have chosen to refer to this book as "The Johanneum Journal," although it is not actually a book. Notes written in the latter portion of "The Johanneum Journal" make it seem as though he had originally planned to release his licentiate thesis as a published book (likely he was planning to further develop it into a doctoral dissertation). Here, he wrote detailed notes about the intended book's format (including paper and type fonts), publisher ("preferably the Diakonistyrelsens Förlag"), and so on ("Johanneum Journal," 163). He later crossed out these passages in the notebook, possibly due to the outbreak of the war and his subsequent need to cancel his research plans. Instead of a book, this study was reorganized into two articles published in *Swedish Theological Quarterly* in 1940: "Skapelsen, lagen och inkarnationen enligt Irenaeus" (1940, no. 2), and "Frälsningens Gud som skapare och domare" (1940, no. 4). The first article contains the more source-oriented study that is also found in his licentiate thesis (51ff.); the second article takes a more systematic approach based on the introductory and concluding portions of the same thesis.

20. Wingren, *Irenaeus och Marcion* (1939), 1.

21. Ibid., 3ff.

Adolf von Harnack had attempted to make the rift between Marcion and Gnosticism as wide as possible in order to remove Marcion from the Hellenistic context and bring him into agreement with Paul the Apostle. However, this also meant that the evil God of creation, the *demiurge*, appeared as fickle, weak and despotic, in a way that drastically diverged from the Gnostic concept where the soul, trapped in the body, was related to the divine. Wingren's strategy was the opposite, in that he did not at all view Marcion as a proponent of Pauline theology: "Marcion is using the same idea of salvation and concept of revelation as the Gnostics. His delight of the natural knowledge of God (i.e., the myth of the fall of man) is a modification *within* the basic view of Gnosticism."[22]

Marcion labored with a tripartite scale of values: first, the material, in which the devil is localized; second, the evil creator-God, the *demiurge* and his law; and third, the alien God, who is ideal love and goodness. Marcion's theology is dominated by the opposition between God and world. However, because the idea of salvation is isolated, Wingren, in what sounds like an idea from Nygren, maintains that it cannot function as *agape*.[23] Thus, God's only act is to save humanity from the material world. Because of Marcion's negative view of the material world, Christ cannot be incarnated; he can only appear in a spiritual body. Normal human birth is not worthy of Christ, and also the resurrection of the body is denied, since Marcion speaks only of the salvation of the soul. For Wingren's later polemics against contemporary theology, it is important to note that the idea that salvation, according to Marcion, is something achieved through knowledge, which Wingren characterized as an intellectualistic approach. However, this refined position also excludes all possibility of articulating the love of God as judgment. When Harnack, in the spirit of Marcion, sought to eradicate the Old Testament in order to save the New Testament from corruption, one may easily identify the opposition God versus the world in the background. According to this perspective, salvation means, briefly stated, that humanity is freed from the world. For this reason, it becomes necessary to maintain a distinct demarcation between the God of creation and the God of salvation. Still, Marcion diverges from Gnosticism by rejecting the myth of the fall, thereby creating an opposition between God and the world.

---

22. Ibid., 100.
23. Ibid., 19, 32.

For Wingren, Marcion stands out as a symbol of the unilateral refinement that attempts to isolate something distinctly Christian, a way of thinking that interestingly enough had many striking similarities with the dominant theological tendencies of Wingren's day. Thus, near the end of his examination, when he states that "the Christian idea of salvation presupposes a particular positive thinking in regard to creation,"[24] it may seem that he is in agreement with Nygren and his *agape* motif. However, later it becomes evident that this only appears to be so on the surface. Even though Wingren speaks of the purity of the idea of salvation and the image of God, his reasoning implies that this purity must instead necessarily incorporate something common to all human beings, that is, something that, in accordance with Nygren's agenda of basic motifs, has a contaminating effect on the pure love of *agape*.

If Wingren's 1936 article in *Swedish Theological Quarterly* and his 1939 licentiate thesis sought to demonstrate the negative image in the form of Marcion's heretical perspective, his ambitions were far more positive and constructive when, eight years later, in his book *Man and the Incarnation: A Study in the Biblical Theology of Irenaeus* (1947/1959), he attempted to describe the positive alternative that is based on the understanding of salvation as a restoration of humanity. As usual, it is possible to discern much of the contents of Wingren's book by studying the dramatic structure evident in its basic organization. The table of contents is divided into three sections: the first covers the movement "From Life to Death," and the last "From Death to Life." In between, as a kind of nucleus of the presentation, appears the section that deals with Christ. Together, these sections illustrate the movement of baptism through death to life.

Yet again, Wingren consciously contextualizes his study in contemporary theology from its outset. In his introduction, he emphasizes that the antiliberal sentiment dominant in contemporary theology has given rise to a situation in which there is a crucial need for "a positive doctrine of *man*—a theological anthropology."[25] Thus, in this, his second published work, the author clearly seeks to come to terms with the tendency to depict man as a competitor of God, so that "positive statements which are made about man then become limitations on the sovereignty of God, and positive statements about the omnipotence of God are seen to be

---

24. Ibid., 102.

25. Wingren, *Man and the Incarnation* (1947/1959), xi. Cf. how Wingren writes, as early as 1938, during his study visit in Berlin, "Anthropology is terribly neglected in all of modern theology." "Johanneum Journal," 179.

limitations on man's freedom."[26] Criticizing this is, for Wingren, a matter of recovering the anthropology that both the Bible and the Reformation assume, but which the early church had been forced to articulate more clearly because it was confronted with powers that wished to negate the idea of creation.

As an alternative to both the deification of humanity in liberal theology and the contempt for humanity in dialectical theology as well as motif research—and which seem to be two sides of the same coin in Irenaeus—Wingren claims to have identified a basic pattern that instead *binds together* God and humanity through the use of the model that *God creates* and *humanity is created*. That God gives and humanity receives is a matter of "the same reality seen from two different aspects."[27] Thus, what Wingren believed he had found in Irenaeus is, in keeping with the title of his book, a possibility for preventing theology from taking its point of departure from the opposition between the divine and the human. Instead, for Irenaeus, it is a matter of a positive determination of the relationship between Christ and humanity, the incarnation and anthropology. On one level, it might seem as though Wingren is following in the footsteps of Nygren with this study, in that he consistently emphasizes that it is God—and God alone—who creates, while it is man that is created.[28] But in Irenaeus, this creation is not limited to a particular isolated point in time or space; and it is not exclusively linked to Christ and the church. God is assumed to be active, although in a concealed way, in *all life*: "By the very fact of our being in the presence of *life* in all its countless forms we are confronted by a wholly divine activity in which God is directly at work in His Creation."[29]

Wingren resumed the implicit criticism of Nygren, which was buried in his licenciate thesis from 1939, in a clear and direct manner in his

26. Wingren, *Man and the Incarnation* (1947/1959), xii. Cf. how towards his conclusion he places his historical study into a context of contemporary theology: "Irenaeus thus displays a primitive Christian line of thought, which cannot always be said about modern theologians who are attempting to free themselves from the liberal Protestant tradition by simply remaining silent about man, or being detrimental in their references to man." Ibid., 93–94.

27. Ibid., 7.

28. Ibid., 7–8. Cf. "God is the creating One, i.e. man is continually in process of becoming" (ibid., 8), and "the function of creation never passes to man." Ibid., 210.

29 Ibid., 14. Cf. "Irenaeus always thinks of life as a manifestation of God's creative power and of death as a manifestation of the Devil's power of destruction." Ibid., 120–21.

book from 1947. Here, he deals directly with the two objections Nygren had made against Irenaeus, clearly signifying a content of *eros*: the natural immortality of the soul and deification. What emerges here is just how the human and the divine communicate and flow into one another, which Wingren calls "the characteristic confusion of divine and human"[30] that characterizes the thinking of Irenaeus, and which at its extreme is founded on his understanding of the incarnation: "The divinity of Christ does not for a moment imply any diminishing of His humanity."[31]

Wingren encapsulates everything that Irenaeus understands by salvation in the concept of *recapitulatio*, which means becoming human again, and presumes an original affirmation of creation-given human life as something to be restored. However, Wingren is careful to emphasize that for Irenaeus, this restoration is not a matter of a static reinstatement. Rather, it is always a matter of something that becomes "even more and richer," a completion that also implies a growth that unites identity and change: "Growth is God's creation, the exact same reality viewed from a special perspective." Through salvation as *recapitulatio*, humankind regains its humanity, but as a result of growth it becomes a matter of humankind receiving a richer humanity. Irenaeus uses concepts such as "raising" and "increasing" to emphasize this dynamic perspective of growth, yet without the creative function ever being transferred to humankind, which Wingren is careful to point out. What humankind is allowed to participate in through salvation is, in other words, not a supernatural addition to humanity, but rather a regaining of lost humanity. Irenaeus' concept of *recapitulatio*, in contrast to *apokatastasis* (the idea of restoration as found in Origen), means that we move beyond a static perspective in that this is a matter of something becoming "even more and richer." Wingren writes:

> Consequently, it is not something *super*natural which is given to us in Christ, but rather it is in the victory and whole work of Christ that this "health" which we have been discussing is to be found—here is the life of perfect health and the absolute and faultless completion of Creation. We might also describe it as nature that has come to full maturity. The gift which Christ bestows surpasses the first Creation, not in the sense that the supernatural surpasses nature, but rather in the sense that the

---

30. Ibid., 94.
31. Ibid., 86.

fully developed and mature life surpasses the undeveloped and immature, or as a man that is stronger than a child.[32]

In his investigations of Irenaeus, Wingren emphasizes the significance of time and history, perspectives that gain their theological foothold in the concept of the incarnation: "To treat the work of God in Christ timelessly is to disregard the humanity of Jesus, and hardly anything is less typical of Irenaeus than this timelessness."[33] This positive emphasis on *change* is of strategic importance, since it further strengthens the undermining function that Wingren's historical investigations employ in relation to Nygren's narrative, which is instead dominated by timeless and unchanging basic motifs. What might initially appear to be refinements to the method of motif research thus turn out to be something that ultimately contributes to its destruction. What finally achieves the break with Nygren's perspective and thus undermines his entire narrative is that Wingren, in his three patristic studies on the early church fathers from 1936, 1939, and 1947, draws attention to the central themes in Irenaeus' world of ideas, which in the work of Nygren also may be labeled *nomos* and *eros*.

Through a number of historical investigations, Wingren had successively undermined the historical foundations for regarding Irenaeus (and Marcion), along with Luther, as heroes in Nygren's grand narrative of pure *agape* love. However, at the same time, he provided the foundations for another narrative, which would come to serve as a contrast of great importance for his theological argumentation. The story of the archheretic Marcion, as he first developed it in the essay he published in 1936, served as a powerful narrative device in his authorship, with which Wingren was able to disarm his opponents. What made this device so effective was that Wingren articulated Marcion's theological position in a way that gave it a striking resemblance to much of the antiliberal polemics that dominated the new theological movements of Wingren's time. When Wingren uses the following terms to characterize the position of the great heretic of the early church, he sounds treacherously like Karl Barth:

> Marcion's theology, for example, can be summed up with this thesis: God has revealed himself in Christ and only in Christ. Against just this view of life the Apostles' Creed with its three parts was built. The fact that the Church Fathers considered this

32. Ibid., 48.
33. Ibid., 116.

theology to be a greater threat to faith than Atheism bears witness to their good judgement.[34]

Here, we see an example of how Wingren used the story of Marcion as a theological instrument to capture his contemporary opponents and incapacitate their arguments. Note that the terminology he attributes to Marcion is typically Barthian. Given the positive role Marcion plays in the framework of Nygren's narrative of pure Christian love, it is not surprising that even Nygren is included when Wingren identifies a Marcionite church life with a creation theology lacuna in the religious revivalist movements and high church groupings of the day. If Irenaeus and, later, Luther serve as positive configurations of a Christian interpretation of life, then Marcion has at least as important a negative function representing an interpretation of the Christian faith in which everything that unites Christianity with a general human position is expurged. The strategic importance that Wingren's Marcionite narrative held for his conclusions concerning Nygren and Barth cannot be underestimated, together with its use as a negative contrast against which he was able to formulate his own theological position.

In retrospect, it may be useful to remember that until the end of the 1930s, Wingren's chief interests were focused entirely on the early church fathers and the adjacent area of Bible exegesis. More specifically, his major interest was, without a doubt, focused on Marcion, and the comparison of Marcion with Paul the Apostle. It was in fact not until several years later that he began to focus on Irenaeus. Luther was added to his investigations only after his project on the early church fathers had been discontinued due to extenuating circumstances. For scholars interested in Marcion, the original source material is associated with great challenges, since we do not have access to any of his own texts. Marcion's world of ideas is known only through the church fathers, who were in conflict with him. Wingren had spent the summer term of 1938 at the archives in Berlin, where the source materials were located and where he could meet the foremost experts on the subject. Upon his return home later that same summer, his private notes still show "Studies on Marcion" at the top of his list of planned writing projects. This order of priority also remained unchanged in the many lists for future projects, which he wrote during the rest of 1938.[35] It was not until 1939 that Irenaeus for the first time appeared

---

34. Wingren, *Creation and Gospel* (1979/1979), 79. Cf. *Credo* (1974/1981), 31.
35. Wingren, "Johanneum Journal," 150ff.

along with Marcion as the planned theme of Wingren's licentiate thesis, and this combination of Irenaeus and Marcion was indeed the topic he pursued.[36] On 15 September 1939, fourteen days after the Nazi invasion of Poland, he received his licentiate degree with the highest honors. A later note, however, shows that he had planned to continue on to his doctoral dissertation with a further adjustment of his topic: "Dissertation should deal with Irenaeus, not with Marcion. Can thus avoid intimate contact with exegetics."[37] However, historical circumstances beyond his control would force him once again, and more radically, to redirect his research interests.

If anyone who found himself in Lund, of all places on earth, given the situation that all the national borders were closed so that it was no longer possible to travel freely, started a research project on Luther, it would not be a very far-fetched thing to do. However, at this time, Wingren was by no means a Luther scholar, even though he had some plans to undertake some studies of Luther in the future. His original research interest had been in New Testament exegesis, but had then gradually moved on to studies of the early church fathers, while maintaining an interest in New Testament materials (Paul the Apostle)—but now he leaped forward fourteen centuries, to the Reformation. It is remarkable to note that it was actually not until 1940 that he decided to change his research topic in this dramatic way. That year, he penned in his journal a new list consisting of three research projects, and the internal order among them:

> Luther's teachings on vocation
> Marcion and Irenaeus. Opposites and similarities.
> Systematic theology in Sweden after 1900.[38]

Due to the fact that the material in which he would now immerse himself was nearly one and a half millennia younger than the texts with which he had worked earlier, and originated in a geographical area in which he had

---

36. In a note from 11 January 1939, Wingren describes what seems to have initially been a planned study on Marcion, with Paul as a contrasting position, as an impossible project, saying that Paul is "a risky subject for a systematician." Ibid., 159. A few pages later he also states, "In general, it will be wise to leave exegetics alone." Ibid., 161. It is also in this situation that the theme that would become the final topic for his master's degree takes form: "It is instead Irenaeus who carries forth the Christian doctrine of creation, as opposed to Marcion. How would it be to call my dissertation 'Marcion and Irenaeus: Studies on the Doctrine of Creation'?" Ibid., 159.

37. Ibid., 268.

38. Ibid., 256.

no specialization, he was in dire need of help in order to quickly make inroads into it. However, since the new direction of his research had in a way brought him closer to the intellectual milieu of Lund University, the help needed was available. When he began to study Marcion, he had taken up his interest in the early church fathers at the suggestion of Bring: the new materials he was now about to study would bring him even closer to Bring. In addition, Herbert Olsson would also be of extraordinary importance to his studies, as mentioned previously.

By the very title of his doctoral dissertation *Luther on Vocation* (1942/1957), he had from the very beginning already allocated his study within one of the most prominent—and disputed—traditions of Swedish theological research, that of the Swedish Luther renaissance.[39] Wingren's dissertation joined a long series of Swedish dissertations on Luther that began with Einar Billing's *Luther on the State* (*Luthers lära om staten*, 1900), which, despite its title, was dominated by subjects dealing more with soteriology and teachings on justification. Wingren adhered to a more specific tradition in which the focus of knowledge was directed toward society, in keeping with the works of notable predecessors who had inspired him, such as Herbert Olsson's *Basic Problems in the Social Ethics of Luther* (*Grundproblemet i Luthers socialetik*, 1934) and Gustaf Törnvall's *Spiritual and Earthly Governments in Luther* (*Andligt och världsligt regemente hos Luther*, 1940). Although Wingren in many ways may be seen as a disciple of Einar Billing, in the case of his dissertation his view can be recognized as almost the opposite. This was because his perspective on the idea of *vocation* (*Beruf*, "calling") as regards Luther, as well as his entire interest in treating social issues without necessarily needing to mix in themes such as gospel and forgiveness of sins, departs from Billing's in a radical way.[40]

Despite their differences in topics and perspectives, the works of the Swedish Luther renaissance show a strong tendency toward the formation of a school of thought, regardless of whether its focus was theocentric or focused on theological anthropology and the varying capacity

---

39. Cf. Anderson, *Gustaf Wingren and the Swedish Lutheran Renaissance*.

40. Consider how Wingren takes pains to point out the contrast between Billing's dissertation and his own by emphasizing how critical Billing is toward Luther's teachings on vocation and work: "According to Billing, Luther has a 'negative' view of superficial, decent work ... Billing never lets the criticism of Luther's concept of vocation, which he presented in his doctoral dissertation in the year 1900, out of his sight." Wingren, "Einar Billings teologiska metod" (1955), 288.

for criticism and self-criticism. When read today it is obvious that these studies were unreflectively shaped from a confessional Lutheran perspective, despite claims of being purely historical descriptions. However, such problems may make it all too easy to forget that the scholars who were part of the Swedish Luther renaissance were in fact extraordinarily radical in their approach through their attempts to break away from rigid interpretations of Lutheran orthodoxy and discover a universal and more or less ecumenical Luther as they focused on his role as an interpreter of the Bible. By making a demarcation in this way between Luther and Lutheranism—taking as its motto "Forward with Luther!"—these researchers were polemically directed against the conservatism that had previously dominated.[41] To what extent this attempt succeeded remains an open issue, but the goal was to discover a "universal" Luther who was relevant not only to Lutheranism. The intention behind the Swedish research on Luther was to develop an ecumenical profile, inspired by Billing and Söderblom, whose importance Wingren described, much later, in the following way:

> When we read Luther, we hear a man from the sixteenth century speak in the pluralistic setting of Wittenberg—and he spoke to the *whole* of Christendom: to the Pope, to the enthusiasts, to his companions in faith, and to anyone who wanted to listen. This sketch is historically accurate, because Luther's real milieu was diversified and un-Lutheran. But this fact makes Luther also remarkably relevant—it is as though he were now speaking to the twentieth century.[42]

There was nothing unusual when Wingren decided to direct his scholarly interest toward Luther. In many ways, his doctoral dissertation was

41. Cf. how Wingren himself, at an early stage, describes this universal, "un-Lutheran" Luther—as early as 1938, in his private journal from Berlin: "This Lutheranism must always be a ferment in our theological and churchly life. As such it is of importance for Christianity all over the world. Yet it can never be more than a ferment. It cannot triumph, achieve a breakthrough, or become a 'movement' without abolishing itself." "Johanneum Journal," 148.

42. Wingren, *Exodus Theology* (1968/1969), 17. Here, in one of his later works, and in keeping with the Swedish Luther renaissance, Wingren returns to the importance of not confining Luther within Lutheranism: "What needs to happen is this: tear Luther loose from Lutheranism! Let him stand alone, with the Bible in his hand, alone as he stood before the Kaiser at Worms! Then he will speak to the entire world, and what is odd is that then the entire world would listen, for then Luther would no longer be locked within Lutheranism—he would be free." Wingren, "Människa först—kristen sedan" (1996), 14.

a typical product of the Luther renaissance. In his method, Wingren followed this tradition, utilizing a strict descriptive approach toward a given set of historical materials. In the foreword, Wingren presents his dissertation as a purely historical investigation, "not intended to be a systematic treatment of basic principles, criticism of contemporary theology, comparison of Lutheran and Romanist thought, or comparative treatment of Luther and his followers."[43] In all these respects, there was nothing original or remarkable about Wingren's dissertation.

What was unusual about Wingren's dissertation was his choice of topic—vocation (*Beruf, vocatio,* "calling")—and its conclusions. He presented an image of Luther that hardly corresponded to the narrative recounted by Nygren, in which Luther was described as the foremost representative of the motif of pure *agape*. Nor can the noticeably dated style of language in *Luther on Vocation* conceal the fact that this book deals with a subject both unusual and modern, namely, an interpretation of everyday work and tribulations as an expression of the activity of God, which God is thought to carry out behind "creaturely masks" and in acts "without name." In Wingren's dissertation, all these acts are identified as acts of God and are thus activities as much associated with *nomos* and *eros* as with *agape*, which clearly undermines the image of Luther as a representative of an isolated *agape* love, according to Nygren's grand narrative. Wingren's point of departure is that previous research had presented a drastically diminished Luther, with single-minded attention to his talk of justification by faith and the gospel, which in turn had served as a negation of the possibilities of human beings themselves. Wingren's dissertation is the first in a long series of Luther studies in which the author, through anti-Pietistic polemics, would emphasize Luther's theological delight in everyday labor, dance, beer, sexual intercourse, and children, based on the conviction that the given, ordinary human community in creation, together with nature as well as work, are portions of God's world. Without mentioning a single word about God, humankind is always a part of the life of God already by living and working in everyday life in the fields, at sea, and in workshops all around the world—outside the monastery. The idea of vocation is therefore not primarily tied to spiritual tasks within the church; instead, the only truly spiritual places, even for Christians, are found in everyday work. Here, Wingren places great emphasis on the fact that when Luther mentions

---

43. Wingren, *Luther on Vocation* (1942/1957), vii.

vocatio in his works, he always presumes a conflict with a monastic life, which is not only negated but actually considered something evil.⁴⁴

The style Wingren employs in his dissertation exhibits traces of Aulén's dramatic presentation of the Christian faith as well as Bring's dualistic perspective on Luther. This is already obvious in the table of contents, where Wingren prepares for the culminating chapter on theological anthropology, "Man" (chapter 3), by the determination of the tensions between "Earth and Heaven" (chapter 1) and the dualism of "God and the Devil" (chapter 2). According to Luther's view of life, man lives in the eschatological tension between earth and heaven as well as the dualism of God and Devil. In this landscape, there is no neutral position; human beings are beasts of burden.

Wingren contextualizes his interpretation of the concept of vocation within the framework of these tensions. In other words, Luther's formula of law and gospel does not exist in a passive and apathetic neutral situation, but rather in a context dominated by persistent adversity. The battle between God and the Devil involves only the "persons," while "stations" and "offices" always remain on God's side. Luther criticizes the pope because he "puts the law into Heaven," with the consequence of deeds being reduced to a means for achieving one's own salvation. Seeking to perform good deeds "before God" destroys faith in heaven, so that we "depose Christ" from his throne; and this "parade before God" means simultaneously a neglect of the neighbor, who is the one who actually needs these good deeds: "Faith is revoked in heaven, and love on earth. Neither God nor one's neighbor receives that which is properly his."⁴⁵

In contrast to this short circuit, faith removes the acts and throws them upon the neighbor, according to Wingren's interpretation of Luther.

---

44. Ibid., ix. Later in his investigation, he speaks of how Luther's works show monastic life as a "a false Stand [station]" (ibid., 2), in contrast to the "true station" maintained by "husbands and wives, boys and girls, lords and ladies, governors, regents, judges, officeholders, farmers, citizens etc." Ibid., 3. In Wingren's writings, we recognize how the story of Luther's break with celibacy points both "backwards," toward Paul's break with the Jewish requirement of circumcision, and "forward" toward the departure from the Pietist "cloister" of the free-church congregation. For this reason, there is an analogy that is constantly present when Wingren presents Luther's coming-to-terms, which came to play an important part in Wingren's interpretations of Luther from the 1970s and onward.

45. Ibid., 13. Cf. "The moral preciseness is not concerned with realities, for it is concerned, not with one's neighbor, but only with a counterfeit irreproachableness which is counterfeit because there is not life without sin, and it ought not to be set up as the standard." Ibid 153–54.

Wingren bases this interpretation on the idea that a Christian lives in Christ (in heaven) through faith, and in the neighbor (on earth) through love. Yet, both of these relationships are expressions of the acts of God.

Because the other is situated at the center of Luther's ethics, the acts are considered as something that approaches human beings from without. Luther takes a strongly critical stance toward situations where ethics is considered more important than the neighbor, the other. This is, in other words, a kind of concrete ethics, or in modern terms, a phenomenological ethics. Luther does not bring moral laws from the Bible, nor does he preach exact moral edicts, since such a rigid kind of ethics does not ask about the actual needs of the other, but is encapsulated in the self in accordance with the egocentric intentions to achieve one's own life as a life without sin. In Wingren's investigations of Luther, vocation is instead described as the "concrete form of the law" (the church is the "concrete form of the gospel"), and it is associated with the encounter with the concrete needs of concrete individuals in particular situations in time and space.[46] In Luther's understanding of the moral of everyday life, the law represents something that forces good actions if they are not found spontaneously in work and family life. God does not approach humanity in the isolated thoughts and emotions of individuals, but rather in what happens to human beings in their outward world, in things that are tangible and close at hand in everyday life. This understanding of vocation is not focused on the church but is located within the relationship to a given reality. Vocation "involves the total of a person's relationship in his situation."[47] It is within this concrete relationship that the particular ethics supporting vocation is inscribed: "If you are a craftsman you will find the Bible placed in your workshop, in your hands, in your heart: it teaches and preaches how you ought to treat your neighbor."[48]

In his dissertation on Luther (1942), Wingren consistently emphasizes the dynamic of action in which *vocatio* excludes *imitatio*.[49] The

---

46. Ibid., 123.

47. Ibid., 192.

48. Ibid., 72. It has sometimes been claimed that Wingren does not deal with creation in his dissertation, but rather with the law only—but this is hardly correct. For example, he speaks of Luther's "rich idea of creation" and continues, "The birds, which sing even though they do not know what they are to eat, are an example for us . . . There is a direct connection between God's work in creation and his work in these offices." Ibid., 8–9.

49. Wingren explores the distinction between *vocatio* and *imitatio* in ibid., 171–84. According to Wingren, the core of Luther's concept of ethics is "that a man's neighbor

radically *local* nature of vocation places it in opposition to the concept of *imitatio*. In the constant process of re-creation and renewal, which characterizes the life of vocation, the individual stands alone in a situation in which he or she must deal with tribulations presented by actual, real-life situations. Here, Wingren points out the German term *Stundelein*, which denotes living in the present, being concrete and alive—as an alternative to a quest for divine plans. God's acts are hidden,[50] and *Stundelein* may be considered quite simply as the modification of *Beruf* (vocation), which is needed to suit the needs of the moment.[51] The place of vocation is thus the world in general, and in particular, everyday work. However, neighborly relationships in everyday life require imagination, empathy, and ingenuity, which means that the law must be understood as something in constant change. It is *fairness* that adjusts the law according to each specific instance. The living and ever-changing character of the situation requires different actions in different contexts, completely in keeping with the idea of the living God who creates *now*. In Wingren's interpretation of Luther, the heart of the ethics of vocation is not sanctification or imitation, but rather *the other*. To meet the needs of the other requires love: "The love commandment both removes all commandments and affirms all."[52]

According to Wingren, the shifting focus of the concept of creation is part of Luther's radicalism: *Creare est semper novum facere*—"To create is perpetually to make new." In Luther's conceptualization, the law is never a final, fixed text; it is neither codified by the Bible nor by tradition, but rather conceived as something continually changeable and unexpected. The acts of God flow to the individual from without. Wingren speaks of how Luther recognizes the individual as "bound" in relation to other people, to the neighbor, because it is the need of the other that comprises the contents of vocation. The world is continually changing, therefore God must continually use new, unexpected and sudden confrontational

---

is the proper objective of his action." He continues: "When a neighbor is given that place, change is introduced into ethics as a constitutive mark. His neighbor is now one person and now another. Now he is in need of one thing, and then of another." Ibid., 231.

50. He explores the term "hiddenness" in ibid., 234–51.

51. Ibid., 231–32.

52. Ibid., 147. Cf. ibid., 230–31. Much later, Wingren returns to how regeneration and movement were the very core of Luther's reformation, when, quoting Luther, he states that "the new man institutes new decalogues, better than those Moses gave us." Wingren, *Creation and Gospel* (1979/1979), 48.

actions to maintain his creation, to create anew. From this perspective, the law does not appear as something that is preservative, as proposed in Lutheran orthodoxy, but instead the law must be understood in terms of a process of constant change. Wingren particularly characterizes the relationship between stability and mobility, between freedom and constraint, as the main point in his presentation; he describes it as a line of thought running throughout his entire dissertation on Luther.[53]

Wingren's entire presentation of the idea of vocation in Luther is an expression of an interpretation of life in which the good is something that the individual receives from the hands of God, regardless of faith and creed, and far beyond the boundaries of the church. This is, in other words, a theological ethics that is not possible to articulate solely from the basis of the second article of faith, according to a situation in which faith becomes a prerequisite for love to stream downward through the individual as through a tube to "lost humanity."[54] The understanding of vocation that Wingren elaborates has strong features of *nomos*, in the same way that this idea of creation bears a strong resemblance to *eros*. If Aulén removed all legalistic reasoning in his teaching on atonement in order to make Luther's understanding of the gospel a *No* to the law (*nomos*), then Nygren's presentation of the Christian idea of love entails that *agape* has an exclusive claim in contrast to *eros*. In this respect, Wingren's examination runs counter to Lundensian theology. Here, we encounter problems, considerable problems.

During the years between 1935 and 1947, Wingren devoted himself to in-depth historical studies of two theologians, Irenaeus and Luther, both of whom every good Lundensian theologian was expected to study. Thus, there was nothing original about this. It was entirely predictable. This was exactly what a researcher embedded in the intellectual soil of Lundensian theology should and would do. What caused a problem, however, and made Wingren diverge sharply from the expected course, was that his focus was directed toward the world, everyday work (Luther), and an understanding of salvation as becoming human again, *recapitulatio*, restored humanity (Irenaeus). Many years later, when defending

---

53. Wingren, *Luther on Vocation* (1942/1957), xii. Cf. how he emphasizes the moveable nature of Luther even more strongly later in his life, by regretting that his investigation on Luther from 1942 was too much influenced by a tendency to strictly separate stability and mobility. Wingren, *Predikan* (1949), 307 n. 22 (not included in the English edition).

54. Nygren, *Agape and Eros*, 740–41.

himself against accusations of a one-sided reading of Irenaeus and Luther, he maintained that the overemphasis of the first article of faith was not his doing, but rather that this is the case in the source material itself. Wingren studied the two theologians in whose works the *agape* motif was expected to be found in its purest form, and not, as in other places in church history, tainted by the foreign *eros* motif. It is precisely here where he finds elements that can be associated with *nomos* and *eros* and an idea of love that is not at all exclusively tied to the church or the existence of faith. While other scholars, perhaps because they were in many cases the sons of clergymen, were occupied by their focus on ecclesiastical themes, and therefore chose to skip over many pages, Wingren, the tanner's son from Valdemarsvik, paused every time he found themes in which he could recognize "the tanning workshop as a place for the work of God."[55]

Anders Nygren had presented a grand narrative about pure Christian love, in which Luther and Irenaeus were featured as historical representatives of *agape*. His protégé, Gustaf Wingren, carried out historical studies in which he presented, instead of pure *agape*, an everyday world of relationships, where God's activity is associated with the circumstance of being alive in the world in general, regardless of the occurrence of faith, or the presence of the church. In the historical sources he studied, the Christian idea of love appeared to be neither as pure or exclusively Christian as Nygren had supposed. Thus, the historical foundations of Nygren's grand narrative splintered.

Sleepless in Basel

Two weeks after defending his dissertation in December 1942, Gustaf Wingren was appointed associate professor in systematic theology. Events had gone well for Wingren for quite some time, which was symbolically manifested by the fact that his hometown of Valdemarsvik asked him to present the annual speech that year at the lighting of the town's Christmas tree in the town square. War was raging on the Continent, and the times were uncertain, making it difficult to plan life projects and careers. On 15 January 1943, just six days after he had been appointed as a church curate in Valdemarsvik, Wingren was called up for military duty. He spent six

---

55. Wingren, *Mina fem universitet* (1991), 69. Cf. "I am a typical Lundensian theologian. I speak of Irenaeus and Luther in precisely the same ways as do Nygren and Aulén. I continue with this work, but I bring out only the elements that my teachers overlooked." Ibid., 70.

months in service, working in the military personnel division at the T1 Garrison in Linköping, all the while continuing his intellectual pursuits. However, important events were also taking place in his personal life. On 4 April 1943, he married Signhild Carlsson, a girl from Valdemarsvik to whom he had been engaged for ten years. The wedding took place in the Valdemarsvik Church, and was followed by a wedding luncheon for the extended family at the Grand Hotel.

Signhild Carlsson grew up at Bergsgatan 6 in Valdemarsvik, in a large single-family home with a view of the ocean and beautiful terraced gardens on the cliff behind the house. Her father, Johan, sailed the world's seas as a first mate and naval engineer, a career that provided his family with a very different standard of living than the Wingren family had known. In Signhild's childhood home, there had been hired help, including baking, cleaning, and laundry staff. The Carlsson home was known for its hospitality, and there was always a fresh pot of coffee on the stove. Signhild had a large wardrobe of handmade clothes that had been brought home from France and other distant countries. Gustaf and Signhild had known one another during their school years. Later, Signhild needed a summer tutor to improve her language skills. When her family hired the poor but gifted university student from Norrgatan for this purpose, the two were instantly attracted and became a couple. On her mother's advice, Signhild went to Stockholm and studied to become a nurse in the tradition of the Swedish order of nurses known as the Sophia Sisters. The certification she received as a Sophia Sister carried with it significant status for a young woman of that era. Once, during Signhild's years as a student nurse, she made something of an uproar in the Wingren family home. Gustaf had come down with a cold, and his sweetheart, the student nurse, was horrified to realize that the Wingren family, despite its many children, did not own and never had owned a thermometer!

Both Signhild and Gustaf shared traits of almost exaggerated exactness and punctuality, which perhaps was only a part of those particular times, but which today seems a little strange. When they later had children, they were extremely vigilant with their care. It was important to keep all germs away, and it was also important that the children receive fresh air each day. In the summertime, the babies were carefully sunbathed for five minutes on their front and five minutes on their backs, neither more nor less, and Gustaf was assigned the task of timing this. When Wingren later became a professor, he practiced extreme punctuality for many years. Before each of his research seminars, he made his closest colleague call Fröken Ur, Sweden's national speaking clock, from his office. When the signal reached 6 p.m., 14 minutes and 50 seconds, the assistant hung up the telephone, and they immediately walked down to the seminar room in order to begin punctually on the academic quarter hour at 6:15 p.m.[56] Wingren was also extremely careful with every detail in his writings. He even proofread and corrected material that had already been published.

During Wingren's tour of military duty in the spring of 1943, the festive occasions continued. At the end of May, during the Doctoral Degrees festivities, he received his doctorate from Lund University. In the late summer of the same year, he accepted employment as a church curate in the town of Motala. This would prove to be his final appointment in the Church of Sweden, as on 1 February 1944 he began work as associate professor on a scholarship grant at Lund University. The relative economic stability that came with this position is reflected in the steady stream of publications, lectures, radio devotions, and sermons that flowed from his pen. The notebook Wingren had kept during his time in Berlin in May and June 1938 and further on—and that I have named "The Johanneum Journal"—contained a number of possible project outlines and titles. Towards the end of this notebook, there is an entry from 2 April 1945, in which he drew up his publication plan for the period 1945–51:

> Beginning of 1947: "Incarnation and Man in Irenaeus"
>
> Beginning of 1951: "The Problem of Reality in Christianity"
>
> 1953: "The Gospel and the Commandments."[57]

Only the first of these publications would become a reality, with the words of the title reversed. However, it was published according to the planned timetable. Nevertheless, as mentioned earlier, the times made it difficult to plan life and work. In 1945 the war ended, and in May, Signhild was called up for nursing duty to care for war refugees. Gustaf traveled to war-ravaged Finland on a long lecture tour. He visited Helsinki and Porvoo, and after twenty days arrived at Turku, home of Finland's Swedish-speaking university. Wingren noted, "20 July: Prof. R. Gyllenberg gave me a tour of Åbo Akademi University and its buildings, primarily the Faculty of Theology."[58]

56. Aronson, "Minnesbilder," 107.
57. Wingren, "Johanneum Journal," 272.
58. Wingren's private journal, 20 July 1945.

The following year, in January 1946, the Wingrens' first child was born, a daughter, Anna Teresia. That spring, Wingren was completely free from instructional duties so that he could pursue research. He worked intensely on the project he had begun before the war, his long-planned-for book on Irenaeus. However, his personal journal from that spring also contains the following entry: "6 April: Met with R. Prenter to discuss current theology." Professor Regin Prenter from Aarhus University in Denmark, as has already been mentioned and to which we shall return, would be of great importance for Wingren's career after the war. The first help Prenter offered was to send Wingren abroad to Basel; later, he provided support as a member of the evaluation committee that nominated Wingren for his professorship at Lund.

An interesting detail that illustrates how the war had disrupted the university world and placed limits on academic travel and communication is that in February 1946, an issue of the American journal *The Augustana Quarterly* (vol. 21, no. 1 [1942]) arrived in Wingren's mail. It contained "The Christian's Calling According to Luther"—an article that Wingren had delivered for publication more than four years earlier, in January 1942.

Nevertheless, the war was now over, Wingren was in Lund, and his career was beginning to take on momentum. He served as acting professor of ethics for four weeks in November-December 1946. On 30 November, he received an invitation from the Faculty of Theology at Basel University, Switzerland. Professor Oscar Cullmann had written on behalf of the Basel faculty to ask if he would substitute for Karl Barth. The position had first been offered to the more established scholar Regin Prenter, who had been forced to decline this flattering offer because he was unable to free himself from involvement in an important study commission. Prenter had instead recommended that the Basel faculty extend the invitation to his less well-known colleague from Lund. At first, Wingren declined the invitation, since his calendar was already full. We can only hope that his family situation also played some part in this consideration (his daughter would turn one year old that January), but after a second letter of invitation a week later, he reconsidered and accepted the offer. The day before New Year's Eve 1946, he completed the manuscript of his book on Irenaeus. All the evidence shows that Associate Professor Wingren was working intently and purposefully to further his academic career. The following year would not be less intense.

The fact that Wingren, during the month of February 1947, had the opportunity to serve as an acting professor at Åbo Akademi University in Turku, Finland, may be comprehended from the background of the shared Lutheran frame of reference, together with his previous lecture tour after the end of the war. It is also likely that Ragnar Bring played a role in sending Wingren to Turku, since Bring's first professorship had been at Åbo Akademi University. After an intense month there, Wingren was able to spend only one and a half months at home in Lund with his young family before he was off again. This time, he traveled through war-torn Germany to Basel, arriving on 19 April, one week after the publication of his book *Man and the Incarnation: A Study in the Biblical Theology of Irenaeus* (1947/1959).

Wingren, the theologian, often himself noted that he arrived in Switzerland as a full-fledged historian, having honed his skills in historical research during the long years of academic isolation caused by the war. With two purely historical studies to his credit, which had as yet been published only in Swedish, his seminar sessions at the University of Basel were less than successful. He was unable to live up to the expectations of Professor Barth's twenty-eight doctoral students, who had a broad collective international background, hailing as they did from Czechoslovakia, Poland, France, Germany, Denmark, Holland, Hungary, the United States, and Scotland. When they gathered around the seminar table (the same table where Friedrich Nietzsche had led his seminars three quarters of a century earlier), they expected insights that the young acting professor from Sweden was unable to provide. He was entirely unprepared for what he encountered and later described the situation as a complete nightmare.

There were structural reasons that made Wingren the wrong person for the position. In some ways, he was the victim of a collision between different academic cultures. The isolation of the war years had led to the development of separate national academic cultures that had no contact with one another. In Lund, Wingren had gained a strong competency as a researcher of historical theology. The Swedish tradition had come to follow Nygren's transformation of systematic theology into historical research, which was further strengthened by the fact that the history of doctrine in Sweden, in contrast to all other countries except Finland, did not belong to church history, but rather fell under the field of systematic theology. This order had no international equivalent. The seminar students expected their professor to guide them through a contemporary interpretation of the Christian faith, but Wingren was unable to fulfill these expectations. In the contemporary theological research milieu of Basel, descriptive, immanent analyses of historical material carried no argumentative weight at all, and two historical studies, weighty as they were, could not help him achieve a dialog with the seminar students. For Wingren, this mental collision was upsetting and painful. Barth's students continually asked questions about the meaning the biblical message might have for them in the current day. Wingren, who was trained as a historian, was ill-prepared to answer such questions. In addition, Wingren disagreed with Barth's solution to the problem. Discouraged, the model student from Lund lay awake at night. But in the midst of his feelings of failure, he began to redirect his thinking. An old paradigm began to die, and slowly, a new one began to grow.[59]

Nonetheless, Basel cannot have been quite the fiasco that Wingren later described, because during his brief months there he was in fact offered a permanent professorship. On the eve of Pentecost, he had an in-depth discussion about the vacant professorship with Oscar Cullmann. The discussion continued on Pentecost Sunday with Karl Ludwig Schmidt. The Basel faculty tried to persuade him, but ten days before he was to begin the long bus trip home, he wrote in his journal, "After careful consideration made the decision to decline permanent professorship in Basel, so that I may instead devote the period up to 1951 to theological research and writing in Lund."[60]

After his return home, Wingren indeed began work on what would become his most puzzling and controversial book, *The Living Word* (1949/1960). But what exactly were the impulses he had received in Basel? What insights had grown during his sleepless nights in Switzerland?

A long-standing and oversimplified idea, which even Wingren himself sometimes furthered, contends that he returned from Basel as a full-fledged Barthian, or at least a semi-Barthian.[61] He certainly showed renewed vigor in his work after his return, and former students recounted how he would now come rushing into his seminar sessions, frenetically

---

59. Much later, Wingren shared his memories of the events in Basel to which I refer in this section—in, for example, Wingren, *Mina fem universitet* (1991), 120.

60. Wingren's personal journal, 9 June 1947. Wingren later writes that in this situation, he had already realized that Nygren would become bishop of Lund in 1949 and that the professorship Nygren had held would be declared open. Wingren, *Mina fem universitet* (1991), 146.

61. Wingren, "Sveriges ende barthian" (1986), 16.

lecturing on his new insights. Could it really be that Sweden had gained its first true Barthian theologian?

While it is certainly true that Wingren was influenced by and often referred to Barth in innumerable articles and books, he cannot at all be considered a disciple of Barth. Here we might remind ourselves of the anecdote already related in chapter 1, in which Wingren passes judgment on Barth ("Barth is the most important theological thinker of our day— who thinks wrongly!"[62]), as well as the fact that Wingren often referred to "the continental Barth" as a tool to use against opponents in theological battles internal to Sweden, rather than as an indication of his positive affiliation with Barth's theological program.[63]

So, was Wingren's theological conversion inspired by Karl Barth? Hardly. Remember the harsh judgment he passed in *Theology in Conflict* (1954/1958): "The removal of the fundamental mistake would mean the destruction of his theology."[64] Wingren could hardly have stated his opinion more sharply or with less compromise. Throughout his career, Wingren perceived Barth's theology as "completely impossible to accept."[65] In fact, he arrived home from Basel charged with a murderous criticism of Barthian theology, criticisms that he later developed in parallel with, and even cross-fertilized by, his own criticisms of Nygren. And Barth himself was of course not in Basel during Wingren's time as acting professor there. The reason why he needed a substitute for those months was associated with the fact that he was to return to the University in Bonn, where he had worked until he had felt compelled to leave Nazi Germany in 1935. On 24 April, the day after Barth was to have begun his classes in Bonn, Wingren wrote in his journal, "Had a detailed theological discussion with Barth for two hours at Pilgerstrasse 25."[66] Then Barth departed for Bonn.

Wingren found himself in Basel, but as a matter of fact his period as a substitute for Barth gave him no opportunities for further discussion with Barth himself. However, some of the people Wingren did meet in Basel, and who would leave indelible marks on his theology, were the

---

62. Aronson, "Minnesbilder," 95.

63. The article in which Wingren comes closest to Barth's position is probably "Ordet hos Barth" (1948).

64. Wingren, *Theology in Conflict* (1954/1958), 28.

65. Wingren, *Mina fem universitet* (1991), 117.

66. Wingren's personal journal, 24 April 1947.

New Testament exegetes Oscar Cullmann and Karl Ludwig Schmidt.[67] For Wingren, the months in Basel meant not only that he underwent a professional crisis but also that he had the opportunity to learn something new. During the period from April to July, he met with Cullmann and Schmidt nearly every week. Both of these men lived alone and had considerable time available to meet with guest teachers. The massive influx of new theological thinking that reconfigured Wingren's world of ideas in 1947 came primarily from these two theologians, but it was perhaps even more true that their thinking, without their being aware of it, helped Wingren bind together the two favorite disciplines that had occupied him before Bring had lured him over to systematic theology: exegetics and homiletics. A glance through the composition notebooks in which Wingren kept his personal journal reinforces the sense that during his study term in Berlin in 1938, it was these two subjects that occupied his thoughts: exegesis and preaching. However, even as late as his period as acting professor in Basel, Wingren was still unsure of how he might bring these two interests together. My own investigations have led me to believe that his time in Basel gave him an important impulse that awoke in him dormant theological resources from his earlier theological interests and studies, and that showed him the possibilities that existed for uniting them. The exegetics he encountered in Basel presumed a homiletic problematization and practice, because these form-critical historians quite simply considered the texts upon which the sermon was to be preached as sermons: *Am Anfang war die Predigt* (Martin Dibelius)—*In the beginning was the sermon*!

According to the fundamental perspectives of the form-critical school of theology that Wingren became acquainted with through his colleagues in Basel, it is not possible to consider the gospels as biographies of Jesus as a historical person. The original sources present no uniform, coherent story of his life; the time line of events described varies markedly between the four different versions that have been passed down to us. The approach that has come to be known as the *kerygmatic* method is based upon the insight that the gospel was originally an oral story, something that from the very beginning was meant to be declared and preached (*keryssein* = to announce, to proclaim, to preach), and as such is something that claims to occur in every new situation in which

---

67. In his memoirs, Wingren repeats again and again that the decisive impetus from his stay in Basel did not at all come from Barth, but rather from Cullmann and Schmidt. Wingren, *Mina fem universitet* (1991), 91, 129, 136, 143.

the gospel is presented. The parables are thus miniature literary works, small texts organized like a string of pearls one after the other in the gospels. Their very form shows that they originally functioned as sermon texts. For this reason, it is entirely in keeping with their original function to arrange them in the book of worship and introduce them on various Sundays, because in this way they are brought back to their original function.[68] This view corresponded with Wingren's own peculiarity, which was that he, while feeling embarrassed over not being able to locate a certain text segment in the New Testament, was nevertheless able to identify the Bible readings for different days in the church year as listed in the Swedish Book of Worship. The recognition is obvious when in his memoirs he states,

> In a historic sense, when they lie on the pulpit and when they are read aloud as the specific gospel message for this or that Sunday, the texts in the New Testament are in their original situation. Thus, thanks to the form-critical school, I suddenly find myself back in my hometown of Valdemarsvik. I am worshipping at the Sunday services of my teenage years.[69]

In other words, there is a connection between the form-critical exegetes with which he came into contact in Basel and his own experience of a very special practice that had captivated his interest since childhood: preaching. Here we discover yet another source for Wingren's thinking, which, although it will certainly remain buried, has nonetheless played a major role and has been normative for the Swedish theological tradition that Wingren adopted—and it concerns Einar Billing. Wingren himself felt that Billing's influence on him had been far stronger than the impressions he had gained from Barth: "What I have written about the sermon and about the gospel from the year 1949 until now is strongly influenced by Billing's work, much more strongly than by continental kerygmatic theology."[70]

Einar Billing's biblical theology also played a major role for Wingren in regard to exegetics and biblical theology. In light of the great importance he attributed to Billing for his own theological development, and

---

68. Cf. "When the texts are found in the books of the Gospel, they are in their rightful place; they are at their 'Sitz im Leben.' There, no one will come up with the idea of making a biography of Jesus out of them." Wingren, "Tro och teologi," (1990), 12.

69. Wingren, *Mina fem universitet* (1991), 127.

70. Wingren, *Exodus Theology* (1968/1969), 59.

his statement that "biblical theology is the richest legacy that Billing left to posterity," the prominent role that Billing's theology played for Wingren is clear.[71]

Furthermore, Wingren spent nearly a decade in Lund while the future archbishop, Yngve Brilioth (1891-1959), was still active there. From 1929 onward, Brilioth combined his duties as dean of Lund Cathedral with a professorship in practical theology. There were also several relationships of a personal nature that brought Wingren and Brilioth together: they both hailed from the same region in the diocese of Linköping, and Brilioth was a faculty adviser to the *Östgöta nation* student association of which Wingren was a member. Later, Wingren was given the task of assisting Professor Brilioth with proofreading and writing articles and reviews for the *Swedish Theological Quarterly* (*STK*), which Aulén had handed over to Brilioth when he moved on to become bishop of Strängnäs. Brilioth encouraged Wingren, and seems later to have viewed the criticisms Wingren leveled at Nygren as nothing more than refreshing.[72] Wingren later stated how important Yngve Brilioth had been for his professional development: "Of the factors in Lund which made me a theologian, those years as Brilioth's assistant were among the most important."[73] Wingren uttered these somewhat surprising words at eighty years of age. Among other reasons, they are surprising due to Brilioth's links to the high church movement; nonetheless, they should be viewed as an important stance-taking and systematic orientation. It is said that it is never too late to acquire a happy childhood, and in the same way, it is never too late to identify an important early factor in one's own intellectual development. When Wingren tells his story in his memoirs, he mentions Brilioth using words such as "reverence" and "inner purity." Brilioth is in particular important to him because of his interest in preaching, a practice that unites his perspectives and brings them back to exegetics and the Bible. In Brilioth, he found the framework that he utilized to bind together the two portions of his book *Theology in Conflict* (1954/1958): the anthropological and the hermeneutical prerequisites for the work of theology.

71. Ibid., 111.

72. Cf. how Yngve Brilioth, who at this time was archbishop in Uppsala, sent Wingren a Christmas letter in which he warmly thanked him for *Theology in Conflict*: "It is according to my view especially valuable that Nygren has gained a disciple who can analyze his master's work with such critical clarity." Yngve Brilioth to Gustaf Wingren, 22 December 1954.

73. Wingren, *Mina fem universitet* (1991), 47.

This allows the approach of creation theology to function within a wider framework, which meant that Wingren had to distance himself, on one hand from Barth, in whose work the *kerygma* seems to appear in a theologically empty situation, and on the other hand, from a liberal theology, in which the glad tidings become both unnecessary and inconceivable, because human beings inherently carry religion within their hearts.

The impulse that Wingren gained through his experiences of sleeplessness in early summer 1947 in Basel led him to begin to reflect on how he might unite the two poles that had dominated his own theological interests, and which he had not been able to bring together: the exegetic interest in particular texts and the homiletic interest in addressing concrete groups of people. Thus, through his discovery of the inner dynamics of the word, he began to develop a theological model supported by the dual pillars of anthropology and hermeneutics—as well as thoughts of how these two pillars dialectically anticipated one another. The Christian message does not enter into an ethically or theologically empty situation; in order to make sense of this message a theological anthropology based on creation is required. In other words, we are dealing with a position beyond a simple kerygmatic program as well as a liberal theological position. It is a matter of a difficult-to-grasp dialectical figure of thought where the theological anthropology is connected to a theological hermeneutics, as well as a hermeneutical theology, revisited in chapter 4. However, Wingren's theological path and stance were mainly influenced by other factors from further back in his life, sources of vital importance for an understanding of his course as a theologian. Therefore, let us go a few more steps back in time.

Berlin 1938

In this study, I have often returned to the question of what inspired and moved Gustaf Wingren to apostasy from Lundensian theology, the attack on his mentor, and his reorientation during the years around 1950. What was the pre-history of his confrontation with Anders Nygren? It is possible to follow this development through Wingren's private journals, from which we may conclude that the basic contours of his theological thinking lie farther back in time than has been previously supposed.

After taking his *kandidat* (bachelor's degree) in theology in 1935, Wingren moved from Hugo Odeberg over to Ragnar Bring for further studies. In the spring term of 1938, he attended Bring's seminars on dogmatics and Nygren's seminars on ethics and philosophy of religion. In May and June of that year he got the opportunity to spend a summer term at the Humboldt University in Berlin, where he would be able to immerse himself in the area that occupied his interest at that time: patristics, the early church fathers, the Gnostics, and Marcion, in particular. Berlin was home to much of the source material on these topics, as well as world-leading scholars, not least of whom was Professor Hans Lietzmann, who at that time was the one to carry on the scholarly tradition of Adolf von Harnack. During his time in the Johanneum dormitory in Berlin, he kept a personal journal, which for once is very complete in regard to ideas and full of reflections and second thoughts about the theological milieu at Lund University.

In 1938, Berlin was the capital of Nazi Germany, a country controlled by a fascist regime that persecuted those who did not agree with its precepts, sought to exterminate entire groups of people, and set out to conquer, dominate, or annex surrounding nations. At the University, the teachers who refused to swear allegiance to Hitler had already been dismissed, and students associated with the anti-Nazi Confessing Church (*Bekennende Kirche*) had to complete their course work secretly because the seminars run by this church had been forced to close. Many years later, Wingren commented on the spirit and environment at the University of Berlin at that time: "In those days, we could truly feel what the struggle for the gospel meant in the twentieth century. It was clear that there was an enemy of the gospel, and that enemy was dangerous and strong."[74]

It is often the case that traveling to other countries provides a healthy perspective on things close to home. For Wingren, it was as if his trip during that last year before the outbreak of World War II gave him the critical distance he needed to distinguish the delineations of Swedish theology.[75]

In his journal entries from the months in Berlin in 1938, Wingren shows signs of an advanced capacity for contextual theological sensitivity, as well as strategic and tactical awareness of the theological field. In

---

74. Quoted from the Lund University Museum's series of videotaped interviews, "Lundaprofiler," in "Lundateologin och världen. En intervju med Gustaf Wingren," with interviewer Göran Bexell (1997).

75. In his journal entry for 25 May, Wingren writes (not without fascination), "A Swede viewing Swedish theology and the Swedish church from a German perspective understands ALL of this." "Johanneum Journal," 113.

Marcion, he identified a position in which salvation was dominant, at the expense of creation. However, he did not merely leave this arch-heretic in his historical framework, where he was positioned in a relationship of tension with Paul the Apostle. Wingren emphasized Marcion's use of Paul as the very reason why Paul was included in the church canon at all; the church needed Paul in order to refute the Marcionite propaganda about him.[76] Wingren's long citations of Adolf von Harnack's studies on Marcion show that he was simultaneously pursuing his readings with an eye to identifying the various positions in the landscape of Swedish theology:

> The most obvious *antithesis* to Marcion can be seen in Billing's view of Christianity (also Odeberg's), while Nygren exhibits similarities in thought to Marcion.[77]
>
> Nygren is right in the middle between Paul and Marcion.[78]

Wingren also implies a strong analogy to the problems of contemporary church politics when he states (in this case considering the Pietistic movement), "The problem of Marcion is an interesting one. Marcion must be set aside in order that the church not embrace a special piety as its own."[79] In his studies, he continually compares what he learned in Berlin with what he knows about theologians such as Ragnar Bring, Anders Nygren, Einar Billing, and Herbert Olsson at home in Sweden. He also reasons at length about the suitability of various strategic and tactical academic maneuvers and the conceivable results they might have in the future. For example, he attempts to isolate a situation in which it would be possible to articulate the idea of creation and a balanced relationship between the Old and New Testament:

> Billing's field was Bible criticism . . . Nygren's field was the victory of liberal theology and the history of religion, which eventually spread . . . Our point of view is the victorious takeover of everything theological as never before, by the message of grace and christocentricity (Brilioth): the definite delineation between Christian and non-Christian; the victory of the New Testament and the crisis of the Old Testament; the crisis of the law and the crisis of the idea of creation; the confused attempts

---

76. Ibid., 3f. Later in his notes, he states that Paul is "hardly Lutheran" and that one should therefore not push the comparison between Paul and Marcion too far.

77. Ibid., 1.

78. Ibid., 10.

79. Ibid., 3.

to re-introduce the law (often in the wrong place), to bring back the idea of creation (but the wrong idea of creation [*Deutsche Christen*]), and to give the Old Testament back its place.[80]

In his reasoning, there is evidence of a strategic openness to the conditions created by a constantly changing context, but Wingren also shows signs of a well-developed tactical consciousness in regard to the conditions and possibilities for his own action. In one instance, he states that it is not practical to draft plans that go too far in the future: "No need to look further than this for now. When these three things have been broached, the entire theological situation will definitely be so changed that a renewed appraisal of the tasks will be absolutely necessary."[81]

His considerations of church politics also witness an advanced strategic ability and tactical consciousness. Quite clearly, Wingren saw both Pietistic revivalism and Lutheran orthodoxy as threatening alternatives, both of which in the long term would lead to isolation.[82] However, the true threat would come from the ever-growing high church movement, which in the future would emerge as the major opponent to Wingren in the arena of Swedish theology and church politics, on the issue of the ordination of women as ministers in the Church of Sweden. At this point in time, Wingren was able to look more leniently upon the high church movement since it offered an alternative to many who might otherwise have become Catholics.[83]

In his notes from his dormitory room in Berlin in 1938, Wingren repeatedly demonstrates strong confidence in his academic advisor, Ragnar Bring. For example, on 3 June, he states that Bring, with his systematic, existential method, is more productive than Billing, Nygren, and Herbert Olsson.[84] He also allows Bring to serve as a representative for the proud tradition of Luther research, and in this area, Wingren's appreciation seems to have no limits:

---

80. Ibid., 128-29.

81. Ibid., 267.

82. Cf. "The church will once again be reclaimed by workers fostered in social democracy and by free church people and idealistically thinking, now-isolated Christians. This is the future situation." Ibid., 87.

83. Cf. "In some ways, it is a good thing that the high church movement is gaining ground. In this way, [the church] is protected from Catholicizing tendencies" (ibid., 136); and further, "thus Rome moves off into the distance again. Crypto-Catholicism is . . . practically extinct." Ibid., 137.

84. Ibid., 92.

> The most important thing in Swedish systematic theology is its modern Luther research. In this area, the foundations have been prepared, upon which a systematician may stand. This heritage must never be wasted. Luther research and our orientation toward Luther must always be kept alive. This basis also makes possible a flowering systematics.[85]

Several of the prioritized lists of future writing projects that Wingren wrote during these months include a study of Luther. Although placed quite distant in the future, he seems nonetheless to have been certain that it could deal with the topic of vocation. But when he maintains here that creation and the law, in his opinion, must once again be made the objects of a thorough systematic treatment, because "justification in general cannot be depicted unless consideration is given to the idea of vocation," he still seems to be supporting his argument mostly through the works of Bring.[86] This confirms that Bring also had an important influence on him in his choice of topic for his doctoral thesis.

One person to whom Wingren devotes a disproportionately large portion of his Berlin reflections is another of his teachers: Herbert Olsson. He seems truly fascinated with, yet at the same time somewhat uneasy about, this man's character, not least because of the difficulties associated with understanding his actual position. Despite the fact that Olsson deals with problems posited by previous development in systematic theology (law, creation, salvation, and so on), he seems to take an "odd side route" as a representative for a "central, churchly Lutheran line of thought that has been pushed aside."[87] The theological position that Olsson seems to have taken could hardly be found on the current chart: "What is odd about Herbert Olsson is that he dismisses Billing as well as Nygren and Brilioth, the circle of young churchmen [*ungkyrkorörelsen*], the Lundensian theology, and the high church movement."[88] In his attempts to place Olsson on his strategic chart, Wingren brings him together with Bring and states that they are, on the one hand, more Lutheran than Aulén, Nygren, and Lindroth, but on the other hand, they seem far less interested in the Confessing Church (*Bekennende Kirche*)

---

85. Ibid., 149.
86. Ibid., 130.
87. Ibid., 138, 142.
88. Ibid., 143.

in Germany. Many times, Wingren revisits the question of how Herbert Olsson's oddly isolated position should be understood.[89]

Wingren's "Johanneum Journal" cannot be read without recognizing the perspective of his contemporary theological conditions, including the smoldering political situation in Europe in 1938. Wingren wrote this journal in Berlin, where the Nazis had been in power since 1933 and had already cleansed the universities of academics who did not agree with their views. His attempts to chart out the Swedish theological scene in his journal must be understood against this background. For example, he describes Olsson's stance as political and sociological, archaic, and traditionalistic, together with a modern political authoritarian tendency. However, Wingren deems it unthinkable that the phenomena of this form of ethics or the modern authoritarian state would recur.[90] In his notes from 23 June, he also states that Olsson combines "an old Lutheran characteristic" with "modern Nazi ideology," and thus in some respects Olsson could be seen as "the most modern, contemporary, and timely theologian in Sweden." He then adds, "This gives cause for a certain measure of care in the treatment of Herbert Olsson's theology."[91]

Wingren's strategic analyses and ponderings about tactical alliances reach their absolute height when he writes about Nygren, the other person to whom Wingren devoted the vast majority of the jottings in his journal. He describes Nygren as a character,[92] and he notes with some admiration how remarkably well known Nygren is in the ecumenical movement, in the Confessing Church as well as among Catholics. Wingren recognized it as advantageous that Nygren, along with Billing and Aulén, had in fact not become engaged in the drawn-out church battle between orthodoxy

---

89. At one point, he seems to recognize Herbert Olsson's isolation as a result of the fact that he did not relate his theological reflection to the Bible. In this sense, he was similar to von Engeström, Cullberg, Josefson, Sjöstrand, Lindström, and Holmström, and on this point, he diverged from Billing and Nygren. Ibid., 139.

90. Ibid., 85.

91. Ibid., 145. Wingren confirms this image of Herbert Olsson in a letter to Gösta Hallonsten on 25 June 1992, in which he recapitulates the lengthy conflict between Anders Nygren and Karl Olivecrona. He also points out that the support Olsson had from Olivecrona, who was favorable toward German views, in fact contributed to the government's decision to appoint Wingren instead of Olsson in 1951: "Based on a reliable source, I understand that the support for Olsson by two major German sympathizers, Olivecrona and Odeberg, was to Wingren's advantage and to Herbert Olsson's disadvantage."

92. Wingren, "Johanneum Journal," 97.

and liberalism—"two equally crazy alternatives"[93]—but had instead occupied himself with problems that lay beyond this struggle: "Even now, this is the only possibility. The problems of the Old Testament, the law, creation and ethics are articulated by this systematic theology, and not by the church battle."[94] As a result, Wingren recognizes Nygren as the one who determines the focus of the Swedish theology, while Olsson and Bring only provide modifications. Furthermore, he believes that Nygren will stand the test of time, and remain long after the Oxford Movement and the high church movement have ceased to be. At the same time, he is careful, in an almost obsessive way, to emphasize the close connection between Billing and Nygren: "Billing's and Nygren's theologies lie along the very same line. I keep coming back to this point. It is the Swedish line within systematic theology, and it is superior to everything else which is currently being promoted from various places."[95]

At this point, Wingren writes a cryptic sentence in his journal that could merely indicate his high regard for Nygren but that might also indicate that his respect was actually a tactical maneuver. He seems to think that for the time being it would be best not to attack Nygren: "He is without a doubt the central figure in Swedish theology *at this time*, and it would be meaningless to attempt to surpass him."[96] Wingren seems to think it would be wisest to wait to attack Nygren for strategic reasons, because he is necessary, but also for tactical reasons, since Wingren was entirely dependent on Nygren for his future career as a Swedish theologian.

There is yet another, darker streak in Wingren's notes regarding his evaluation of Nygren. He believes he can see a general trend in Lund that theologians oppose Nygren's program for philosophy of religion, and that Nygren, with a few exceptions, which of course includes Bring, is isolated in his philosophy: Nygren had in fact "never been modern and never will be."[97] For that reason, it is no coincidence that he identifies signs that Nygren in his great narrative on the basic motif of Christian love "had difficulties bringing the material together."[98] He also recognizes another particular tendency, to which he would often return in the future, namely,

---

93. Ibid., 134.
94. Ibid., 135.
95. Ibid., 152.
96. Ibid., 96.
97. Ibid., 98.
98. Ibid., 37.

that Nygren's philosophy is being used by the high church movement to support orthodox ends. At the horizon here, we see a glimpse of a future confrontation, which would explicitly deal with the resistance against women as ordained ministers.

Wingren's recurrent reflections about Nygren give evidence of an ability for strategic and tactical assessments, which is not necessarily to be considered as a false tactical strategy; it may instead be comprehended as an expression of strategic sensitivity in relation to the conditions and possibilities of the contemporary situation in which he found himself.[99] The message he seems to send to himself must be understood in the light of such contextualism when, in what almost comes across as an attempt to convince himself, he writes about the importance of positively grappling with the issues he plans to research and write about, without unnecessary polemics. It is thus not so surprising when he states that "polemics against Nygren are unnecessary, as polemics against Billing are also unnecessary from 'Lundensian theology.'" He continues, "Swedish systematic theology must nonetheless be based upon the work of Billing and Nygren."[100] This attitude does not however imply eternal peace with Nygren. The times and the context may change, but for *the present*, the changes possible within the near future motivate him to remain in agreement with Nygren, for good reasons:

---

99. In a letter to Gösta Hallonsten on 25 June 1992, Wingren emphatically denies any treacherousness on his part and maintains that it was in fact Nygren who concealed the truth. At the same time, things seem to have been complicated by the smoke screens he set up in his earlier writings, which can give the impression that he was taking an extremely tactical approach. As early as his licentiate thesis (1939), it is unclear as to just how straightforward he had been about his opinions, which became especially obvious when the contents of his thesis reached the public eye in the two articles he published in *Swedish Theological Quarterly* in 1940. Near the end of the second article, he is so eager to point out his affinity with Nygren that it almost feels as though he wants to take back some of what he had written earlier. Suddenly, he begins to speak of how God is the subject in Christian love and emphasizes how the concept of *agape* encompasses both faith and natural ethics, and concludes at last with the formulation "Creation, the law and salvation mutually affirm one another, and together comprise one idea: God is love, but this love is sovereign, and may only be obtained through faith," Wingren, "Frälsningens Gud såsom skapare och domare" (1940), 339. Cf. also ibid., 337-38. His book *The Living Word* would play a role in the competition for the professorship in which he received strong support from Nygren. In a note close to the conclusion of *Predikan*, Wingren emphasizes his distance from Barth and his proximity to Nygren (301 n. 2). This particular note is, however, not included in the English edition of the book, issued in 1960, when their relationship had collapsed.

100. Wingren, "Johanneum Journal," 131.

> If the same situation which now prevails in Germany were to occur in Sweden, which is plausible and believable, the name of Nygren would stand out as the great name in Swedish theology. His resolute purification does not fit in the current spiritual situation in Sweden, for which reason he is now generally dismissed. But in Germany he would be the foremost theologian, better than Barth (who is now losing ground on all fronts in German theology). It is precisely his removal of major portions of accepted Christianity that makes him, in an actual sense of the word, a *radical* theologian.[101]

This quotation shows very clearly that Wingren recognized and appreciated the great strategic value of Nygren's theology; it would serve as a bulwark against a development similar to that which had taken place in Germany, a situation that truly required a radical purification of theology in order to stand against the movement of the *Deutsche Christen* and the Nazi regime. In keeping with the methodology that Wingren would later call *confrontational analysis*, it is clear that Nygren was necessary, and at the time he was unavoidable, and should not be criticized, given the atmosphere of the late 1930s. With the current situation in mind, Wingren rightly decided to pursue positive work on the main problems, such as the Old Testament, the law, the idea of creation and the concrete problems of ethics—areas in which Nygren had not expressed himself comprehensively. At the same time, Wingren was obviously certain that a new time would come when Nygren could—and even should—be criticized.[102]

What were the personal implications of these ponderings for a student from Lund as he sat alone in his dormitory room in Berlin, researching and contemplating the future? For Wingren, it meant continuing to work with his advisor Bring in the tradition of Billing and Nygren, and this could be better achieved "by actually working in their spirit than by making their theology the object of one's own presentation."[103] Thus, he

---

101. Ibid., 93. Cf. how he writes that "the shortcomings in our cultural religion, which is based on the Enlightenment, become all the more evident," and further, that "the breakthrough of Nazism thus has a meaning that cannot be underappreciated." Ibid., 148.

102. Ibid., 132–33.

103. Ibid., 154. This is followed by a section written in large, underlined letters:
Studies on Marcion
For the discussion of various "contexts of meaning"
Paul and Luther
The christological struggles of the early church.

chose not to write *about* them, but rather to work in their spirit. At a time in which he saw a tendency toward orthodoxy, it was necessary to begin anew and go one's own way in order to tackle the main problems, which he also called the new problems, which implied the Old Testament, the law, creation and ethics: "This is my intention with my planned dissertation on Marcion."[104] Thus, at this time, Marcion remained at the top of the list and still seems to be the topic for his planned dissertation. However, his Berlin journal ("The Johanneum Journal") reveals his concern over whether he is capable at all of writing a dissertation and which topics he might best write about, given his skills. On midsummer eve 1938, he writes a few lines seemingly addressed to himself that indicate that he was still uncertain about his chosen topic:

> Write it only as a quiet examination, in the style of Herbert Olsson's dissertation on Luther. I am hardly mature enough to treat the problems of ethics and the word systematically. It would be best to continue with purely historical studies. Why not "The Conflicts of the Early Church," "The Idea of Vocation in the Works of Luther," or "The Theology of Albrecht Ritschl"?[105]

A few quiet historical studies were exactly what Wingren would write—until he gained the impulse for a *practical turn*.

---

104. Ibid., 140–41.
105. Ibid., 147.

4

The Practical Turn

IN HIS BOOK *COSMOPOLIS: The Hidden Agenda of Modernity*, Anglo-American philosopher of science Stephen Toulmin outlines a perspective on how the Western concept of knowledge has throughout the ages swung like a pendulum between theoretical-minded Platonists and practical-minded Aristotelians. This tension between *theory* and *practice* was also evident when the new interest in practical wisdom (*phronesis*), which occurred in the carnival-like scientific atmosphere of the sixteenth century, with its focus on concrete, practical life and time-bound local practices, was supplanted around 1630 by an abstract and universalistic scientific paradigm, which instead took as its point of departure theoretical understanding (*episteme*). If one follows Toulmin's account, European thought took an unfortunate turn in the early decades of the seventeenth century, when Descartes and his followers forsook the tolerant, skeptical philosophy of the sixteenth century to the benefit of a focus upon abstract, geometrical ideals regarding mathematical precision and logical strictness of a kind of knowledge without context. The sixteenth century had mainly been interested in ethnography, history, and poetry—each a different form of thinking characterized by a high degree of being context-bound, and developed to completeness by thinkers such as Montaigne. With the turn towards theoretical philosophy in the seventeenth century began a three-centuries-long cognitive era in which a rigorous scientific paradigm of timeless logics prioritized the written word over the oral, empirical evidence and formal logic over argumentation and rhetoric, and the abstraction of generalization over the multiplicity of the local and time-bound. Toulmin identifies signs that the pendulum had begun to swing back during the second half of the twentieth century.

Renewed interest in local life forms, language games, and in the concrete and individual led him to speak of *the return of practical philosophy*.[1]

To understand the breadth and potential variation in this general turn towards practical knowledge, it may be helpful to remember that the leading representatives of the two worlds of philosophy that dominated the previous century—Martin Heidegger (1889–1976), proponent of Continental philosophy, and Ludwig Wittgenstein (1889–1951), representing analytical philosophy—were both characterized by the way in which their thinking was shifting from a *theoretical* to a *practical* pole. In the case of Heidegger, the result was a *hermeneutics of being* based on an understanding of human beings as never disinterested in their surrounding environment, but rather always engaged in the world in constant care (*Sorge*). For Wittgenstein, it was a matter of a shift within his own philosophical project from his earlier, strictly theoretical critique of language, in accordance with the ideas of logical positivism, to his later philosophy focused on everyday language, a philosophy of action based on contextualized life forms and language games.

Thus, both Heidegger and Wittgenstein may be recognized as parts of a more general turn that characterized twentieth-century philosophy: from a unilaterally theoretical epistemology to a more profound understanding of practical knowledge, including all its ontological determinations. When the theoretical bent of modern science was questioned in the second half of the twentieth century and was in part replaced by a neo-Aristotelian interest in everyday practices as a source of knowledge, concepts such as *tacit* knowledge took on a central role. Michael Polanyi coined this concept as an expression of knowledge of which we may be bearers, even if we do not possess the representational theoretical terminology needed to express it. Polanyi emphasized that "we know more than we can tell,"[2] indicating the existence of implicit knowledge extant in human action, institutions, and traditions, beyond formalization. In the extension of this idea, which also could be named *knowledge-in-action*,[3]

1. Toulmin, *Cosmopolis*. Cf. my presentation in Kristensson Uggla, *Slaget om verkligheten*, 201–4.

2. Polanyi, *Tacit Dimension*, 4.

3. This concept comes from Bengt Molander. In his book *Kunskap i handling*, he provides an overview of discussions and experiments associated with practical knowledge and concludes by summarizing his presentation in a tension-filled theory of knowledge in action, which is supported by a series of dialectical oppositions and exchanges: partiality-wholeness, proximity-distance, criticism-trust, action-reflection. Ibid., 247ff.

a broad spectrum of philosophical attempts has developed, in which a new sort of epistemological culture has emerged, with an emphasis on the relationship between intuition and complexity, art and knowing, knowledge and action, and knowing and ethics. At times, there has been a tendency to mystify this tacit knowledge by presenting it as something that generally cannot be articulated, and thereby to risk developing it into an anti-intellectual stance. For this reason, I believe that we ought to talk about the tacit *dimension* of knowledge as an expression of an *extended concept of knowledge*, which transcends both a one-dimensional theoretical understanding of what knowledge is, and a diffuse pragmatism that celebrates unreflected action in the absence of all theory. As Ludwig Wittgenstein states in his *Philosophical Investigations*, rules—and the obeying of rules—always imply a practice.[4] This means that the question of obeying rules is equally as interesting as, or perhaps more important than, the rules themselves. However, how one obeys rules cannot be captured in an axiom or a rule; there can be no rules for how we are to obey rules. Instead, we have to cope with practical knowledge and the necessity of new interpretations in ever new situations, which require a judgment. Rules cannot save us from the uncertainty that is often present when we engage in new situations. Practical knowledge is not the result of formalized manuals, but rather is often example-based and founded upon analogical thinking, which calls upon a rich repertoire of examples. However, this area of knowledge is far from uniform and has been researched from different perspectives during the last half-century.

The development of an extended concept of knowledge is important for our discussion in this chapter, when we will examine Gustaf Wingren's most arcane and controversial book, *The Living Word: A Theological Study of Preaching and the Church* (1949/1960). I have previously touched upon how this book elicited widely varied responses, and how it functioned as a point of controversy and a tipping point in the drawn-out process by which Wingren finally received his professorship at Lund. The author himself seems, at least in retrospect, to have had no uncertainties about this work: "In my own estimation, *The Living Word* is my most important book, the only one of my works which reveals a spark of talent in its author."[5]

4. Wittgenstein, *Philosophical Investigations*, 81, para. 202.

5. Wingren, "Den springande punkten" (1974), 104. Cf. how Aulén praises the book *The Living Word* (1949/1960) to the skies in a thank you letter: "It belongs among the books that will leave a lasting mark on theological 'development.'" Gustaf Aulén to Gustaf Wingren, 11 December 1949.

However, the last six decades have left this book somewhat hanging in the air, without a theoretical framework that might make it comprehensible. Neither Wingren nor the many critics and denigrators of his book have provided such an intelligible framework. For this reason, it may be said that a more nuanced understanding of the book's contents and message is needed. In this chapter, I intend to contextualize *The Living Word* in its original situation, then decontextualize it, and finally recontextualize the book within the framework of a context that makes it possible to understand its message from a different horizon of understanding: the practical turn in contemporary epistemology. By doing so, I hope to disclose the contribution of the book to contemporary theology and present a frame of reference that makes it possible to elaborate a critical discussion of its contents. To achieve this, it is necessary, on the one hand, to recognize Wingren as an academic theologian, and, on the other hand, to move beyond the limitations of his own self-understanding and context. In the contemporary situation, some sixty years after the book was first issued, it is important to not simply recapitulate the book's basic structure within the context of the post-World War II cultural climate, but also to go beyond the limitations of its original intention and context. Only in this way will it be possible to benefit from the contents of this work and achieve a balanced critique of its shortcomings.[6]

Science versus Science

Gustaf Wingren's book *The Living Word* (1949/1960) is really difficult to comprehend, and there are significant challenges associated with any attempt to conceptualize its contents. Those who try to read through it at a single sitting can easily lose their way and be left with a lasting lack of comprehension concerning its message. The book is truly challenging. In regard to its style, we might speak of Wingren's Nietzschian moment, or view the book as a reply to another theological work of equally volcanic

---

6. Armgard is one of the exceptions in the Wingren literature. In an article from 1987, he sketches out the possibilities for discussing Wingren's theology from the point of intersection between theory and practice and emphasizes in particular "participatory observation." However, he does so with reference to Wingren's later authorship, disconnected from the book *The Living Word*. Armgard, "Gustaf Wingrens senare författarskap," 16. In Karlsson's dissertation, *Predikans samtal*, the problem of theory/practice is part of the presentation, as well as a recurring discussion of its theological background.

emotion, Karl Barth's *Epistle to the Romans*. The fact that the book is equally as fascinating as it is difficult to comprehend may be a result of the unusual level of energy with which the text is charged, but it may also be due to its immense mixture of materials, styles, and, I would claim, messages. The reader is left with the feeling that here can be found nearly everything in Wingren's theological thinking in a somewhat unstructured concentrate: all of his topics, all of the various sources and groupings of materials that he used for his theological reflections except the extension of sources in his later works, his most central theses, and so on and so on.[7] Readers who pass by too quickly and do not pay attention to the unusually detailed table of contents (especially in the Swedish edition) may easily become confused about its structure and message while reading the text. This is because, in contrast to the particularly well-structured table of contents, the materials seem arbitrarily placed throughout the book.

The Living Word became controversial in Sweden as soon as it was released. As we have seen, it went to press in early summer 1949, only days before the deadline for submission of materials to the evaluation committee for the vacant professorship at Lund. In the foreword to the second Swedish edition (1960), Wingren wrote that after some consideration, he had decided against reworking the text for the reason that it was simplest for the reader if the text was allowed to remain "without changing the target at which it had been fired."[8] This statement (which is not found in the English translation) may be read as an ironic reference to the critical judgment Professor Hjalmar Lindroth issued as a member of the evaluation committee in 1950, when he emphasized the book's lack of merit "in a strictly scientific respect," and continued with the claim that "even in its details, [the book] offers a large target area for critical objections."[9]

---

7. This impression is more or less confirmed by Wingren's own retrospective comment in an article from 1974, in which he seeks to show "how organically necessary my book about preaching was in 1949, how clearly everything that I have written during the last quarter century is built upon this book, and how it is impossible to skip over it in a backward look." Several pages later, in discussing the book's main structure, he states: "Nothing in my later authorship can be fully understood without this fundamental construction." Wingren, "Den springande punkten" (1974), 101, 105.

8. Wingren, *Predikan* (1949), xv, in Swedish edition, not included in the English edition, *The Living Word* (1960).

9. Lindroth, in Appendix 26C of the Faculty of Theology's protocol, meeting 24 October 1950, 152.

There were also critical objections from other people involved in the appointment process, and as we have seen, the book was critically reviewed and dissected in a pamphlet written and privately published by Karl Olivecrona, *What Is the Deciding Factor for a Professorship: Science or Proclamation of Faith?* When the matter of the professorial appointment reached Lund University's Greater Academic Council, the arguments from committee members and the faculty regarding the book's merits and shortcomings were repeated. Philosophy Professor Gunnar Aspelin felt that the book diverged from "the impersonal objectivity deemed necessary for a scientific work" on the basis of its methodological shortcomings and "existential" and "subjective" style.[10] History Professor Sten Carlsson saw no other course of action than to sit down and study with his own eyes this most contested of all the works submitted in the appointment process. He reached the following conclusion:

> I have thus—to the extent it is possible to do so without any previous opinion—concluded that I can state that it is a remarkable and in many respects interesting specimen. It is truly, as attested by Prof. Kjöllerström of the faculty, *stimulating*; as a historian, I have benefitted greatly from my study of it. I can comprehend it in no other way than that it is at its heart biblical interpretation and interpretation of Luther in a broad context of the history of ideas and fundamental theology. In addition to its captivating historical perspective, it distinguishes itself by a refreshing and, as far as I can determine, unusually independent view of the problems of contemporary theology and the contemporary church.[11]

What nonetheless decided the council to go against the committee and the faculty, and instead recommend Olsson as the appointee to the professorship, was the recurring complaint that Wingren did not distinguish between academic theology and churchly preaching, and saw no difference between the classroom lecture podium and the pulpit, which may have been reinforced by the Swedish title, *Predikan (The Sermon)*. Because of these alleged serious shortcomings of scientific scholarliness, the contents of the book were reduced to a sort of Christian proclamation, which claimed to be able to determine the true nature of Christianity. Yet,

---

10. Aspelin, in Appendix 1010 D of Större akademiska konsistoriets i Lund protokoll den 16 december 1950, par. 101.

11. Carlsson, in Appendix 1010 N of Större akademiska konsistoriets i Lund protokoll den 16 december 1950, par. 101.

for the same reasons, the book has found many enthusiastic readers ever since it was first published. Both its critics and defenders converge on this point. Moreover, if this is the entire truth about *The Living Word*, then Lindroth is probably correct in his complaint: theology has made itself superfluous. But is this really a reasonable interpretation of a theologian who at the time was applying for an appointment at Lund University? The confusion and uncertainty characterizing the many divergent evaluations of the book may more readily be evidence of a lack of categories for determining its theoretical status. Against this background, I feel it is important to posit the serious question of how we may read and understand this book, and move beyond either issuing uncritical, enthusiastic repetitions of its contents or simple, categorical dismissals of it because it seems foreign and inaccessible. In both cases, there seems to be a lack of concepts to comprehend it and elaborate on an appropriate critique of its contents. Because of this, contemporary theology runs the risk of not being able to use the book at all as a resource for theological thinking. The text is thus left hanging in midair, without a context.

The style of language Wingren employs in *The Living Word* is colorful, and he often seems to present ideas without explanation of their background; the reader may also feel the lack of a proper review of the assumptions upon which the author's reasoning is based. However, only someone who has made a superficial reading of the book would reach the conclusion that it contains purely sermon-like proclamation. In the same way that Hans-Georg Gadamer's magnum opus, *Truth and Method*, raises hopes that the reader might gain an insight into truth as well as method, when in fact the book is a critique of the grandiose (and vainglorious) hopes of discovering truth by the use of methodology, the Swedish title of Wingren's book—*Predikan (The Sermon)*—may indeed prompt expectations that this is an instructional text on how one should preach, or might even itself *be* a sermon. In order to cope with these uncertainties, one should take note of the book's Swedish subtitle: *En principiell studie (A Fundamental Study)*, which reveals that it is a *fundamental* study dealing with general issues and ought to be related to the field of systematic theology. The book is, despite the expectations that its Swedish title may elicit, neither a textbook on homiletics (although it has in fact been used as a textbook in this respect) nor a collection of sermons. It is rather a fragmentary, nearly aphoristic rough draft of a treatise on theological hermeneutics—and on hermeneutical theology as well. But more on this aspect later; let us further examine the book's relationship to the sermon.

In the journal notes that he kept as a graduate student in Berlin during the summer of 1938, Wingren had already jotted down thoughts that point toward *The Living Word*, but at that time he seems to have thought of it as a possible doctoral dissertation that he might write in the spirit of Yngve Brilioth's—or Karl Barth's—works. This is obvious when the Berlin student writes, "In a review in the *Swedish Theological Quarterly*, Brilioth has pointed out the need for a dissertation on the *word* (exegetic, systematic, homiletic). Cf. Barth's *Das Wort Gottes und die Theologie*."[12] The broad range of topics he here indicates—exegetic, systematic, homiletic—also point the way towards what would later become *The Living Word* (1949/1960). However, as we have seen previously, these notes that Wingren wrote on midsummer eve 1938 show that at this time he did not feel "mature enough to treat the problems of ethics and the word systematically," and for this reason he decided instead to "continue with purely historical studies."[13] Eleven more years of studies and an intellectual head-on collision with a different theological world changed these circumstances, and the result was finally—*The Living Word*.

In *The Living Word*, preaching as a concrete, ongoing practice is of general significance for the understanding of the conditions and possibilities of theology. However, this does not mean that theology and the sermon implode into one another. In this book, as with other of his works and in his inaugural lecture, Wingren is careful not to allow theology to be reduced to proclamation, a fact that is strengthened by the sharp criticism he directs toward Karl Barth for his deficient ability to maintain a clear distinction between the sermon and theology.[14] Even though Wingren became known early on as a gifted preacher, he did not preach

12. Wingren, "Johanneum Journal," 141.

13. Ibid., 147.

14. In *The Living Word* (1949/1960), 22–24, Wingren pursues a discussion about theology considered as "a science like other sciences." Ibid., 22. Luther, however, did not know anything about science in the modern sense of the word. Nevertheless, Wingren seemed to recognize contemporary trends that overlooked this fact: "In contemporary theology certain definite tendencies have been revealed, and efforts made towards returning in this direction, with the desire of obliterating the distinction between preaching and theological science." Ibid., 23. Here, he mentions and criticizes Barth, for whom theology at once turns into preaching or is being reduced to a science that aids preaching. In contrast with the Lundensian theology of Nygren and Bring, Wingren still finds good reasons to continue an investigation from the point of view that "preaching is a relatively independent entity, which can be made the subject of a systematic theological analysis." Ibid., 23. But this requires the existence of two separate entities.

sermons when he lectured at the university. His work is characterized by a clear ambition to pursue scientific scholarship. Even in the introductory methodological discussion he presents in this controversial book, he emphasizes that theology is a science among other sciences.[15] Throughout the years, Wingren often repeated the statement that there was nothing unscientific in his book from 1949.[16] Wingren researcher Johnny Karlsson clearly states that "throughout the years, Wingren constantly and consistently upheld the need for theology to be kept scientific."[17] Moreover, Wingren often expressed regret that the Church of Sweden during the twentieth century had lured away so many leading scholars and academics by appointing them as bishops, which resulted in harsh losses for Swedish theology. Yet, what is new in Wingren's book from 1949 is his departure from Nygren's historicizing methodology in that the task Wingren sets for himself is not purely historical; instead, he deals with a systematic theological analysis—in other words, an analysis of the concept of the sermon. Thus, the fundamental questions in focus are, "What does it *mean* to preach? What is *the content* of preaching?"[18] In an analysis of Wingren based on *The Living Word*, Edgar Almén concludes that Wingren is not only an argumentative theologian, but in fact one of the most systematic thinkers he knows: "He interprets everything as systems of thought dependent on their foundations, and must therefore be discussed as systems of thought according to these foundations."[19]

What then is the problem? Why has this book been subjected to such strong criticism? Karl Olivecrona and others have pointed out its style of language, and quoted long sections of the book to inform their readers about what kind of text was to be found in *The Living Word*. Indeed, the reader may be struck by the powerful, mythic-poetic language—as well as Wingren's failure to provide interpretative links of mediation. This seems obvious, for example, when he uses formulations

---

15. Ibid., 22.

16. This was the position he consistently took in *The Living Word*, and much later he underscored it and defended the scholarliness of that book: "There is not one single piece of anything specifically unscholarly in my book about preaching from thirty-three years ago. That is how I was in that book, and that is the way I have remained. And I maintain that a theologian should remain as such." Wingren, "Pensionärer och avlidna" (1982), 20.

17. Karlsson, *Predikans samtal*, 264.

18. Wingren, *The Living Word* (1949/1960), 21.

19. Almén, "Gustaf Wingrens teologiska argument," 15.

such as this: "Forgiveness destroys the tyrant who causes the guilt—the Accuser, Satan, the Devil—and hunts him down out of the conscience, cleanses man's conscience from the army of evil spirits."[20] However, the problem with this objection to *The Living Word* in particular is that in respect to language, it is really no different from Wingren's two earlier books. In respect to its language, tone, and rather terse methodological reasoning, along with the fact that the examination undertaken in the book is governed by a systematic theological focus, there is no decisive difference between *The Living Word* (1949/1960) and Wingren's two earlier works on Luther (1942/1957) and Irenaeus (1947/1959).[21]

I believe that one element behind some of this criticism is connected to the biblical theology that Wingren develops in *The Living Word*. The Swedish edition of the book contains about one thousand references to the Bible. Already from the beginning, Wingren's academic career was, as we have seen, marked by a firm interest in exegetical theology. He had attended Hugo Odeberg's seminar on New Testament exegetics before Ragnar Bring entered the scene and redirected him toward systematic theology. His interest in exegetics prevailed even after he began his studies on the early church fathers in the second half of the 1930s. In his journal from his 1938 stay in Berlin, he often refers to the need for biblical theology, as for example in this note: "But what I feel a painful lack of in Sweden is a central and in-depth biblical theology."[22] In his "Johanneum Journal" from Berlin, he also complains that the Old Testament has been left to "lie completely fallow." In this context a strong inspiration from Einar Billing's biblical theology is evident. Wingren declares that he misses biblical theology in the works of all contemporary systematic theologians—"except Einar Billing."[23] This reference to Billing is important,

---

20. Wingren, *The Living Word* (1949/1960), 173. Later in Wingren's theological project, this dualistic theological imagination is being demythologized.

21. Eklund's statements in the faculty point out the confessional framework that in the works of Wingren direct his examinations of both Luther and Irenaeus. Among the area experts, Prenter has fewer comments on Wingren's study on Irenaeus from 1947, and Hjalmar Lindroth directs sharp criticism toward Wingren because he "sometimes abbreviates the material, and utilizes it often only when it stands in agreement with the primary systematic stance that he has established." Lindroth, in Appendix 28B of the Faculty of Theology's protocol, meeting on 24 October 1950, 153. Yet, at the same time, there are no objections in regard to the immediacy of his language.

22. Wingren, "Johanneum Journal," 114. Cf. "Currently, the great shortcoming is the absence of a respectable biblical theology." Ibid., 113.

23. Ibid., 114ff.

because it illustrates Wingren's own position, since Billing, along with Nathan Söderblom, was of almost emblematic importance in the defense of free and unfettered biblical research that embraced historical-critical methods without any reservation—not only in the academic world but also in the church.[24]

In *The Living Word*, Wingren's strategy of increasing the number of indexes in the book from two to three by adding an index of Bible references (something he had cautiously tried for the first time in his 1947 book on Ireneaus) resulted in a veritable explosion of Bible references.[25] This may of course elicit questions of what theoretical status and argumentative value Bible references may hold and how Wingren's use of the Bible should be considered. Yet, at the same time, it must be clear that Wingren did not represent some sort of naïve fundamentalism or biblical literalism. He was in many ways an especially well-informed researcher for his day, one who, in the spirit of Billing and Söderblom, without a doubt and with great enthusiasm affirmed all the achievements of biblical criticism.

Nonetheless, I believe that Wingren's critics are heading in the right direction, even though they draw faulty conclusions, or at least think too narrowly, when they claim that the reasoning presented in the book is better suited to a discussion held within the church. Ragnar Bring mentioned this argument in his statement to the appointment committee in 1950, although he immediately refuted it. Others presented this idea as well, among them Harald Eklund, to whom in turn Karl Olivecrona

---

24. In his later work on Billing, he allows his presentation to begin with Billing's indignation over the fact that his academic teacher at Uppsala in the late 1800s hid the results of critical research from his students, and also that Billing made it a virtue to "include discussions of the results of biblical criticism in his sermons or describe those results in other contexts of worship." And furthermore: "The critical view of the Bible belongs in worship because its views and discoveries are 'edifying': they promote faith and songs of praise in the congregation." Wingren, *Exodus Theology* (1968/1969), 6.

25. Wingren consistently followed the pattern of equipping his books with three indexes. However, *The Living Word* (1949/1960), in which he (especially in the original Swedish edition) includes a gigantic index of Bible references, is a notable exception, for it has no index of subjects. In the English edition this has been added, but the number of Bible references as well as footnotes is radically reduced. This may be related to the fact that *The Living Word*, in its original Swedish edition, has a particularly detailed table of contents, but may also indicate how disorganized the material in this book is and how impossible it would have been to create an index of subjects for it. At some points in the book it can seem as though Wingren is discussing all subjects simultaneously.

referred, stating that the book "is limited to arguments which function only in a practical and churchly context."[26] The combination of the terms "practical" and "churchly" may give the impression that they refer to one and the same thing, which is by no means the case, either in general or in the case of Wingren. Certainly, Wingren's work is characterized by a distinctly *practical* perspective; his text is rife with verbs and references to things that *occur* and *happen*; he speaks of things that emerge, spring forth and continue to this day, people who are being created and recover, and he talks of wandering and listening, and so on. Actually, the central theme of the book is that there is something that *occurs* in the meeting between human beings and the Word.[27] Wingren presents this occurrence as a scientific thesis, with the determination that it would be incorrect to take the content of the texts for granted. What is read in texts always takes on a coloring; every interpretation contains a personal and existential element. To this he adds exegetical arguments from the form-critical school, which implies that the course of events of Christ's death and resurrection are to be apprehended as the heart of the New Testament texts. To describe this occurrence, and to describe the human existence that identifies itself with it, requires a systematic narrative perspective that clearly places the stories at the center of the presentation. To preach is to tell a story. The sermon may be considered as a link in the chain of events between the resurrection of Christ and the resurrection of the body and life everlasting. In this context, according to Wingren, preaching is to be considered as a *practice*—"preaching is a continuing function in the actual life of the Church today"[28]—which maintains the continuity of the phenomenon we refer to as Christianity: "In this way the Bible finds its unity when it preaches and is preached. If preaching is suppressed, then the book of God's acts falls apart as into *disjecta membra*."[29] This means that it is not possible to use a purely theoretical determination of the unity of the Bible based on something that exists in these texts; instead, the unity of the Bible must be constituted by the means of acts of interpretation in "the world *in front of* the text," to borrow a phrase from Paul Ricoeur. It is not, however, in any way necessary that the context of

---

26. Eklund, in Appendix 28E of the Faculty of Theology's protocol, meeting on 24 October 1950, 9. Olivecrona, *Vetenskap eller trosförkunnelse som merit för professur?*, 1.

27. Wingren, *The Living Word* (1949/1960), 25.

28. Ibid., 24.

29. Ibid., 39.

this practice be a churchly one, or that it must necessarily withdraw from scientific argumentation and criticism.

In the book *Religious Language* (*Det religiösa språket*), by philosophy lecturer Sven Wermlund, *The Living Word* plays a significant role. At the outset, Wermlund finds it refreshing that Wingren here departs from Bring and Lundensian theology by "upholding the 'weight of the issue of facticity' with clarity." He thus does not dismiss the question of whether the biblical texts are true in the usual sense as pure metaphysics, referring to religion as a separate area of human experience.[30] Then, however, he becomes disappointed that Wingren does not posit the question of facticity in accordance with what he considered as the principles of a scientific examination of truth. The reason for this, according to Wermlund, is that Wingren refuses to separate "the facticity of the resurrection" from "the facticity of our enslavement."[31] It is as if Wermlund is confused regarding which categories the book actually treats when he criticizes "the tremendous laxity of Wingren's language."[32] Nevertheless, he also points out that Wingren in fact takes pains to de-psychologize faith, which moves the focus to Wingren's refusal to separate subject from object, and how faith can both "rest upon" and "wait for" occurrences. Thus, even if Wermlund feels the lack of what he himself considers a scientific frame of mind in Wingren, there are at least some interesting openings in his analysis of Wingren that in the presence of other intellectual resources and evaluation criteria could lead to another conclusion.[33] Let us follow this path.

Wingren's conviction that it is necessary for theology to in some way consider the question of truth seriously is strongly influenced by Einar Billing's ideas about the undeniable relationship of the Christian faith to history and outward reality: "If this relationship is discarded, Christian faith cannot survive."[34] Theology is, according to Billing, always related to a historical context; along with the prophets, it is a matter of "interpreting

30. Wermlund, *Det religiösa språket*, 78–79.

31. Ibid., 80ff.

32. Ibid., 86.

33. This circumstance is strengthened by the fact that he finds reasoning in the book that is worthy of further examination (ibid., 88), and also by the fact that two of Wermlund's young students, Tore Nordenstam and Mats Furberg, wrote an essay in the later 1950s—an essay that amounted to an *Ehrenrettung*—in which they maintained "that Wingren could be read more favorably." Furberg, "Filosofiskt 50-tal i Göteborg," 104.

34. Wingren, "Einar Billings teologiska metod" (1955), 282.

the history of God's election," which implies that the task of theology is neither a matter of writing psychology nor a matter of reproducing a system of doctrines.[35] Billing considered the struggle and tribulation that a scientific study of the question of truth and the question of reality may bring the theologian both necessary and beneficial. He dismisses every attempt at escapism, demanding instead that theology maintain continual connections with science and the historical disciplines.[36] Wingren wholeheartedly shared this basic view of Billing's, although the concrete challenges associated with how this program should be set into operation in different times and scientific contexts is another question.

In his presentation in *The Living Word*, Wingren indeed shows a tendency to develop a sort of immediacy in his thought, and some sections of the book lack background explanations and clear presentations of the assumptions on which his reasoning is based. *The Living Word* appears as a hermeneutical book that, paradoxically, remains hermeneutically unmediated. Yet, once again, on this point there is no major difference between this particular book and Wingren's previous historical books. In his dissertation, he claims that he seeks to pursue a purely historical study, yet his presentation nonetheless takes the form of an interpretation so immanent that the author almost takes on Luther's voice. In long sections of the book, his presentation also presumes a confessional pact between the text and the reader, something that cannot be presumed without prior explanation. Here, once again, the presumptions on which the presentation is based are not explained, as for example to what extent these examinations are determined by the agreement between Lutheran orthodoxy and Pietism. Instead, Wingren simply enters into Luther's world, and all that is said there immediately becomes a current truth. Wingren consistently uses an "immanent analysis," which in its historical form is in one sense equally as problematic from an epistemological perspective as the hermeneutically influenced approach he elaborated on in 1949. Both of these analyses lack contextualization; he does not clarify the prerequisites for his reasoning, and the process of interpretation is not mediated by a variety of explanations. In this way, even his earlier books on Luther (1942/1957) and Irenaeus (1947/1959)—the scientific nature of which no one seriously questioned—also involved the dilemma created by simply including the reader in a "we" that presumes a common

---

35. Ibid., 283. Cf. "Faith lives in a story that lies open for observation and research." Ibid., 284.

36. Ibid., 291.

(Christian, Protestant, Lutheran, Billingian) world, something that simply cannot be taken for granted. Neither Bible quotations nor references to Luther may hold any argumentative value in themselves, without clarifications and explanations.

A more serious problem is that some passages of *The Living Word* tend to mystify the process of interpretation. This tendency becomes obvious in unfortunate formulations, as for example when Wingren relates that "the unity of the Bible is 'an interpretation of faith.'"[37] Yet this passage of *The Living Word* diverges from Wingren's general pattern of taking a very skeptical stance toward all attempts to spiritualize theological processes.[38] This sort of spiritualization and lack of clarity is all the more remarkable if we consider Wingren's unreserved acceptance of biblical criticism and the historical-critical thinking that he claims to use in the tradition of Billing and Söderblom. Wingren also developed strong theological justifications for accepting the critical methods of science based on the idea of creation as well as incarnation theology as critical standpoints against monophysitism, which acknowledges only Jesus' divine nature and not his humanity. It is clear that already in his early theological thinking he wholeheartedly accepted the breakthrough of the historical view of the Bible; he actually considered it to be the most significant theological development that had occurred since the Reformation. This position is equally as evident in *The Living Word* as when he nearly a decade later writes,

> The Bible is a literary product with a simple account of human origins, the investigation of which requires no more than accepted rules of procedure. But only to a very limited extent has this insight made any impression on the preaching or teaching of the Word, so far as such preaching or teaching is carried out by the ministry of the Church.[39]

Also the theological argumentation for this position is always present and clear:

---

37. Ibid., 39.

38. In a way, Jonny Karlsson has drawn a conclusion concerning this when he makes use of Mikhail Bakhtin's philosophy of dialogicity to demonstrate the inner structure of Wingren's practice of preaching, and how through the use of this linguistic theory one may "avoid a one-sided theological determination" of preaching. Karlsson, *Predikans samtal*, 283.

39. Wingren, *Gospel and Church* (1960/1964), 136.

Those who make the humanity of Christ a living reality for the people to whom they speak are able to incorporate the findings of biblical criticism into the ministerial acts of the Church. To support that this will make us lose sight of the divinity of Christ indicates that we have failed to accept that the incarnation ever took place at all.[40]

In light of this background, the question of what is *really* so problematic about *The Living Word* bears repeating. For this reason, let us approach this much-debated book in another way.

Hermeneutics as Practical Philosophy

On numerous occasions, in spoken and written words, Gustaf Wingren related that beginning in childhood he had been fascinated by a particular kind of practice, the meaning and function of which occupied his thoughts: preaching. This practice involves a profound dimension of interpretation and thus brings the problems of hermeneutics to the fore. What actually takes place in preaching, when someone presents a Bible text for a group of people who listen to it in the framework of a worship service? What conditions are necessary in order for this practice to function at all, to be maintained over the course of centuries, and still be experienced as meaningful? And what fundamental problems may be identified when this practice does not function? *The Living Word* deals with this set of problems, and much more. As mentioned, the Swedish title of the book, *Predikan* (*The Sermon*), invites misunderstanding and may raise faulty assumptions that this is a book on homiletics, which in fact is not the case at all. Instead, the practice of preaching is made to serve as a model for the more general practice of interpretation, the theological presumptions and consequences of which Wingren sets into play within the framework of a Christian tradition in general, and a Lutheran one in particular. The problem, however, is that the academic context in which Wingren found himself offered limited preconditions for articulating a relevant epistemology and ontology for his examination. On a purely immanent level, his argumentation is strong; but on a metalevel and in a broader interdisciplinary context, the book is weak. The practice at the heart of Wingren's interest is the act of interpretation, but the concept of both the text and the context for the theological hermeneutics he

40. Ibid., 136.

develops must be reinforced with other intellectual resources than those to which he himself had access.

The historical distance offered by the passage of more than six decades makes it easier to recognize the limitations of the scientific paradigm of the postwar years in Sweden, and also makes it easier for us to qualify a more adequate epistemological context for the understanding of Wingren's 1949 book. Quite simply, it is a matter of identifying a culture of knowledge that can provide the book with meaning—in other words, of suggesting a context for this text. I affirm that Wingren himself, and the predominant scientific infrastructure of that time in Sweden, lacked the philosophical resources to disclose the real significance of this book. The author himself also stated that neither the idealistic solution of neo-Kantianism (in other words, the work of Anders Nygren) nor the different variants of analytical philosophy (in other words, partly the work of Axel Hägerström and, primarily, that of Ingemar Hedenius) offered acceptable alternatives.[41] However, we cannot ignore the fact that we are reading the book today and that our contemporary epistemological context, which is in many ways different from the one that prevailed when the book was first published, will thus influence our reading. While this provides us with advantages, it is of course also associated with risks. For this reason, the utilization of our contemporary philosophical resources must be tempered with sensible criticism and self-criticism. Nonetheless, it is difficult to ignore the feeling that the context of our day has finally caught up with Wingren's text.[42] However, let me emphasize that despite the different frame of reference available today, Wingren's book remains controversial in many ways, even if some of the points of controversy have shifted somewhat.

I regard *The Living Word* as the first great manifestation of the *turn toward practical knowledge* that occurred in Wingren's work as a theologian near the end of the 1940s. This practical turn was a result of the new resources for theological thinking brought into play through his "Basel impulse." Using terminology that Wingren himself would never have used, I would like to describe this change as a *hermeneutical variant of a general turn toward practical knowledge*. As such, the book exhibits

---

41. Wingren, *Mina fem universitet* (1991), 55–57.

42. Cf. how Wingren himself comments on the changing context in the foreword to the third Swedish edition of *Predikan*: "The cultural shift has now taken place, even in Sweden." "Förord" (1996), x.

evidence of surprising hermeneutical insights and is associated with profound philosophical implications.

Modern hermeneutics presents itself as one of the most ambitious attempts to develop a contemporary understanding of the emerging new paradigm focused on practical knowledge. What is the basic structure of this hermeneutical variant of the turn toward practical knowledge? Hans-Georg Gadamer has developed the most extensive philosophical investigation of the limits and possibilities inherent in hermeneutics as a practical philosophy. His most significant contribution is *Truth and Method*, in which he synthesized the most important ideas from German hermeneutics. However, as mentioned earlier, although this book may appear as a utopia for every researcher, eliciting hopes that it will deliver both truth and method, its purpose is actually just the opposite: Gadamer delivers a penetrating coming to terms with the grandiose expectations of what may actually be achieved through abstract methodology based on the ambitions of theoretical reason. Hermeneutics, too, had at an earlier stage been developed into a methodology that promised to deliver a purely theoretical path toward truth. For Gadamer, however, hermeneutics was first and foremost a *practical* philosophy, which emphasizes the necessity of involvement, understanding, and innovation in the hermeneutical process, based upon an understanding of interpretation as *application* and with the metaphor of play, as well as dancing, as its dominant model.

In a chapter titled "The Recovery of the Fundamental Hermeneutic Problem" in *Truth and Method*, Gadamer positions the question of *applicatio* at the very center of hermeneutics. In his extension of the concept of practical wisdom (*phronesis*) in Aristotle, he seeks to show what he refers to as "the exemplary importance of legal hermeneutics."[43] In this way, he brings out the original context of regional hermeneutics in a tradition of literary, legal, and theological hermeneutics, which consistently finds its point of departure in "recognizing application as an integral element of all understanding."[44] Legal hermeneutics as well as literary and theological hermeneutics are constituted by the tension between a specific text and its use in concrete situations of interpretation: "A law does not exist in order to be understood historically, but to be concretized in its legal validity by being interpreted . . . to be understood properly . . . in every

---

43. This section is found in Part Two, "The Extension of the Question of Truth to Understanding in the Human Sciences," in Gadamer, *Truth and Method*, 334–50.

44. Ibid., 319.

concrete situation."[45] What is required for achieving a legal decision or writing a sermon is concrete acts of interpretation; the text finds its full significance only when it is made concrete in a specific context. However, this also means that the claims of the text in each new situation must undeniably be understood in terms of new and different interpretations: "Understaning here is always application."[46]

The resurgence of regional (or disciplinary) hermeneutics is tied to the rise of neo-Aristotelianism. By bringing Aristotle to the fore, this hermeneutics has thus sought to emphasize the limited regularity of human action and the necessity of seriously considering that only practical wisdom (*phronesis*) can provide guidance in the application and appropriation of texts in different specific situations. Against the background of how, for example, a skilled handcraft transcends taught technical knowledge (*techne*), Aristotle shows that all aspects of crafts exist in a state of tension with concrete action. The capacity for judgment thus takes on decisive importance for dealing with the challenges of concrete situations. Here, too, regional hermeneutics assumes an exemplary significance, because the concrete law case reinstates the unity of hermeneutics, in the same way that the concretization of a proclamation occurs in and through the sermon. Thus, Gadamer aims to redefine the hermeneutics of the human sciences in terms of legal and theological hermeneutics.[47] The Aristotelian analysis of *phronesis*, the well-informed action in the concrete situation, thus functions as a determination of the meaning and inner cohesion of the practice of interpretation. Gadamer sums up his view of hermeneutics in his theory of historically effected consciousness (*Wirkungsgeschichtliches Bewusstsein*), which is present in the fusion of horizons (*Horizontversmeltzung*) characterizing all interpretation. In other words, here is a practice of interpretation that does not limit its interests to that which is present before us. The hermeneutical experience that occurs when the horizon of the text, or the work of art, fuses with the horizon of the reader, or viewer, is an expression of a practical philosophical perspective focused on a reality that reveals itself only if we allow ourselves to be involved in this process of interpretation.

Paul Ricoeur has also been deeply engaged in the question of what it means to interpret a text. He developed a hermeneutical theory that in

---

45. Ibid., 319–20.
46. Ibid., 320.
47. Ibid., 321.

part aligns with, and in part diverges from, Gadamer's position. Ricoeur takes his point of departure in the fact that text and interpretation mutually define each other, which presupposes, on the one hand, the text's paradoxical position as a bearer of meaning and, on the other, the dialectical nature of the act of interpretation. The text can be said to convey a *surplus* of meaning, and at the same time be characterized by its *lack* of meaning. Thus, the text demands interpretation, which in analogy with the various determinations of the text may both take the form of a *reduction* of meaning and function as a *completion* of the inherent semantic possibilities of the text. The hermeneutical experience, which comes into being between the text and the reader in and through the act of reading, has however a far more critical and alienated character in Ricoeur than in Gadamer. This is reinforced by the fact that Ricoeur speaks of the hermeneutical experience as a *heterogeneous synthesis*. Yet, this hermeneutical theory also functions as a paradigm for how practical and theoretical reasons are intertwined with one another in an inseparable way. The meaning of a text is not conclusively given in the text itself; its semantic possibilities open themselves to different interpretations in "the world *in front of* the text." The text *speaks*, but it *does not speak on its own*. Rather, it can only speak through human action, in and through the act of reading. Furthermore, the text speaks in new ways in different contexts. It is only in "the world *in front of* the text" that what exists in the text's own realm can be realized and determined. Interpretation is, therefore, not a free act of imagination but is regulated and limited by the horizon and semantic possibilities of the text. Yet, because each text may be interpreted in different ways, Ricoeur posits that hermeneutics, given the absence of absolute knowledge, must necessarily treat the *conflict of interpretations* in responsible as well as creative ways.[48]

The hermeneutical epistemology and ontology that I have outlined here makes it possible to develop a better understanding of what occurs in and through the practical turn in Wingren's theological project. He himself was also embedded in a particular vein of regional hermeneutics, namely that of theological hermeneutics, as configured by the tension between exegetics and homiletics. In the mid-1930s, he had begun his

---

48. Ricoeur, *From Text to Action*. For a presentation of Gadamer's and Ricoeur's hermeneutical projects and their similarities and differences, see my examinations in Kristensson Uggla, *Ricoeur, Hermeneutics, and Globalization*, 38–52. For a theological appropriation of Gadamer and Ricoeur in systematic theology, see Tracy, *The Analogical Imagination*.

research career in New Testament exegetics, but had then been drawn to Ragnar Bring, who had encouraged him to pursue systematic theology instead. Bring even sketched out a route for him and gave him good advice for his future historical investigations.[49]

Given Wingren's fascination with preaching as a practice of interpretation, it was primarily the book *The Living Word* that allowed him to bring together his interest in exegetics with a parallel interest in homiletics. If on the basis of hermeneutics we understand the sermon in terms of a practical philosophy, it becomes possible to develop the intellectual resources needed to bring together the two interests he had cultivated earlier: on one hand, Bible exegesis, which takes its point of departure in the text, and on the other, homiletics, with its orientation toward the listening audience. Thus, the book contains both a hermeneutical theology, a hermeneutically reflected theology in which the story of death and resurrection is at the heart of a process, which is paralleled with the process of becoming human—both of God and each person becoming human in Christ—and a theological hermeneutics, a theological understanding of the process of interpretation as a process of death and life, which implies that the individual must be prepared to lose himself in order to regain himself in "the world *in front of* the text."

In *The Living Word*, Wingren draws a number of analogies between different regional hermeneutics to reveal the meaning of the process of interpretation in preaching. Later on, to emphasize the necessity of transcending the dichotomy of objective/subjective, he also draws direct analogies to illustrate how the relationship functions. He elaborates on analogies between a professor of law and a judge in the courtroom within the framework of judicial hermeneutics, and the relationship between a professor of exegetics and a local church minister's task when preparing the sermon, as an expression of theological hermeneutics, in this way:

> It is not the case that the professor of law is acting objectively and the judge subjectively. Both have entirely objectively fixed tasks and both can display a personal subjectivity in carrying out their duties that is injurious to the matter in hand. The exposition of, and commentary on, a biblical passage given by a professor

---

49. Thus, on the one hand, in Bring Wingren gained an enthusiastic adviser who gave him advice and support, but on the other, he also gained an enemy in Hugo Odeberg, who would work against him when the opportunity arose, as he did during the faculty's decision-making process in association with the appointment of the new professor (1949–51).

of exegesis is no more objective than that of the preacher; both exegete and priest are charged with wholly factual tasks, because they are both dealing with passages of the Bible—though, undeniably, *different* tasks, just as the legal scientist and the judge have *different* tasks *vis à vis* the laws.[50]

In the footnote to this quotation, Wingren pursues an argument in which he confesses that "the temptation to subjectivism is greater in the case of the latter [the preacher] than for most men, since he comes under the influence of an (objectively incorrect) theory of preaching according to which the preacher should reproduce his own personal experiences and nothing else."[51] What is interesting about this quote is his dismissive stance toward a "spiritualistic" solution to the problem of interpretation. This also strengthens the impression that the area of application for science should not in any way be limited only to the university, but rather that its validity should be generalized. One dimension of Wingren's theology that has rarely been noted is his criticism of the type of personality split Sven-Eric Liedman has criticized and characterized by this motto: "One may even be a worshipper of fetishes in his free time, as long as he produces the most objective knowledge during his working hours."[52] According to Wingren, one contributing factor to why Nygren's program became so successful was that it offered a scientifically defensible task for theology and provided the church with a sheltered position, due to the fact that the basic motifs were considered as belonging to an independent cohesion of meaning outside the domain of science. To Nygren, religion could neither be scientifically criticized nor scientifically supported, but it could be *described*, and only in that way could science be applied to theology. However, through this definition of theology as a descriptive study of the history of ideas, the discipline of dogmatics avoided not only appearing normative or evaluative, due to the elimination of the question of truth, this way of determining the division of labor between academy and society (the religion that exists in society, including the church), but also involved an approach to the relationship between theory and practice that Wingren did not share.

Wingren often highlighted Einar Billing's unwillingness to insert himself into this schizoid situation and stressed his capacity never to

---

50. Wingren, *The Living Word* (1949/1960), 120.
51. Ibid., 121 n. 2 (note starts on 120).
52. Liedman, "Humanistiska forskningstraditioner i Sverige," 23.

allow a churchly longing for security to overshadow the ordeal of biblical criticism, which he considered as both a necessity and an opportunity for theology. For Billing, it was obvious that the same free and critical atmosphere that characterized the university should also prevail in pastoral training and in the life of the church. For this reason, Billing came to criticize what had increasingly become the dominant attitude in his time: "Theologians were proud that they could 'gather' the church and bring even the enemies of historical research of the Bible into the fold. One cultivated a sort of double behavior: a scientific behavior inward toward the forges of education and research, and an extremely ecclesiastical one outward toward the congregations."[53] This link to Billing strengthens the impression that Wingren's theology is deeply rooted in an academic tradition that refuses to renounce the scientific approach, even when it directs itself toward theology's other two public arenas: the church and society. Today, as we face the challenges of the Information Age, when science has been transformed from an external factor in the development of society to an internal element in all of society, the discussion of scientific methodologies can no longer be limited to the academic sphere or be claimed as an exclusive academic specialty.

I claim that it is possible to read Wingren's 1949 book as a theologically oriented attempt to take part in the age-old Western discussion on the relationship between theory and practice. However, the really innovative and interesting aspects of *The Living Word* do not become evident until one takes into account the extreme theoretical stance that characterized the work of Nygren, in which theology, according to a positivistic spirit, was transformed into a pure description of historical sources. In Nygren, the answer to the question, "What is Christian faith?" is given a unilaterally theoretical bent, which in turn is determined by a distinctive strategy primarily focused on Christian faith as something that is distinguished from everything else. Agape is an eternal motif, which unchangingly allows itself to be determined by its characteristics, which in turn distinguishes it from all other interpretations of life. The answer is purely theoretical and presupposes a distinctive isolation of the Christian faith from humanity in general.

Wingren defends the idea that neither the law nor the gospel may be determined by purely theoretical means. The law, written in the form of a letter of demand emerging from the concrete needs of the other person,

---

53. Wingren, *An Exodus Theology* (1968/1969), 167.

regardless of belief or religion, as with the gospel, which brings people liberty and forgiveness, must be understood as something concrete that *occurs* in the listener, an occurrence that again and again must be varied because it will be repeated in new situations. From this point of view, we may claim that the gospel does not become the gospel until it addresses concrete people at the moment of their specific need. In the same way, Wingren describes the sermon as a phenomenon constituted in the form of an address, that is, something contextually bound that occurs as a result of the listening that is initiated by a certain practice of interpretation. The answer to the question, "What is Christian faith?" thus does not allow itself to be answered to the disadvantage of general humanity, or in a unilateral theoretical way. The phenomenon we refer to as Christianity is not an empirical fact or something fixed and permanent throughout history. In other words, it is not the case that Christian faith exists *first*, and that we *thereafter* interpret this faith. The process of interpretation already exists even before every beginning, and it is through the hermeneutical experience that takes place in the "meeting" between "Word" and "men" that the phenomenon we call Christianity comes into being and exists. Much later on, Wingren likens the Bible to a musical score. In both cases, it is a matter of something that must be played and performed. Wingren continues to elaborate on this analogy: the Bible is "a musical score which has now been played in a two-thousand-year-long series of concerts." And furthermore: "Thus the word of the Bible is at work as long as there is Christianity. When the word has ceased to function, it is no longer Christianity."[54]

From this background, it is patently incorrect to ascribe to Wingren the idea that theology itself must preach; what is at stake is instead a matter of how we should determine the matter of Christianity. Using Ricoeur's terms, we could say that the phenomenon we name Christianity does not exists in a collection of texts, but rather is something that is constituted in "the world *in front of* the text." We could continue to employ later terminologies and say that it is a kind of non-foundationalism, which for Wingren's part is rooted in the stance taken by the form-critical school, which states that we can find nothing beneath or more stable than the *kerygma* approached in the gospel texts. When Wingren makes analogies between the necessity of interpretation in theology and law, in his emphasis on the normative character of the musical score as something

---

54. Wingren, "Den springande punkten" (1974), 104.

that may be accepted through free will, there is also an exciting parallel to Gadamer's claim of the importance of tradition as something that people trust of their own free will: "The composition is played; it is the conductor, the musician and the listener who voluntarily offer the score normative character—as a result of their appearance at the concert and as a result of the piece being played."[55]

It is obvious that Wingren's practical turn is based upon his point of departure in the *acts of God*, that is, the interpretation of events and occurrences in history. Wingren considered Billing and Söderblom representatives of the idea of the *acting* God whose workshop is the external world together with its events and conflicts. For Billing, biblical faith is to be considered as condensed history, or continuous consciousness based on historic events, which distinguishes it from the intellectualism of Greek philosophy, and this is reinforced by the crisis that in Israel is generated in the inner person.[56] This is a distinguishing characteristic for a presentation that to a remarkable degree is based upon an understanding of baptism and communion as *acts*, along with a narrative theology that informs the entire presentation. There is a specifically close connection between the narrative constitution of the Christian faith, which is based on an interest in the gospel parables, the story of Christ, and the definition of the sermon itself as storytelling, and the practical knowledge that regulates this practice of interpretation. The narrative form of knowledge is in fact a sort of practical knowledge. Within the framework of this implicit narrative theology, the gospel of the day serves as a story about every human being on her way from life to death. When the listener hears the story of Christ, this means that she is simultaneously traveling the same journey and is drawn into the same events. In this context, the function of the biblical texts changes from serving as a source of information to becoming a narrative that seeks to achieve an act of recapitulation, restoring humanity. Yet, from this perspective, there is nothing like a purely theoretical solution to the challenges of interpretation. At the heart of Wingren's understanding of the nature of Christian faith, we do not find any information, message, or theory, but rather practices, occurrences, events, and narratives.[57] In this sense, the act of preaching is *but*

---

55. Ibid., 104.

56. Wingren, *An Exodus Theology* (1968/1969), 24-30.

57. Cf. the way in which Wingren criticizes how neglecting "the time for preaching," the time between Easter and the Parousia, means "to skip *preaching itself*" and results in a situation where the kerygma is cut away and preaching supplanted by seeing:

one example, which Wingren is most careful to emphasize in an article from 1974, in which he also indicates a wealth of side references to show that this was also the case in his books from this particular period.[58] The title chosen for the 1960 English translation of *Predikan* (*The Sermon*) indicates more clearly its actual contents: *The Living Word*. As a paradigmatic model for the general practices of interpretation, the sermon is not considered as a treatment of information but an event, which can only occur through that kind of creativity that characterizes all good interpretations. This means that all theology is, and should be, contemporary and contextual—and therefore also changing and dynamic. Only then can that which is distinctly Christian be articulated in accordance with the incarnation. The unity and continuity of the Christian faith is something that must be maintained in "the world *in front of* the text." In the same way that Christ is a person and an event, the sermon is described as something that at its furthermost extent *occurs* with the listener, a story about life in which the listener is also involved. This is the meaning in Wingren's many nearly aphoristic formulations, such as, "*The Word* exists to be made known; only when it is preached is its objective content fully disclosed."[59]

Together with its intertwined hermeneutical theology, this theological hermeneutics implies that a series of dichotomies must be transcended. First, it is a matter of the dichotomy between subjectivity and objectivity, as mentioned above. Furthermore, a radical separation of theory and practice risks rendering the entire endeavor incapable of describing what the sermon is, and in a figurative sense, also all of the interpretative practices that sustain theology:

"so that the hearer sees (has a theory of) Christ, instead of dying and rising again." Wingren, *The Living Word* (1949/1960), 146.

58. Wingren, "Den springande punkten" (1974), 103. The references that Wingren makes to his own books are *Theology in Conflict* (1954/1958), 156ff., where the author makes a parallel with musical compositions on paper and in concert, and also states, "There is very likely no part of the Bible which is not intended to be used in one way or another in a practical situation" (ibid., 158–59); further developed in *Växling och kontinuitet* (1972), 22, but primarily in *The Living Word* (1949/1960), 191–203.

59. Ibid., 13. In this formulation, we can discern inspiration from Billing and also an "impulse from Basel," and more specifically an inspiration from Oscar Cullmann, who in works such as *Die Christologie de Neuen Testaments* (1957) pursued the thesis that the various titles given to Christ describe not who he is but rather what he does, that is, an occurrence.

As the function of preaching is to effect a meeting between the Word and men, as we have argued above, so the dilemma of preaching is that this *meeting* does not take place, and a wrong antithesis arises. *Either* preaching is concerned with the Word, the objective element, *or* with men, the subjective element.[60]

A second dichotomy deals with the division between pure Christian love, as expressed in God's *agape*, and all the *other forms of love*, which have their origin in the human world and thus, according to Nygren, cannot be said to be Christian—that is, the strategy of determining what is distinctly Christian through isolating it:

> It is misleading to try and cut away the human element so as to arrive at a point where the Word is entirely divine, without any human admixture. Such an effort implies that God can be found and grasped beyond the human sphere whereas, as Luther says, the true God lies in the straw of the manger. From human mouths are heard the voice and tones of God.[61]

By transcending these dichotomies, Wingren puts himself in direct confrontation with the Lundensian school of motif research. Nygren's view of the work of theology, trying to determine a separate cohesion of religious meaning and identifying the distinctly Christian, is inscribed in a long tradition of dualisms, in which theory is separated from practice, subject from object, Christianity from humanity. This results not only in the ambition of defining Christian faith by isolating a distinguishing characteristic, separate from that which is common to humanity in general, and a unilaterally theoretical determination of what this specifically Christian characteristic is, but also in a mindset that elaborates on the academy and the church as dual systems, in keeping with the tendency toward a split personality as discussed above. The reverse side of Nygren's approach is that he offers the church peace and quiet in that its activities are removed from scientific criticism and external interference. The consequences of this approach, which became evident many years later, Wingren articulated in a drastic way: "The surprising thing about Nygren is his combination of a strictly scientific attitude and a directly reactionary ecclesiastical attitude."[62]

---

60. Wingren, *The Living Word* (1949/1960), 25.

61. Ibid., 27. Cf. "the Word and men belong together." Ibid.

62. Wingren, *Creation and Gospel* (1979/1979), 85. What Wingren was primarily thinking about here is the tragedy Nygren's program would result in on the practical

What is then Wingren's alternative to the theoretization and isolation that characterizes Nygren's approach? We have already seen how Wingren's use of creation theology when identifying the Christian faith emphasizes the importance of ideas from both Irenaeus and Luther, dealing with God's presence in common human life shared by all people regardless of faith or creed. Through his book *The Living Word*, Wingren introduces a hermeneutical perspective, which from a fundamental point of view includes the entire spectrum of interpretative practices that constitute Christianity as a phenomenon. To put it more directly, it could be said that according to Wingren, there is no timeless theoretical answer that conclusively defines what the Christian faith is. First, the answer must be practical, in the sense that it is contextually bound as something immediate for tangible human beings. Second, we cannot understand what the Christian faith is without emphasizing its necessary and positive connection to the human bodily existence that is common to all people. Many years later, Wingren formulated it in the following manner: "To abolish this undue theorization and to return the Christian faith to those human situations where it belongs is perhaps the most important task for contemporary theology."[63]

However, this means neither arbitrariness in the determination, which is the risk inherent in focusing on practical knowledge, nor general theoretical vagueness, which is the risk of focusing on the positive determination of the relation between human and Christian. Here, it is interesting to note that Wingren chose to use the final chapter of *The Living Word*, in which he summarizes the book's many perspectives, to deal with *communicatio idiomatum*, a concept from incarnational theology that attempts to explain how the two natures, human and divine, are united in one person, Jesus Christ. This is tied to a polemic that Wingren for decades directed against *monophysitism*, a theological position that emphasized the divine at the expense of the human, and thus states that Christ had only one single, divine nature. According to Wingren, this position had experienced a boost in the postliberal theological situation during most of the twentieth century. However, because Christ is a human being and because his divinity is poured out into his humanity, humanity can never be downplayed and placed in conflict with his divinity:

---

level when he joined ranks with Bo Giertz, Gustaf Adolf Danell, and Bertil Gärtner and took a position against the ordination of women. Ibid., 10–11, 84–85, this a theme to which I shall return in chapter 8.

63. Ibid., 80.

"If Christ is not man, man is lost. If, on the other hand, Christ is man, Satan is lost. But *God* is not lost; he retains his glory in the cross and the humiliation. God's glory consists in this, that he redeems. And he does that by coming *sub contraria specie*, clothed in his opposite."[64]

Wingren's point here is that the divinity of Christ exists exactly in his humanity—and cannot be placed above it. For this reason, according to Wingren, the sermon cannot evade or avoid the humanity of Jesus, his hunger and thirst, uncertainty and anxiety over death, his ultimate fate and his interaction with humans of flesh and blood. To escape from any of this is equivalent to escaping from the living God. Wingren ties all of this together by emphasizing the preacher's own humanity: "The *communicatio idiomatum* means that the priest may venture to belong to his own age and mix in the ordinary life of society without thereby losing the divine life."[65] In Wingren's work, divine and human are united in the action of self-giving. The divine contents of the message are not lost because they move outward; quite the opposite, they are lost when the message does *not* move outward, "when it keeps within the temple walls and fears being in the world, in the depths, among the doubters, prisoners and sinners."[66]

Wingren also connects the *communicatio idiomatum* with a theological approach that does not emphasize knowledge and information but is instead focused on God's acts according to a process in which divine and human cannot be separated. It is impossible to divide one from the other: "To listen to the divine voice is to live a human life."[67] His entire presentation on the *communicatio idiomatum* is infused with an anti-Barthian polemic, and while we may discuss to what degree this is justified, it does anyway serve as a productive background against which Wingren's own anti-speculative ambitions become clear.[68] Quite simply, he argues that "Barth knows entirely too much about God"—and at this point he contrasts Barth to how unknowledgeable Luther seems to be regarding God, and how Luther was in general reluctant to speculate about God: "For this reason he has nowhere else he can go but to the humanity of Christ when he wants to seize hold of God."[69] Yet, rather than tying

64. Wingren, *The Living Word* (1949/1960), 210.
65. Ibid., 211.
66. Ibid.
67. Ibid., 212.
68. Cf. Sigurdson, *Karl Barth som den andre*.
69. Wingren, *The Living Word* (1949/1960), 212.

the *communicatio idiomatum* and the dual nature of the person of Christ (*diphysitism*) to metaphysical speculations, Wingren moves in the opposite direction and attempts to connect the processes in question to the *kenosis* hymn in Philippians 2:5-11, in which the unity with God through faith and the unity with the other through love in themselves *are* the very connections between the divine and the human. Everything is brought together in the figure of Christ, who comes down to earth and makes himself destitute *for others*: "Christ is changed into us, and therefore we are changed into each other."[70] All this takes place in a world that is God's world, a world imbued with divine presence and action. We shall now examine more closely the systematic cohesion for this Wingrenian theology, and then conclude this chapter by returning to Wingren's explosive presentation in 1949.

A Concrete Systematic Theology

In addition to his work with historical sources (Luther and Irenaeus) and his polemical confrontation with the leading theologians of the day (Nygren, Barth, and Bultmann) in *Theology in Conflict* (1954/1958), the "early" Wingren wrote three major works that demonstrate his ambitions to develop a constructive systematic theology: his controversial *The Living Word* (1949/1960) and the single work that, due to the publisher's technical limitations, had to be released as two books: *Creation and Law* (1958/1961) and *Gospel and Church* (1960/1964). In these three later books, we face what might be described as the positive, constructive version of the same theological conception that Wingren had only implied in his critical break with Nygren, Barth, and Bultmann, a discussion carried out from the perspective of the hermeneutical and anthropological assumptions of theology. The basic idea of *The Living Word* goes to the heart of this model of thought when it speaks of the sermon as a meeting between human beings and the Word. This remarkable book contains a rough draft of nearly everything that would later be presented in *Creation and Law* and *Gospel and Church*, but in *The Living Word* the material is presented in a disorganized manner. The supporting systematic structure is still missing.

Part of the originality of Wingren's dogmatics is that he sketches an overall picture of the Christian faith using four concepts: *creation*,

70. Ibid., 213.

law, *gospel*, and *church*. Another original aspect of this systematic presentation of the Christian faith is the thoroughly theological basis in *the concrete* when he focused on the acts of God through material bodies, the presence of God in the encounter with the ethical demands of the other in concrete everyday life, the *kerygma* as a contextually determined concrete proclamation, baptism as an act effected on concrete bodies, the concrete presence of the church in the world, and so on. In his conception of dogmatics, we may also discern an anti-speculative tendency, informed by a pre-Constantinian theological reflection inspired by Irenaeus from a period of time when the formation of dogmas had not yet truly taken flight; an unsystematic tendency, which instead makes the confrontations important for determining the presentation of the Christian faith inspired by Luther; a consistent use of biblical theology that characterizes both Irenaeus and Luther, and also Billing; and a dramatic tendency from Aulén—but almost nothing from Nygren.

Behind both of Wingren's attempts to develop a constructive systematic theology, in what he presented in 1958–60 and later in *Credo* (1974/1981), we can discern two specific models of argumentation that he used consistently in his conception of dogmatics: first, the organization of the *canon*, divided into *two testaments*—the old and the new—and second, the *tripartite structure of the creed*—God as Father, Son, and Holy Spirit—in accordance with the doctrine of the Trinity. Based on the *two testaments* and the *three articles of faith*, he thus developed *four organizing concepts* to structure his systematic theology: creation, law, gospel, and church. As is always the case with Wingren, the structure is extraordinarily well thought out and deliberately assembled, and it is foremost in this meaningful cohesion that Wingren's aim and position should be sought.

Within the framework of his *analysis of confrontation*, Wingren often recalled the two fronts on which the early church had to struggle as a framework of understanding for the structuring of canon and creed. In order to preserve faith, the church had to make demarcations in two directions: on one hand toward Judaism, the original context in which Christianity emerged; and on the other, Gnosticism, whose enmity toward the body and the material world constituted a threat to any form of creation theology. His work on Marcion provided Wingren with profound opportunities to consider these two fronts, since Marcion lived during a very decisive time for the early church.

The basic order of this structure is thus determined by the confrontation with positions that annihilate the Christian faith. His idea is that it is precisely the perspective of conflict that extracts a clearer articulation of the structure and contents of the Christian faith. Under the surface of these confrontations with Judaism and Gnosticism there is a more contemporary polemic of church politics that deals with Lutheran orthodoxy, Sweden's high-church movement, and resistance to the ordination of women, and also with the great revivalist movements and Pietism.

In addition to these ideas, we need to add yet another concept from Irenaeus, which has a more comprehensive capacity in the sense that it served as an organizing principle for Wingren's conception of dogmatics—*recapitulatio*. This term assumes a comprehensive view in which the human condition is articulated and seriously taken into account. Without a theological anthropology based on creation theology, the meaning of salvation as restoration of a damaged humanity becomes incomprehensible. Thus, the concept *recapitulatio* implies the entire comprehensive context for Wingren's conception of dogmatics from two testaments, three articles of faith, and four organizing concepts.

The first organizing concept in Wingren's dogmatics is the concrete point of departure in the given, creation and the body, which also implies the importance of the resurrection of the body. The idea of *creation* otherwise invites misunderstanding due to the problems that are associated with the concept and that have not been lessened with the passing of time. What Wingren is definitely *not* talking about when he speaks of creation is some sort of fundamentalist creationism that considers the creation story as a historical description of the formation of the earth. Neither does creation theology form the basis for a theology of orders of creation, a German tradition where the idea of creation is instead part of a reactionary defense of the status quo, a way of thinking expressed in the racial ideologies of the twentieth century that led to the Holocaust and widespread destruction. Wingren's creation theology has *nothing* to do with an idea of creation that legitimized the Nazi ideology of how God created the Germans as a superior master race. According to Wingren, creation, like the law, is first and foremost a matter of *change*. Within the framework of the Trinitarian creed, it serves as an expression of God's work in the world. In contrast to what he considered Barth's "odd antiliberal frenzy," which because of the dominance of the concept of the revelation posits *knowledge* as the heart of the presentation of the Christian faith, Wingren maintains that the divine *action* in all living creatures should serve as the organizing principle, if we are to take canon and creed seriously.[71] Yet, the clear demarcation that Wingren makes between an information-oriented and an action-oriented view of Christian faith, or his predilection for the latter, is by no means based upon an assumption that his critique of Barth is necessarily correct. His primary argument is connected to the basic narrative structure of the salvation history that configures canon as well as creed. However, a prerequisite for this reasoning is that we again read the Bible as a single, long story, as was done prior to the Reformation, and practiced not least by Irenaeus. Here, once again, we recognize how Wingren brings together the categories of narration and action, narrative theology and the emphasis on God as an *acting* God.[72]

Nevertheless, the point of departure is not the Old Testament creation story, but rather the fact that God creates *now*. Wingren maintains that even our birth means that God creates us. In other words, we cannot live our lives without constantly being in relationship with God: "Man bears his relationship to God about with him wherever he goes."[73] The idea of creation should thus not be comprehended as part of an anthropocentric humanism that places an autonomous human subject at the center of the universe; rather, it serves as a de-centering through which we may discover life as a gift.[74] It is within the framework of the idea of creation that our humanity is articulated and apprehended as something that will be restored in and through the gospel (*recapitulatio*).[75] A unique aspect of this restoration is that it is not achieved by a lessening of or avoidance of death, but rather in that we radically incorporate death as a judgment over our own lives.[76] God creates thus something new *from*

---

71. Wingren, *Creation and Law* (1958/1961), 12. Cf. "It is not man's knowledge but the works of God which are central." Ibid., 81 n. 85.

72. In this context, it is interesting to point out the central role that baptism plays in Wingren's concrete systematic theology, since baptism comprises a course of events or passages; it is an epic act that reconfigures human life with the help of a very special story about Jesus' death and resurrection. It is thus not a matter of information but of recapitulation: salvation as the restoration of creation.

73. Wingren, *Creation and Law* (1958/1961), 89. Cf. "Birth and death have a particular meaning, and point to the receiving of life and judgment from the hand of the Creator." Ibid., 119.

74. Ibid., 38–39.

75. Cf. "The life which Christ gives to the world through His victory . . . is the life which Adam lost." Ibid., 35.

76. Cf. "God gives life by putting to death, and forgives by judging. Law and Gospel are thus closely related." Ibid., 74. In this context, Wingren also elaborates on a

nothing, and God justifies *that which has been rejected*. For Wingren, being in communion with Christ in death is also at the same time to be connected to Christ in life.

As we saw earlier, Wingren's presentations are often marked by seemingly arbitrary placement of the materials within the overall structure of his works. This is obvious when in the above reasoning he has already tackled what logically ought to be found in the second portion of his dogmatics, namely, *the law*. Here, however, we meet an observation that clearly strengthens and accentuates the consequences of his practical turn, when he elaborates on an ethics that distances itself from theorization and instead is anchored in the concrete human life. According to Wingren, ethics is in general not something that can be retrieved from the Bible but is instead based on the anonymous "letter of demand" containing the concrete needs of the other. Ethics is thus not a matter of some abstract basic motif, but is instead written in the concrete face we encounter in each meeting with the other.[77] In keeping with this theology, a distinctly Christian ethics is not needed, nor can it be found. We may hear an echo of his research on Irenaeus, when he emphasizes that also

---

comparison in which he maintains that while Pietism tends to understand forgiveness in terms of milder judgment, Luther goes in the opposite direction by radicalizing judgment, yet forgiveness provides strength to remain in judgment. Ibid.

77. Here, it may be interesting to tie into the reflections that Wingren made as early as 1938 in "The Johanneum Journal," where he emphasizes the importance of separating oneself from "the theoretical treatment of an ethical problem": "It is characteristic of Christian action to . . . act forthwith, and without looking to the side, take hold of the problem as it is found; this is revolutionary, it means that in ethics, the point of departure must be the concrete ethical problems, not some basic Christian motif or such, not some form of Christian observation." Ibid., 90. Cf. also how he continues on the following page: "Precisely the matter-of-fact treatment of them (the concept of creation!) is the right one, even from a Christian perspective. Then there is the matter of discovering how this leads to the law, what faith, the Word and Christ mean—and then anew grappling with the concrete ethical problem (the concept of vocation). Through the constant contact with the ethical problem, one is preserved from psychology. Even the gospel, the Word, Christ, must be shown to be something that reaches us at the exterior. This is the method of ethics. Ethics must be built up in this way. We must, in other words, maintain a pure systematic nature, not a historical-descriptive one. But naturally, such a presentation requires constant contact with history, primarily the Bible, Luther, the most recent history of ideas, the nineteenth and twentieth centuries. These things must constantly touch upon one another, both positively and negatively." Ibid., 91–92.

the persecuted church was able to firmly hold to the idea that worldly power is ordained by God, acting as God's servant.[78]

This part of Wingren's dogmatics contains a series of determinations, such as that the application of the law is not graded, and that both the social (*usus politicus*) and the spiritual (*usus theologicus*) use of the law also implies a possible abuse. Here, furthermore, there is a warning concerning abuse of the first article of faith, in reducing the creation faith to idealism and anthropocentrism.[79] As a corrective to such an interpretation of the idea of creation, Wingren points to the combination of total judgment and total forgiveness that characterizes the Christian view of faith and life, and that applies not least of all to the judging function — the conscience in accordance with the theological or spiritual use of the law.[80] Similar to the interpretation of Luther that Wingren presented in his doctoral dissertation in 1942, the law is here considered as something dynamic and changeable, for it is only when old laws are abolished and new ones are enacted that they are able to serve as expressions of God's work in creation. God's hidden work in creation is, so to speak, the source of the law — the law is not an effect of ecclesiastic proclamation. Not taking the law seriously, as something already at work before the gospel enters the scene, has devastating consequences: "For where it is denied that the world is God's world, the attempt is soon made to regulate it by some other 'religious' standard."[81] This provides a background for understanding the fundamental importance of the order and organization of the canon, the creed, and the four fundamental concepts that configure Wingren's systematic theology.

The second volume of Wingren's dogmatics, *Gospel and Church* (1960/1964), strengthens the impression that his theology may, to a great extent, be characterized as a baptismal theology, that is, a theology that integrates the reconfiguration process by which the individual becomes human into the inner structure configured by the story of Jesus' death and resurrection. The fact that this pattern has already characterized the presentation in the first volume may be viewed as a structural shortcoming but can also be taken as evidence of the strong continuity in his presentation. Through his great attention to the order of his presentation, in

---

78. Wingren, *Creation and Law* (1958/1961), 148.

79. Ibid., 147-48.

80. Cf. "We might say that man's conscience has a continual foretaste of the Last Judgement." Ibid., 174.

81. Ibid., 160.

the section on *the gospel*, Wingren clearly sought to distance himself from any form of Marcionite theology, including its modern guises, which hold that God's work with an individual does not begin until he or she comes into contact with the Bible or the church, and which thus transforms the life of the church into a community superior to everyday human life. Instead, the proclamation of the church through *viva vox* is presented as part of God's restoration of humanity, a process with the healing of the individual as its primary aim. Baptism makes us human, and does not give us churchly life or liberation from humanity.[82] Nonetheless, it is not by preserving one's life that one becomes fully human but rather by facing death, in accordance with the story of Christ: "His victory was not won separately from his humiliation but in the midst of it."[83] Thus, there is a noticeable structural similarity between anthropology, christology, and ecclesiology in Wingren's theology, as we have seen earlier, and shall see repeatedly in the course of this examination.

The closing section of Wingren's presentation of Christian dogmatics deals with *the church*, interpreted as a way to regain humanity. He describes the church as a fellowship that does not constitute itself; instead, its focal point is located outside the church: "The Church is the community of those who receive from Christ."[84] The significance of baptism as a dramatic configuration of the basic story of Christianity accentuates the fact that this faith is not something that the church itself can maintain and control.

Due to technical limitations at the publishing house, Wingren's study in dogmatics from the late 1950s had to be released as two volumes. Two entire years went by before the publication of the second volume, and in the meantime some important events took place that strongly influenced the book. Circumstances brought about a more radical break in the middle of the presentation than Wingren had planned. This is evidenced by the fact that the second volume was less popular with readers of a conservative and high-church persuasion; in particular, it was certainly not popular with opponents of the Church of Sweden's 1958 decision to allow women as ordained ministers. In some ways, *Gospel and Church* can be recognized as a second "apostasy" by Wingren, but this time the result was that a number of readers stopped reading his books. Thanks

---

82. Cf. "Baptism makes a man truly human and not just a member of a particular Church." Wingren, *Gospel and Church* (1960/1964), 11.

83. Ibid., 50.

84. Ibid., 41.

to his pointed criticism of high-church ideas of episcopal succession and any idea of channels of office of unbroken episcopal succession, his conflict with the opponents of the ordination of women became irreconcilable and made continued dialog impossible. Yet in the same context, he also attacked the Pietist obsession with conversion, which he likens to "an indirect denial of the first article of the creed."[85] For this reason, he maintains that even the clergy is always subordinate to the Word, which alone creates the church. He confronts both the high-church movement and the Pietist revivalist movements with the astonishing outspokenness that characterizes the New Testament: "Nor would the one say about its bishops or the other about its revivalists what the New Testament says about the apostles, if there were not some obscurity in regard to episcopal ordination or conversion."[86]

However, *Gospel and Church* also contains rather lengthy discussions of what the increasing urbanization of twentieth-century society might mean for the church in a post-Constantinian situation. The original theological aim of territorially organized church congregations was to link humanity with Christianity in keeping with the theology of the incarnation. But as everyday life began to be separate from the home, and the workplace separate from the house where people live, it became difficult to maintain this type of ecclesiology. Given this situation, attention is needed so that the relationship with creation and the law will not be severed. Wingren urges the church to look for other ways to defend and maintain this connection. This need is reinforced by the absence of theological anthropology in the antiliberal theology of the day, which is alarming because of the risk of distorting the understanding of the church's communication in the world with word (mission) and deeds (*diaconia*). In the same way, he maintained that the idea of calling (vocation) must be renewed when the spheres of the church and everyday life are being separated. Here, Wingren made somewhat unexpected analogies to the United States—as a kind of evidence of his many trips to that country and his theological contacts on that continent—where the situation of the church differs noticeably from that of the Old World, due to the "lack of Middle Ages" there. Thus, in this situation the connection with creation has to be achieved through other means. The entire book concludes with a discourse dealing with such future challenges—questions concerning,

---

85. Ibid., 163.
86. Ibid., 168.

for example, where a church should be located given the new, disjointed infrastructure of society, in which the distance between places of worship and workplaces may be considerable. In such situations, where the immediate cohesion is broken, escapism may easily become an attractive, alternative life view.

Grain-of-Wheat Eschatology

By the end of the 1950s, Gustaf Wingren seems in many ways to have completed his system of theology. The second volume of his dogmatics, *Gospel and Church* (1960/1964), may in retrospect be seen as the grandiose conclusion of an extraordinary productive period in the career of this Lundensian theologian. Following his two earlier historically focused studies in 1942 and 1947, in 1949 he started to publish a sequence of theological investigations that covered the period of his appointment as a professor and that materialized in four larger books in which he qualified his stance and developed his theological program. In a personal note that he wrote in 1964 in which he summarized his production, he describes his books *The Living Word*, *Theology in Conflict*, *Creation and Law*, and *Gospel and Church* as the most important works he had written. In this context he states that his "theological production from 1949 to 1960" is to be considered his "greatest contribution."[87] Considering these major works, how should we comprehend his theology?

Despite the contents of Wingrens constructive systematic theology from 1958 and 1960, which I have covered in the previous section, a number of obstinate misunderstandings arose and persisted for many years. One of these suggested that Wingren's theology should be comprehended as a sort of unilateral creation theology containing but a single idea of creation. Another suggested that Wingren attempted to create a sort of harmonious balance between creation and gospel, a sort of in-between stage as a more or less poor compromise between Christian uniqueness and what we generally share as human beings. Still others have held that Wingren's theological project should be regarded as a kerygmatic theology that he had quite simply learned from Karl Barth. A fourth misconception described him as a churchly theologian who only sought to edify pious congregations and who merely proclaimed. According to the fifth

---

87. The uncatalogued personal papers of Gustaf Wingren in the Lund University Library.

and final of this series of misconceptions, from a list that could be made significantly longer, Wingren's creation theology is described as romantic anthropocentrism in which an elevated experience of life promotes an optimistic belief in human possibilities.[88]

These misconceptions may be evidence of an insufficient frame of reference for comprehending Wingren's aim within the framework of the existing theological infrastructure of the day. What may at first appear to be indistinct or unclear points in his production may also be signs of the originality of his theological project, and thus help explain why his position, despite his repeated clarifications, is nonetheless so easily misunderstood. Therefore, before we enter into the tumultuous era of the 1960s and 1970s, let us pause for a moment and depart from chronology, take a look both backward and forward in time, and employ a sort of summarization to identify Wingren's position, starting from a theme that spans his entire theological project.

During the summer term of 1947 in Basel, Switzerland, Wingren had good cause for headaches. The experience of encountering a different theological tradition had been painful. His journal entries from that time reveal a feeling of powerlessness in the face of this situation. Yet, the impulse that resulted from this experience brought into play a number of elements that had not previously been visible among the array of intellectual tools at his disposal. His academic education at Lund had simply been too narrow, both epistemologically as well as ontologically. However, there were also other experiences with which he wrestled that lay farther back in time—dilemmas that had occupied his mind long before he came to Lund and that were now resurfacing. Wingren's deformed hand was a constant reminder of the tangibility of the body but also of his roots in another world—the manufacturing town of Valdemarsvik, where his daily life had been colored by the radical tension between the world of manual labor and the Sunday worship service. In the opening chapter of his autobiographical work, *My Five Universities* (1991), where he recounts his growing up in a simple tanner's home that suddenly came under grave threat when his mother died and his father was unable to manage the situation, we may sense an unreconciled tension between creation and the word. This was even amplified by the painful contrast he was forced to live with from the age of ten onward, between the Methodist piety of the aunts who took over the household and in practice saved the

---

88. I refrain from giving examples here, but it can be stated that a number of these variants are represented in Petrén's book *Skapelse och frihet*.

family, and the religious views of his father, who had chosen to leave the local Methodist congregation and thereafter faithfully attended services at the local Lutheran parish church. The general contrast between church and world, between Sunday services and weekday labor, was heightened by the family's internal tension between free-church Methodism and state-church Lutheranism, which reinforced an "unbroken obsession throughout my entire career as a student," as Wingren wrote in his memoirs.[89] In this writing at the age of eighty, he described in retrospect these life dilemmas from the Valdemarsvik context. However, he had already dealt with these issues twenty-five years earlier in an article published in 1966 in the Christian journal *Vår lösen*, later published in English translation as chapter 1 of *The Flight from Creation* (1971). In this article, he highlights that sense of division and fragmentation that he had felt in his childhood environment as a background to his theological agenda:

> The lack of integration, the feeling of discord, was an essential part of adolescent distress. There was nothing to link together the facts of eating, singing hymns, playing football and going to the cinema. Sexuality and the sordid fact of women giving birth to children were forgotten pieces of reality when one played the violin or sang in the choir ... Death was completely ignored ... Religiousness was included there, too. One was converted and shook off certain habits. But life was not integrated by piety. On the contrary, religiousness was still only a speciality, one among all the others.[90]

Against this background, we may consider Wingren's dogmatic conceptualization—with its threefold organizing principle of *two testaments, three articles of faith,* and *four structuring concepts*—as an attempt to articulate, in contemporary theological terms, that the world of work, nature, and culture in creation, from which we draw our humanity, is also God's world. In our given, natural community, which is supported by numerous "deeds without names," there is a hidden divine presence, regardless of faith. However, this anonymous presence awaits theological interpretation. Here, theology finds its task, and if it is not completed,

---

89. Wingren, *Mina fem universitet* (1991), 37. Cf. the way in which he returns to this theme several times in his autobiography, as on p. 31, when he speaks about "the problems of my youth," and toward the end of the book returns to "the actual problem of faith throughout my entire youth" and furthermore "the unresolved problems of my youth." Ibid., 169.

90. Wingren, "Creation: A Crucial Article of Faith," (1966/1971), 14.

then the horizon of understanding necessary for the gospel to be heard as a gospel will not exist. For if salvation means restoration of humanity and becoming human again (*recapitulatio*), we will need a concept of humanity in order to understand what, so to speak, it is all about. The life problem that Wingren carried with him from his youth in Valdemarsvik dealt with the issue of how to bring about a meeting between human beings and the Word. Wingren's own experiences with free church piety, which tended to limit the presence of God to the inner religious experience and community, further strengthened the tendency toward individualization that characterized church services in which the message was directed toward the individual and his or her inner life, thus distancing the Word from the network of human relationships in everyday work and pastimes. In this situation, the gift of creation and the demands of the law have no relation to the worship service.

Wingren focused his theological interest on what he understood to be a significant lacuna in contemporary theology, namely, how the concept of creation, the idea of God's presence in everyday human life, regardless of faith or church context, had become relegated to a such a rear position. But Wingren's theology by no means only deals with creation, as has sometimes been suggested. Even worse is the perception that this idea of creation is regarded as a romantic heightened sense of life.

Let us at the outset make it clear that Wingren's primary interest deals with the question, "What is Christian faith?" He criticized the many attempts made in his day to determine the content of Christian faith through methodological isolation of the distinctly Christian. The reasons for his criticisms are connected with his paradigmatic use of the story of Marcion and Gnosticism. Here we face a radical attempt to isolate something distinctly Christian, but because this paradoxically resulted in the necessary exclusion of vital elements of the Christian faith, this maneuver brought a *de facto* distortion of its contents. According to Wingren, to correctly depict what Christian faith is, we must also take seriously that which *unites* the Christian view of faith and life with basic realities shared by all human beings, in other words, parts of Christianity that are not at all original or unique. The clarity that may be achieved concerning what Christian faith is by the use of methods only concentrating on isolating something unique carries the risk of devastating consequences for our understanding of the Christian faith. The idea of creation is, according to Wingren, not an appendix to the faith, but rather the necessary horizon of understanding that allows us to understand the gospel at all. We cannot seriously comprehend salvation as *recapitulatio* if we do not recognize that there is a *positive* relationship between the specifically Christian and the universally human. Every determination of the Christian that is made to the detriment of the human leads to incorrect conclusions. The unique characteristic of the Christian faith can never be qualified at the cost of its openness.

Wingren thus takes his place in twentieth-century theology as a critic of the dominant antiliberal movements that utilized isolation of the distinctly Christian as a methodology. There are of course unique elements within the Christian faith, but a prerequisite for these elements to be at all understood and embraced, Wingren claims, is that the universally human is articulated and taken seriously. This is not a matter of an *external* relationship that must be established outwardly to something outside the faith, but rather of an *integral* part of the Christian faith itself. Against this background, Wingren claims that any attempt to identify opposite pairs of human and Christian, anthropology and christology, creation and salvation, the world and the church, will obscure, or even eliminate, the Christian view of faith and life.[91]

Now let us cope with the question of to what extent the idea of creation in the works of Wingren implies a harmonizing tendency. We may easily be enticed into believing that a creation theology is nothing more than a natural-romantic version of liberal theology. There has even been a profound tradition in which the law has served as the theological basis for the orders of creation, with dangerous preservationist effects. This is, however, not at all the case with Wingren. With his point of departure in creation theology, he directed sharp criticism against liberal theology's unlimited faith in human reason, its romantic view of creation and lack of eschatological dimension. This bright creation faith, with its optimistic view of human potential, stands in strong contrast to the central importance of concepts such as sin, guilt, and death in the creation theology that Wingren developed. At the same time, as we have seen earlier, he maintains that the strong antiliberal movements within theology during

---

91. This was the theme of my presentation at the symposium arranged in 1995 on the occasion of Wingren's eighty-fifth birthday: "Against all potentially divergent views, it must first and last be understood that what has occupied Gustaf Wingren's interest throughout his entire career is the issue of the unique nature of the Christian faith. Only when this has been stated can we understand the radicalness and originality of the fact that Wingren has rejected every attempt to identify the unique nature of Christianity at the cost of its openness." Kristensson Uggla, "Möjligheter i Gustaf Wingren's teologi," 80.

the twentieth century risks throwing out the baby with the bathwater. There are elements within the liberal theological tradition that are absolutely essential.

At the heart of Wingren's theology (although never isolated) is the gospel as a message of Jesus' crucifixion and resurrection. The same gospel that comprises the unique aspect of the Christian faith also stresses the openness of this faith, and even strengthens and radicalizes this openness, entirely in keeping with the dialectical figure of thought that holds together change and continuity, death and life, crucifixion and resurrection. This makes it impossible to imagine creation theology as an expression of a romantic interpretation of human life, in which faith works as a sort of elevated sense of life. Instead, a Christian interpretation of human life is, from beginning to end, a matter of *interpreting death*.[92] But in what way might death be seen as a central component of a Christian interpretation of life?

In a review of Philosophy Professor Mats Furberg's book *Everything a Rag? About the Meaning of Life* (*Allting en trasa? En bok om livets mening*, 1976), Wingren makes several remarks about the author's views on death, which also reveal his own position. He makes the somewhat surprising interpretation that Furberg's plea for the meaning *in* life rather than the meaning *of* life necessarily requires that we make everyday matters and things such as physical objects of central interest, which in turn implies that the meaning *in* life lies outside ourselves, in keeping with the idea of living for others.[93] Wingren maintains that experience shows that people who live their lives with this simple acceptance, in terms of receptivity and giving of oneself, in fact find it easier to die when that day comes: "Because they know how to live, they know how to die." He appreciates that Furberg so openly speaks about his fear of death, yet at the same time points out the prerequisites for this particular interpretation of death:

> It makes for a grim calculation when we localize death to a certain day, the day in the obituary with a cross upon a single date. Yet, all of us who will one day die have actually been dying all the time; we have been used up and worn out without ceasing,

---

92. Cf. Karlsson's examination of Wingren's methods of preaching. In his concluding discussion, Karlsson maintains that his analysis and study reveals "that Wingren's theology should sooner be described as a theology of the cross." Karlsson, *Predikans samtal*, 294.

93. Wingren, "Livets mening" (1976).

in the way that tools become worn out. That is what was meaningful about life.[94]

Here, Wingren seems to be of the opinion that what is meaningful about life is associated with the experience of being used up and worn out in terms of a sort of everyday experience of death. Thus, the question of how to interpret death is at the very center of his focus of interest. He maintains that Furberg's fear, however, originates from a misplacement of death:

> After life comes death. Before death lie concrete, meaning-filled aims in the midst of life, such things as are stopped and obliterated by death; this is what Furberg seemingly wants to say. But this is in fact not the case at all. Life is death; life is a way of dying. There is an old saying about the grain of wheat that comes to life just when it dies—a New Testament saying with multi-leveled meanings, and a saying that farmers yet today understand. Nothing in life is truly meaningful if I am not in some way put to use. When I am put to use, I become worn out. Death on the day of my death is only a special instance of this meaningful process of being worn out.[95]

Here, we see how the grain-of-wheat metaphor plays a central role as a model for the contrasting interpretation of death that Wingren presents and that ties the meaning of life together with the ideas of being taken into use and being worn out. To understand this grain-of-wheat theology, we must extend our perspectives. The review of Furberg's book was written in the wake of the publication of Wingren's second attempt to write a constructive dogmatics, *Credo: The Christian View of Faith and Life* (1974/1981). In this book, Wingren includes two sections characteristically titled "In Destruction One Perceives What Creation Is" and "To Find Meaning Is to Interpret Death."[96] Wingren articulates the Christian faith as an interpretation of life based on the encounter with unavoidable situations of meaninglessness. In the Christian tradition, the cross stands as a symbol of absolute meaninglessness, which also offers us the opportunity to consider our own meaningless death. According to Wingren,

---

94. Ibid.

95. Ibid.

96. Cf. two sections in Wingren, *Credo* (1974/1981), 45–49, within the framework of the presentation of the first article of faith, in a context in which Wingren qualifies the human condition in the tension between "creation is happening now." Ibid., 37 and "destruction is happening now." Ibid., 43.

this is the message contained in the Bible's remarkable speeches about obedience. Within the framework of this world of ideas, the confrontation with death is simply a matter of facing what must be accepted as something necessary: "This is something I must accept."[97] To live and believe means that we must unavoidably face meaninglessness—that is, death. In Western cultures, however, there is a risk that death goes without interpretation. In this situation, the Christian interpretation of faith and life has an important contribution to make, in that death in this tradition is the key to understanding the life of God as well as the life of humankind. Here, the grain of wheat serves as a model that shows the conditions for recognizing one's own existence, but this model is also associated with profound ethical implications as a configuration of a human life that is lived *for others*: "To obediently 'take' the loss, accept the meaningless work and the meaningless death, this is to be 'in God.' This is the life form of the grain of wheat: its purpose is to fall into the earth and die."[98]

Here we encounter the same pattern that characterizes baptism, an act that for Wingren plays a central role in the presentation of the Christian faith. Baptism has the advantage of being a matter of an *act*, an *occurrence*, a *process*—rather than a set of theoretical statements of faith that people must embrace. In *Gospel and Church* (1960/1964), Wingren incorporates Oscar Cullman's concept of "general baptism"—once for all, and for all—to speak of Jesus' death and resurrection in theological terms, also including everyday life as "a life of baptism."[99] Thus, Wingren's interpretation of human life is paradoxically focused on interpreting death. It is interesting to note that this view of life was symbolically honored, probably unwittingly, a number of years ago when the town of Valdemarsvik named a street—a street that runs past the town cemetery—in honor of Wingren. This choice of street might serve as a sort of reminder that the idea of creation is not at all an expression of a romantic view of life. According to Wingren's view of faith and life, man's path through life runs through the neighborhood of death; to find meaning is to interpret death.

We have mentioned several times previously that Wingren regarded the story of Jesus' death and resurrection as the central, fundamental

---

97. Wingren, *Credo* (1974/1981), 48.
98. Ibid., 49.
99. Wingren, *Gospel and Church* (1960/1964), 7.

story of the New Testament. The pattern of this story also configures the narrative structure of the rite of baptism, the worship service, the rhythms of the week and the church year, the confession of the faith and the history of salvation. Among these processes, the central hub that supports this narrative theology is always death and resurrection, entirely in keeping with the *kenosis* hymn in the book of Philippians, in which Paul the Apostle speaks of the one who was in the very nature of God but who gave up everything and made himself nothing, and was therefore exalted over all else. This pattern of baptism not only characterizes Wingren's entire theology but also serves as a characteristic of his theological anthropology. I have chosen to use the term "grain-of-wheat eschatology" to capture this composite figure of thought. It is a term that Wingren himself uses in only a few isolated instances but that I have chosen to give extended meaning in order to cover all of his theological work.[100] This grain-of-wheat eschatology comprises the very core of Wingren's theology and offers what may be the most pregnant way to summarize his interpretation of the Christian view of faith and life. There are, however, great challenges and risks associated with interpreting death in terms of life. When placing the story of Christ and the life story of humans in parallel, and interpreting these events according to the logic of a grain of wheat, it is important that we maintain the tension in the eschatological perspective between an "already now" and a "not yet." Even here, we sense a strong influence from Oscar Cullmann in Wingren's work. The concept of a grain-of-wheat eschatology can thus be said to contain two elements, which are linked to two tension-filled conceptual pairs: one of *death/life*, a paradoxical interpretation of life based on death; and one of *actual/ideal*, a time-related tension between "already now" and "not yet."

The same composite logic that is implicit in the concept of the grain-of-wheat eschatology also occurs in Wingren's understanding of the hermeneutical theology that he develops in his book *The Living Word* (1949/1960). This is, specifically, a view of the inner structure of the hermeneutical experience that is characterized by the same kenotic logic, in which individuals must lose themselves and their understanding in order to find themselves and a new, different, and unexpected self-understanding. The metaphor of the grain of wheat can thus stand as a model for the inner structure of the process of interpretation, a pattern that characterizes christology as well as theological anthropology

---

100. Wingren, *Credo* (1974/1981), 21.

in Wingren's hermeneutical theology. This is almost overexplicit in *The Living Word*: "In fact the message of Christ's death and resurrection has as its most prominent objective that we who hear it should die and rise again."[101] Wingren writes further,

> We are talking about him when we talk about *Christ*. We do not first speak of the objective event and then try to find a way of applying it to men, for in the *kerygma* concerning Christ's death and resurrection man is already present; the hearer is there in the passage when the minister opens the New Testament.[102]

Yet, in Wingren's theology this idea is joined by the eschatological insight that each interpretation is provisory and may be revised. This eschatological perspective has profound roots in Wingren's theological project, not least of all in his studies of Irenaeus, in which he depicts humankind as being created as a *child*, destined to *grow*. Through growth, a person changes all the time and yet remains the same person. When a person is restored through salvation, he or she eradicates injuries, yet through growth also becomes something more than he or she was from the beginning. In his study from 1947/1959, Wingren writes, "By *recapitulatio*, man comes into being as man in accordance with the first decree for Creation."[103] In other words, it is a matter of a process of *becoming human*, which is equally as dynamic as it is paradoxical. In keeping with this theological anthropology, one *is* not human; human is what one *becomes*. Wingren's interpretation of Irenaeus thus places us in the face of the utmost *aporia* that may be linked to our identity, which can be articulated through the following question: Why must we *become* the persons that we *are*? This is a classic theme that is developed in many settings, from folk tales to Hegel's reflections on the *Geist*-process. In a similar way, the eschatological perspective of this theological anthropology deals with the conditions for our *becoming* who we *are*. Eschatology thus becomes a general intellectual construct, which simultaneously motivates and limits all projects.

Already in his early writings about Irenaeus, we may recognize the basic structure of the parallel placement of what Wingren perceives to be the heart of the Christian narrative: the affinity between the internal structure of the hermeneutical experience and the internal logic of the

---

101. Wingren, *The Living Word* (1949/1960), 18.
102. Ibid., 28.
103. Wingren, *Man and the Incarnation* (1947/1959), 201.

process of becoming human, later developed thoroughly in his book *The Living Word* (1949/1960). Being human is a matter of *becoming* human, and a Christian interpretation ties this process of becoming human to the necessity of descent. *Kenosis* thus functions as the axis around which the hermeneutical motion revolves. Not only does *kenosis* prevent the transformation of creation theology into a romantic, harmonious interpretation of life, but *kenosis* also prevents us from transforming the Christian view of faith and life into a sort of extended egoism. In a later book, Wingren comments on this form of egocentricity: "Every time I perceive the eternal life as something that I myself receive while another is left without, I can however be sure that I am not imagining the eternal life. The grain of wheat that falls into the earth and dies—what has this grain gained as an isolated grain?"[104]

In the works of Wingren, the sermon becomes a paradigmatic model for the practice of interpretation that can bring about the meeting that in turn constitutes Christianity as a phenomenon. The interpretation of texts and the interpretation of life, christology, and anthropology are all intertwined in a common dialectical cohesion, and this witnesses to "an event that belongs to our own lives."[105]

In an article on the meaning of work, published in 1949, the same year in which *The Living Word* was released, Wingren integrates his grain-of-wheat eschatology in a way that makes it the very framework of his presentation. In the opening section of his article, Wingren maintains that the meaning of work is something that each person, regardless of faith, can understand and discover: "The meaning of work is the good of our neighbor." Expressed in negative terms: "Ceasing to work is an attack on the existence of our fellow human beings."[106] Since this is something that each person is capable of comprehending, the Bible really has nothing to add; it only verifies what is already general knowledge. Understanding this requires only a little common sense. The problem—"sin"—is that we as human beings cannot help thinking of our own selves, and when this self-absorption gains the upper hand, the meaning of work disappears in the same instance that other human beings disappear from our view: "My own heart constantly asks the opposite question: What will I gain from

---

104. Wingren, *Växling och kontinuitet* (1972), 28.
105. Wingren, *The Living Word* (1949/1960), 49.
106. Wingren, "Arbetets mening" (1949), 278.

doing this work?"¹⁰⁷ But this egocentric focus, according to Wingren, leads us to "beat the meaning of work to death."

Yet, the loss of a comprehensive view of Christian faith and life in modern times has also weakened the meaning of work in a crucial way:

> If one among us carries out a trade, for example, tends a shop or repairs shoes, and at the same time "wants to be a Christian," as we say, then what is thought to be specifically Christian is relegated to some place outside the store or the workshop. We think that the "sanctification" cannot occur here in this tiresome, everyday place. We think that our love for our neighbor must certainly be expressed in a more "spiritual" way.¹⁰⁸

When we try to understand the meaning of work through this sort of striving after sanctification, we transform others into a means of achieving our own sanctification or blessings. Wingren is harsh in his criticism of such pious instrumentalization, which in its turn leads to a transformation of the church into a sect: "Not until this religiosity is eliminated and the experience of the everyday prevails will it be possible for the other to become the center of our focus."¹⁰⁹ In accordance with this *humanism of the other*, life is a permanent encounter with the other, and the meaning of work emerges only when others become the center of our actions.

Wingren believes that this view of the meaning of work—evident in his article from 1949, where the law takes the form of pressure, of weight or a burden that each person must shoulder in order for his or her labor to benefit the welfare of other people—is easier to understand in regard to others than in regard to one's self. Nor is this a matter of some theory that can be assimilated through instruction; rather, it is a matter of taking seriously the actual demands that occur in everyday life. He develops a theology of work and economic life in which the death that characterizes work and the everyday wear and tear of life in all its earthliness takes on the same meaning as our meeting with our actual, final death. There is an autobiographical ring to Wingren's words when he expresses this idea in concrete terms:

> When I read a book or write a few lines, I employ and build upon a bit of my old grade school teacher's work, though she herself lies forgotten and unthanked in her grave somewhere—she who

107. Ibid., 279.
108. Ibid., 280.
109. Ibid.

taught me to read and write. When death goes forth among us, it often helps us perceive the meaning of life. Sometimes at the grave, the lives of many who were much admired are revealed to have in fact been empty; while the lives of others who were without splendor, and were given away by those who were always faithful in fair weather as well as foul, and whose faithfulness we, too, always took for granted and for which we never said thanks, are shown to have been deeply meaningful.[110]

It is interesting that Wingren in this context uses Christ's death and resurrection, along with baptism, as a pattern for interpretation in order to understand the everyday death in work. In other words, baptism becomes not a baptism into churchliness, but rather into true human life, which is lived in thousands of variations in professions and in homes. The conclusion of this exciting article is strong and significant:

If we flee from our neighbor to God, we come not to God but to ourselves, to our own selves. When the other is pushed from the center of our lives, Christ is also pushed from the center. For Christ is given to the world, he is human, in the form of a servant. The journey outward toward the people of the earth is a journey in the direction in which the cross stands and in which death occurs; that is, a journey in the direction toward where He is, and where there is hope, the hope of resurrection.[111]

This idea, too, has a personal resonance in Wingren's own background. In his autobiography, he recollects how his mother, Engla Teresia, died when he was only ten years old, an event that was utterly meaningless to him. He often returned to the memory of seeing her wooden casket being lowered into the soil in Valdemarsvik's town cemetery on a March day in 1921. It was a memory that forever influenced Wingren's view of life. But in order to understand how he could interpret this tragic event from his childhood as "a happening charged with death, charged with an indomitable hope," we must recall the exemplary importance of the grain-of-wheat eschatology for his theology. He makes explicit use of Jesus' words from the Gospel of John as a paradigm for interpretation: "Truly, truly, I say unto you, unless a grain of wheat falls into the earth and dies, it remains alone; but if it dies, it bears much fruit."[112] The grain-of-wheat aspect of this event was strengthened by the fact that the funeral

110. Ibid., 282.
111. Ibid., 286.
112. John 12:24.

took place during Lent, so that Swedish Passion hymns were sung during the service, for example, Erik Gustaf Geijer's hymn "Du bar ditt kors" ("You Carried Your Cross").

With the help of a grain-of-wheat eschatology, this tragic experience during Wingren's childhood years would later be combined with the knowledge he gained through his studies in biblical theology. From the form-critical school, he learned that there is only one important exception to the careful placement of the gospel parables in the New Testament: that of the account of the passion. Among the gospel narratives of Jesus' crucifixion and resurrection, there is a surprisingly high level of agreement regarding the order of events, which indicates that this is a course of events that from the very beginning was of vital importance for an understanding of the Christian faith. The dominant position of the passion story in each of the four gospels places the Easter drama at the center of Christianity. In comparison with the total dominance of Easter, Christmas is actually a marginal event. In a manner of speaking, the gospels are to be read "backwards." They are stories of the passion of Christ, with lengthy introductions. In the drama of the passion, only losers win any victories. Wingren is clear in his opinion: the more Christ suffers, the more human he becomes. Thus, it is not by avoiding darkness but rather by losing oneself that the individual can gain his or her life. For Wingren, the secret of the grain of wheat is a matter of being *for others*. Yet, the grain of wheat, as an interpretation of life, also becomes a model for his own life project. It is specifically against this background that we should view the metamorphosis that he underwent during the 1970s. The grain-of-wheat eschatology may be seen as the role model for *the practice of transformation* that characterized his own life during that period of time. This concept has theoretical as well as practical dimensions, which seek to "do justice to religion as a dynamic phenomenon, which in itself contains an idea of change or transformation."[113] In other words, religion understood as a practice of transformation is always already political. After his triumphal successes of the 1960s, Wingren's life became part of a practice of transformation for which the grain-of-wheat eschatology was obviously the model. This is the subject of the next chapter.

---

113. Sigurdson, *Det postsekulära tillståndet*, 68. In this book, the author uses the concept "practice of transformation" to develop an adequate heuristic concept of religion for his study. But the concept "practice of transformation" was originally coined by John Swedenmark. Cf. Swedenmark, "Bortom bortträngningen," 72.

5

Metamorphosis and Recontextualization

THE 1960S APPEAR AS a remarkable period of transformation in modern history, when many things came to an end and so many new things began. The decade of the 1960s saw the convergence of a number of processes of change that would continue to alter the world toward the turn of the millennium. On a superficial level, the changes were evidenced by the emergence of an entirely new youth culture and new social movements on the world scene. One lasting image of the new expressions of popular culture and the new ways of life that were developing during this time is the enormous hysteria that surrounded The Beatles. Yet it was Bob Dylan who put the spirit of the time into music when he sang, "The times, they are a-changin.'"

On a more profound level, these expressions of popular culture pointed to a destabilization of the basic infrastructure of society, in economics and technology as well as in politics and culture, which in turn led to a long series of crises, with growing uncertainty about the direction future developments might take. As sociologist Manuel Castells has stated, the 1960s can be seen as a watershed in modern history: signs of discontinuity appeared in almost all areas, including economics, technology, politics, culture, and society.[1]

In hindsight, it is clear that the two economic systems that dominated the world during most of the previous century were both heading toward a deep crisis at this time: by the end of the 1960s, the Western

---

1. This is the larger picture that Manuel Castells outlines in *The Rise of the Network Society* (1996), but also in the following volumes of his great trilogy: *The Power of Identity* (1997) and *End of Millennium* (1998), and their later revised editions.

market economy as well as the Eastern planned economy had reached the limits of their capacity for exploitation, and in many ways they even seemed to have reached the ends of their respective roads. Around 1970, a process of decay began in the East that eventually led to the downfall of the Soviet Union and the final collapse of the entire collection of communist regimes in Eastern Europe. At around the same time in the West, important technological breakthroughs were made, laying the foundations for the coming information revolution. The post-communist convulsions and the growth of a global economy were two parallel stories that would dominate the latter half of the twentieth century. But in the 1960s none of this could even be imagined.

On a geopolitical level, the world of the 1960s was dominated by the American story. After World War II, Europe became decentered and brutally split, as manifested in the erection of the Berlin Wall in August 1961. The United States dominated the world scene economically, politically, and culturally; its only imaginable competitor was the Soviet Union. The era was marked by these two superpowers, two ideological and economic systems that stood in irreconcilable opposition to one another. A series of events that became world events, including the Hungarian uprising, the Cuban missile crisis, the Six-Day War between Israel and its Arab neighbors, and the 1968 invasion of Czechoslovakia by the Warsaw Pact countries, resulted in protests that threatened the uneasy balance between the two.

In other parts of the world during this era, the post-World War II process of decolonization was in full swing, with the result that numerous new countries began to make their uncertain and shaky way into the community of independent nations. The range of postcolonial complications and failures brought a growing awareness of the unequal distribution of wealth in the world. A wave of solidarity movements swept through the developed world. Young people, in particular, gathered around causes such as the antiwar movement, demonstrations against the Vietnam War, anti-imperialism, protests against the violence in the former Portuguese and French colonies in Africa, engagement against the apartheid regime in South Africa, a new environmental consciousness, growing awareness of the limitations of capitalism and economic growth, criticisms of commercialism and consumerism, the emergence of the new left and neo-Marxism, feminism, etc. The list of new movements and causes that arose in the 1960s could be made much longer indeed.

One of the demographic reasons for the convulsions of the 1960s and the political radicalization of youth was that the social effects of the large post-WWII generation became visible. Over time, the ideals of the youth culture of the 1960s gradually influenced society as a whole. Suddenly, the universities became crowded as the student body increased with the changing demography. Previously, students had been part of an elite minority with considerable freedom of movement and clear privileges. Now, the old status quo was threatened. These conditions led to government reforms in the Swedish university system that were aimed at transforming the old elite universities into mass universities. These reforms generated powerful student revolts that made their influence felt in many directions. Soon, many attractive career fields became crowded, and frustration grew as graduates found that they were not enjoying the economic advantages traditionally gained from university studies. At the same time, the media brought the issue of world poverty ever closer, and many young people felt that they were unjustly enjoying privileges that were in harsh contrast to the conditions of the world's poor.

The technological advances of the decade reached a peak with the manned moon landing of the Apollo 11 mission on 20 July 1969. Optimism about the future and the belief that the development of society could be predicted, planned, and exploited were still strong. The "grand society" elaborated plans as to how to colonize the future, and for the sake of this future, severe urban renewal programs were undertaken in downtown areas of many older cities. In Sweden, the urban renewal programs reawakened a question from the days of writer August Strindberg: "We are tearing down our cities to get air and light; is not that enough?" The era was characterized by increased urbanization, and the population of Sweden's rural areas shrank at an ever-increasing rate. Beginning in 1965, a Swedish government initiative known as the Million Program aimed at creating one million new dwellings over a ten-year span, temporarily saving the day for many new urban residents—even though the high-density apartment complexes that were built led to their own set of problems later on. Before the 1970s had even begun, Harry Aronson hinted at Sweden's transformation from an industrial to a postindustrial society: "Modern-day humanity's sense of life is determined to a large degree by the rapid rate of change and the feeling that practically everything is fundamentally changeable."[2]

---

2. Aronson, "Från industrialism till postindustriellt samhälle," 188.

What impact on theology can we expect from societal change, and how does the spirit of the day influence theology? It would be a mistake to imagine religion and theology as timeless phenomena, from which we may gaze serenely out upon a contemporary scene in tumultuous change, and it would be equally as mistaken to simply dismiss religion as being out of touch with the contemporary situation. In a similar way, we sometimes think of the Christian message as something that has been transmitted untouched through the turmoil of history, and that the foremost task of theology is to defend pure and unchanging doctrines through time. This sort of ahistorical positioning runs the risk of becoming laden with anachronisms, as in the story of an elderly English lady who, upset that the Church of England was issuing a new translation of the Bible, said, "If King James' Bible was good enough for Jesus, it is good enough for us."

History itself, however, teaches us that religion is an elastic and changeable phenomenon. Furthermore, Christianity is not merely a historical phenomenon closely associated with a history of change in both time and space. A Christian self-understanding also includes the idea that faith *should be* contextually determined, entirely in keeping with the theological implications of incarnation theology.

A Stranger in 1968

The year 1968 is so rife with symbolic overtones that it seems almost equated with societal transformation. Yet it is easy to be captured only by the social changes and forget some of the monumental technical and economic changes that also occurred that year. As a matter of fact, 1968 not only saw the founding of Sweden's Group 8 feminist organization, but it also experienced the largest Swedish industrial merger ever when truck and bus manufacturer Scania joined with SAAB to form the SAAB-Scania megacorporation. For Swedes, it is impossible to think of 1968 without recalling the image of the country's then minister of education, Olof Palme, marching arm in arm through the dark, wintry streets of Stockholm with North Vietnam's ambassador to Moscow, in a protest action that later concluded with Palme's now legendary and oft-quoted speech in criticism of the US bombings of Hanoi. Two weeks after Palme's famous speech on Swedish Radio, the United States recalled its ambassador to Stockholm, and relations between the two countries remained chilly for years afterward. During the 1960s, Swedish public opinion toward the United States swung dramatically from admiration to strong criticism, if not anti-Americanism. Culturally, 1968 was also a year when the traditional values of Swedish society came into question, as marked by avant-gardistic Swedish films such as *I am Curious (Yellow)*, by Vilgot Sjöman, and *They Call Us Misfits*, by Stefan Jarl and Jan Lindquist, as well as the American musical *Hair*, which had its Stockholm premier in September.

The year 1968 was also a dramatic year politically. Martin Luther King was assassinated on 4 April, and two months later, Robert Kennedy also fell to the bullets of an assassin. On the Continent, the Prague Spring brought hopes of a softening of the totalitarian communist regimes of Eastern Europe, but these hopes were brutally dashed when the Warsaw Pact countries invaded Czechoslovakia on 20 August, bringing an end to the dream of "socialism with a human face." Earlier that summer in Sweden, demonstrators had succeeded with their slogan of "Stop the Match!," shutting down the Davis Cup tennis match between Sweden and Rhodesia at the beginning of May. Moreover, in May 1968, Sweden was the host for another world event when the World Council of Churches held its General Assembly in Uppsala.

University students increasingly came to dominate the public sphere. During Lund University's traditional Walpurgis celebration, radical students burned their student caps and threw eggs at the police. The acts of the Swedish students seemed mild, however, in comparison with the uncompromising conflict of the May Revolt in Paris. During the so-called Occupation of the Student Union House in Stockholm (which was not really an occupation), students took over the Student Union's headquarters for a few days in May of that year. To Swedes in 1968, this act was almost unbelievable. The winds of change even blew among established Swedish politicians, as the parliament abolished its long-standing bicameral system. Nonetheless, it is clear that Sweden's political establishment failed to keep up with the dramatic and rapid radicalization of society, especially among young people.

On 9 May more than one thousand students demonstrated in Lund to demand that the Swedish government sever its ties to South Vietnam's US-supported Saigon regime and recognize Hanoi. Ten days later, five thousand people in Lund attended a public meeting to demand increased aid to developing countries. In early summer, the dramatic student radicalization clashed painfully with the celebration of the University's three hundredth anniversary on June 12–14. The organizers of the anniversary celebration felt that it was necessary to protect their twelve honorary doctoral candidates and one hundred fifty specially invited international guests with police barricades and mounted police. The fact that the University did not even consider involving the students in the anniversary celebration says something about general attitudes of the day and serves as further evidence that different worlds were colliding during this period of change.

The wave of radicalization was also noticeable within the churches, and not least among the youth. The 1968 General Assembly of the World Council of Churches in Uppsala came to be a source of inspiration to the young people of Sweden's churches. The theme of the assembly—"See, I make all things new!"—seemed so contemporaneous that people almost forgot the biblical background of this quotation. It was as if the entire world had come to Sweden, and Swedes found the spirit to be radical. On the afternoon of 7 November 1968, a group of diplomats, including representation from white-ruled South Africa, visited the Cathedral of Lund, where Bo Fredrik Kjellin, manager of the local tourist office, was to give them a tour of the building and show them the cathedral's famous medieval astronomical clock. Outside the church, they were met by boos from demonstrators, who shouted, "Abolish racism!" Still, they were able to make their way into the quiet of the cathedral. Pastor Martin Lind (later bishop of Linköping) had applied for permission to hold a prayer service in the cathedral at the same time, but instead followed the visitors through the cathedral with a group of students singing "We Shall Overcome." Third Secretary Vorster from the official diplomatic representation of South Africa in Stockholm later related that he and his wife felt uncomfortable when the students sang "Black and white together..." in protest against South Africa's apartheid regime. This was as threatening as the students became that day, and seen from the perspective of the present day, when protests can be truly violent, the incident seems rather innocent.

However, the way in which the incident was handled is indicative of how shocking the new radicalism was for the established society. Legal accusations were made and a court case ensued, first at Lund City Hall on 5 and 6 March 1969, then at the Swedish Superior Court in Malmö in December of that same year. The Swedish establishment condemned the cathedral protest. The bishop of Lund, Martin Lindström, thought that it was "distressing that the action had taken such expression that we must now feel shame before the diplomatic representation from South

Africa."³ Along with young people such as Per Frostin and Göran Bexell, one of the few representatives of the establishment who appeared in court for the defense of the accused students (Claes Hellborg, Martin Lind, Dag Sandahl, Herman Schmid, and Anders Westerberg) was Wingren's younger colleague in systematic theology, Per Erik Persson. In contrast to the official reaction, Professor Persson witnessed that he had felt a liberating joy when he heard about the protest. Earlier that year, he had been a delegate at the World Council of Churches in Uppsala, where the General Assembly had likened indifference to world poverty and need to heresy. For that reason, he expressed his surprise at finding himself alone in his support for the Lund Cathedral protesters, yet at the same time expressed his happiness "that there were nonetheless a few who were not only hearers of the word, but also its doers."⁴ In the wake of the Cathedral protest, Persson released a book with the significant title *Sharing God's Stance against Evil* (*Att dela Guds hållning mot djävulskapet*, 1972), in which he repeated the conclusion of *The Uppsala 68 Report* from the World Assembly of Churches that indifference in the face of the world's needs was equal to heresy.⁵ In his foreword to Persson's book, Göran Bexell, who would later defend his doctoral dissertation for Wingren, assume Wingren's professorship, and eventually become the president of Lund University, brought the different perspectives together with the following words: "After this, the world will never be the same again . . . Prior to 1968, we diligently devoted ourselves to questions regarding the church and church office. In 1968 and the years following it, issues of social, economic and political development came to the center of interest."⁶

---

3. Westerberg et al., *Världsproblem och kyrkofrid*, 98.

4. Persson, in ibid., 100. Cf. "as an expression of the fact that some in our church have, despite it all, heard this cry to awaken, and have taken it seriously, not only as non-binding and beautiful words, but also as the word of God, which binds the conscience and spurs us to action." Ibid., 101. On the final day at the Malmö Court of Appeals, there was a large gathering of young people through whom ran a feeling of outrage, as expressed for example in fliers with the text "The District Court supports a racist representative, and thereby shows its true face." These fliers were handed out at various schools in the city of Malmö and were signed "In holy wrath" by a number of people, including Gunnar Wetterberg. Ibid., 252ff. In the final court decision, Lind, Westerberg, and Hellborg were convicted of "anger-provoking behavior" and made to pay 75 Crowns, plus 93 Crowns 50 öre, to cover the costs of a court witness. Ibid., 186.

5. Persson, *Att dela Guds hållning mot djävulskapet*, 53.

6. Bexell, in his foreword to ibid., 5.

In the midst of this historic turbulence, in the midst of the legendary year of 1968, when international challenges from all directions seemed to call for immediate intervention, Wingren published a book with the entirely implausible subtitle (to the Swedish edition) *A Study of Swedish Theology before 1920* (*En studie i svensk teologi före 1920*), published in English the following year as *An Exodus Theology: Einar Billing and the Development of Modern Swedish Theology* (1968/1969).

At first glance, Wingren's book on Billing may seem almost unbelievably out of touch with the spirit of the times. When the entire world seemed to be in flames, and Swedish universities had been transformed into epicenters for worldwide activism, the theology professor from Lund published a book focused on a period of time—*before 1920*. Wingren's thoughts seem to have been somewhere else entirely. While the Lund Cathedral protest dominated the consciousness of many theologians during the years 1968–69, Wingren did not mention it at all in his personal journals. His thoughts were occupied by the University's anniversary, his international lecture tours—and the period before 1920.

After his book *Gospel and Church* (1960/1964) had been released on his fiftieth birthday, Wingren's system of theology was more or less complete. Indeed, although the following decade saw no decisive innovations in Wingren's writings, he seemed to surge forward on a wave of success.[7] He was involved in numerous international theological committees and gatherings, and his influence and network of contacts spanned five continents. In addition to being an important representative for Lutheran theology in national and international ecumenical circles, he received requests from several bishoprics in Sweden—but his answer was always the same: "I decline." His academic work saw the translation of his books into several languages, and invitations to lecture abroad continued to be

---

7. Wingren's contacts with the Swedish publishing house Gleerups during the early 1960s gives rise to the impression that he nurtured plans for more books of a more comprehensive nature, which obviously were never realized. I am unable to determine whether this was due to lack of time or flagging inspiration. On 7 April 1962, he entered into a long-term agreement with Gleerups involving several books, including one on Billing. At that point it seems to have been a much more ambitious project than the one that eventually resulted: the original Swedish version of *An Exodus Theology: Einar Billing and the Development of Modern Swedish Theology*, about five hundred handwritten half-folio size pages completed sometime in the mid-1960s, including about one hundred handwritten half-folio pages of footnotes. He mentioned one other book: "a book of speeches and sermons will be published by Gleerups." Discounting the smaller pamphlets of morning prayers and such that he did publish, it was quite a while before even this book project was realized.

showered on him. He was among the leaders of the international society on ethics, *Societas Ethica*, and in 1968, he was inducted into the prestigious editorship of *Theologische Realenzyklopädie*, in which capacity he was entrusted with responsibility for encyclopedia entries relating to ethics. During the 1960s he was awarded honorary doctorates at the universities of Kiel (1965), St. Andrews (1966), and Rostock (1969).

His personal journals bear witness to his frequent travels, often in the company of one of Lund's associate professors in his subject, Harry Aronson. In early 1961, he made a lecture tour to London, Cambridge, and Birmingham. The following year he spent all of December in Saint Paul, Minnesota, to deliver eight lectures based on his book *Gospel and Church*. He journeyed to Montreal, Greifswald, Hamburg, Bonn, Durham, St. Andrews, and other places—while at the same time maintaining a media presence in Swedish television, radio, and newspapers and publishing frequent contributions in Swedish journals such as *Vår Lösen*, *Kristet Forum*, *Swedish Theological Quarterly*, and *Svensk Kyrkotidning*, not to mention his numerous articles in Sweden's popular religious press. New articles and lecture manuscripts seemed to flow from Wingren's pen each week, and he was frequently interviewed in media, where he expressed his opinion on current issues. From midsummer 1967 he traveled almost nonstop, lecturing in Saint Paul, San Francisco, Minneapolis, Philadelphia, Cambridge, and Bristol. It was a summer full of travel that culminated in his appointment as chairman of *Societas Ethica* in late August. This series of international successes for Wingren seemed to reach its climax in 1969. April that year saw the publication of *Theology in Conflict* in Japanese, and Wingren spent the summer months traveling almost hectically: from 21 July through 1 August he was in Tanzania to deliver lectures, from 2 August to 10 August he made a lecture tour in Germany, from 16 August to 22 August he lectured in Canada, from 8 September to 12 September he attended the meetings of *Societas Ethica* in Strasbourg—and he even managed to get home to Lund before the last of these trips to attend an international meeting of Lutheran theologians, from 28 August to 30 August.

However, in the wake of all these international triumphs, Wingren's situation at home in Lund began to deteriorate in his professional as well as his private life. While he participated in the gala events of Lund University's three hundreth anniversary celebration with gusto, he dismissed the student protests completely, seeing them only as some sort of minor disturbance on the margins of the University. Wingren's lack of interest in politics contrasted starkly with an era when *everything* seemed to be political, and the "second article of faith theology" that dominated the new radicalism in the churches was foreign to him. Almost without exception, his doctoral students remained strict adherents to the methods of Nygren, though they did not employ Nygren's focus on basic motifs but maintained his strictly historical approach. Wingren's seminars on ethics dealt with almost no contemporary ethical problems whatsoever. Yet, the *context* was moving further way from the *text*, until finally, in the face of an era marked by exceptional discontinuity, not even Wingren could maintain continuity. Society (the context) suddenly began to *speak back* in a more powerful way.[8]

The events around 1968 were frustrating for Professor Wingren. Students began to use a tone to which he was not accustomed. He complained that not only professorial authority but also the economic advantages traditionally associated with a professorship were being undermined. He was clearly out of step with the rapid changes of the time and made it clear that he did not like what was going on around him. For the most part, Wingren tried to ignore what was happening. It is interesting that only a few years later he would place his hopes in this generation of young radicals as forerunners of a better future; but in 1968, he perceived them as something threatening, or in the best case as a disturbance. It is no wonder that so many of the more gifted and politically engaged doctoral students, especially those with left-wing leanings, turned their interest toward Wingren's younger colleague in systematic theology, Per Erik Persson. Professor Persson had a completely different capacity for identifying contemporary trends, reading the signs of the times, and attempting to meet the new demands that this generation of students was making. If Wingren's months as a guest professor in Basel in 1947 had been his first collision with an environment of foreign ideas, the events of the late 1960s may be considered his second serious confrontation with a seemingly foreign set of surroundings, and it hit him hard.

Nonetheless, the radical transformation of the social climate of the 1960s and 1970s would change Wingren in profound ways, although it took some time. Against the background of the alienation he felt toward the events of 1968, what happened to him in the 1970s seems almost improbable. The change may be comprehended by three personal events that determined the course of Wingren's life in the 1970s. These defining

---

8. Cf. Nowotny et al., *Re-thinking Science*, 1.

events brought on a metamorphosis of the Lundensian professor's life and work and are important for understanding his views and the changes that were about to take place.

The first event occurred in 1974, when the same man who over the years had been seen as an obvious candidate for a number of bishop's seats after thirty-five years withdrew his ordination as minister in the Church of Sweden. He felt forced to take this dramatic step because of the Church of Sweden's conduct over the issue of the ordination of women, a question that had occupied his theological interest since 1958. In the letter that he sent to the Diocese of Lund, dated 1 October 1974, he wrote:

> The undersigned hereby respectfully asks to be relieved of the office of minister which was entrusted to me through the rite of ordination in Linköping Cathedral on 15 December 1939 . . . Through recent developments, the ordained ministry which I received through the rite of ordination has become an object of exchange, being used to hawk and buy peaceful relations between brothers, without considering the legal rights of individuals, without considering the wishes of the congregations, and without deference to the compulsions of personal conscience . . . For my own part, it is my intent to no longer look passively upon what is taking place. I have no wish to retain an office that has become a means of exchange for the purchase of false peace.[9]

These somewhat cryptic constructions should be considered as a criticism directed first and foremost toward the bishop of Växjö, Sven Lindegård, and his attempts to control the warring fractions by the decision to allow no ordinations of women during his first year in office. Wingren wanted to demonstrate his discontent over this double-dealing in the treatment of women as ordained ministers, as well as the failure by the church leadership to deal with the resistance to the ordination of women. He sought a more open support for the ordination of female clergy. His action brought the attention that he expected, not only in the Swedish mass media, with which he had shared his letter and his opinions, but also within the church. On 16 October, the same day that the chapter of the Lund diocese consented to his request and he ceased to be an ordained minister of the Church of Sweden, Wingren's former doctoral student Olof Sundby, now the archbishop, wrote in a personal letter to Wingren:

---

9. Lund Cathedral archives, dossier C23, register number 41/74.

I certainly need not waste many words to tell you that I strongly question your actions in response to the entire Växjö affair. If everyone who disagrees with Sven Lindegård's dealings in the current case were to resign their ordination, our ranks would probably thin out considerably. Those of us who are left will have to make the best of the current situation, as we always do. I admit that I better understand the motivations that you have revealed afterward, but which were not in your initial, indignant letter. The catch is that if we are to follow the actual legal determinations, a diocesan chapter can actually only separate a person from the ordained ministry on the grounds of apostasy in his teachings! But as you certainly know, in the last few years, we have also granted withdrawal from ordination on the grounds of personal requests.[10]

The drama in Wingren's life would continue. Two years later, in 1976, to the surprise of many people, he divorced his wife, Signhild. They had two grown children and had been married for thirty-four years. Throughout those years, Signhild had managed their household and had kept herself engaged in her husband's teaching and research. She was a down-to-earth person who in many ways lived out Luther's idea of vocation and calling. For many years, she typewrote her husband's manuscripts, and she organized the Wingren household. Signhild had managed almost everything in his life, except theology. Even though Gustaf Wingren had exhibited a pronounced liberal stance on lifestyles and relationships, including same-sex relationships, and had argued for the right to divorce according to Luther's theology, his separation from his wife was unexpected, not least because he had also often argued the virtue of remaining in and enduring difficult relationships. Yet, what was probably most surprising, both to those close to Wingren and to the public at large, was that he then married a woman who was a leading figure on the Swedish political left—Greta Hofsten.

Gustaf Wingren and Greta Hofsten had met for the first time in 1967 at a meeting in Stockholm. The two soon formed a friendship that revolved around discussions carried out in person and through correspondence. In his personal journals, Wingren mentions Hofsten for the first time on 31 March 1970, when he breaks his pattern of rather dry journal entries concerning academic and churchly tasks with a note about a "daylong discussion with Greta Hofsten about 'social ethics in

10. Olof Sundby to Gustaf Wingren, 16 October 1974, written on the official letterhead of the archbishop of Sweden!

Stockholm."¹¹ The following year, Swedish public radio's P1 Channel broadcasted a studio discussion between the two on the theme of "Church, State, and Society."¹² She is mentioned in his works already in 1972, and in the foreword to *Credo* (1974/1981), Wingren's second book of dogmatics, there is a section in which he thanks not only his professorial colleagues Birger Gerhardsson and Per Erik Persson, but also "my very good friend Greta Hofsten."¹³ In the early 1970s, the relationship was purely platonic. Greta was a regular dinner guest in Signhild and Gustaf Wingren's home during this time. The three of them even made a trip together to Hinseberg, Sweden, to see the women's prison where Greta faced possible incarceration for her involvement in the magazine reportage that led to Sweden's IB affair (a kind of Swedish version of the Watergate affair). Greta also frequently spent Christmas at the Dominican Sisters' cloister at Rögle, outside Lund, and while there she often took the opportunity to visit the Wingrens.

However, by December 1974, the same year in which he renounced his ordination, there were hints that the relationship between Gustaf Wingren and Greta Hofsten had become more than platonic.¹⁴ It became obvious that Gustaf was going astray. One year later, around New Year's 1976, the Wingrens and their two children consulted a lawyer in Lund to agree on the terms of a divorce on mutual grounds. In the spring of 1976, Gustaf and Greta procured the apartment at Warholmsväg 6B in Lund.

---

11. For many years, Wingren was involved in a debate regarding the Social-Ethical Delegation, which he later documented in the little pamphlet *Socialetik i Stockholm* (1970), the one to which he refers in his journal. The controversy surrounding the Social-Ethical Delegation was complicated, and I have chosen to exclude it from this book. For those interested in this conflict, there is a dissertation covering the topic: Sandahl, *Folk och kyrka*.

12. This program was broadcasted on Swedish Television, 4 October 1972.

13. Wingren, *Credo* (1974/1981), 15. When Wingren mentions Greta Hofsten in this context as one "who is not afraid of being nonconformist" (ibid., 15), we should keep in mind that these words were written at a time when she was involved in Sweden's infamous IB affair. She was forced to defend herself in court on the basis of the freedom of the press, and faced a prison term.

14. In his journal, Wingren has saved a card from a Chinese restaurant at Drottninggatan 71C in Stockholm. On the back of this card he has jotted the following note: "December 13, 1974 + Alviksvägen 88" (Hofsten's address in Bromma). A week later, Gustaf and Signhild Wingren were invited to the home of Harry Aronson and his family on Lauritz Weibulls väg in Lund. The spur-of-the-moment entry Wingren wrote in the Aronsons' guestbook after this Christmas gathering almost seems a careless boast of his confused relationships at this time: "Oh, all these women . . ."

The Wingrens' divorce took effect on 12 May, and the events that followed occurred quickly: on 13 May, Gustaf and Greta filed a preliminary application for marriage; on 15 May they moved into their new apartment together; on 16 May they were engaged; and on 7 June they were married in the chapel at the Sigtuna Foundation (*Sigtunastiftelsen*). The location for their wedding was not chosen at random, for both Gustaf and Greta had often been involved in cultural and theological meetings at the foundation. Their choice of author and hymn writer Olov Hartman, director of the Sigtuna Foundation, to officiate at their wedding ceremony was not random either. Greta had spent much time at the Sigtuna Foundation together with Swedish author and translator Gunnel Vallquist, later a member of the Swedish Academy, along with many other Swedish authors who gathered there around Olov Hartman, who had long been Greta's spiritual advisor. In the evening following the wedding ceremony, Greta's twin sister, Karin "Kajsi" Rössel, a renowned psychiatrist who served as a witness at the wedding, organized and hosted a reception for the couple's closest friends at her apartment in Stockholm. Among the guests at the reception was Gunnel Vallquist, who less than two weeks earlier had received an honorary doctorate in theology from Lund University.

Leaving his first marriage and renouncing his ordination were two life-changing events for Wingren, and they were followed by yet another when he retired from Lund University in 1977. Although his retirement was necessitated by purely perfunctory reasons, Wingren also imbued it with great personal importance by refusing to allow the University to formally recognize him with a traditional gala retirement dinner and festivities, which would have been a matter of course following the departure of one of the Faculty of Theology's most well-known professors. But no, Wingren wanted instead to end his career like any other laborer, by simply walking out through the gateway for the last time. He also made it very clear that he wanted nothing to do with an emeritus position at the University. Wingren researcher Jonny Karlsson states, "This afforded Wingren the opportunity to cultivate to a higher degree than had been previously possible the image of himself as *l'enfant terrible* of Swedish theology and church life."[15] It became clear that his identity as professor, which Wingren had borne for so many years, would now be practiced within an entirely new sort of university, namely, that of society.

---

15. Karlsson, *Predikans samtal*, 236.

The processes of profound change that began in Wingren's life around 1970 became evident in these three biographical events that would define his life in the decade that followed. His renunciation of ordained ministry, his divorce, and his retirement all bear a resemblance to his idea of the grain-of-wheat eschatology. This idea was now being incarnated in the course of his own life through these events in the form of a *practice of transformation*. His transformation was also evident on a purely professional level in that his authorship during the 1970s and 1980s took on a new vitality and a level of production that would have been difficult to achieve otherwise. On both a personal and a professional level, things in Wingren's life were dying. This was probably very painful, but out of this death grew something new and different. Wingren, the Lundensian theologian, underwent a metamorphosis. What brought about this remarkable transformation?

A New Colleague Enters the Scene: Greta Hofsten

One of the main ideas in this book is that it is not possible to comprehend Gustaf Wingren's later authorship without moving *outside of* the domains of theology and academia. The sources of the new theological thinking that he developed during the 1970s and later, when society became his new university, are tied to a new professorial colleague, someone who held no academic or theological position but who nonetheless influenced his theology in a profound way—Greta Hofsten. It is no exaggeration to say that academic studies on the theology of Wingren have without exception ignored this relationship. At best, Hofsten is mentioned as Wingren's second wife, but never as a decisive influence upon his theology. Her importance has been rendered entirely invisible. This lack of contextualization in these presentations is probably the result of a narrow focus of traditional academic studies and a tendency to overlook the achievements of women. Because of this, the most important source for Wingren's later years and the developmental logic behind his writing during this period have remained largely unrecognized. Who was Greta Hofsten?

The family name of Wingren's new wife, seventeen years his junior, was Bagger-Sjöbeck, and she came from an upper-class context in Djursholm, an exclusive suburb of Stockholm. Greta was the child of the CEO of a Swedish film company, Eduard Bagger-Sjöbeck, and his wife, Edith, née Bagger-Jörgensen. She had five siblings, all of them gifted: the oldest brother Hans, older sister Inga (married name Thorsson), older twin brothers Lennart and Bertil, and Greta's own twin sister, Karin (married name Rössel). In 1942 the family moved to the city of Malmö in southern Sweden due to their father Eduard's work with the film company *Svensk Filmindustri*. Greta was fifteen years old at the time of the move, and she began studies at the girls' school in Sweden's third city, where the family had old ties. At the age of eighteen she became pregnant by her teacher, adjunct instructor Henrik Petrén (1896–1970). They married in March 1946, and in September of that year their son, Finn, was born. Greta and her new little family moved to the nearby city of Helsingborg, where they took up residence at Kungsgatan 18. In 1948 their second son, Kåre, was born. After a few years, Greta left Henrik and took the children with her to Lund so that she could complete her studies in philosophy and sociology at the Social Institute (now known as the School of Social Work, part of Lund University). She had to work hard as a single mother, but at the same time cultivated intellectual networks and became actively engaged in the political scene in Lund. During the academic year 1951–52, she and her sons lived at Sandgatan 12, in a house that stands halfway between the Theologicum building and the great Bishop's Mansion below the University Library. This was the same year that Gustaf Wingren was installed as professor and began his breaking away from Anders Nygren with his inaugural lecture—but these things were taking place in a different world with which Greta had no connection. In 1952, she and her sons moved to the city of Kalmar in southeastern Sweden, where she worked as a children's healthcare assistant. In Kalmar, Greta deepened her political involvement in the Swedish Social Democratic Party. In 1954, she was elected to the city council in Kalmar and took up a role as an unusually young and driven chairperson for the local party's women's club.

Three years later, in 1957, she moved to Stockholm and assumed the name of Greta von Hofsten when she married statistician and election expert Erland von Hofsten. She and her sons moved into his large home in the Stockholm suburb of Bromma.[16] However, the relationships between Greta and Erland, and between her children and his, were not happy. Just one year later, she and Erland divorced, and Greta and her sons moved to a small apartment in the Äppelviken section of Bromma.

---

16. After marrying Gustaf Wingren in 1976, she expanded her name to Greta Elisabeth Wingren von Hofsten, even though she never presented herself as, or was referred to by, any name other than Greta Hofsten.

During their summer vacations in the 1950s, Greta's sons lived with their father while she spent extended periods in Paris where she established an extensive network of contacts among authors and intellectuals.

In addition, Greta's small apartment in Bromma, with its tiny galley kitchen, was visited by numerous figures from the Swedish cultural elite, such as Olof Lagercrantz, Kai Henmark, Birger Norman, and Vilgot Sjöman, making it the scene of intense intellectual discussions. In Stockholm, Greta worked as an abortion counselor at RFSU (Sweden's National Association for Sex Education). However, when she became involved in a conflict with Elise Ottesen-Jensen, the founder of RFSU, she had to make a career change of her own. At the threshold of the 1960s, Greta thus found herself as an unemployed single mother, but she managed to begin a long, successful career at AMS, the Swedish Labor Market Administration, where in just a few short years she rose from the position of job counselor to bureau director. In addition to her demanding job, responsibility for her two children and her extensive political involvement, Greta was somehow also able to invest considerable time and effort in reading and travel in pursuit of her personal spiritual quest. Like many others at the time, including the members of The Beatles, she was drawn to the Maharishi Mahesh Yogi and Transcendental Meditation. In many respects, Greta was a passionate person, and during these years she pushed her energies to their uttermost limits.

Greta Hofsten first became known to the general Swedish public through her connection to the infamous IB affair. She was unemployed and an avowed communist, but as yet held no position of leadership within the Swedish Communist Party. On the contrary, to many within the party, Greta may have seemed like some sort of foreigner, given her strong interest in spirituality. She was a free spirit, an outsider who felt at home among anti-Vietnam War protesters. When she was elected to succeed Jan Myrdal as chair of the board of directors for the left-wing Swedish magazine *Folket i Bild/Kulturfront*, no one could foresee the stormy years that lay ahead. Few in her new environment understood the composite nature of her personality, her intense drive, or her strong faith. The IB affair began when journalists Peter Bratt and Jan Guillou, together with their source Håkan Isaksson, published articles in *Folket i Bild/Kulturfront* magazine, revealing that Sweden's Social Democratic party was operating a top-secret spy organization known as "IB," which had been cooperating with government and military institutions to gather evidence on left-wing sympathizers. The Swedish government reacted to these reports with the force that only an unholy political alliance can muster. As the accountable publishing editor of the magazine that had revealed these secrets, Greta Hofsten found herself in the public spotlight. By this time, she had developed into a full-fledged political professional. In 1970 she had left the Social Democratic party, and a year later she left her career as bureau director at the Swedish Labor Market Administration.

Lurking behind all of this in her life were complex religious problems. After having been "afflicted" (that is the word she herself used) with a religious awakening in the mid-1960s, as a thirty-eight year-old single mother in the midst of a promising professional career and with two children in upper secondary school, Greta had "come out" as a Christian. This announcement was not received with any enthusiasm by members of her family or her social networks. Neither did she garner any great understanding when she began to donate half of her wages as a bureau director to Church of Sweden Aid and other organizations that worked to provide help to developing countries. Around 1970, she accepted the consequences of her religious and morally motivated radicalization and drifted to the political left. She had begun to define herself as simultaneously Christian and Communist, and after several years of unemployment, she took an ordinary job as a postman. She said that she wanted a job that involved physical movement, that she could enjoy, and that would not corrupt her. Despite her simplicity, she still seems to have been a kind of Epicurean who was happiest when she could take part in discussions, read a variety of newspapers, and enjoy a cup of coffee with the obligatory cigarette. Although she was certainly not ingratiating, many people remember her warm smile and how she always had time for anyone who needed to talk. There were those who admired Greta Hofsten, such as author and public intellectual Anders Ehnmark. In his political memoirs, many years after the furor surrounding the IB affair and *Folket i Bild/Kulturfront* had subsided, Ehmark asked himself:

> Whatever happened to Greta Hofsten, our brilliant chairperson who always seemed to be coming in from the rain while others sat resting? She was always standing out in the rain for hours, selling hopeless revolutionary newspapers. No one else lived up to her willingness to sacrifice herself, and that is the way she wanted it. Her medicine was hard manual labor, hard office work, and on top of that late evenings filled with intellectually

brilliant meetings at which angels danced on the heads of pins. She was a wonderful chairperson, and we missed her greatly.¹⁷

In contrast, Jan Guillou—journalist and editorial chief at *Folket i Bild/Kulturfront*, later successful author and public figure—had a complicated relationship with Greta Hofsten. In his autobiography, he expresses not only his lack of understanding, but also his lack of respect for her:

> She had descended from a higher position at the Swedish Labor Market Administration, and after that had undergone some sort of total transformation. She had a bowl haircut, began wearing old-fashioned blue worker's smocks and practical shoes, had stopped wearing makeup, and had taken a job as a postman. She had thus proletarianized herself . . . The strictness with which she made her change of class was quite unusual.¹⁸

It is clear that Jan Guillou did not understand Greta Hofsten, and during the most dramatic period of the IB affair, he had also gone behind her back.¹⁹ However, his text hints at a sort of grudging respect, which raises the suspicion that he might not have dared write what he did were Greta still alive and able to reply. At the same time, there is not much else to say about his characterization of her outward appearance, other than to note his teasing tone, which indicates that he never came to terms with her and may have felt the need to defend himself against her criticism. However, when Guillou comes to the theological reasons behind Hofsten's transformation and lifestyle choices, it is obvious that he did not at all understand what was going on:

> Greta suffered physically, and enjoyed it. She got up incredibly early in the morning to deliver mail before the political work began. I saw her as a deeply religious person, a Christian who found it necessary to suffer and go without, and thus be subjected to trials sent by God, so that after a life lived in His spirit, she might reach Heaven . . . Later on, Greta became extremely

---

17. Ehnmark, *Arvskifte*, 116f.

18. Guillou, *Ordets makt och vanmakt*, 166. Cf. how Guillou derisively claims that she exaggerated her change of social class: "She had disguised herself to the extent that even I could hardly recognize her as a member of the upper class, other than by a few expressions in her speech. I had not disguised myself." Ibid., 167.

19. For Guillou's own version of what happened when he went behind Greta Hofsten's back, as well as that of the rest of the board of directors, and of Greta's reaction, see ibid., 201–14.

Christian. Who the hell knows, she might even have worn a hair shirt under her blue mason's smock.[20]

It is strange to read these lines by Guillou. Despite his insightful portrayal of religious psychology in his internationally best-selling trilogy of historical novels about the medieval Swedish crusader Arn, which is full of depictions of how people viewed the world through religious eyes, he seems tone-deaf to the religious and moral thinking that Greta Hofsten developed.

Jan Stolpe, later a literary critic and translator, also worked with Greta Hofsten at *Folket i Bild/Kulturfront* during this stormy time. He gives a much more balanced picture of Greta's personality and spiritual psychology:

> It was easy to take her to be an enthusiast of self-flagellation, and to see her post job as some sort of working-class romanticism. But that is completely wrong. Greta Hofsten was a complex person who was seriously engaged in the issue of how to create a meaningful life in harmony with the deepest values and life experiences, without making compromises that were all too humiliating.[21]

This more composite image of Greta Hofsten is confirmed by her own writings in which she depicted her wanderings during the spiritual crisis she underwent after her religious awakening in March 1965, and which she later gathered in a book, *By Way of Conversation* (*Samtalsvis*, 1969). Originally, Greta intended these journal entries only as an aid to herself in her regular discussions with her spiritual advisor. In her entries from the years 1965–67, she writes that she wanted to "make it clear to myself what is happening" after having been "afflicted by faith" and after which, like Jacob at the ford at Jabbock, she wrestled with a God who did not seem to want to let go of her. The life that awaited her after she had taken her Kierkegaardian leap over a depth of seventy thousand fathoms was neither one of peaceful balance and harmony nor a pilgrim's self-flagellation with sights set on the coming glory. Such ambitions of holiness were foreign to her. Instead, for her it was a matter of finding a meaningful context for her life and work, based on an experience of radical grace. Not least of all, she sought to meet the realities of life in an uncensored

---

20. Ibid., 167.
21. Stolpe, "Greta Hofsten 1927–1996."

way: "I can honestly just say that I want reality."[22] Her faith and spiritual life were influenced by a profound materiality in a palpable way, clearly rooted in the experience of her own lived body. Her confrontation with reality would also be a severe one. In the past, Greta's well-developed intellect and her political and religious involvement had always allowed her to maintain rational control over her own life, but this control was now being broken down in a brutal and painful way. Her previous spiritual quest during the early 1960s had been focused on self-realization, as she sought to find balance in her existence through Buddhist and Hindu wisdom and meditational instruction. Now, however, she found herself drawn into a world of unceasing tension and battle; she faced a genuinely political and moral situation. Greta tells about the shock she felt when she realized that she actually shared responsibility for the poverty and suffering in the world, a shock that she had been able to effectively neutralize for twenty years. The radical experience of grace made it possible for her to open herself to this painful reality. In her existential battle of life and death, through what the mystics refer to as "the dark night of the soul," she came to identify herself strongly with the suffering Christ. In her own life, like Christ, she experienced a long and agonizing passion, and a very dark Good Friday. It would take a considerable time before she would be able to experience the first Easter morning of her own life: "All questions are now gathered around the cross. Here, there is no language to express it, no parallels, there is nothing other than a unique fact. Here, in the end, language refuses to serve its duty."[23]

In other words, this experience of faith was an imposition that in no way made life simpler for her. Instead, it was a major complication for her as she struggled to piece together the fragments of her life that were impossible to fit together into a harmonic order. On New Year's Eve 1965, she writes, "*This entire year:* my life has been shaken to its foundations by the disorder of grace! I must leave the order of grace behind. Wonderful!"[24] Greta's desire to be truly alive and meet life earnestly came at a high price. This was not a faith that bestowed harmony or offered a firm footing, yet neither was it a pilgrimage to some distant paradise;

22. Hofsten, *Samtalsvis*, 19.
23. Ibid., 30.
24. Ibid., 90. The "disorder of grace" *(nådens oordning)* is part of the anti-Pietistic rhetoric of Lars Ahlin's novel *Pious Murders (Fromma mord,* 1952). Cf. Gunnar D. Hansson, who fittingly used this expression as the title of his dissertation on Ahlin, *The Disorder of Grace (Nådens oordning).*

instead, it was as if everything in her life was falling apart. At the heart of her religious breakthrough was the experience of guilt, cross, suffering of the Passion and Good Friday, themes that form an obvious parallel to Wingren's grain-of-wheat eschatology. In contrast to categories such as *development, growth,* and *ascent,* faith instead forced her to face the necessity of *annihilation, diminishment,* and *descent.*[25] The way in which this remarkable chapter ends is significant for Greta's attitude toward life and for her dawning theological reflections: "I am prepared to lose my way many times over, to say yes to your no—but not without great trembling."[26]

Much later, in the mid-1980s, she described how she felt linguistically handicapped after having become a Christian through a terribly rapid and thorough process. She found herself standing before an existential chasm that she was unable to find language to describe. In addition, she had begun to visit St. James's Church (*Jakobs kyrka*) in central Stockholm to listen to organ concerts, which had helped draw her into a spiritual awakening. However, she felt compelled to filter the high church religious language that she encountered because it clashed completely with the political language that she knew so well, the language of "the Social Democratic worker's movement, of the local organizations of the social democrats, women's clubs, district congresses and the Worker's Educational Association."[27] It was not until she came into contact with the writings of Wingren that she found an appropriate theological language by which she could express her faith.

Greta Hofsten's spiritual journal from the middle of the 1960s hints at a somewhat sad daily experience, as she was often short of money and struggled to find time for all that she needed and wanted to do. She

---

25. Hofsten, *Samtalsvis*, 82.

26. Ibid., 171.

27. Hofsten, "Kristet språk och vänsterns språk," 3-5. In the conclusion of this article, she also presents a sort of vision for a functional radical theological grammar: "We need a language in order to be human, a language that liberates our identity. We need a language in order to be fellow human beings, a language to give expression to that which divides and that which unites, the combination of distance and proximity that makes a 'you-relationship' possible. We need a language in order to function as social beings, as political beings who can take part in collective work for a common, human future. We need a language as historical beings, a language that can make us aware of our past, the past in which every living community must be rooted. And finally: we need a language for the utmost, a language of faith for our hope and the sake of our healing." Ibid., 5.

attended communion almost daily, and she prayed: "After work and the practical chores of the day have taken what is theirs, I spend almost all of the time that is left over in prayer . . . But this turning in the direction of God increases the pain."[28] In the midst of this vulnerable situation, when language refused to serve its duty, there were also hints that this experience, which desperately sought a form of verbal expression, had begun to point Hofsten in the direction of Wingren's theology:

> I could also express it in this way, that if my decision in March 1965 was to a high degree a decision to accept the second article of faith, atonement, and the Savior; then, what happened in August was the culmination of at first my lack of clarity, then of growing tension, and finally a crisis in relation to the first article of faith, the Creator, and to my own existence as well.[29]

It is thus in the theological writings of Wingren that Hofsten found a language for expressing her faith. She was thus inspired by a theology based on creation theology, with a marked trinitarian structure, which rather than focusing on achievement and activism was based on the fundamental experience of both life and faith as a gift. However, this inspiration also ran in the opposite direction, in that Wingren was simultaneously taking important influences from Hofsten's social analyses and ideological criticism. In fact, it seems to have been Hofsten who showed him the way to the descent that he made in the 1970s. She had already made the three major life changes that radically changed her social position a number of years earlier than her soon-to-be husband. The first step was that, after having lived her life as a confirmed atheist, she became a Christian in the mid-1960s. The most significant factor behind this decision was the growing moral agony that she felt over Swedish labor market policies at the time. The second step was that, for this reason, she felt forced to leave the Social Democratic party. The third step was that she therefore felt that she also needed to leave her job as a bureau director at the Swedish Labor Market Administration. After several years of unemployment, Hofsten took a job as a postman, first in Stockholm and then in Malmö after her marriage to Wingren. She often related how well she got on in her new job, and how surprised she was by how much the camaraderie at her workplace meant for her. Hofsten's downward move, her descent, clearly served as a spiritual and political homecoming, and

28. Hofsten, *Samtalsvis*, 160.
29. Ibid., 167.

as a precursory model for the downward move that Wingren would make a few years later. Together they would take a journey that in theological terms would resemble a kenotic process in which they, using Paul's words in his letter to the Philippians, "emptied themselves of everything," but that in political terms could probably be described as a process of self-proletarianization.

Hofsten found important inspiration in Wingren's theology, but as early as the beginning of the 1970s there is also a powerful influence in another direction, noticeable in the strong inspiration Hofsten provided for Wingren's later authorship. Their relationship was a reciprocal one, and a pattern emerges in which their writing is interspersed, such that two distinct voices can always be discerned, each one presenting its reflections from the point of its respective sources. This can be clearly seen in such books as *A Small Catechism* (1983) and *The Courage of the Living* (1991). The very first major literary manifestation of this new partnership came in 1978 through a series of articles published in the daily newspaper *Sydsvenska Dagbladet*, which were later published as a book, *Faith and Alienation* (*Tro och främlingskap*, 1979). The work consisted of eight letters that present a mutual dialectical movement denoted by, on the one hand, "the way outward to the periphery" (Wingren), and on the other, "the way inward to reality" (Hofsten). Both authors claim that their faith had caused them to feel estrangement toward various unjust and inhuman circumstances—on Wingren's part, toward circumstances in the church, and on Hofsten's part toward circumstances in society. A closer examination of the letters they exchanged in this series is worthwhile, as it demonstrates in an exemplary way how their respective voices form a unified message.

Early in his first letter, Wingren describes his personal journey: "As a young man, I lived on the periphery of the church, and now I have returned to the periphery."[30] With concern, he tells of how he was quickly seduced by the feeling of being an important person when he became a clergyman, as well as the way in which he was charmed by the growing ingratiation of a milieu that began to see him as a rising power figure. He criticized a church that focused on the clergy and the problems of the clergy. The critique that he had cultivated for more than two decades was further strengthened by his acquaintance with Hofsten. He claimed that

---

30. Wingren, in Wingren and Hofsten, *Tro och främlingskap* (1978), 9.

the example of her life had played "a decisive role for me and the path I have chosen." He continues, in an almost ceremonious way:

> She was an atheist, had left the church, and held a relatively high position in a government institution. In the space of a few years, she took three steps: she rejoined the church and began attending worship services each Sunday, she became politically radical and left the political party most suitable to the furtherance of her career, [and] she resigned from her career and instead began working as a postman.[31]

Long before their relationship developed into a romantic relationship and during several years of conversations, critical and self-critical questions were raised about the spiritual stench Wingren experienced himself. He felt a distinct contrast to Hofsten, with whom people in broader society seemed willing to share their sorrow and degradation because she was not seen as a power figure but as a rehabilitator and liberator.[32]

Greta Hofsten's letters are based on the experiences that she had described in detail ten years earlier in her book *By Way of Conversation* (*Samtalsvis*, 1969) of the widening chasm between her own well-controlled life and the bloody drama of brutal reality. Rather than providing a path out of this painful experience, her journey into the Christian faith had led her on a path into life, toward an unreserved affirmation of life, and had brought her to confront her own existence and the life of every other person in an uncensored way:

> The challenge of faith, which I experienced as a disturbing interruption, as something which would not let me be, the challenge of the cross around which everything was at last gathered, was a challenge from reality itself: this is what it looks like; just as at Golgotha, everywhere in the world the cross is raised. Reality is neither harmonious nor in balance. To believe that it is so is to live a lie. Reality is struggle. And what are you doing? The recognition was forced out of me, that the price I had paid for my security was life itself. My well-organized existence, in which all experiences had been interpreted beforehand and placed into prearranged patterns, was lifeless. Death was already ruling life—the death of a lukewarm life.[33]

---

31. Wingren, in ibid., 10.
32. Wingren, in ibid., 12.
33. Hofsten, in ibid., 19.

The reality of faith brought Hofsten an increased awareness of the nearly bottomless need and suffering in the world. For several years she floundered in a theoretical vacuum in search of language adequate to express it. This was the spiritual crisis that she documented in the form of a diary in her book *By Way of Conversation* and that dominated her life until 1967, when she discovered the works of Wingren, an author whom she now began to read in a voracious and systematic way.[34]

Hofsten began weaving together the inspiration she took from Wingren's theology with the political analysis of society and culture that she had developed on her own. The resulting amalgamation is illustrated by the analysis of contemporary nihilism that she developed, based on the mystically shaded perspective of Gnosticism. The duality expressed in the Gnostic idea that the soul could be liberated from material imprisonment in the body through insight (*gnosis*) was made into an analogy by Hofsten, who sought thereby to develop a critique of both new spiritual movements and the ideologies she identified within the natural sciences, psychology, politics, and lifestyle consumerism. She felt that contemporary nihilism and the Gnosticism of the first centuries AD were united in their extreme antisocial individualism, in which their similarities emerge in a striking way over the course of seventeen centuries:

> When the world seems chaotic, and the future is filled with more threat than hope, and it becomes ever more difficult to find meaning in life, it is tempting to see human existence as slavery, a life in exile. Especially if, by way of your higher instincts, you are holding the keys of your prison cell in your hand, and have a passport and visa for passage to the homeland. Longing for a better world thus takes on the flavor of a pilgrimage, as does so much of spirituality. It becomes spirituality without any purpose toward the world, and without the will to change it according to the world's own, creation-given terms.[35]

Nevertheless, the price we have to pay for the lifeview of nihilism and Gnosticism is high, according to Hofsten. If we subscribe to this interpretation of life, we are also forced to give up the Christian confession of God as Creator of the world and all living things, a God who cares for bodies, food, and drink. The understanding of faith as a gift is thus also lost. From a theological point of view, the result is devastating: "What

---

34. Here, Wingren's article "Creation: A Crucial Article of Faith; My Selection of Topics" (1966/1971) played an important role.

35. Hofsten, "Klyvnad och troløshet," 76.

remains is a spirituality more spiritual than Jesus ever was, and much less human than he was. Or not human at all, but rather, nothing other than a flight from and a denial of that which is human."[36]

When Hofsten makes use of antique Gnosticism as an interpretive model for understanding contemporary nihilism, she also presents an interpretation of life that is nourished by a crisis of political-moral values. When the world becomes unbearable and no longer deals with human beings, the solution offered by the Gnostic-nihilistic idea of the soul's estrangement within the body, which can lead to either asceticism or hedonism, becomes as tempting as it is potentially devastating. This analysis of her times carries a definite echo of Wingren's works on the early church fathers.

The most important arena in which Hofsten articulated her philosophical view and political position was the tension between Christianity and socialism. The way in which she brought together these two major views of life in her thinking is clearly stated in a lecture she presented during a summer meeting of the Forum for Christian Socialists (*Forum før kristne socialister*) in Norway in 1978, where she had been invited to speak along with Martin Niemöller and Rudi Dutschke. In her lecture she made an unexpected use of Luther's Catechism, such that her definition of the Christian faith took on a decidedly trinitarian structure, as a belief in the Father, the Son, and Holy Spirit: "The Father, who created the world and continually creates anew ... The Son, who became human like us, yes, more than we are able to become, and who died to free those bound by oppression and sin in every age ... The Spirit, who calls us to fight the good fight for a more humane society."[37]

Quite the opposite of what might be feared when uniting Christianity and socialism, what Hofsten presents is not an activist theology, nor does she make an instrument of theology such that it is reduced to a weapon in her political battles. We could say that her horizontalization of the world is even more radical than that. Inspired by Wingren's creation theology, she instead sought a foundation for the Christian faith based on the gift:

> No education, no social class, no specific language, no special ethics, no particular lifestyle makes us Christian. No special characteristics, neither good nor for that matter bad, make us

---

36. Ibid.
37. Hofsten, "Kristna i kamp för socialism," 5.

Christian. Nothing more than this confession, this faith . . . Human life, received in faith.[38]

Yet this form of life, in which one gratefully receives his or her own existence as well as that of the other as a gift, is not one of harmony and health, but is a life filled with conflicts, tensions, and defeats. This echoes the conflictual interpretations of Luther developed by Bring and Wingren, in which life is always presented as a battle between good and evil. Hofsten, however, uses this perspective of conflict in a way that might be characterized as a sort of political theology. Furthermore, she speaks of the necessity of affirming a dialectical life between opposites, where we are not only spectators of the forces that battle for domination of the world but are ourselves involved to the utmost:

> For this reason, the life of faith is a battle, and not rest. To live dialectically means affirming the battle and joining it. It also means living in a provisory, living in an eschatological now . . . The Christian life is a life of opposites: living in faith is to live in the eschatological paradox. To affirm a limited and threatened now, in which nothing more certain than our individual deaths awaits us, and faith that the future is already present in the now, open and full of hope.[39]

After this determination of what it means to be Christian, she continues by qualifying the implications of the word *socialist*, a position that she maintains requires insight into the driving forces behind the development of society, the basic oppositions that characterize society, and the necessity of choosing a side in this opposition out of solidarity. Here, the possibility of choosing social class was important for Greta, not least in light of her upper-class background and her past as a prominent civil servant: "It may be a solidarity that you were born into, or one that you have chosen through a break with your original social standing. I would call this choice a class position."[40] In this text, Hofsten talks about socialism as a *necessary*, but not at all *sufficient*, prerequisite for a humane society. She describes socialism as "a risky venture, a social experiment that can go wrong" and that "has degenerated into openly inhumane societies" which "we can look upon coldly or embrace in burning sorrow," and which thus should also be strongly criticized. She introduces a sort

38. Ibid., 5.
39. Ibid., 6.
40. Ibid.

of eschatological corrective, when she dismisses any thought of a realized socialist human being, and instead emphasizes that such a human being can only be understood in terms of someone who is *in the making*. In the same context, she describes Christian socialism as an explosive combination, a standpoint that provokes upper-class Christians as well as atheistic socialists, and which demands comprehensive theological reflection and careful integration.[41] Hofsten's Christian socialism thus dismisses any possibility of ulterior motives or of making mere instruments out of either Christianity or socialism. Instead, she emphasizes perseverance, resistance, hope, and forgiveness as the virtues of Christian socialism.

Hermeneutical Mediations: Continuity through Change

When viewed *in toto*, Gustaf Wingren's authorship seems to be divided into two major sequences. In some ways, his theological system was complete and had been concluded by the 1950s; during the decade that followed, he more or less harvested the fruits of a long series of well-received books, which were being translated into several languages, but without producing anything that was really new. Then, however, during the 1970s and 1980s, it was as though he started to revisit all his sources and themes of his earlier, academically oriented works and recontextualized their contents in a new long series of books through the use of a social-political prism. The role that Greta Hofsten played in Wingren's theological recontextualization and personal metamorphosis was vitally important and far beyond the role she played as his spouse. It is interesting that in her own spiritual quest, after having discovered the writings of Wingren, Hofsten disclosed an *implicit* political theology in his books—of which he himself had not been aware. In the context of the year 1968, Wingren had recognized the new political left as something foreign and threatening; yet in his books, Hofsten had found the mediating link that she needed in order to be able to connect her newfound faith to her radical political stance: "Gustaf Wingren's creation theology gave me the most important basis for reflecting on the relationship between my Christian faith and my political convictions."[42]

41. Ibid., 8.
42. Hofsten in *Tro och främlingsskap* (1979), 24. Cf. "It is indiciative that these books helped me rework my political views, without my having much of an idea of the author's own political views." Ibid., 24.

One of my theses in this book is that anyone wishing to understand the logic of the development of Wingren's theological project during the 1970s and 1980s must be aware of the successive shift he made in the primary focus of his work: from academia to society. The prerequisite for the success of this maneuver was the earlier *turn toward practical knowledge* that he had made in the 1950s, beginning in 1949. While his earlier turn dealt with a move from a historical to a hermeneutical methodological approach, his later turn was a move from academy to society in which he expanded his theory of interpretation in a critical direction, in the form of a *critical* hermeneutics. From this point onward, he considered the primary aim of theology not only to write *history* or to *interpret*; his *historical* endeavors as well as his *interpretive* ones had to function first and foremost as *criticism*. He now transformed his entire systematic theology into social criticism. However, it was Greta Hofsten, before anyone else, who recognized this potential in his theology, and it was Hofsten who provided the impulse that launched the significant authorship that comprises Wingren's later works.

The creative repetitions that Wingren presented in his works during the 1970s and 1980s add unquestionably important elements to the unique character and strength of his theological project. His book *Theology in Conflict* (1954/1958) led to the later works *Change and Continuity* (1972) and *The Silent Interpreter* (1982). His *Luther on Vocation* (1942/1957) was followed by *A Small Catechism* (1983); and *Man and the Incarnation* (1947/1959) was followed by *Human and Christian* (1983). None of these later works were simple repetitions of his earlier writings; they were rather *creative* reinterpretations in which a new social context was actively generating new meanings in the texts.

The implications of the recontextualization that Wingren employed in his later authorship become most obvious when we compare the books in which he sought to present a comprehensive view of the Christian faith in its entirety, that is, in the two dogmatic works that he published. A comparison of his earlier two-part work *Creation and Law* (1958/1961) and *Gospel and Church* (1960/1964) with his book *Credo* (1974/1981) shows that the basic structure of the two are nearly identical. In both cases, the reader faces Wingren's unique dogmatic structure, in which two testaments and three articles of faith become four structuring concepts: creation, law, gospel, and church. This presentation is also characterized by its basis in the *acts* of God (along with the works of Einar Billing), which in the later works of Wingren generates a discussion about theorization as the great risk for any doctrine of faith. The fixation on the Revelation and the Bible as definite limitations of the work of God is "killing faith," according to Wingren's view.[43] This means that the interpretation of the human condition that Wingren elaborates as a rallying cry, so typical for him during that era—"Adam, that is 'we', 'I'"—is focused not on information but on life.[44] He explained the story of Jacob wrestling with God at the ford at Jabbock, stating that "one can wrestle with God without knowing his name, and one can be blessed by God without knowing the One who gives the blessing."[45] As previously, Wingren's creation theology provides a perspective that favors neither theology nor church; on the contrary, the first article of faith is directed as a critique against religious individuals and groups; it says that *"God is larger than the congregation."*[46] However, as a foundation of his presentation of the first article of faith we find the grain-of-wheat eschatology, centered on the death and resurrection of Christ, a baptismal theology that flows over into the paradoxical determination of what is distinctly Christian: complete judgment—and radical forgiveness.[47]

Readers who only take a quick look at the table of contents, the main source materials, and the three indexes at the end of the book may easily be led to believe that *Credo* is only to be considered a repetition of Wingren's dogmatics from fifteen years earlier.[48] But as a matter of fact, in this book we face a series of significant shifts of profound importance to Wingren's theological transformation.

Firstly, this book makes use of the *worship service* as a framework for the creed—a context characterized by certain practices. In the introduction to *Credo* he included a liturgical text, the creed (both the Apostles'

---

43. Wingren, *Credo* (1974/1981), 29-30. The words about "killing faith" are excluded from the English edition of the book.

44. Ibid., 37. Cf. Wingren, *Trons artiklar* (1986), 9-18.

45. Wingren, *Credo* (1974/1981), 38.

46. Ibid., 39.

47. Ibid., 69.

48. An examination of the dominant sources Wingren used for his systematic presentations of the Christian faith shows that his understanding was already articulated in the notes he jotted down in his dormitory room in Berlin in 1938: "Systematic theology must be pursued in constant contact with three determining elements: (a) the Old and New testaments, a central and comprehensive biblical theology, (b) Luther, a scholarship on Luther that never entirely ceases and is constantly renewed, and (c) the specific Swedish tradition, both that of the church and of systematic theology (from Billing to the present day." "Johanneum Journal," 112.

Creed and the Nicene Creed). He continues in the same way by including a number of prayers and hymns. The framework of a worship service in this book has been considered controversial, but we need to remind ourselves that this is a textbook and not a research report.[49] Along these lines, it is important to note the generous thanks that Wingren extends to a particular theologian, who probably played a much more important role in his work than has been recognized in general, namely, Gustaf Aulén. Wingren writes about Aulén as "Sweden's foremost author of textbooks on dogmatics." As always in his works, this book reflects how much Wingren was inspired by the dramatic structure in Aulén's interpretation of Christianity, as well as Aulén's profound interest in liturgy. In his foreword, Wingren also refers to conversations with Aulén and extends him effusive thanks: "It is a priceless privilege for me to be able to publicly thank Bishop Aulén for this."[50]

Secondly, *Credo* exhibits a *socio-political contextualization*. Earlier, we saw how Wingren acknowledged Hofsten in the foreword to his book, noting that she seemed to have found it easier than his university colleagues to swallow a textbook with rhyming sentences. The very first page of his foreword also signals the clear social context for a theology that has now taken on more political overtones. Although it is only an analogy, Wingren uses a vocabulary that is remarkable and that would have been inconceivable also for himself only half a decade earlier, during the 1960s, when he writes,

> Class interest is a central concept in Marxist ideology. It has its assigned place both in the exposure of "the anatomy of the bourgeoisie community" and in the liberating, forward-looking aspect of its theory, namely, the political victory of the working class. The working class ought to be driven by class interest; it is thus that the whole society is to be rescued.[51]

However, these statements do not indicate that the theologian had become a Marxist. Instead, Wingren uses comparisons with Marxism, as well as

---

49. In light of the fact that the author is a wordsmith of considerable skill, one might expect higher-quality results from these efforts: the prayers work well and have been frequently used, but the psalm texts have never really found any widespread use.

50. Wingren, *Credo* (1974/1981), 15.

51. Ibid., 12. Cf. the way in which this contrasts with two years earlier, when he spoke of "present-day socialistic dictatorships," and writes, "It cannot be a coincidence that all of the Marxist revolutions that we know of have resulted in dictatorships, and have become immoveable." Wingren, *Växling och kontinuitet* (1972), 178.

other life views, in order to propose a basic structure for the Christian faith. In regard to Marxism in particular, he raises objections to its view of destruction, namely, that we underappreciate that there is something "in the human being as such which hinders the development of the new socialist person."[52] With regard to humanism, he criticizes its individualism, its lack of recognition of the body, and its stress on the importance of human community. In this respect, he uses a Marxist concept of class as a corrective to the individualistic view of the human being found in humanism.[53] In regard to existentialism—although he draws together thinkers such as Martin Heidegger and Søren Kierkegaard in a somewhat confusing way as if they represented identical positions—he raises the issue of its lack of creation faith.[54] When elaborating on existentialism, he soon slides into a Danish context, in which he places Kierkegaard's lack of an idea of creation in juxtaposition to the prevalence of material images of eternal life, such as bodies, flowers, birds, and other natural phenomena, found in the theology of N. F. S. Grundtvig. Here, the final judgment is interpreted as the definitive expression of *recapitulatio*, which is by no means a matter of a reactionary regression into an original condition but rather is connected to the concept of a God who continually creates anew.

The reference to Grundtvig directs us to the third new component characterizing *Credo*, in comparison with Wingren's earlier dogmatic works from 1958/1961 and 1960/1964, namely, the profound importance of Danish philosopher K. E. Løgstrup (1905–81) of Aarhus University. In fact, *Credo* is the first book in which we face a more systematic influence from Løgstrup on the theology of Wingren. Løgstrup's ideas had of course been present in Wingren's work earlier on. The two Scandinavian theologians had first met in Basel during the summer of 1947 and had maintained contact and cooperated academically, although previously, Løgstrup had not been of such importance for the work of Wingren as he now receives. The index in *Credo* bears witness to this change, as it shows that Løgstrup is the most cited person in the book; only Martin Luther

52. Wingren, *Credo* (1974/1981), 149.

53. Ibid., 154–57.

54. Wingren sometimes distinguished himself as a surprisingly good reader of certain works by Heidegger, but in this context, his very use of these concepts is confusing. For example, he uses the concept of "existentialism" in a questionable way, allowing it to cover everything from Kierkegaard to Heidegger. Even more problematic is that he does not see that Heidegger's fundamental-ontological perspective is not at all an expression of a humanistic anthropocentrism, but rather part of a tradition that seeks to decenter the individual.

comes close to receiving as much attention as Løgstrup.[55] It is no exaggeration to state that with this book Løgstrup becomes The Philosopher in Wingren's theology. Furthermore, it is no coincidence that Wingren's foreword makes a special note of one of his graduate students, who wrote his dissertation on the Danish phenomenologist: "With regard to modern philosophy, I am less well read than is the docent in my field, Lars-Olle Armgard, and I engaged in a continuous exchange of ideas, and I think that I received more from him than he did from me."[56] The foreword also includes several pages introducing how a phenomenological philosophical analysis of the human situation may clarify the basic structures of a biblical perspective of life. By utilizing Løgstrup's terminology concerning spontaneous (given and definitive) and confining (locked-in and destructive) life-expressions, Wingren gained effective tools for demythologizing God and the Devil; and in the extension of Løgstrup's phenomenological description of a human existence in which "God's activity encounters opposition," they can actually be spoken of as life and envy.[57]

In 1972, two years before the release of *Credo* (1974/1981), Wingren published a book titled *Change and Continuity: Theological Criteria*. On one hand, this book may be recognized as a successor to *The Living Word* (1949/1960), but on the other, it may also be considered as a review of the theological criteria that directed the extensive recontextualization that Wingren accomplished from the 1970s onward. Through the titles of the four chapters—"Textual Continuity," "The Addressees," "Change," and "The Criteria"—this theological hermeneutics puts into play what might be described as a *confrontational analysis* that clearly places the perspective of conflict at the heart of the developmental logic of his theology: "Confrontation plays a decisive role for the factual, objective judgment of continuity and change in the history of Christianity."[58] The basic thesis, that continuity in the phenomenon we know as Christianity can only be maintained by change, is intended as a contribution to the field of

---

55. In his biography *Historien om K.E. Løgstrup*, Jensen describes Wingren as a Swedish "parallel phenomenon" to K. E. Løgstrup. Ibid., 122–23. He points out how they became sources of mutual inspiration for one another but feels that it was more a matter of Wingren taking inspiration from Løgstrup, an opinion that is supported by the relatively tiny role that Wingren plays in Jensen's presentation.

56. Wingren, *Credo* (1974/1981), 15.

57. Ibid., 267–69.

58. Wingren, *Växling och kontinuitet* (1972), 178.

religious studies and directed as a critique against the idea of faith as a phenomenon external to society. Like a two-edged sword, it is directed against Christian radicals, who tend to equate the message of the church with a progressive political ideology, and against conservative Christians, who want to defend Christianity as an invariable phenomenon.[59]

Here we can clearly recognize how Wingren employs a model in which formulations in the text are being *re-directed*, so that they may be intended for new audiences and take on new content. In effect, this is a sort of *re-addressing* that had paradigmatic importance for the great recontextualization that Wingren undertook in the 1970s and 1980s.[60] He takes his point of departure in Irenaeus and Luther's factual practice of Bible commentary, but in this context, he also includes numerous references to concrete examples from Marxist movements, apartheid regimes, and from other religions. Wingren's point is that Luther, in his battle against the medieval institution of indulgences, found himself in a completely different situation than Irenaeus, who faced Gnosticism as his enemy. This also means that Irenaeus and Luther were involved in completely different confrontations, and yet there is a clear continuity. The secret is that continuity is maintained by constant change, in accordance with this radically contextual understanding of the Christian faith: "There is no gospel above the environment. Gospel is *always* colored by a local, human, limited environment. A gospel raised above the limited human environment has never been historically transmitted to us."[61]

Change is connected with the necessity of recontextualization: it is quite simply necessary to say and do new things in order for the same phenomenon to recur and for the same thing to be achieved in new, concrete contexts. In accordance with this analogical theology, it would be meaningless for Luther to speak of circumcision in sixteenth-century Germany; instead, he must interpret, or *re-direct*, the text so that it makes an equivalent point in a new context. Today, we too, like Luther, must ask ourselves the following: "The question is where we stand *now*, what is *our* confrontation?"[62] Recontextualization is thus determined by the

59. Ibid., 9–10.

60. Ibid., 30.

61. Ibid., 23. Cf. how he maintains that "the gospel does not exist at all if it does not exist within a milieu, colored by that milieu and confronted by that milieu." Ibid., 24.

62. Ibid., 54. Cf. "The preacher is faithful to the Bible on only one condition, namely, if he brings something new." Ibid., 25. Textual continuity results in constant change; to emphasize this, Wingren presents three concepts: speech, listening, and use

contemporary confrontations in which theology is involved. A theology that seeks only to repeat an unchanging history will no longer be dealing with Christianity. Here, the grain-of-wheat eschatology once again serves as a model of interpretation, in that it describes a process in which the reader must die, in the sense that he or she must let go of his or her original understanding, in order for a new understanding to grow forth. As we saw in our examination of the book *The Living Word* (1949/1960), the gospels' basic christological structure of death and resurrection also functions as a theological hermeneutics in which the Christian faith is continually recontextualized in new situations. Death and resurrection are thus central not only to the texts of the New Testament but also to the process through which these texts are appropriated.

According to this theological hermeneutics, creation theology plays a decisive role in the determination of the situation of the addressees, since it indicates that God is always already present and active in the world, long before the gospel and the church come into existence. Wingren mounts a polemics against the idea of revelation, where Christ conveys knowledge of a God who has not entered the world before Christ, a position that Wingren ascribes partly to Barth and partly to Marcion.[63] In the framework of Wingren's hermeneutics, the addressees are given a key position in interpretation: "What comes 'out of' the texts depends to a large degree on what the addressees 'find themselves in.'"[64] But because the addressees are different, and because "the word in the text says more than what can immediately be realized in the milieu in which the text came into being," the contextualizing process of interpretation also serves

---

of pronouns. Ibid., 30, 48. He also uses Grundtvig to argue for the importance of one's mother tongue as an organ for company with God, in keeping with the image of Christ incarnate, and whose speech is presented in his mother tongue.

63 One of the consequences of creation faith is the idea of "a God who is greater than the church and who acts in the world, even where the church is not." Ibid., 74. According to Wingren, Karl Barth maintains that "the good must come from the church. God's direction of the human action are based on the place where human beings know something about God." Ibid., 76. Yet, because the addressees find themselves with the framework signaled by the idea of creation, he polemicizes against Marcion, who imagines God as "a remote island that no one has known." Ibid., 89. Wingren rejects the idea that the revelation in Christ conveys knowledge of God, who has not been present in the world before Christ. He uses the following argumentation: "This idea is not presented anywhere in the New Testament (if it were, the Old Testament text could not be used as holy scripture, a conclusion that Marcion quite correctly makes." Ibid., 89.

64. Ibid., 130.

as a specification of a contemporary meaning.[65] It is this relationship that makes change a necessary prerequisite for maintaining continuity in the interpretation of the Christian faith.[66]

Two years after retiring, Wingren published *Creation and Gospel: The New Situation in European Theology* (1979/1979), a book that summarizes and, I would like to posit, subsequently seeks to correct the picture of his own theological project for the reader. The book was written specifically for English-speaking readers, which has the advantage that it requires the author to examine and make explicit his own assumptions, to explain things that may have been taken as obvious but that can easily become invisible in one's mother tongue. In this book, the horizon of understanding for creation and law is provided by secularization theology and the perception that work, in contemporary society, has been robbed of its meaning, while the horizon of understanding for gospel and church are provided by K. E. Løgstrup's anthropology and nonreligious Christian interpretation of life, along with the church's reticent position. In this way, the same four dogmatic concepts that Wingren had used earlier now once again function as organizing principles for his systematic theology.

Creation and Gospel also involved the two dialectical configurations that guided the great recontextualization that occurred in Wingren's theology during the 1970s and 1980s: first, a *synchronic* dialectic between openness and individuality, and second, a *diachronic* dialectic between change and continuity. This double dialectical model should not be considered as some sort of compromise or a balancing act. Rather, these dialectics presume that the recognition of that which is present in one pole is also always implicitly present in the other, as well as an interplay between opposites that presuppose one another. First and foremost, however, it is the recognition of new meaning being created. To emphasize this idea, and to limit the perception that this is a matter of compromises or balancing acts, it might be helpful to reword Wingren's concept of "change

---

65. Ibid., 132.

66. Cf. "That the 'gospel' in practice brings with it different sorts of definitions of the meaning of the biblical word for different people does not imply contradiction or theological conflict between these people. The differences in interpretation exist in the New Testament, and they must exist there if the gospel is to be the gospel, that is, a message that brings liberation and support to the milieu of the listener. The four gospels tell of the same events; they paint four different pictures of Christ, and this is done for the sake of the addressees: only through variety can the unified gospel reach individuals in their different milieus (those of language, terminology, and ways of thinking) in order to bring liberation in that situation." Ibid., 159.

and continuity" as "continuity *by* change." In the same way, his concept of "openness and individuality" might better be reworded as "individuality *by* openness," entirely in keeping with the following statement by Wingren: "Individuality does not decrease the openness of the church, but increases and radicalizes its openness."[67] And furthermore: "The continuity of Christianity can paradoxically only by preserved by change."[68]

Since his grammar school years, Wingren had a strong interest in literary fiction. Prominent Swedish poets such as Gustaf Fröding, Verner von Heidenstam, and Erik Axel Karlfeldt had made a strong impression upon him. He was able to recite many of their poems by heart, and their work influenced his use of language in profound ways.[69] As an adult, Wingren regularly wrote newspaper and magazine reviews of new works by leading Swedish fiction writers. Later, he took significant cultural impulses from Greta Hofsten, who had a considerable network within the Swedish cultural sphere. Another important influence on his personal cultural development was the Sigtuna Foundation, as it developed during the leadership of Olov Hartman. Another influence came from Margit Sahlin, one of the first women ordained as a minister in the Church of Sweden and the founder and longtime director of the St. Katharina Foundation (*S:ta Katharinastiftelsen*). In addition, K. E. Løgstrup was an inspiration regarding the use of literary fiction as a source for theological reflection.[70] Not only did Wingren take inspiration from literature, he was himself a source of inspiration for literary writers, including the author Lars Ahlin. However, it was not until his later writings that Wingren made explicit and programmatic use of literature as a source for theological thinking. In the foreword to the collection titled *Grief and Grace in Swedish Literature* (1991), in which Hofsten gathered several of Wingren's essays and some jointly written texts, he wrote, "Oddly enough, the Christian faith is often articulated more clearly there than from our church pulpits."[71]

---

67. Wingren, *Öppenhet och egenart* (1979), 8 (this quote only in the Swedish edition)..

68. Wingren, *Växling och kontinuitet* (1972), 10.

69. Karlsson, *Predikans samtal*, 287–88.

70. Cf. the way in which Wingren writes in his memoirs, emphasizing how important Løgstrup was for him to begin using culture and literary fiction as sources for his theological reflections: "Previously, I had been somewhat unilaterally focused on professional theologians." Wingren, *Mina fem universitet* (1991), 134.

71. Wingren, *Tyngd och nåd i svensk skönlitteratur* (1991), 5.

When Wingren approached literary fiction, he did not use a religious microscope in search of pious code words or spiritual experiences that point the direction to another, religious world. Instead, he employed a sort of literary analysis to elicit what he referred to as a *hidden* theology in the seemingly unreligious. The dialectical relationship between life and storytelling provides a context in which we may perceive the often incomprehensible basic biblical pattern. In an analysis of Lars Ahlin's novel *Night in the Market Tent* (*Natt i marknadstältet*, 1957), he states:

> But Paulina *lives* in that way. She lives, without theology, and without quotations from the Catechism. To depict her existence in an epic way is to depict the gospel, and thus a novel writer in our day risks being seen as incomprehensible.[72]

Entirely in keeping with his interpretation of Luther, Wingren believed that God is at work in everyday life, but as if hidden behind a mask, in the human experiences of suffering and joy as well as in the erotic love between man and woman. At the center of Wingren's interest we find a sort of narrative theology, focused on the narrative structure itself. Instead of religious terminologies, quotations, or references, Wingren is focused on the epic depiction itself to identify how the configuration of the human existence itself may serve as a Christian interpretation of life. In these contexts Wingren locates more of the reality of the grain-of-wheat eschatology than an elevated sense of life. Furthermore, there is an obvious political dimension in his focus on the lowest and weakest and those on the fringes of society. It is, in other words, not a matter of stories with a happy ending. Wingren is rather carried by a conviction that the broken life that we all live is a life in God, and that only those who relinquish their grip on life will be saved: "Arching above each human destiny is God, he who also knew a human destiny, laid in the manger, and hung on a cross."[73]

Two prominent Swedish authors held special positions in Wingren's literary universe: Lars Ahlin (1915–97) and Sara Lidman (1923–2004). Thanks to Hofsten, Wingren formed a personal relationship with both of them. Sara Lidman was an old friend of Greta Hofsten from her days in the solidarity movement. Lars Ahlin lived just a few hundred meters away from her in the Äppelviken section of Bromma, in the house the Swedish Writers' Association had made available to him and his wife,

72. Ibid., 23–24.
73. Ibid., 13.

Gunnel. Over the years, Wingren and Hofsten made many visits to the Ahlin home for conversations and mutual exchange of ideas. Wingren had in fact nurtured plans to write about the works of Ahlin as early as the 1950s but had hesitated due to the difficulties inherent in the sources. Two decades passed before he finally did so, and it was Greta Hofsten who put the process in motion and who brought about a personal relationship between Gustaf Wingren and Lars Ahlin.

It is clear that the influences between Wingren and Ahlin flowed in both directions, in the sense that the theology of Wingren also influenced Ahlin in his work as a writer and novelist. Wingren saw Ahlin as a modern equivalent to Sweden's beloved eighteenth-century poet, songwriter, and composer, Carl Michael Bellman (1740–95). Like Bellman, Ahlin portrays the lower levels of society and the individuals who inhabit them, while depicting poverty in an almost stately way. In their depictions of ragged human existence, both employed a sort of humor that avoided comic ridicule or sympathetic sentimentality. As with Bellman, Ahlin's form of expression, although burlesque, is nonetheless characterized by respect and warmth. Wingren found that Ahlin's novels were remarkable in that "he maintains an attitude toward the downtrodden that is *Christian*, founded upon faith."[74] Ahlin's works are not to be considered as "religiously edifying literature that transcends death." Rather, they are focused on everyday suffering, by which we may die many times before our actual day of death comes, as for example when a person accepts the blame for a wrongful act, without seeking to flee: "To sacrifice oneself and die before dying is the only thing that gives meaning to life."[75] In *Grief and Grace in Swedish Literature* (1991), Wingren presents an analysis of Ahlin's systematic use of classical baptismal terminology to interpret human existence. Using a voice that sounds almost like Luther, Wingren examines how baptism serves as a paradigmatic model for the performance of our daily work for the good of our fellow human beings: "I want us to die with open eyes and a willingness to take up the cross every day. Our death is life; this is how it is. Each day, we receive life from the death of others."[76] Yet, this baptismal narrative is never transformed into a program or a common thread that we can clearly identify in our own lives. It remains the result of a paradoxical interpretation of what it

---

74. Ibid., 22.
75. Ibid.
76. Ibid., 23.

means to become human, a process that is otherwise incomprehensible: "Lars Ahlin is unfathomable, bottomless as a biblical text."[77]

In his dissertation on Lars Ahlin's novel *Pious Murders* (*Fromma mord*, 1952), Gunnar D. Hansson, poet and later professor at the University of Gothenburg, highlights the importance of Wingren for Ahlin's work. Hansson maintains that Wingren's *Luther on Vocation* (1942/1957) was "of the utmost importance for Ahlin when he wrote *Pious Murders*" and was in fact a guiding force for him in his work.[78] Wingren's treatment of Luther's concept of *Stundelein* (the time) as a localized, time- and situation-bounded identification of the paradoxical position of human beings as both free and unfree in creation strongly influenced Ahlin's literary depiction of the human condition. Gunnar D. Hansson refers to poet Karl Vennberg, who stated that Ahlin had found "support for [his] creative process" in Wingren's study on Luther and emphasized that the problem faced by the character of Aron in Ahlin's novel was in fact formulated in accordance with Luther's teachings on vocation.[79] In his portrayal of the process of becoming fully human, Ahlin uses the baptismal message of dying and being buried with Christ, so that all earthly life becomes a life of resurrection. He maintains that in this way, the mystery of love between the characters of Aron and Evangeline "bears the characteristics of both death and affirmation at one and the same moment."[80] Anders Tyberg follows Gunnar D. Hansson's line of thought, but also points out how Ahlin's special form of rhetoric, in which the spoken word and those who receive it are focused in a specific way, may be linked back to Wingren's book *The Living Word* (1949/1960).[81]

During the period 1978–86, Greta Hofsten and Gustaf Wingren coauthored (as an exceptional example of producing common texts) a series of articles about author Sara Lidman's five-novel Railway Epic about the colonization and modernization of the Norrland region of northern Sweden.[82] In the 1970s, after university studies, a career as a successful

---

77. Ibid., 25. Cf. the very title of Wingren's review of Lars Ahlin's novel *Night in the Market Tent* (*Natt i marknadstältet*, 1957): "Lars Ahlin = gospel = incomprehensibility" ("Lars Ahlin = evangelium = obegriplighet"), originally published in *Sydsvenska Dagbladet*, 5 January 1975.

78. Hansson, *Nådens oordning*, 113, 115.

79. Ibid., 272–73.

80. Ibid., 347. Cf. 346.

81. Tyberg, *Anrop och ansvar*, 83ff.

82. Sara Lidman's Norrland Epic is comprised of five novels: *Din tjänare hör*

writer and international activist working on behalf of Vietnam and South Africa, Lidman had returned to her home village of Missenträsk in Norrland. Gustaf and Greta visited Sara at Missenträsk several times, and these visits were significant for all three of them. The first visit occurred at the end of August 1982, just before their departure for the conference of *Societas Ethicas* in Dubrovnik in the former Yugoslavia. The second visit took place in November 1984. An overview of their schedule during that visit gives a good idea of what the many joint lecture tours that Wingren and Hofsten undertook during that time could entail: first, Wingren preached at a special worship service at Luleå Cathedral, after which both Wingren and Hofsten participated as special guests at a retreat, speaking on the topic of "The Theology of Luther in His Small Catechism." Wingren then addressed the Luleå chapter of the Swedish Christian Students' Movement on the topic of "On the Side of Life, Against the Destruction"—and finally, they made their way to Missenträsk.

In their joint readings of Sara Lidman's railway novels, Wingren and Hofsten used the creation story as their model of interpretation. Writing in the dialect of northern Sweden, Lidman portrays the struggles of the far-flung inhabitants of Norrland to break their isolation and join the rest of modern Sweden by having a railway brought to their region. This story about the conditions for achieving full humanity echoes the narrative of the suffering Christ, who died outside the walls of the city. The book portrays heavy manual labor and drudgery performed "in the sweat of their brows" as a life "after the fall." Unbearable living conditions and the desperate struggle for survival foster anger and wrath among the people. In their analysis of the novels, Wingren and Hofsten state not only that this anger is "closely related to love,"[83] they even recognize it as a tool used by God to create life—an idea taken from Luther's concept of the law. In Lidman's story, this divine wrath is blended with the rhetoric of revivalist preachers and ancient heathen traditions. The tragedy of Didrik, the main character, is that the railway that he has fought so hard to obtain does not improve the living conditions of the poor local inhabitants. Their oppression by the rich continues, and the day when the railway is finally to be dedicated finds Didrik on the train in handcuffs, en route to his prison sentence in Stockholm. Yet, the overall story ends not in tragedy but in a paradoxical interpretation of the great mystery of the creation, that of

---

(1977), *Vredens barn* (1979), *Nabots sten* (1981), *Den underbare mannen* (1983), and *Järnkronan* (1985), amounting to more than fourteen hundred pages all told.

83. Wingren and Hofsten, *Tyngd och nåd i svensk skönlitteratur* (1991), 66.

realizing the fullness of humanity: "The savior has gone down into Hell, into our anguish."[84] Wingren's and Hofsten's joint theological reading of Sara Lidman's Railway Epic brings out an inner connection between life and work, something that they believed had been made invisible, given the way that the modern Swedish welfare state had normalized the condition of unemployment.

Is There a University in Valdemarsvik?

The summer of 1989 found the seventy-year-old Gustaf Wingren at Revhaken in the southern Swedish town of Åhus, an area of gleaming white sand beaches on the Baltic Sea. It was there that Greta Hofsten's first husband, Henrik Petrén, had purchased a summer house in 1940. The house had been passed down from Henrik and Greta to their two sons, Finn and Kåre, and family and friends often gathered there during the summer months. As so often, Wingren was hard at work during these days, outlining the major features of what he intended to be his intellectual autobiography. In his journal entry for 8 June he wrote that he had "conceived" what later would become the book *My Five Universities: Memories* (1991) on exactly that date in the pine forest behind the sand dunes of Revhaken. After taking his usual period of time to elaborate on and think out the structure of the new book, he finally decided on a sampling of the universities that had been the most important to him and that had provided him with the most significant impulses in his theological work. He counted his five universities to be Lund (Sweden), Berlin (Germany), Basel (Switzerland), Århus (Denmark), and Oslo (Norway).

Six months later, however, on 28 January 1990, he had changed his mind, and he reworked his outline. In the style of Maxim Gorky, he had broadened his definition of the word *university* to include places that had made significant impressions on him, regardless of whether they were actually centers of higher academic education. He wanted to describe "the forces that have shaped me"[85]—and so decided to include Valdemarsvik, the little manufacturing town on the Swedish east coast where he grew up, among his most important "universities." To keep his planned number to five, he had to remove one of the other universities from his book, and the choice fell on Oslo. I maintain that Wingren's decision

---

84. Ibid., 71.
85. Wingren, *Mina fem universitet* (1991), 13.

to include Valdemarsvik as one of his universities shows the high level of consciousness he had developed about how important nonacademic sources had been for his thinking as a theologian.

As the son of a tanner from Valdemarsvik, Wingren had made a rather phenomenal social ascent. His successes at Lund and on the international theological scene meant that he had become increasingly more separated from the environment of his youth. It seems that his homesickness became the most acute when he finally realized that he would never truly be able to return home. As we have seen earlier in this book, he had commented on the importance of his childhood for his choice of career in an article he wrote for the journal *Vår lösen* in 1966 (translated and reprinted as chapter 1 in *The Flight from Creation*, 1971). But with the great process of recontextualization that occurred in his work during the 1970s and 1980s, he turned his own past into source material by making it an explicit part of his theological work. This process also made it clear to him that Valdemarsvik had indeed been one of his most important universities. It is evident that it is his relationship with Greta Hofsten that helped him realize how important Valdemarsvik actually had been for his theological work, and joining forces with her had put him into more intense professional contact with his own past.

Reading Wingren's intellectual autobiography *My Five Universities* (1991) today, one is struck by the idyllic tone and the author's tendency to idealize the past. This stands in sharp contrast to childhood days that seem to have been anything but happy for him. Valdemarsvik has never had, and probably never will have, a university, and yet he came to a gradual, growing insight that this place had made a vital impact on him and had directed the course of his life as an intellectual. He goes through a long process of redefining the term *university*, and re-evaluates the intellectual importance of his childhood—and in the end, he finds that Valdemarsvik had indeed been a university to him. It is said that it is never too late to have a happy—or unhappy—childhood. Perhaps in the same way, it is never too late to discover the factors and sources of inspiration that have shaped one's intellectual life.

For Wingren, there was yet another important element, which he referred to in his autobiography as his "sixth university," namely, the circle of young theologians and others who regularly gathered at Wingren's and Hofsten's apartment at Warholmsgatan 6B in Lund.[86] He relates how much

---

86. Ibid., 173ff. Cf. Wingren's article "My Six Universities" ("Mina sex universitet," 1983), which does not, however, tie into the meaning that he gives this concept in his autobiography.

he had learned from his contact with these students, who lived their lives on the margin of the academic world: "As a professor, I knew a lot about source materials written in ancient languages, but almost nothing about society. Now I know much more about the actual conflicts in society."[87]

Because the idea of salvation as restoration and completion of creation (*recapitulatio*) had taken on political dimensions for him, Wingren now found the need to identify a clearer political aspect also in his childhood. The way in which he projected the ideals he had embraced from the 1970s onward invites the current reader to deconstruct his presentation. Using such an analysis, we may disclose the story *underneath* this story.

In Wingren's memory, life in Valdemarsvik emerges as the ideal image of Luther's view on everyday work. Also the historical examination, which comprised Wingren's doctoral dissertation, had taken its direction and intensity from Valdemarsvik's organic world of everyday manual labor and drudgery. With his political conversion, his theological project took a corresponding sociological turn. As a result, as he analyzed his first university in Valdemarsvik, he seemed to be motivated by a strong need to identify in it the same values he had found in his sixth university among students in Lund. This led him to idealize, and this idealization was heightened in particular when he came to the subject of his father, Gustaf Fabian Wingren, who became the hero in his son's autobiographical portrayal of Valdemarsvik. In his story, Gustaf Fabian stands out as the very icon of a conscientious worker in an organic community in which everything is tied together, a world full of a Lutheran spirit. The life of Valdemarsvik was in fact full of deeds without name, serving as an expression of the hidden presence of the divine on earth. In keeping with Wingren's need to make identifications, Gustaf Fabian thus becomes The Worker—although he was not truly a worker, since by the time he became a shop foreman he belonged to the other side in labor negotiations with the workers. His father's relationship with his family thus became more difficult when one of his daughters, Maj, married the chairman of the local workers' union.

While I certainly believe that it is important for us to take Wingren's autobiographical writings seriously, we should not do so unreservedly. Once again, we must remember that it is never too late to re-evaluate one's past and discover that certain places, individuals, and times have had a greater importance in one's development than had been realized.

---

87. Wingren, *Mina fem universitet* (1991), 174.

Yet, perhaps there were other things that Wingren learned at the University of Valdemarsvik. Besides the great catastrophe of his mother's untimely death and the chaos that followed, the family home was also dominated by a violent man who sometimes lashed out unexpectedly, especially if he had been drinking. When things were at their worst, the father would retreat to a small cabin in the forest to distance himself from society and from alcohol, and would not come back until he was completely sober. Thus, Gustaf Fabian seems both threatening and fragile. The children avoided confronting him, not only because of the risk of receiving a beating but also out of sympathy for a man who had been dealt a hard life. Might it be that Gustaf Wingren took out some of the rebellious anger he felt toward his father against Anders Nygren instead? This is pure speculation, and yet not an entirely unreasonable thought. In any case, it does not change the fact that there were obvious and real differences of opinion between Wingren and Nygren.

In addition, the life story cultivated by Wingren's new partner, Greta Hofsten, may also be deconstructed. She often claimed that her early childhood was not at all as wealthy and well-established as might be expected for a family who lived in a large home in the exclusive Stockholm suburb of Djursholm. She relates that they had to scrimp on how much butter they spread on their bread and that the younger children had to wear mended clothing handed down from their older siblings. She made it seem that the lack of money was a recurring topic of conversation in the family. While wartime rationing certainly affected even the upper levels of Swedish society, the fact remains that Greta began life in one of the finest homes in Djursholm, which was later purchased by world-famous film and theatre director Ingmar Bergman. The new home to which the Bagger-Sjöbäcks moved in Malmö was also exclusive and was the scene of frequent dinner parties with stars from the early Swedish film industry. Greta's mother was descended from the powerful Bagger family of Denmark, further reinforcing the image of a well-heeled childhood. It was this background that Greta sought to escape. Her siblings must have felt some of these impulses, too, for several of them became politically radical as well. One factor in the children's radicalization was the conflicts they experienced in school with classmates and teachers who sympathized with Nazi ideology during the 1930s and 1940s. It is another matter that the entire family became left-leaning and identified with the Swedish Social Democratic Party. In the final analysis, it was probably the case that even Greta Hofsten sometimes felt the need to claim a more radical background than the one in which she had actually grown up. Perhaps this was merely an expression of her desire to tone herself down and live an ordinary human life.

6

The Final Academic Battlefield

GUSTAF WINGREN RETIRED IN 1977 after an academic career spanning more than forty years. His position as a tenured professor at Lund University had allowed him to fully engage himself in his work. The basic structure and frame of reference for his theological project were largely complete by the 1950s and were magnificently concluded with the Swedish edition of his book *Gospel and Church* (1960/1964). In any case, he penned no other books of the same caliber or scale for the rest of the 1960s.

Then came some dramatic changes. The sixty-year-old professor underwent a metamorphosis. Beginning in the 1970s, his theological creativity flowed anew, and he authored a long series of significant works with an energy that was brought to a halt only by old age, in the 1990s. The theological ideas that he developed in his later authorship were the fruit of a radical recontextualization that transformed his theology into a critique of civilization. He underwent a metamorphosis on a personal level as well. Together with Greta Hofsten, he embarked upon a kenotic process of descent, or as I might call it, a process of self-proletarianization. When he set aside his academic guise, he seemed almost ecstatic over the experience of being part of society—mainstream society—which then also became the most important context for his theological work.

However, no more than four years passed before he was tempted to return to the academic battlefield. In doing so, he re-employed every theological resource he had at his disposal to launch what would be his second great attack against the leading contemporary representatives of theology. His first major attack on theology had occurred in 1954 with his book *Theology in Conflict: Nygren, Barth, Bultmann*. However, this time his perspective was limited to Sweden. Even though the ideas that he presented contained some very important points, they caused theological conflicts and confusion that hardly helped his purpose or his reputation. Let us begin this chapter by looking back in time.

Echoes from 1949

Two important books on theology were published in Sweden in 1949. As we have already mentioned several times, this was the year when Gustaf Wingren published his controversial book *The Living Word* (1949/1960). The same year saw the release of another controversial book that would have a huge effect on the discussion of theology and worldviews in Sweden as well as on the general intellectual climate in which Wingren's theological project would come to be viewed, *Belief and Reason* (*Tro och vetande*, 1949), by philosophy professor Ingemar Hedenius. Although it was a coincidence, it almost looks as though the release of *The Living Word* and *Belief and Reason* had been planned. The two books were influenced by two widely divergent ways of thinking and are seemingly unrelated, and yet, considered as a pair, they denote the two opposite poles of the public discussion in Sweden about religious faith and worldviews—two poles that set the agenda for the theological discussion in Sweden for years to come.

The final years of the 1940s saw the publication of a number of significant books in Sweden. Author Vilhelm Moberg published his four-novel epic, *The Emigrants* (*Utvandrarna*), and Astrid Lindgren embarked upon a career that made her a world-renowned children's author. Elsewhere, French philosopher Jean-Paul Sartre published his programmatic work, *Existentialism Is a Humanism*, which initiated a great debate with many international offshoots that have lasted to the present day. One year later, German philosopher Martin Heidegger countered Sartre with an essay that also became a classic—"Letters on Humanism." However, these events were taking place in other parts of the world.[1]

That year in Sweden, Professor Anders Nygren followed his older academic teacher and colleague, Bishop Gustaf Aulén, by making the transition from university to church to become a bishop. Two years later, Wingren assumed Nygren's professorship in systematic theology after a long, hard competition. Not everyone appreciated Wingren's

---

1. In sketching the contours of the historical context, I have benefited greatly from Hans Ruin's essay "Filosofen som hade rätt men fel" ("The Philosopher Who Was Right, yet Wrong"), published in *Dagens Nyheter*, 23 January 2010, on the occasion of a new publication of Hedenius' *Tro och vetande* (1949) in 2009.

appointment. In the daily newspaper *Stockholmstidningen*, lawyer and legislator Vilhelm Lundstedt went so far in his criticism as to call this event an antidemocratic encroachment: "Never has the choice between scientific and unscientific views been clearer than in this case. Contrary to the suggestions of the Academic Council and the Chancellor [of universities], the government has chosen to award the victory to the unscientific viewpoints."[2]

Yet as we know, the situation was not at all so simple. Wingren had enjoyed support from the faculty as well as area experts, the best informed persons regarding this appointment, and thus the fact that some perceived his appointment as a scandal must be understood in light of the very special intellectual spirit that prevailed in Sweden at this time. To gain perspective on this particular event, we must again broaden our view from text to context—while reminding ourselves that contexts are phenomena that change over time. Sometimes, the changes are quite dramatic.

Because *Faith and Reason* and *The Living Word* were published in the same year it was not possible for the authors to comment on each other. Nevertheless, they gained an opportunity to do so later as they looked back on the literary events of 1949. In 1959, Ingemar Hedenius (1908–82) described the new star of systematic theology in Lund, Professor Gustaf Wingren, in the following way:

> Wingren made his debut as a student of Professor Nygren (later Bishop Nygren), and with the help of this great mentor, he was ushered into his professorship. In his very inaugural lecture, he strongly distanced himself from Nygren's theology, and today stands out as an independent thinker, in whom many hopes have been placed.[3]

However, these expectations were in vain, according to Hedenius, as evidenced by the drivel that he felt he discovered in Wingren's foremost work as professor, namely, *The Living Word*: "Its contents are so confused that finding a single reference that might determine his points of departure, conclusions or even his objects of study and basic idea is hardly possible."[4] Meanwhile, Wingren's evaluation of Hedenius was hardly any milder. He

---

2. Lundstedt, "Vetenskap eller trosförkunnelse som merit för professur?," *Stockholmstidningen*, 1 May 1951.

3. Hedenius, "De teologiska fakulteternas framtid," 43.

4. Ibid., 45. His use of the word "drivel" occurs on the following page.

regarded Hedenius as a joker who was hard to take seriously, since it seems that he was making fun of his readers. Regarding Hedenius' book *Faith and Reason*, Wingren wrote in an article published in 1950 that it was difficult to determine whether "Hedenius had consciously chosen the path of the warrior" or whether it was all simply some sort of macabre farce, since this was a book "which during the summer months last year became the success of the season, and which even today is still a folk farce of high value."[5] Many years later, Wingren made a clear reference to Hedenius in his autobiography when he stated, "I have always tended to find questions of the existence of God to be afflicted with a certain degree of intellectual weakness, a bit stupid in their very formulation."[6]

Belief and Reason gained wide acceptance in Sweden and gave rise to the greatest debate on theology and religious belief in Sweden during the twentieth century. In his book on the Hedenius debate, Johan Lundborg writes, "After this, nothing was ever the same again in regard to the question of religious belief or unbelief in Sweden."[7] Hedenius' book shaped the philosophical prerequisites and the cognitive infrastructure that would be used by several generations of Swedes in their conversations about theology and Christian faith. However, the book as well as the debate remained a purely Swedish phenomenon. One major reason for Hedenius' rise to celebrity was the tone he used in his attacks on a whole series of Swedish bishops, which was at once both cheerful and without respect. Hedenius presented the archbishop of Sweden, Erling Eidem, as "officially *primus inter pares* in this entire series of religiously uninteresting administrators and dissertation writers, moral weapons dealers and tacticians, who are called Sweden's bishops."[8]

Ingemar Hedenius was a member of a prominent, religious family of doctors in Stockholm. His father was eventually appointed private physician to the King of Sweden, and his grandfather had served as president of Uppsala University, the institution where Ingemar Hedenius would spend his entire academic career and where, in 1947, he was appointed

---

5. Wingren, "Tro och sanning" (1950), 20–21, 10. In his dissertation, Karlsson has shown how Wingren also worked significant portions of "Tro och sanning" into the sermon he gave on 7 April 1950. Karlsson, *Predikans samtal*, 211–18.

6. Wingren, *Mina fem universitet* (1991), 23.

7. Lundborg, *När ateismen erövrade Sverige*, 7. For a detailed presentation of the philosophical infrastructure in an era dominated by characters such as Ingemar Hedenius, cf. Sigurdson, *Den lyckliga filosofin*.

8. Hedenius, *Tro och vetande*, 141.

professor of practical philosophy. Yet it was in his alliance with another professor, Herbert Tingsten from Stockholm, who by this time had become editor-in-chief of the major Swedish newspaper *Dagens Nyheter*, that Hedenius became known as a man who created controversy.[9] In his 1949 book, he made a frontal attack against the leading Swedish theologians. While many of these men had left university life by this time and become bishops, it was their earlier academic works that Hedenius scrutinized and declared unscientific, or in the best case described as expressions of "quasi-science." Because these professors had now become bishops, Hedenius was also able to bring together his criticisms of theology and of the church. In addition, because bishops at that time (far more than today) were part of the powers that be in Sweden, Hedenius was able to present himself as an underdog who happily and mischievously cried out, "The emperor has no clothes!" Hedenius claimed in his book that theology contains purely logical self-contradictions, and in addition, it presupposes personal faith on the part of its practitioners. Much of Hedenius' book had first appeared in Tingsten's newspaper in the form of articles, but its introduction was a newly written essay that had given its name to the entire book, *Belief and Reason*, the dominant theme of which was an attack by Hedenius on what he called "the hard-boiled school of thought," namely, Lundensian theology.[10] Anders Nygren's ideas about religion as an independent realm of experience seemed to make all philosophical objections impossible, and Hedenius dismissed this Schleiermacher-like model of thought as empty speculation and an unsustainable position for theology. In a section on "The Lundensian Theologians and the Truth," in which these "apologists" in actuality stand out as "a theology in decline, a systematic sense of shame over the gospel," he maintained, "Nygren ought to hold God's existence as true, in order for his theology to function."[11]

Hedenius formulates three postulates that together aim to support the maxim of the intellectual ethic, that one should not believe something

---

9. Tingsten was a professor of political science in Stockholm between 1935 and 1946, and thereafter editor-in-chief of the major Swedish newspaper *Dagens Nyheter* (1946–60). He became known not least for his criticisms of ideologies, which he considered not only unreasonable but dangerous because they lend support to totalitarian thinking and societies.

10. Hedenius, *Tro och vetande*, 163–221.

11. Ibid., 167, 169–70, 180, and 218–19.

if there are no reasonable grounds for regarding it as true.[12] The first, his *religion-psychology postulate*, states that religious belief contains metaphysical assumptions that are held to be true in the usual, literal meaning—for example, about the existence of God or the immortality of the soul—that science or empirical evidence can neither verify nor deny.[13] The second, his *language theory postulate*, states that religious comprehension and experience can be communicated to people who do not share the same faith.[14] The third, his *logic postulate*, states that two truths cannot contradict one another; of two contradictory statements, at most one can be true.[15] Through these three postulates, Hedenius encircles the theologians and can then simply state that Christianity goes against what we know about reality, and furthermore contains unsolvable problems such as theodicies; nor can theologians claim that its truth cannot be communicated to others. Christian belief is unreasonable.

Hedenius bases his arguments on the current views of science and modern scientific philosophy and assumes that the level of truth in science is determined entirely by its capacity to depict reality according to truth, which can sometimes give the impression of a relatively unproblematic attitude toward the changeable nature of science.[16] At the same time, there are occasional glimpses of a more problematic stance, as when he writes, "To continually revise, discard that which is unsustainable, and strive for new cohesions is, as we know, the only course for a philosophical quest for truth."[17]

In regard to theology, Hedenius' stance is clear: the authors of teachings on faith cannot claim to be men of science. But religious psychology is also debatable: "To hunger and thirst for righteousness is usually a neurotic condition."[18] His conclusion is clear: "As far as I can understand,

12. Ibid., 35.
13. Ibid., 65ff.
14. Ibid., 68ff.
15. Ibid., 75ff. In this context, there is more than just the problem of theodicy; Hedenius attacks every form of dramatic structure and reference to paradoxes. It is not difficult to see that individuals like Aulén or Bring were the target of his critical observations, such as "they make use of artistic terms such as 'tensions,' 'antinomies,' and 'paradoxes,' and avoid the simple and adequate expression 'self-contradiction.'" Ibid., 143.
16. Ibid., 31, 157, 31.
17. Ibid., 157.
18. Ibid., 33.

great portions of faith ought to be thrown away."[19] At the same time, it is impossible to escape the impression that what he describes as his results seem also to have been his points of departure, namely, "that there is no harmony between Christianity and human reason. They contradict one another. Evangelical Lutheran Christianity is in conflict with certain purely logical truths, which our reason knows, independent of all experience."[20]

Hedenius' criticism of Christianity was hugely successful. Neither Swedish theology nor the Church of Sweden has fully recovered from the fateful power of his attack. Hedenius dramatically changed the philosophical and intellectual climate of Sweden. Professor of History of Ideas Svante Nordin states, "The lasting impression is that Hedenius won the debate. Where the theologians were grumpy and obscure, Hedenius was cheerful and brilliant. His attack had taken his enemies while they were asleep."[21] But time has passed, the philosophical and scientific climate in Sweden has changed, and Nordin also notes retrospectively that Hedenius' views were marked by a narrow concept of reason. For example, regarding Hedenius' third postulate, he makes the following remark: "In everyday life, as in fiction, we find that two truths often contradict one another, that one and the same person may be both cruel and good, that a novel can be simultaneously naïve and insightful, that an experience can be both delightful and painful, and so on."[22] Nordin also points out the risk inherent in an overly strong faith in science, which may lead people to develop dual natures. He takes Hedenius' companion, Herbert Tingsten, as an example:

> In this way, Tingsten is at once two persons: "the vital, energetic, aggressive, talking editor-in-chief, and the worried, needy human being, harried by the fear of death, feelings of guilt, and wet dreams of salvation" . . . Doubt, worry, and the longing for salvation are relegated to the sphere of the private, the emotional, the purely psychological complication. Officially, what is preached is the milk of reason and independence from ideology. If stronger drinks are sometimes enjoyed, it is done in privacy.

---

19. Ibid., 36.
20. Ibid., 130.
21. Nordin, *Från Hägerström till Hedenius*, 179.
22. Ibid.

In the fancy parlor, rationalism rules the day, while the demons are locked in the cellar, which they must share with the angels.[23]

It is also important to place Hedenius and the power of the new analytical philosophical thinking that he represented in the greater context of the general cultural shift in post-World War II Sweden, from a Germanic cultural influence to an Anglo-Saxon one. For example, at universities in Sweden, the individuals who assumed professorships in philosophy after the war were all, with the exception of Gunnar Aspelin at Lund, influenced by analytical philosophy: Konrad Marc-Wogau (1946) and Ingemar Hedenius (1947) in Uppsala, Anders Wedberg (1949) and Harald Ofstad (1949) in Stockholm.

The philosophical ideals that came to characterize Sweden in the postwar era dealt with analysis rather than synthesis and were carried by the conviction that problems are often based on a lack of reason. The analytical philosophers perceived themselves as a sort of cognitive cleaning crew or scientific police force, or to use another metaphor that Nordin uses to interpret the situation: "Analytical philosophy becomes a sort of house mother in the temple of reason, who keeps 'romantic historical philosophy' and other irrational false teachings at bay."[24] What must be especially guarded against were the so-called unscientific philosophies, that is, various forms of Marxism, neo-Thomism, phenomenology, existentialism, and so on.

In his dissertation, Jan Bengtsson describes the reception and influence of phenomenology in Sweden and also provides an outlook on the dominant analytical philosophy. The result is something resembling a history of the heretics of Swedish philosophy. All of the philosophers who established themselves after World War II broke with earlier tradition, and in particular with the tradition that had been colored by Continental philosophy. During the first half of the twentieth century, phenomenology was in fact generally known in Sweden, and it was also "represented and discussed at all universities and colleges in the country . . . and the leading philosophers showed themselves to be familiar with Husserl's phenomenology," a circumstance that has now been forgotten.[25]

23. Ibid., 191.
24. Ibid., 153.
25. Bengtsson, *Den fenomenologiska rörelsen i Sverige*, 148. In this context, it can be noted that Jan Bengtsson mentions theologian and bishop John Cullberg as the person who made phenomenology known within Swedish theology. Furthermore, he maintains that "Cullberg's work is original, and perhaps Sweden's foremost contribution to phenomenology." Ibid., 136.

The criticism that analytical philosophy directed toward Continental philosophy is interesting, since it shows that Wingren was not the only person who stood out as singularly bizarre in Sweden's new philosophical and scientific climate.[26] Anders Wedberg speaks of existentialism as a philosophical-literary revivalist movement that gives a confused and hysterical impression, and Göran Hermerén writes of "the sort of speaking in tongues and wordplays that we find in Heidegger."[27] Jan Bengtsson compares analytical philosophical centrism with the developmental logic of ethnocentrism. In the first phase, other peoples are perceived as strange, confused, unreliable, prejudiced, primitive, and uncivilized, in the same way that analytical philosophy perceived existential philosophy as poor, unimportant, unscientific, and, in general, not as philosophy at all. In the second phase, the structure of subordination and superiority is so well established that there is no longer a need to argue one's position, and the subordinate accepts expressions of derision and ridicule.[28] For example, Harald Ofstad feels no hesitation in stating that Heidegger "writes like a pig" and continues by characterizing his texts as "truly first-class drivel."[29] This same philosopher maintained emphatically and in full earnestness that only analytical philosophers should be included in books on modern philosophy; "the only and the true philosophy" was not to be questioned in any way.[30] Ingemar Hedenius is no more gracious toward philosophers like Martin Heidegger: "What Heidegger says is incoherent, and should anyone stoop to understand it, it would be because he is stupid or has been duped. That I, Hedenius, do not understand a bit of it is proof of my philosophical competence."[31]

This is an important context to consider, because it shows that the intolerance of analytical philosophy afflicted not only theologians such as Wingren but also philosophers such as Martin Heidegger, Jean-Paul Sartre, Karl Jaspers, Martin Buber, and many others. Texts always exist in contexts. In the closing chapter of his book, Bengtsson pauses to

26. Wingren, *Creation and Gospel* (1979/1979), 97.
27. Bengtsson, *Den fenomenologiska rörelsen i Sverige*, 207, 211.
28. Ibid., 217.
29. Ibid., 218.
30. Ibid., 220ff. In an article titled "Tolerance and Responsibility" ("Tolerans och ansvar"), the same Harald Ofstad writes that his colleague Arne Naess should have prevented his students from reading Heidegger and that he should not have treated them so mildly, but rather should have "kneaded them and fried them." Ibid., 225.
31. Ibid., 224.

make note of what a contradiction it is that the same analytical philosophers, who always maintained the importance of rational argumentation, used such a high degree of irrationality in their own references and interpretations:

> They constantly expressed their disgust over dogmatism, but their own relationship to "the other philosophers" was a shining example of dogmatism. They often held forth a democratic method as the ideal for discussion and education, but were both totalitarian and authoritarian in their irreconcilable dismissal of "the other philosophers."[32]

No one who studied philosophy in Sweden during the 1950s and 1960s could resist taking a stance on the subject of Ingemar Hedenius. He was present everywhere.[33] The pressure he exerted on Sweden's theologians led to permanent changes, for better or worse, in Swedish theology.

As a matter of fact, Wingren did not reject everything that Hedenius represented. For example, he agreed with Hedenius' criticism of Nygren's attempts to establish religion as a separate cohesion of meaning, and he agreed with the necessity of allowing a critical trial of theology and faith. The crucial question, however, was how this should be done. One nearly overlooked fact in this context is that in 1949 Wingren actually wrote a sort of review of *Belief and Reason*, an article that was published in 1950 as a contribution to Sweden's debate over belief and reason. Many years later, in 1992, he commented on this article in a letter:

> For that matter, it is not true that I left Hedenius unacknowledged. Early, in fact in 1949, I wrote the article "Belief and Truth" ["Tro och sanning"], published in *Swedish Theological Quarterly*, 1950, pp. 7–23. Had Swedish theology taken the stance which I took there, immediately and without unnecessary reverence, we would have a healthy theology at our universities today. Not one Swedish theologian has ever mentioned my article from the year 1950.[34]

---

32. Ibid., 299.

33. In *Expressen*, Ivar Harrie cleverly wrote, "Wherever two or three of them are congregated—or wherever any of them has a congregation, even one of only two or three—Professor Ingemar Hedenius is there with them." Harrie, "Striden om Hedenius," *Expressen*, 15 July 1949.

34. Wingren to Gösta Hallonsten, 25 June 1992.

In his long, convoluted article "Belief and Truth" ("Tro och sanning," 1950), Wingren maintains that Ingemar Hedenius has constructed the problem of belief and truth in such a way that the truth of belief is neutralized. What is left is a poetic and dreaming faith, a religious poetry that no longer makes any claims. Wingren points out that in other contexts, Hedenius had maintained that there are different sorts of truths—but this does not seem to be true in regard to morality, and it is absolutely not true in the case of theology. Only reason is allowed to test its own truth, with the following consequence: "Belief expresses itself unilaterally on the same plane as reason. But it is not reason."[35] Hedenius has thus excluded all other components of reason, except for mere statements. He strongly maintains that if we are to believe, then we must have complete knowledge, which has remarkable consequences for the very concept of belief in Hedenius' writings: "What is peculiar about belief is not what it has, but what it lacks."[36] Yet, when Hedenius claims that "to really be Christian, one must believe that there was something about Jesus that was unexplainable from a scientific perspective," this seems to be the only thing that interests him and, in the next phase of his book, makes it possible for him to completely dismiss belief. Here, Wingren sees circular reasoning: the stage is already set, the curtain can rise and the play can begin—but "the conclusion that is reached is always smuggled in at the start."[37]

Therefore, Wingren wishes to take a few steps backward in this process and posit the question of "who has been allowed to make the decision when the two parties in the discussion are at odds."[38] If we disregard the obvious personal aversions to religion, which have made Hedenius a warrior—and the sentimentality and pious egocentricity of the revivalist movements, which in a misdirected way determine his understanding of religion and which he subjectively ascribes to the theologians he criticizes, but who in fact belonged to the same school of thought as Hedenius' own family, especially on his mother's side—then we ought to be able to state simply that the conflict between belief and reason seldom comprises a conflict "between factual truths within zoology, the history of science, etc., and the statements of belief—in any event, this is not where the

---

35. Wingren, "Tro och sanning" (1950), 8.
36. Ibid., 9.
37. Ibid., 11.
38. Ibid., 9.

heart of the problem lies."[39] Wingren also questions in general Hedenius' claim that belief ought to result in a more split personality. Further, he has difficulty seeing that belief must necessarily be placed in opposition to science: "When victory is won over an egocentric position, reason is not crushed."[40] To state this using a different terminology, the Christian faith that serves as a *practice of transformation* that reconfigures a human being from self-absorption to a life for others can certainly collide with reality, but it can hardly be placed in general opposition to reason and knowledge. Nonetheless, there is something fundamental that does not correspond with the opposition between belief and reason, faith and knowledge—and for Wingren's part, this is connected to the fact that faith "itself contains a demand to be faith, and not a 'viewpoint.'"[41] Based on the expanded concept of truth that Hedenius allows himself to work with in other areas, Wingren's conclusion pursues an argument about the difference between hearing and seeing. In contrast to a "religious statement" that deals "with something," the language of faith is something that we "hear"; it is a *kerygma* that is "directed toward" someone. While the optical metaphors of the Enlightenment deal with casting light and seeing, the knowledge of faith is characterized by an eschatological perspective that places faith in contrast to seeing and observing: "We do not see *now*, but we shall see. To believe is to wait and thus to live precisely in *the word*."[42] Somewhat later, he writes, "In the expression 'faith' there is a distance from observing."[43] Within the framework of this reasoning, the difference between "see" and "hear" gains its understanding from the eschatological tension between "already now" and "not yet." Thus, Wingren maintains that Hedenius does not present a correct picture of belief and faith but instead has quite simply constructed his own dragon, which he can then easily slay.[44] Here, Wingren sounds almost like Wittgenstein,

---

39. Ibid., 17.
40. Ibid., 14.
41. Ibid., 19.
42. Ibid.

43. Ibid., 21. Wingren examines the relationship between "to see" and "to hear," that of visible proof and reliance on the word, in, for example, *Living Word* (1949/1960), 63–65.

44. Cf. "When Hedenius, as far as can be determined, has failed in his task as a warrior, it is fundamentally due to the fact that his basic description of faith is so crude and misleading. Even those Christians who are quite unversed in theory may set down this book without harm after having read it." Wingren, "Tro och sanning" (1950), 20.

who once claimed that his text contained two things, that which was written and that which was not written, and that it was the latter which was important.[45] In other words, there are things that are important, even if they cannot be the objects of a scientific study. Wingren writes:

> This is stating beforehand that what is not science is nothing, only "emotion," without correctness and without truth. You thus break down the very possibility of encountering the truth about your own innermost being ... do not deal with anything other than truths about facts and circumstances outside your own being, scientific truths ... If you take the expanded concept of truth that Hedenius presents in the introductory section of *Belief and Reason* (*Tro och vetande*, pp. 30ff. and 42ff.) as your point of departure, then an auxiliary method should, quite the opposite, be natural; in any case, it ought to be tested. But now everything that is not scientific is stuffed into a box labeled "emotions" and thus any discussion and continued examination of it is prevented.[46]

It is interesting that Wingren concludes his article with the complaint that Hedenius has made a maneuver preventing further questions regarding faith and that by reducing it to an attitude of emotion has eliminated continued critical examination. In his analysis, Hedenius isolates the claims of faith—with the devastating result that he "kills the questioner's question."[47]

I would like to add, briefly, two additional perspectives on the relationship between Hedenius and Wingren, which tie into other portions of my presentation. First, we might redefine the collision between the views of the philosopher and the theologian as a conflict between theoretical and practical paradigms of knowledge. Thus we once again tie into the discussion of the respective Platonic and Aristotelian traditions of knowledge that we examined in chapter 4. In Wingren's article, this discussion is especially close at hand when he discusses "the split between knowing and acting."[48] Second, I want to point out the fact that

45. Ibid., 22.
46. Ibid., 23.
47. Ibid., 23.
48. Ibid., 12ff. In an article from 1974, he also comments that theologians with an interest in the sermon, and who have taken *kerygma* as their point of departure and thus have been characterized by an interest in practical knowledge, have not been in the habit of using analytical philosophy: "It is important to observe the incredibly elementary way in which the conceptual apparatus of analytical philosophy blocks

Wingren comes ever closer to a tradition of critique of reason, not least of all via his ties to K. E. Løgstrup. In doing so, he presents an exciting parallel phenomenon to Georg Henrik von Wright, as I shall demonstrate in chapter 7. In light of this background, it is possible to view the opposition between Hedenius and Wingren as an opposition between two diametrically different types of critique of reason: on the one hand, a critique *based on* reason, and on the other, a critique *of* reason.

In the article he wrote for *Theologische Realenzyklopädie* about his predecessor at Lund, Wingren stated, "It is Nygren who has given Swedish theology a face."[49] Writing this article was in fact a task he had tried to avoid, because by that time his personal views on Nygren were already known. If Einar Billing and Nathan Söderblom had been pioneers in making critical historical research into a self-evident tool in the theological workshops of Sweden, and had fought to free Martin Luther from conservative churchly orthodoxy, then Anders Nygren took on an almost opposing function. The other side of his positivistic, purely historicizing theology was, according to Wingren, a directly reactionary position on church issues, especially in regard to the question of the ordination of women in the Church of Sweden. All of this was made possible by the focus that Swedish motif research elaborated with independent contexts of meaning, a position that Nygren further developed in his later years through his ties to Wittgenstein's philosophy of language games and life forms when he used new philosophy—but with the same results:

> The basic motif is part of an independent context of meaning which lies outside the domains of science, which can never be attacked, and which science can only *describe*. At the bottom of the philosophical reasoning lies a well-hidden apologetic interest. The point is that the church and Christianity shall hereafter be allowed to exist in peace: values that are foreign to the church shall be left outside the walls of the church, and not disturb its members. This is what comes unimpeded out of the debate over my office in 1957–58.[50]

In one sense, Wingren thus welcomed Hedenius' philosophical attacks on Nygren's watertight theological compartments, entirely in keeping with Wingren's affirmation of biblical criticism and his positive approach

---

the possibilities for theology to have a phenomenological beginning in the sermon." Wingren, "Den springande punkten" (1974), 105.

49. Wingren, "Anders Nygren och svensk teologi av idag" (1988), 11.
50. Ibid., 13.

to secularization. At the same time, however, he had been influenced by a completely different epistemology and ontology than both Nygren and Hedenius. It is paradoxical that Hedenius, this philosopher who fought Christianity, stands out as one of the most important individuals in the history of Swedish theology in the post-World War II era.[51] Hedenius frightened the entire theological establishment of Sweden, and he demanded changes in its leadership. He thus transformed the entire infrastructure of theological discourse in Sweden. At the end of the 1950s, he presented concrete suggestions as to how Sweden in this way might "abolish the isolation of the theologians":

> Theologians should be trained by always being in the minority on committees that determine grades, make faculty appointments, and organize university curricula. We must take away from the current generation of theologians the power that they hold over the further development of Christian religious research in this country.[52]

Wingren was also involved in this debate, which in some ways served as a preliminary exercise in the heart-rending discussion about the methodology of theology that would break out in the early 1980s. In his memoirs, he made the following comment about Ingemar Hedenius: "It is clear that *all* of Swedish theology has been affected."[53]

While Wingren's early debates regarding theological methodology centered around Anders Nygren, no one who took part in the corresponding Swedish debates during the 1970s and later could avoid another Uppsala University professor by the name of Anders—Anders Jeffner (b. 1934). Jeffner made the most serious reply to the challenges Hedenius directed toward theology. He also presented a completely new program for systematic theology, so radical in its design that the name of the entire university program was changed from *dogmatics* to *studies in faith and worldviews (tros- och livsåskådningsvetenskap)*. Jeffner was guided by *the principle of integration* and refused all kinds of cognitive isolation. Epistemological claims need to be founded on argumentation and openness for logical examination, and also need to be tested according to personal

---

51. Wingren makes this point in his article "Pensionärer och avlidna" (1982), 17–18, with reference to Anders Jeffner's article "Dogmatik in der nordischen Ländern," in *Theologische Realenzyklopädie* (1982).

52. Hedenius, "De teologiska fakulteternas framtid," 21. Cf. ibid., 50.

53. Wingren, *Mina fem universitet* (1991), 97.

experiences. Jeffner criticized Wingren for not having developed a meta-theory aiming to connect his theology to other kinds of knowledge. Jeffner elaborated an extended concept of knowledge, always connected to science, but where scientific claims are confined.[54]

In his major overview of the study in faith and worldviews research program at Uppsala University, Mikael Lindfelt points out Jeffner as the program's great figurehead and emphasizes that Hedenius' concept of worldview (*livsåskådning*) is to be considered as the background for Jeffner's position. Lindfelt also states that Hedenius' critique of religion in general served as the great theological challenge, which in fact changed the life of Jeffner's entire generation, as well as that of subsequent generations of Swedish theologians.[55] According to Jeffner's mature theory, a worldview contains three components: a central value system, a basic view regarding existence, and certain theoretical convictions.[56] Even if Jeffner, unlike Hedenius, emphasized from the outset that a worldview could not be exclusively defined as a theoretical construction, Lindfelt believes that Jeffner's concept of worldview shows a development toward a more cognitive and substantial focus, so that the cognitive component tends to form the basis for the other components: "Increasingly, the perspective deals with knowledge and the reliability of this knowledge."[57]

For many years, there was a prevailing stereotype that the theological programs of the universities of Uppsala and Lund were at odds with one another in unresolvable conflict, and that this conflict was especially bitter in the relationship between Jeffner and Wingren. This is both true and untrue. It is obvious that they had differing views about what tasks could be considered within the framework of scientific theological research at universities in Sweden, perhaps best expressed as the difference

---

54. Jeffner, *Kriterier i kristen troslära* and *Vägar till teologi*.

55. Lindfelt, *Att förstå livsåskådningar*. This book contains an in-depth analysis of Jeffner's development, as well as a comprehensive overview of the great reception of the concept of worldviews (*livsåsåkådningar*).

56. Cf. Jeffner's summary: "A worldview seems to be an entirety consisting of certain values and attitudes linked with certain theoretical convictions." "Livsåskådningsforskning—material och metoder," 36.

57. Lindfelt, *Att förstå livsåskådningar*, 65. After a thorough review, Lindfelt criticizes the toned-down existential dimension in Jeffner's concept of life views, something that he finds rather surprising: "It is very clear that Jeffner's definition of life views may be said to provide space for an existential dimension only in an indirect way," Lindfelt states, but adds that there is an exception in regard to "the possibility of defining a life view as a whole that answer a person's life questions." Ibid., 81.

between *religious study* and *theology*, respectively. And it is also evident that the two had backgrounds in different cultures of learning. At the same time, it is impossible to deny that Wingren hoped to find links and bridges to Jeffner—for example, regarding the necessity of integration in theology.[58] Even though their ideas of integration took different expressions, both agreed that theology can and should be critically examined, which in some ways implies a return to the situation of liberal theology. Neither of the two defended a religious compartmentalization into which faith and theology may withdraw and remain immune to criticism, even though Jeffner's idea of integration tended toward vertical thinking, while in Wingren it tended more toward horizontal integration. There were also evident connections between the two in regard to their focus of interest on *current* faith and worldviews, in contrast to the previous focus on pure historical studies. First and foremost, however, they were united in their resistance to the use of a methodology focused on singularity and the distinctly Christian in theology. Furthermore, Wingren truly respected Jeffner, not least because he would engage in close-fought academic skirmishes and was thus a colleague with whom Wingren could associate, which for Wingren often meant someone he could *confront*—and fight with!

There could have been an exciting trial of strength between these two, but it was not to be, for a number of reasons. Primarily this was due to the explosive theological debate that broke out in Sweden in the early 1980s and that, in the end, burned all bridges. In its wake, Wingren found himself completely marginalized in the field of academic theology, while the Uppsala school of theology took on a dominant position. With the passing of time, the studies in faith and the worldview research program were eroded. It is a real irony of history that after Jeffner retired from his professorship at Uppsala, the label systematic theology has been reintroduced at the University. No one has, however, been able to explain why.

---

58. When Wingren delightedly mentions that Jeffner continuously returns to the meaning of integration, and how important it is that convictions truly be tested in a critical way, he does so as an implicit critique of Anders Nygren, whom he treats earlier in the same presentation: "No part of a person's convictions can be left floating loose in the air." Wingren, "Anders Nygren och svensk teologi av idag" (1988), 15. But he also recognizes it as a lack of proportion to place a question mark on Lutheranism in the contemporary period when exegetics has in fact become the normative idea in the conflict over women priests: "It would be a task worthy of Anders Jeffner to deal directly with these exegetic theses in a critical analysis." Ibid., 17.

Quarreling Professors

In June 1980, on Monday morning following the Swedish midsummer holiday, almost exactly three years after his retirement from Lund University, Gustaf Wingren began writing his book *The Silent Interpreter*, a debate book with the provocative subtitle *What Theology Is and What It Ought to Be* (*Tolken som tiger: Vad teologi är och vad det borde vara*, 1981). He worked intensively on this book project during the latter half of 1981 and finished the manuscript on 19 January the following year. As a retired professor he had no access to the services of the departmental secretary at the Faculty of Theology, so he called on Greta Hofsten for help. From 28 January to 16 February she struggled to edit and type the manuscript, in addition to her regular job delivering the mail. Finally, the manuscript was submitted to the publisher.

During the period that followed, Wingren worked almost unceasingly. His high level of activity that spring was typical of the way that he lived his life the first ten to fifteen years after his retirement. In late February he held one of his many radio worship services; this time, Greta Hofsten also participated, and together they chose the following themes for their meditations: reflection, work, offering, resistance, losses, and keeping the Sabbath. These meditations then became the body of a book that he and Greta Hofsten published through Bonniers. They had originally titled it "The Blessed Day" ("Den signade dag"), but the book was finally renamed *The Courage of the Living* (*De levandes mod*, 1981). As those two titles indicate, during this period of time, Wingren was moving, also in a theological sense, from J. O. Wallin toward N. F. S. Grundtvig.

The mix of projects that Wingren undertook in the spring and summer of 1980 shows how he continued to live the life of a professor also after his retirement. He wrote, lectured, and preached in various places and capacities. At home in Lund he lectured to groups of theologians connected to different dioceses of the Church of Sweden and to the local chapter of the Student Christian Movement, LuKRISS. He made frequent trips to Stockholm, where he spoke in the Stockholm Cathedral and at the Theological Seminary at Lidingö (later merged into the present Stockholm School of Theology). He wrote newspaper reviews of new books, spent a significant amount of time and work on his responsibilities for *Theologische Realenzyklopädie* (TRE), and participated in a panel debate against the Synod (Bertil Gärtner and Dag Sandahl), while representing the Exodus movement (together with K. G. Hammar and Per Erik

Persson). In April of that year he traveled to the United States to deliver a series of lectures at Dana College in Nebraska, in conjunction with the release of the English translation of his book *Credo: The Christian View of Faith and Life* (1974/1981). This stream of varied activities continued at the same pace throughout that summer. On 1 June he was at the local chapter of the Student Christian Movement facility in Lund to participate in a constitutional meeting of a Christian support mission for the churches of El Salvador. In addition, he devoted a major portion of his time that month to proofreading, writing articles, and preparing lectures. Despite all this, he also found time to spend his traditional one-week vacation in his hometown of Valdemarsvik, just before attending the summer meeting of Christians for Socialism at the monastery Rögle Kloster. At that meeting Greta spoke on "The Crisis of Marxism and Our Socialist Vision," and he himself spoke on "Creation Faith and Christ Confession: The World and the Church." During this period, his academic assignments came mostly from Norway and Denmark. For example, during the summer of 1982, he was appointed area expert to assist in deciding a professor's appointment at the University of Oslo, a center of learning that often called upon him at this point in his life. In mid-August, he spent a week together with Greta, family, and friends at Greta's summer house at Revhaken on the Baltic coast in southern Sweden. On 21 August, *The Courage of the Living* (1981) was released. A few days later, both Gustaf and Greta traveled north to Oslo and its University, where Gustaf lectured and where, on 2 September, he was made an honorary doctor.

Two days after the festivities in Oslo came the release of the book that would mobilize the entire establishment of Swedish theology against Wingren: *The Silent Interpreter* (1981). There was no doubt that this book was meant to stir controversy, nor did Wingren make any attempt to hide this fact. He got right to the point in the introduction, declaring, "Should anyone interpret my book as an attack on theology in Sweden, then he has understood the matter correctly."[59]

As with all of Wingren's books, *The Silent Interpreter* follows an obvious dramatic structure and was written and edited with a strategic focus. Let us approach the book first by an overview of its table of contents, structure, and main thesis, then its indexes of names and subjects, and finally, make note of its numerous Bible references.

---

59. Wingren, *Tolken som tiger* (1981), 10.

In the first chapter, Wingren presents his point of departure, namely, that the task of theology is to serve as an interpreter. In his fourth and final chapter, he returns to the hermeneutical basis for his attack by illustrating how the task of interpretation returns, but he does so in the form of a sharp warning: if the theological faculties at the universities in Sweden will not adopt the new orientation, a new home will have to be found for the necessary hermeneutical work of theology. In this context, he discusses the role of pastoral theological education at the institutions for pastoral training, where future ministers of the Church of Sweden are being trained. In between he also presents two chapters that outline the serious dilemmas facing theology as an interpretative science. In the first of these (chapter 2), he writes of how a particular theory of science that has come to dominate at Sweden's theological faculties has resulted in a flight away from the hermeneutical task. In reality, theologians have redeemed its scientific nature by limiting its activities to descriptive and historical studies, but by so doing, theology has become a prisoner of what was at hand. Wingren chose to refer to this as positivism, although this is certainly a rather unusual understanding of the concept. He maintains that it is strange that the disagreements that characterize theology as well as all academic activity had suddenly become an indication of arbitrariness. In his third chapter, he describes the ordinary Swedish primary schools as theology's last resort, referring to the fact that Swedish teachers of religious studies usually study theology as part of their academic education. The problem, according to Wingren, is that the needs of teachers and pastors are so different that there is a risk that neither school nor church will get what it actually needs.

This is the major outline of the drama Wingren presents in *The Silent Interpreter*. We may now ask, who are the major players in this drama, and what are the major issues? This question is answered by Wingren's indexes. The book follows the basic model he had used in his Swedish books for more than three and a half decades, in which he uses three registers: one index for names, one index for subjects, and one index for Bible references. As we have noted earlier, one of the distinctive characteristics of Wingren's books is that they are full of Bible references. To a large degree, his theology is a biblical theology, and although *The Silent Interpreter* is a book in the form of a debate dealing with the future of theology, it is also one of biblical theology. In this book the Swedish Bible exegetes are subjected to Wingren's criticism, primarily for the arguments they had made against the ordination of women.

Besides his ranting against biblical exegetes and the resistance to the ordination of women, Wingren identifies two individuals as scapegoats for the derailment of theology: Axel Gyllenkrok and Sven Kjöllerström. Regarding Gyllenkrok, once again Wingren attacks the way in which theology has been coupled together with philosophy: "theology becomes subservient to philosophy, one philosophy after the other. The result is that the process of interpretation ceases: the themes of theology become copies of the themes of philosophy."[60] Yet, neither Anders Nygren nor Anders Jeffner are themselves in the line of fire; instead, Wingren directs his attack against Axel Gyllenkrok. In his book *Systematic theology and scientific method with particular focus on ethics* (*Systematisk teologi och vetenskaplig metod med särskild hänsyn till etiken*, 1959), Gyllenkrok argues that the Bible contains nothing more than contradictory texts without any inner unity, and that theology as a contemporary interpretation of the Christian faith is thus impossible. He argued that dogmatics should be discarded, and that the only component of systematic theology that should remain and be a worthy academic discipline, was ethics. Wingren was outraged that a book—he called it a pamphlet—that had not even been properly reviewed, let alone publicly debated, had been allowed to influence theology in such a decisive and devastating way.[61]

Wingren's attack against Sven Kjöllerström deals with how his former colleague had prepared the way for theology to forsake the present in favor of historical studies by his transformation of practical theology into church history. Despite his profound competence, Kjöllerström had not been appointed professor of church history, since this post had more or less been reserved for Hilding Pleijel. Thus, Kjöllerström had become a historically focused professor of practical theology, and consequently, Yngve Brilioth's two flagship subjects within practical theology, homiletics and pastoral care, soon had disappeared from the scene. The full weight of blame for the transformation of Swedish theology into pure

60. Ibid., 27.

61. In his memoirs, Wingren writes ironically about his having been a professor of a true scientific discipline (ethics), despite the fact that his scientific scholarship was questioned, and that the situation was more or less the opposite in the case of Gyllenkrok (who was a professor of dogmatics). However, there was little in the way of noticeable polemics against Gyllenkrok during his time as a professor of dogmatics and symbolism at Uppsala. Wingren did send a telegram to the newly appointed Gyllenkrok with the following wording: "Best wishes to a true professor in an illegitimate scientific discipline, from an illegitimate professor in a true scientific discipline." Wingren, *Mina fem universitet* (1991), 183.

historical investigations, which Wingren had previously always ascribed to Nygren, is now laid upon Kjöllerström. Throughout his career as a practical theologian, Kjöllerström had remained a church historian. Wingren found no limits to the negative effects this had: "The injury brought to Swedish theology by this loss has never healed."[62]

Apart from the statement of the issues themselves, it may seem somewhat remarkable that Axel Gyllenkrok and Sven Kjöllerström were awarded the dubious honor of being named as the two theology professors who had destroyed Swedish theology. Three decades earlier, Kjöllerström had played a key role among the supporters who had made it possible for Wingren to receive his professorship at Lund, and in many ways, their views on theology and church politics were similar. At the same time, however, it was well known from the early 1950s onward that Kjöllerström and Wingren had been in almost constant disagreement with one another.[63] Regarding the other accused professor, one could state that Wingren's position differs from Gyllenkrok's in almost every area. Yet, they had worked together as advisory experts on a number of projects over the years, and perhaps it was for this reason that the professor from Lund chose never to go to open conflict with his colleague from Uppsala.

Other than the personal conflicts contained between its covers, Wingren's *The Silent Interpreter* (1981) makes a broad attack against Swedish theology: systematic theology; exegetical theology; the shortcomings of theological education as proper training for Swedish ministers due to its adaptation to the needs of primary school; the lack of contemporary and critical interpretation from a theology that had fled to the matter of what was at hand, regardless of whether it was history or the present day. Everywhere he looked, the quality was poor, and nowhere did Wingren find a theology that sought to act as an interpreter for the present day.

62. Ibid., 96.
63. This conflict was rooted in the events that took place when the then-student and later archbishop Bertil Werkström became one of Wingren's doctoral students. After Kjöllerström showed no interest in Werkström's subject (confession in the works of Luther, Thurneysen, and Buchman), Werkström turned to Wingren, who immediately took him on as a doctoral student. Wingren even made the effort to telephone his colleague, and is supposed to have said something like the following: "I hear that you are not taking care of your responsibilities. Here we have a man who you are unable to advise. I will take care of him!" After this, the conflict between the two was irreconcilable. Interviews with Bengt Hallgren on 20 January 2010, Harry Aronson on 20 January 2010, and Bertil Werkström on 23 January 2010.

The book could be considered as an extension of the practical turn that occurred in his overall theological project with the publication of *The Living Word* (1949/1960). At the heart of his argumentation, we find the idea that it is education that is the connection to a concrete practice in society, rather than research, that holds theology together.

In order to understand the book *The Silent Interpreter* (1981) at all, the reader must be aware that beneath its surface, it is organically connected with the complications of a theology of ordination that had made only half-hearted and disingenuous arguments to those who opposed the ordination of women. In the second volume of his two-volume work of dogmatics, *Gospel and Church* (1960/1964), there were already clear signs that this was becoming a major issue for Wingren. His defense of the right of women to be ordained as ministers may be considered an integral part of his theological project as a whole. The issue of the ordination of women involves and integrates exegetical theology, systematic theology, and ministerial theology together with church organization, church history, and national church politics into his thinking. His intentions with *The Silent Interpreter* cannot be understood without considering this dimension.

Although it is not clear whether they are ex post constructions, Wingren makes numerous references to how Oscar Cullmann and Karl Ludwig Schmidt undermined the churchly dream of their day about apostolic succession and hierarchical superiority by the ordination of bishops. They so clearly showed that priests did not gain this position or charge until the 1200s. Thus at its heart, it is to be considered that this was an attack against the ministers who were opponents of the ordination of women as priests—and what he indicated as these opponents' habit of being married and having many children—when Wingren wrote, "Celibacy is much clearer."[64] At the decisive 1958 assembly of the Church of Sweden, which was to decide the matter of the ordination of women, leading Swedish theologians had argued against the ordination of women as priests. Wingren's bitterness regarding this fact would last for the rest of his life, as we shall see in the final chapter of this book.

The Silent Interpreter was published on 4 September 1981, and even before the end of that year, a reply came from the Swedish theological establishment in the 1981/6 issue of the Swedish theological journal *Faith & Life* (*Tro & Liv*), which arrived in the nation's mailboxes on the day

---

64. Wingren, *Tolken som tiger* (1981), 83.

before Christmas Eve. It made a dubious Christmas gift for the retired professor from Lund. Sven Hemrin, the attentive editor of the journal, who in fact had a licentiate degree in systematic theology from Lund, selected the reviews and edited what probably turned out to be the journal's most loaded—and vociferous—issue ever. With this issue, the professors' quarrel began. Seldom have Swedish professors of theology argued so roughly and quarreled so openly as in the debate that ensued.

The headlines of the editorials and reviews show the anger and energy that Wingren's book had elicited: "Painting in Black and White" (Per Erik Persson), "I Will Not Be Silent, Said the Exegete" (Birger Gerhardsson), "The Battle with the Constructed Dragon" (Lars Eckerdal), "Some Reflections on Wingren's Latest Fight Book" (Anders Jeffner), "The Roaring Interpreter, or the Retirees' Quarrel" (Ragnar Holte), and so on. The less strident and more sober analyses seem to have come from the few reviewers who did not hold academic chairs (Holsten Fagerberg, Lennart Molin, Kjell-Ove Nilsson and Torsten Bergsten), but Wingren never really included them in the debate and they remained outside the battle. The main argument made by the various professors was that Wingren's analysis of the situation in Swedish theology was not only one-sided, but extremely misleading as well. The tone of the editorials and letters that followed Hemrin's matter-of-fact review of Wingren's book was almost unbelievably shrill. One way to comprehend this heated response is that the debate was not merely about the contents of the book; the professors were also taking the opportunity to settle years of unresolved mutual injustices.

Per Erik Persson had been a professor of systematic theology with responsibility for instruction and examinations in dogmatics and symbolism at Lund University since 1963, and was thus not only a successor to Gustaf Aulén and Ragnar Bring, but also in many ways Wingren's closest colleague in the faculty for almost one and a half decades. In his article in *Faith & Life*, Persson was thus astonished at the condemnation his former colleague had declared over a theology that Wingren himself had been part of and responsible for: "The reader may obtain the impression that Gustaf Wingren himself had not been part of or active upon this scene."[65] Further, he wondered why Wingren had not begun this discussion earlier, and asked why, for example, the severe criticism of Gyllenkrok had not been heard until now. He then attempted to add nuance to his former

65. Persson, "Att måla i svart och vitt," 9.

colleague's black and white image of the present, and recommended that this picture ought to be painted using a spectrum of nuanced colors. Persson also stressed that there is actually no single theological method. In science, there are, and ought to be, different methodological approaches which must confront one another. Persson then goes on the defense as one of the educators responsible for the program in which teacher education was combined with the longer theological course of study pursued by those who intended to become pastors in the Church of Sweden and which Wingren had criticized so harshly. He states that the situation is not at all as new and alarming as Wingren wants to make us believe: teachers-to-be have always taken courses along with theology students. Furthermore, therefore, this cannot be considered a great problem in the present day, since it is a matter of such small numbers of students. Why make such a great issue of this?

Per Erik Persson was probably the individual who had the greatest reason to feel treated unfairly by Wingren in his picture of the state of Swedish theology, since his views did not differ dramatically from Wingren's. Furthermore, they both shared a basic hermeneutical view of the task of theology, including its consequences in regard to the necessity of change in order to preserve a tradition.[66] However, Persson was missing in Wingren's presentation. If readers were to believe Wingren, Persson did not seem to exist at all on the Swedish theological scene. For an author who made such important use of indexes, it hardly seems coincidental that Persson was missing from the book's index of names.[67] In hindsight, it seems like nonchalance bordering on impudence that Wingren ignored the colleague who in fact delivered much of what he had claimed was lacking. We can almost hear the weariness in Persson's voice when he writes, "This type of condescending judgment is not especially conducive to joy in one's work."[68] Worst of all, Wingren behaves as though he was not even aware that Persson was in fact a professor

---

66. In a series of books, Persson has developed a clear hermeneutical perspective on contemporary systematic theology; see, for example, *Att tolka Gud i dag*, a much-used textbook that introduces various new theological movements and uses hermeneutics as a common focus.

67. It is certainly true that other of Wingren's active colleagues are missing from the register of persons (which mostly covers "retirees and deceased persons"), but the difference is that Wingren treats areas in which Persson in specific had been active—for example, that of the coordination of theological education with teacher education, and the meaning of hermeneutics in contemporary systematic theology.

68. Persson, "Att måla i svart och vitt," 11.

of dogmatics—the subject that he claimed Axel Gyllenkrok had already done away with in Sweden; a directly false statement that Wingren would nonetheless repeat during the coming years.[69]

Birger Gerhardsson (1926–2013), professor of New Testament exegetics at Lund University and one of the many successful disciples of outspoken Wingren antagonist Anton Friedrichsen, took the same line as Persson regarding Wingren's lack of nuance. He was disturbed by the uncompromised tone expressed in a flood of categorical words such as "all," "none," "never," and so on. He also countered the criticism that he was operating a univocal Jewish exegesis, by stating that from a purely historical perspective, the background of Christianity is in fact Judaism. Gerhardsson did not recognize the isolation of Swedish theology that Wingren had claimed, and to counter Wingren, he therefore reported on the numerous lectures he had delivered at university departments of theology as well as at freestanding theological seminaries.

Lars Eckerdal (b. 1938), who would eventually become bishop in Gothenburg, had served for years as acting professor of the chair in practical theology once held by Sven Kjöllerström, which had since been converted to a professorship in ecclesiology. Eckerdal complained somewhat unjustly about the miserable disposition of the book, and then launched into a defense of what had occurred in practical theology. In his article, he wondered whether Wingren really believed that practitioners of practical theology should devote themselves to rehearsals of the art of preaching. He then provides a reminder that such "practice preaching" had been removed from theological studies at both Uppsala and Lund at the turn of the twentieth century. He also wondered whether Wingren, after his own retirement, really wanted theologians to leave their universities and instead become active at pastoral training institutes.

The tone became more elevated when Anders Jeffner, professor of studies in faith and worldviews at Uppsala University, entered the discussion. His indignation hung heavily in the air from the very first sentences of his editorial:

> In my opinion, Gustaf Wingren has written many interesting books. In these books, he lays forth his own personal reactions to the Christian faith. On that count, I have appreciated him, and have been prepared to overlook the catastrophic theoretical stupidities he has also achieved, as well as his polemical prejudices and exaggerations. However, his latest book, *The Silent*

69. Cf. Wingren, *Mina fem universitet* (1991), 182.

Interpreter, has changed my entire attitude toward him. In it, we get his bad sides in concentrated form, and this is more than what is bearable.[70]

Jeffner emphasizes that through his polemical tone, Wingren has sketched a picture of Swedish theology that is not only one-sided and twisted, but also fundamentally false. His selection of theologians is arbitrary, and is comprised mostly of retired or long-dead colleagues; furthermore, his analysis is superficial and distorted, and he has overlooked how much things have changed since the day when these colleagues were active. Jeffner notes that Wingren tends to describe Swedish theology as a lonely island, while he himself represents an international development. He then asks how Wingren has actually thought to answer the challenges that Gyllenkrok presented. He finds no substantial answer. Instead Wingren's book seems to be a strange sort of medicine: "Homeopathic drops supplied with pompous labels."[71]

When Ragnar Holte (b. 1927), professor of ethics and thus Wingren's closest colleague from Uppsala, enters the debate, it comes to its stormy culmination in this particular issue of *Faith & Life*. The taunting title of his review, "The Roaring Interpreter, or the Retirees' Quarrel," hints at what is coming. The professor from Uppsala proudly recounts all that he has done during one single week in September, just to show how much actually takes place within theology at Swedish universities and in contrast with Wingren's sad picture of the situation of theology in Sweden. He had written articles, proofread, participated in conferences, been awarded grants for research projects, spoken at local churches, and so on. Against this background, he judges the presentation made in *The Silent Interpreter* to be extremely misleading: "It is an insolent lie. The book does not fulfill even the most elementary academic requirements for the correct review of facts."[72] Clearly, this is a poisonous old disagreement that has bubbled up anew. Holte, the successor of Herbert Olsson in Uppsala, focuses on what he has always felt was the great problem and weakness in Wingren's theology: his methodological lacuna, which he also sees as the reason for the lack of success of kerygmatic theology. He considers Wingren's theology as characterized by a sort of intuitive talent which is difficult to teach to others, and for this reason, it has "stiff-

---

70. Jeffner, "Några reflektioner kring Wingrens senaste stridsskrift," 29.
71. Ibid., 31.
72. Holte, "Tolken som röt eller pensionärernas gräl," 35.

ened into a sort of self-righteous dogmatism."[73] Holte skillfully re-directs Wingren's polemics against the descriptive dissertations being written at Uppsala, due to what he sees as theology's captivity in what is at hand, back at Wingren—whose doctoral students, with a few exceptions, wrote strictly descriptive theological dissertations. Toward the end, Holte's tone rises again: "It is as if he wants to cry: 'Don't any of you understand that you are all wrong, and that I am the only one who is right?' He then follows an old, familiar homiletic recipe: 'Loud voice, if your argumentation is weak!'"[74]

In conclusion, it is clear that the theological establishment rejected Wingren's presentation as one-sided and misleading. Yet, the reviews were not only about the shortcomings of the book. It is obvious that the reviews were written by a group of greatly offended former colleagues, even though few of them had been directly attacked. We can also note that they all avoided the two major questions that had been of such decisive importance to Wingren's discussion and pre-understanding. First, the old issue of the role Swedish theologians had played by delivering arguments against the ordination of women that was entirely central to Wingren's argumentation and the composition of his presentation. But no one, not a single one, considered this issue. The same was true of the second question, regarding the social perspective, which in fact provided the horizon of understanding for Wingren's presentation. Only the editor, Sven Hemrin, mentioned it. Above all of this waited the question of how to understand the task of the theologian as an interpreter in accordance with the theological hermeneutics and hermeneutical theology that had occupied Wingren for more than three decades. The debate did not cope with this question at all.

Confusions: Lack of Social Contextualization

Gustaf Wingren composed his rebuttal to the collective theological elite after the holidays, between January 12 and 31, 1982. This may seem like a long period of time, but his long twenty-two page reply, which was published in *Faith & Life* (*Tro & Liv*) issue 1/1982, was almost a small book. The article had the profoundly ironic title: "Pensioners and Deceased Persons: A Small Guide to Close Reading" ("Pensionärer och avlidna:

73. Ibid., 36.
74. Ibid., 38.

En liten hjälpreda vid innantilläsning"). Here, Wingren presented many arguments, not all of which were connected, but all consistently aimed toward demonstrating that it was the *social perspective* that was the most important horizon of understanding when he wrote his book. *The Silent Interpreter* (1981) was not intended to focus solely on academic work, and to show this, Wingren referred to the index of subjects, and even more to the table of contents, which shows that the first chapter is called "Theology and Society," and the final chapter is titled "Society and Theology." In other words, the book deals with the *social function* of theology, and Wingren complained that his critics had failed to notice this: "They have disregarded the book's main issue."[75] Later in the article, he again returned to the fundamental importance of the social perspective when considering the purpose of the book, which stands in sharp contrast to the complaints lodged by the university theologians that he had not devoted enough attention to theory of science: "We are not sitting in the academic ivory tower, occupied with the task to determine who may be declared to be scientific. Rather, we find ourselves in *society*, and our task is to decide where in our society our centers for the education of ministers should be located."[76]

In Wingren's reply to his academic colleagues, there is one person who he treats especially harshly, and who seems to bring out strong feelings in Wingren, namely, his former colleague in ethics at Uppsala University, Ragnar Holte. Wingren states that each of the five professors (Gerhardsson and Eckerdal, and the three systematic theologians Persson, Holte and Jeffner) only defends his own university discipline. He then declares that he intends to give four of them a concrete answer, and then states: "To Ragnar Holte, whose article is a parody, I will make no reply."[77] However, this was not to be the case. In fact, Wingren's article, while it does deal with the issue of the ordination of women and the social perspective on theology, it actually also deals to a great extent with Holte. Three pages later, Wingren makes a powerful attack on him:

> As I have mentioned earlier, I will disregard Holte's article. In the first page of his article (p. 38), he declares that he does not intend to waste more time on the debate over my book, a statement which I received with happiness. Otherwise, I would have

---

75. Wingren, "Pensionärer och avlidna" (1982), 3.
76. Ibid., 19.
77. Ibid., 5.

to reply to a person who in the course of a conversation about the task of theology counts the sums of money he has received from Central Bank [i.e. The Swedish Foundation for Humanities and Social Sciences, financed by the Central Bank], who describes his own smirk when the cheers are flowing towards him, who tells derisively of the low level of the conferences he has visited, and of the way in which his presence at these events raises their quality, all things notwithstanding, and in addition someone who on top of all this, uses the word "pensioner" as a term of abuse. Obviously, I could reply even to these things, but it would be difficult to do this without descending to Holte's level, and acting in the same insulting way as he. But now, I will not have to do it.[78]

After this, Wingren comments again and again on Holte, in an ever-rising tone—and this is being done in an article in which he had declared that he would not reply to Holte at all. At one point, he suddenly gives Holte yet another polemic blow: "Anyone who imagines that they are telling about a victory, when they count up their thousand-crown notes from the Central Bank's Tercentenary Fund, does not know what he is doing."[79]

He returns to the topic of Holte once again when he comments that Holte seems to believe that he, Wingren, had been sitting in Lund, listening to *Erevna* with Hugo Odeberg as he tried to reconstruct the worship services of ancient Christianity—which he did not. In triumph, Wingren believes that he has revealed Holte for the person that he really is:

> Now, it is interesting to learn that Ragnar Holte, this master in critical distance-taking, belonged to the travelers from Uppsala who listened to the wisdom of Erevna. Yes, I believe that this is very suitable. There were many there who at that time, full of spirituality, spelled Church with a capital C (today, Holte spells Central Bank with a capital C and B). However, I was never at Erevna; I was namely interested in *exegetics*.[80]

Holte's revenge came two years later in the form of a wrathful attack on Wingren, poorly camouflaged as an overview of Swedish research on Luther. Hidden under the seemingly innocent title of *Luther and the Image of Luther in Sweden* (*Luther och lutherbilden*, 1984) was a highly tendentious presentation in which the organizing principle seems to be

78. Ibid., 8.
79. Ibid., 12.
80. Ibid., 13.

that Wingren, and anyone who might be associated with him in any way, are stuck in an indefensible academic ghetto, or downhill methodological slide, which has "declared war against human thought's attempt to test the possibility of faith in God in the present day, and the conditions for mankind's moral insight and responsibility."[81] Meanwhile, in this book it seems sufficient for a researcher to be a critic of Wingren in order to have his work elevated to "the most mature fruit of Swedish Luther research," as in the case of Axel Gyllenkrok.[82] Although Holte only had fifty pages at his disposal, he allows his attack on Wingren to cover issues that goes far beyond his research on Luther, while seemingly forgetting his decleared task: to provide a research overview of the Swedish reception of Luther. To compound the insult further, he points out Wingren's former teacher and competitor for the professorship, Herbert Olsson, as "certainly the most learned of all the Swedish Luther researchers"[83] who was wise enough to move to Uppsala "after having been treated unfairly in Lund,"[84] and who represents a "correct" perspective on creation. I must say that it is rather sad to recognize the contentious relationship between these two researchers, who in fact were so close to one another on many issues, although not methodologically, and how they used the scientific infrastructure mostly to express their personal aversions.

After this divergence, let us return to the conclusion of Wingren's long journal article, in which he discusses the future of Swedish theology based on the reasoning that he identifies in three theological generations: the first, "retirees and deceased persons," the second, the in-between generation who currently hold faculty positions, and the third group, in whom Wingren placed his hopes:

> *The young persons who have just completed their theological education or who are still pursuing it*: concealed in this group are the really interesting people, as yet unknown. This third generation has not yet expressed itself in the debate over [my] book, *The Silent Interpreter*. When these young ones finally do express themselves, it is possible that they will talk about the book's subject matter.[85]

---

81. Holte, *Luther och lutherbilden*, 43. I want to emphasize that the (strong) words that I used just prior to the quotation are directly taken from Holte's presentation.

82. Ibid., 33.

83. Ibid., 34.

84. Ibid., 35.

85. Wingren, "Pensionärer och avlidna" (1982), 23.

It is exciting to note that while the Wingren of 1968 had viewed this same group of young, radical theologians as nothing more than noisy and threatening, the current Wingren now ascribed to them the role of precursors with utopian energies who would play a key role in a brightening future.

The battle with his former professorial colleagues, which the seventy-year-old Wingren was now fighting at the beginning of the 1980s, would place an unfortunate, and in many ways unjust, stamp upon his theology as "unscientific." Not only had a unified academic cadre of professors loudly defended their territory; many of them had banished Wingren to a place outside the borders of the academic world in Sweden. Nonetheless, with a little historical distance, we may wonder whether it is an oversimplification when the Swedish theological debate of the 1980s, which centered around *The Silent Interpreter*, is described as one in which the major front lines ran between Uppsala and Lund, with Jeffner and Wingren as the main combatants. The lines of battle were in fact not only between Uppsala and Lund. Furthermore, we must not underestimate the value of the potential points of contact between Jeffner and Wingren's respective projects in regard to their common focus on the current situation, as well as their unwillingness to focus solely on the distinctly Christian, regardless of whether it was a matter of systematic theology or studies in faith and worldviews. In Swedish theological circles, it is seldom noted that Wingren actually used the studies in faith and worldviews (or lifeviews) concept almost literally in the subtitle of (the Swedish edition of) his second book of dogmatics, *Credo: The Christian View of Faith and Life* (1974/1981). Considering the way in which the Swedish theological debate of the previous century has been portrayed as a debate between the Universities of Uppsala and Lund, and later, as one between Jeffner and Wingren, it is worth noting how little energy Wingren devoted to attacking Jeffner. Furthermore, a number of times he explicitly expressed hopes for his relationship with Jeffner, as for example in a text from 1977, when he presents the following thoughts regarding Jeffner's installation as a professor at Uppsala:

> Most important among these fundamental principles is his insistence upon the methodological basic principle for the comparison between the Christian faith and the contents of other worldviews: our comparisons should not be based upon that which is unique to Christianity (the gospel), but rather, just the opposite, upon the points of Christian faith which express

what is common to all people (creation and the law). This basic principle should also have a certain relevance even for the program that Anders Jeffner has now introduced; the program of research on faith and worldviews.[86]

Wingren himself maintained that in his book *The Silent Interpreter* (1981), he focused his discussion on bridges to the surrounding society, but at the same time he stated that the answers he received were comprised of purely academic defenses for the discipline that the respective author represented. For this reason, he complained that his discussion partners did not in general speak about theology and its tasks outside of the universities; instead, the discussion was stuck within the borders of the limited academic territories of the discussants.

Yet, the way in which Wingren himself carried on the debate also contributed to a series of complications. First, it seemed as if he had stepped back into his old role as a hierarchically superior professor. Lars Eckerdal makes an interesting comment here, pointing out that Wingren seems to count only professors, or more precisely, only full professors with tenure ("with the exception of a few associate professors of ethics") as legitimate references and partners in the debate.[87] This is indeed a striking observation, because in *The Silent Interpreter*, Wingren largely disregards all other actors and hardly takes them seriously at all.[88] He counts only professorial colleagues. The most objectionable aspect of *The Silent Interpreter* is simply the fact that Wingren seems to have suddenly left his new focus on the social context behind, and once again put on his traditional academic clothing—at the same time that he declares that the horizon of understanding for his entire reasoning is society: *the role of theology in society*.[89]

---

86. Wingren, "Livsåskådningarna och frågan om kristendomens egenart" (1977), 200.

87. Eckerdal, "Kampen mot den konstruerade draken," 25.

88. Wingren employs this pattern throughout the actual book, but in the article he wrote in reply in *Tro & Liv*, no. 1, 1981, there are several small exceptions: Wingren briefly mentions Sven Hemrin's commentary on the organization of pastoral education, and the analogy Torsten Bergsten draws between the respective work situation of pastors and teachers. Wingren, "Pensionärer och avlidna" (1982), 21–22.

89. Considering his fixation on the office of professorial chairs within the institutional hierarchies of academia, it may seem somewhat odd when we read Wingren's polemics against Nygren and Nygren's marked interest in an absolute academic focus, which led to his obsession with concepts such as science, scholarliness, true scholarliness, and strict scholarliness (ibid., 20). One may wonder whether Wingren made a

Secondly, the confrontation was being pursued so vehemently, in the way that Wingren loved and found so attractive, that all nuances were at risk of being lost. When one side of a discussion holds categorically fast to its viewpoints, the conversation can easily become blocked, and the parties incapable of receiving the arguments being presented. In the debate that followed in the wake of *The Silent Interpreter*, not only ideas, but also individuals, were mistreated and relationships that had already been fragile now disintegrated. As so often, Wingren seemed to have been blind to the potential alliances he could have built in order to support a constructive theological agenda.

When all parties involved had had their chance to vent their frustration, the great debate about the organization and methodology of theology remained. However, no one had become much the wiser. In addition, in these debates Wingren's own recontextualization, together with his move from academia to the public social sphere, became invisible. Disregarding the studies in faith and worldviews program that had been established earlier, Swedish theology has not yet been able to bring about any new movement or school of thought. In the end, the debate over *The Silent Interpreter* resulted in Wingren's own marginalization. In the best case, he was able to strengthen his position in society and in the church; in the worst case, the result was that he became unilaterally perceived as a churchly theologian who sought to offer encouragement to pious communities—far away from the critical discussion that was actually an integral part of his theological agenda, in both its academic and its social contextualizations.

The Romantic Narrative: Continental Thinking

Throughout his lifelong disagreement with Swedish theology in general, as well as in the debate over *The Silent Interpreter* in particular, something that I would call "the romantic narrative of continental thinking" played a central role in Gustaf Wingren's self-perception and rhetoric. Prior to World War II he made two life-changing trips to Berlin. On his first visit, he attended a meeting of the World Student Christian Movement in Berlin-Spandau over the New Year's holiday 1935–36, at which he had opportunity to meet many individuals who would later take on

---

more or less conscious decision to return to pure academia when he again takes up a discussion of the problems, challenges, and future of theology.

leading positions in ecumenical theology internationally, such as Martin Niemöller and Visser't Hooft. On his second trip to Berlin in 1938, he spent a summer term at the Humboldt University. It was during this period that he lived in the Johanneum dormitory where he also wrote the journal that I have referred to as his "Johanneum Journal" (see chapter 3). After the war, he served as a guest professor for a number of months at the universities in Åbo (Turku), Basel and Göttingen. Over time, he received a steady stream of invitations and assignments that took him out into the world, primarily to the European Continent. His inaugural lecture at Lund University in November 1951 contained an echo of his many trips southward to Europe, both before and after World War II, with numerous of references to the state of theology on the Continent. Here, Wingren did refer to the Lundensian school of motif research as "Swedish motif research." However, with only one single exception, in his inaugural lecture Wingren did not include or mention any other specific country. Instead, he spoke of "dialectical theology on the Continent." In other words, Wingren's inaugural address dealt with a comparison between Lundensian theology, which he made synonymous with "Swedish" theology, and "continental" theology, which at least in the beginning mostly meant dialectical theology.[90] In addition to the fact that this reasoning may be considered as an expression of Eurocentric thinking and an exclusive fixation on Protestant theology North of the Alps, where "continental theology" is presented as though it were a uniform phenomenon, it also implies that everything is better on the Continent. In times to come, when this comparison between Sweden and the Continent was established, it would take on great importance in Wingren's theological argumentation.

Over time, Wingren assumed an increasingly romantic view of how well everything worked on the Continent—in contrast to Sweden, where everything was clearly so much worse. He surely would have agreed with August Strindberg, when he wrote about the Oresund (*Öresund*), as "the waterway that separates the Banished Ones from the Continent." In a concrete rhetorical context, the romantic narrative of Continental Thinking describes how isolated and dead Swedish theology seems to be—in comparison with the liveliness that characterizes the Continent. Gradually, this romanticizing tended, more and more, to be focused on Denmark. There is considerable evidence of Wingren's interest in Denmark.

---

90. Wingren, "Några karaktäristiska drag i modern teologi" (1951), 241, 244, 247.

After all, Scania (*Skåne*), the southern Swedish province where Wingren lived for most of his life, had historically been an eastern province of the Kingdom of Denmark, and to this day, this region of Sweden still shows some distinctly Danish traits. When Wingren writes in his memoirs about the homeward journey after his rather difficult time in Basel in 1947, there is no mistaking the enthusiasm and ease that he felt when the train reached Kolding in Denmark, where he heard "the wonderful Danish language."[91]

For Wingren, the Danish paradise that gradually came to represent the Continent lay in the heart of Denmark, in the city of Aarhus. It almost seems more than a coincidence that in February 1954, Wingren was in Aarhus as he prepared the important book where he further elaborated on the criticism that was initiated by his inaugural lecture in 1951. During his three weeks at Aarhus University, he lectured and led seminars on Barth, Bultmann, and Nygren, and, as he carefully noted in his personal journal, wrote a third of the book *Theology in Conflict* (1954/1958). Furthermore, Wingren seems to have visited Denmark on a number of important events in his life, for example when he celebrated his sixtieth birthday at the home of Harald Østergaard-Nielsen, who at the time was dean of Roskilde Cathedral. The numerous requests Wingren received to serve as an area expert on various Danish university committees helped him establish ties with colleagues there. The fact that Wingren's later colleague, Per Erik Persson, had been supervised by a Dane, Professor K. E. Skydsgaard of Copenhagen, further strengthened the faculty's relationship with Denmark. In fact, no less than five of Wingren's own doctoral students wrote dissertations investigating Danish materials: Per Wagndal wrote about Søren Kierkegaard, Tord Ehnevid wrote about Christian Pontoppidan, Lars-Olle Armgard wrote about K. E. Løgstrup, and Gert Nilsson wrote about Jens Møller. This Danish-Swedish angle was manifested in a special event in 1971, when K. E. Løgstrup was both the object of Lars-Olle Armgard's dissertation and a prominent guest during Armgard's defense, as well as at the traditional dinner that followed. In addition, Løgstrup's favorite disciple, Ole Jensen, served as an extraordinary opponent on Armgard's dissertation committee. It was no coincidence that Løgstrup was awarded an honorary doctorate at Lund in 1965, or that Wingren received the same honor at Aarhus University

---

91. Wingren, *Mina fem universitet* (1991), 147.

in connection with the University's fiftieth anniversary in 1978. For Wingren, Denmark increasingly resembled the promised land of theology.

The Danish theological scene is both rich and complicated due to the country's connections with two outstanding theological schools of thought that stem from two significant thinkers in the ninteenth century: Søren Kierkegaard and N. F. G. Grundtvig. These two theological giants have been a boon for Danish theology. Both were geniuses and unusual men, and yet their contemporaries must have found them difficult to cope with on a personal level. Throughout the last two centuries, Danish philosophy and theology has been characterized by the tension between these two very different and powerful traditions. In modern times, this tension has been embodied in the conflict that arose between K. E. Løgstrup, a proponent of the Grundtvigian tradition, and Johannes Sløk, an adherent of the Kierkegaardian tradition—both professors at Aarhus University.[92] Early on, the two had a good relationship; they shared much in common and traveled in the same social circles. In the 1950s, however, their relationship abruptly ceased due to personal reasons. The disagreement began when Sløk denounced Løgstrup's critique of Kierkegaard, which Løgstrup found unacceptable. Løgstrup became enraged and terminated all contact with Sløk, to the point where he even stopped acknowledging Sløk's presence. After two or three years, the men's wives stepped in and sought to bring them together again. They finally agreed that outwardly they would behave as if the other did not even exist; they would neither speak of the other nor attack the other. All possible communication would occur behind closed doors. This agreement probably saved Sløk's career, so that he was able to attain a professorship a few years later, and at the same time allowed Løgstrup to maintain his position of power. But it also resulted in some odd situations and episodes, and worse, their students and colleagues were not able to benefit from what is the lifeblood and entire purpose of academia—public discussion.[93] Wingren clearly but unnecessarily chose sides in his relationship with his Danish

---

92. Personally, I am convinced that Wingren could have benefited even more from his exchanges with the Danish theology if only he had not emphasized the tradition passed down by Grundtvig in such a "strict" and unilateral way, or dismissed the rich possibilities for productive theological thinking that the tradition of Kierkegaard can demonstrate.

93. Kemp, "Den religiøse lidenskab," 28ff. In this context, Kemp relates that Løgstrup found it very difficult to accept criticism, a fact that had affected Kemp's own career. Ibid., 24. Løgstrup's rage could last for decades. For example, he refused to speak with his colleague P. G. Lindhardt at all during the last twenty-seven years of his life.

colleagues. This probably served only to caricature a relationship that was complex and further deepen the disagreement, but it also blocked Wingren himself from the potential inspiration that he might have found in a more profound spectrum of sources for theological thinking.[94]

Gustaf Wingren's love of Denmark and Danish culture may also have been strengthened by his marriage to Greta Hofsten, who was of Danish descent. In fact, one member of the prominent Bagger family, of which Greta was a member, had served as the first president of what would become Lund University, when Lund and the province of Skåne were still part of Denmark. Other members of the Bagger family had been bishops and important public figures in Denmark. Greta and Gustaf's respective personal connections with Denmark probably reinforced their shared love of that country. Wingren also made a considerable contribution to introducing Danish theological traditions into Sweden. In the Swedish theological context, Wingren-Hofsten found a common tie with another couple, Henry Cöster and Margareta Brandby-Cöster, both of whom worked to disseminate, translate, and further develop Danish theological ideas in Sweden.[95]

The romantic story of continental thoughts also played an important role in Wingren's book *The Silent Interpreter* (1981). For example, the book contains a systematic comparison between the Uppsala tradition (Gyllenkrok) with that of Aarhus (Løgstrup)—and it will not surprise any reader as to which tradition came out more favorably in this comparison.[96] Yet, it is primarily in the two books in which Wingren wrote about himself in which his romantic ideas of the Continent, as opposed to sad, old Sweden, reaches its true climax. In *Creation and Gospel* (1979/1979), Wingren writes, "Swedish theology seems to be, more and more for every year, like an isolated theological island—a peninsula—in

---

94. In this context, we might also wonder whether some of the delight that Wingren took in Denmark and Løgstrup were actually directed toward ideas that had to a high degree been inspired by his own theology; in other words, Wingren's admiration for Denmark contains a certain amount of self-admiration. His standpoint of irreconcilable opposition may also have made him blind to the fact that Løgstrup's earlier work had been inspired by John Cullberg, a Swedish theologian who stands out as the real dark horse in twentieth-century Swedish theology.

95. Margareta Brandby-Cöster's Swedish translations from the Danish and Norwegian include Knud Hansen's *Den kristna tron*, K. E. Løgstrup's *Det etiska kravet*, Leif Grane's *Vision och verklighet: En bok om Martin Luther*, and Johannes Møllehave's *Där kärleken bor: Predikningar*.

96. Wingren, *Tolken som tiger* (1981), 52-58.

northern Europe."⁹⁷ In his memoirs twelve years later, Wingren continued to elaborate on this theme, with some small variations: "We have become a mere province in the world of theology," "theologically, we are a hinterland," "Sweden is both exegetically and systematically a province, an island in Europe," the humanities and theology live in "isolation in Sweden." Theology in Sweden is "from a scientific point of view, a province, an island. " and so on and so on.⁹⁸ At some points, Wingren seems to take his own legs out from under himself, as in his book *My Five Universities*, when on the one hand, he writes derisively of ninteenth-century Sweden as "nothing more than a copy of general European tendencies," and on the other hand, contrasts it with Grundtvig's and Kierkegaard's Denmark, the unique character of which (also itself a sort of isolation) is now described as something positive: "Not anywhere in Europe is there anyone who equals either of these two."⁹⁹ In the same way, we can wonder at his method of argumentation when he states, in a Grundtvigian way, that it is entirely correct to be Danish in Denmark—but that it is far from sufficient to be Swedish in Sweden.

The continental-romantic Wingren combines this story about the isolation of Swedish theology in relation to the wider world with the myth of his own position as an outsider. In the book he originally wrote to present his theological ideas to an American audience, he returns to how remarkable and problematic his Swedish readers found his book, *The Living Word* (1949/1960), and that Nygren's view of the scientific nature of theology lived on and dominated the scene, resulting in the consequence "that during my whole stint as full professor at Lund I stood outside what is considered respectable in Swedish theology."¹⁰⁰ In his autobiography, he speculates about what might have happened had he not listened to the biblical scholars in Basel: "I might then not have been as isolated among Swedish theologians as I am," but then adds that he is "satisfied with my isolation." He avoids any form of regret, presenting himself instead as an outsider who "embraces the isolation."¹⁰¹ Toward the end of his memoirs,

---

97. Wingren, *Öppenhet och egenart* (1979), 85. This particular passage seems to have been deleted from the English edition, *Creation and Gospel* (1979), where the reader, a few lines earlier, finds only this short sentence: "It is unfortunate that Swedish theology is becoming more and more isolated." Ibid., 81.

98. Wingren, *Mina fem universitet* (1991), 98, 118, 139, 173, 176.

99. Ibid., 151.

100. Wingren, *Creation and Gospel* (1979/1979), 84.

101. Wingren, *Mina fem universitet* (1991), 145.

he writes about himself as the "only theologian in the nation" who pursues dogmatics and biblical theology using the present as his horizon of understanding. He continues: "Since I am alone in doing so, I am unscientific, a judgment upon my work that I willingly accept."[102]

Referring to the context of another country or place in order to demonstrate the faults of one's home country is a well-proven rhetorical device. Nonetheless, it must have been difficult for Wingren's former colleagues to deal with him when he assumed the role of a martyr and outsider. While the process of self-proletarianization that he underwent during the 1970s may be considered as a sort of homecoming for him, it was not easy for those in his circles to deal with a colleague and friend who suddenly began cultivating a self-image of himself as an outsider. Sometimes it is almost comical, for example when he wrote in his memoirs about his debates with former colleagues. Wingren, a world-famous professor from one of Sweden's top universities, who had a *curriculum vitae* that included almost 800 published works, suddenly refered to himself when he spoke about "those of us in the working class."[103]

With a few exceptions, none of Wingren's followers have come to hold leading positions in any of the Swedish academic institutions where theology and religion is studied. Wingren joined many conflicts, but did not win an equal number of victories. Despite his great sense of strategy, the final results of his endeavors were meager. After he retired, not one of his academic followers applied for his old professorship. On the other hand, he did little to maintain continuity in the direction of his professorship. For example, when his colleague, Per Erik Persson, sought to make sure that the label by which Lund University would refer to their field would continue to be systematic theology, Wingren took no interest. Persson was unsuccessful in his efforts; the new label was not even theological ethics, but simply ethics. This change of name virtually eliminated any possibility for the continuation of Wingren's program at Lund. In his later years, he even wrote of himself as a loser, and felt that he had not been of any importance for the future development of Swedish academic theology.[104] While this can certainly be discussed, it is definitely not true in regard to Wingren's influence on Swedish society and cultural life in

---

102. Ibid., 181.

103. Ibid., 23. Even though this comment is uttered in a context in which he is talking about his youth in Valdemarsvik, in its actual rhetorical context it serves as a construction that at least partly includes the author in his current situation.

104. Wingren, "Pensionärer och avlidna" (1982), 16.

general, and in particular in regard to his influence on the third public sphere of theology, namely, the church. For these reasons, the final two chapters of this book will examine the two public spheres outside of academia in which Wingren's theology came into play: society (chapter 7) and the church (chapter 8).

7

Systematic Theology Turned Critique of Civilization

THE SAME PROCESS OF modernization and industrialization that successfully transformed the entire world by materializing the project of the Enlightenment has always co-existed with a tradition of critique of civilization that aims to disclose a darker reality beneath the surface of this success story. One does not need to use words such as *Wideraufklärung*, expressions of a sort of anti-Enlightenment, in order to recognize that every civilization in history tends to be blind to its own barbarism; it is sufficient to state that the Enlightenment has always been imbued with a sort of Romanticism. Somewhat as belated second thoughts, like shadows cast by the Enlightenment, darker aspects of our civilization have increasingly become evident to us. In accordance with Friedrich Hegel, who claimed that "the owl of Minerva spreads its wings only with the falling of the dusk," we may recognize this critical stance toward civilization as a sort of self-critical awareness, which in many ways also forces us to reconsider this historical process.

Post–World War II Sweden experienced an incredibly rapid development. War-torn Europe had to be rebuilt. For a country that had not been involved in the war and had thus kept its industries and population intact, the 1950s and 60s became a period of technological optimism and belief in progress. Yet, just around the corner awaited the economic malaise of the 1970s, with its serious economic problems and dramatic demographic changes. Furthermore, a few years into the 1970s the oil crisis afflicted the world, forcing the global economy to its knees for the rest of that decade. Today in hindsight, it is easier to comprehend that the world had at the time been drawn into a profound structural transformation.

For Western countries such as Sweden, the 1960s had been the peak of the process of industrialization, and thereafter the development was characterized by a new, post-industrial logic. In retrospect, it seems as if the current political economy and its dominant ideologies were caught by a lagging self-understanding. In the years since, we have experienced the emergence of a new form of society characterized by global financial markets, a de-regulated world economy and a digital information system that has brought about a new compression of time and space.[1]

How is it possible to cope with and comprehend a century that was so full of progress that in many ways it exceeded the highest-flying utopian fantasies—and yet at the same time, may be considered as the most violent hundred years in the history of humankind? As a matter of fact, history has never seen a more well-educated or shining barbarism than that of the twentieth century. The past century experienced the great triumph of democracy—and yet during the same century totalitarian ideologies and states dominated the world, harvesting human sacrifices on a scale never seen before. Thus, the framework of this single century encompasses both the height of civilization and the most brutal barbarism. Considering this intertwinement of civilization and barbarism, it is not difficult to understand why it has been associated with significant difficulties to develop a balanced view of the state of the world.

A philosopher who realized very early what was taking place, and who identified the problems that waited beneath the surface of this optimistic belief in progress, was Friedrich Nietzsche (1844–1900). Long before anyone else, he identified a different kind of reality and a darker logic of development. With his hypersensitivity to flaws and contradictions, he seemed to assimilate all of civilization with a passionate ambivalence—and went insane as a result. Before the twentieth century had even begun, Nietzsche directed his philosophical gaze toward the future and saw with horror what was coming:

> What I relate is the history of the next two centuries. I describe what is coming, what can no longer come differently: *the advent of nihilism*. This history can be related even now; for necessity itself is at work here. This future speaks even now in a hundred signs, this destiny announces itself everywhere; for this music of the future all ears are cocked even now. For some time now, our whole European culture has been moving as toward a catastrophe, with a tortured tension that is growing from decade to

1. Harvey, *The Conditions of Postmodernity*.

decade: restlessly, violently, headlong, like a river that wants to reach the end, that no longer reflects, that is afraid to reflect.[2]

The two German-Jewish philosophers Max Horkheimer (1885–1973) and Theodor W. Adorno (1903–69), who had personally experienced some of the catastrophe Nietzsche seemed to prophesy, further developed this tradition of critique of civilization through philosophical reflection that focused on the inherent contradictions in the process of Enlightenment. In their aphoristic book *The Dialectic of Enlightenment*, these two esoteric intellectuals, who had fled Hitler's Germany and the Holocaust for sunny California, wrote forthrightly about the self-destruction of the Enlightenment:

> We are wholly convinced . . . that social freedom is inseparable from enlightened thought. Nevertheless, we believe that we have just as clearly recognized that the notion of this very way of thinking, no less than the actual historic forms—the social institutions—with which it is interwoven, already contains the seed of the reversal universally apparent today.[3]

Viewed from this perspective, the Enlightenment should not be considered as a singular, linear process of progress, but rather is characterized by fundamental contradictions. The Enlightenment is determined by a break with myths—but results in its own mythology. The Enlightenment is associated with progress—but seems to the same degree to result in regression: "The fully enlightened earth radiates disaster triumphant."[4]

A philosopher who developed his thinking in the direction of this critique of civilization was Georg Henrik von Wright (1916–2003). His pessimistic philosophical reflections gained a wide audience among intellectuals in Finland and Sweden during the 1980s and 90s. He had a background as a logician with an interest in practical philosophy and entered the international philosophical scene in 1948 when he succeeded Ludwig Wittgenstein as a professor at Cambridge University. In the later (post retirement) works of this Swedish-speaking Finn, the reader is confronted by a quiet, yet harsh, critique of a worldview shaped by modern technology and science. He warns of the deadly influence of science on the conditions of human life when it finds social realization in the form of modern technology and an industrial production system. While von

2. Nietzsche, *Will to Power*, 4.
3. Horkheimer and Adorno, *Dialectic of Enlightenment*, xiii.
4. Ibid., 3.

Wright's earlier work had been carried out within the tradition of analytical philosophy, he tied his later authorship on the critique of civilization to a continental philosophical discussion associated with the crisis of reason, primarily inspired by the Frankfurt School of Critical Theory, to which Horkheimer and Adorno belonged. Against this background, he discusses the limits of the mechanical and deterministic models of explanation. However, as a result of this, his intellectual project had entered into an area where it is no longer only a philosophical critique *based upon* reason, but to an equal degree may be considered as a philosophical critique *of* reason, or more specifically, of instrumental reason. Georg Henrik von Wright feared a development where humankind is destroying the natural environment, with the devastating consequence of alienation and "a deepened sense that life is without meaning." He actually speaks about a "double alienation," due to the fact that it not only separates human beings from nature, but also from work, resulting in unhappiness and dissatisfaction.[5] Despite the fact that von Wright mobilizes all of his reason in order to make this disheartening diagnosis of modern life, his conclusion is clear: it is scientific reason itself that is generating the most serious problems that we face today.

In the closing chapter of his book, *Science and Reason* (*Vetenskapen och förnuftet*), von Wright takes a dire tone. According to him, there seem to be no reasons why the dominant trends should not continue, adding: "One perspective that I do not see as unrealistic, is that humanity is headed toward its demise as a zoological species."[6] Given this conclusion, von Wright's final words about hope seem anything but hopeful. He completed these thoughts several years later when he identified his position as one of "the optimism of powerlessness" and "provocative pessimism," once again employing a dire tone: "It is not impossible that we are standing on the threshold of an era when we may be afflicted by scourges of great scale."[7] Of particular interest to us is that von Wright here articulates a philosophical critique *of* reason: "Much of what makes our existence problematic arises from an over-estimation of our ability to rationally control development, using science and technology."[8]

5. Wright, *Vetenskapen och förnuftet*, 148.
6. Ibid., 151.
7. Wright, *Myten om framsteget*, 150–51.
8. Ibid., 151.

I maintain that we may view the work of the later Wingren as a theological variant of the critique of modern civilization that also the later von Wright developed. These two intellectuals worked somewhat in parallel. Both were born in the second decade of the twentieth century, and both became politically radical in their later years.[9] After the social turn in Wingren's theology and his political transformation during the 1970s, he re-directed his interests, making society, rather than academia, the primary context for his own theological texts. In his autobiography, he describes his new focus in this way: "One may indeed write books against Barth; that is a small thing. Yet the real battlefield lies out in society, in the newspaper press, in mass media, and last but not least in one's personal lifestyle."[10]

In this way, the professor transformed systematic theology into a socially critical contemporary theology by mobilizing all of his sources and texts, moved them from the disputes in the academic seminar rooms and re-contexualized their message in a social context. One of the prerequisites for him to succeed at this endeavor, without descending into trivialities and predictable instrumentalization, was his unique ability to develop an interpretation that was equally as creative as it was responsible.

How should we then understand Wingren's new political theology and his socially critical stance? I maintain that the dominant perspective that determined his new position may best be described as a critique of civilization. Furthermore, it is more a critique of the Enlightenment and the industrialized life form, aligned with the tradition I have outlined here, than some kind of socialism, albeit with a more human, or in fact a Christian, face. I will argue that Wingren's position becomes more comprehensible if we view him through the lens of a tradition that is critical toward the Enlightenment and science, and as such his theological project is more or less a parallel to Georg Henrik von Wright, as well as K. E. Løgstrup, who also influenced him in profound ways. Seen from this perspective, it is easier to comprehend the ways in which he contrasts with a tradition of Enlightenment and science that has taken a more unproblematic point of departure in reason. Wingren's social critique is thus also a critique of reason. Thus, it is interesting to ask what might

---

9. The only example of a corresponding parallelization that I have seen is Håkansson, *Vardagens kyrka*, 248–52.

10. Wingren, *Mina fem universitet*, 135. Cf. "The consequences were that I, in my capacity as a theologian, had to develop creation theology through active social criticism." Ibid., 134.

have happened if Wingren had not been forced into his profound process of recontextualization. Most likely, his authorship would not have become anywhere near as exciting, creative, current or relevant. In his later books, Wingren's theological project takes a turn which is by no means unproblematic, but it is nonetheless impressive, and cannot be ignored in any evaluation of his work.

"If a Baptized Person Runs a Hot Dog Stand . . ."

The power and intensity of the process of transformation that characterized Gustaf Wingren's partially new theological project from the 1970s onward can hardly be exaggerated. His obvious ambition and ability to recontextualize his earlier sources resulted in the development of a sort of political theology. At the same time, Wingren, the theology professor, was taking his first shaky steps out into a society about which he knew little. After all the years in the ivory tower of the university, it was as though he was peeking out at the world "out there" with wonder and horror. His early attempts in this period to develop socially oriented examples for his new, politically radical theology are as elucidating as they are labored. Sometimes they are even comical, as in the quotation I have chosen as the heading for this section. It is taken from Wingren's contribution to a Swedish collection of essays on ethics published in 1971, in which he writes:

> If a baptized person runs a hot dog stand, he has numerous opportunities to secretly battle the temptation to make money by using poor-quality ingredients. Yet, if he succeeds in his fight against this temptation, he will not record it in his bookkeeping with a triumphant note of "The church sells only the finest hot dogs!" It is quite sufficient that his customers satisfy their hunger without becoming sick. This is a matter of doing what is best for the other, and nothing more. If the baptized person is captain of an oil tanker, then the secret enemy with which he struggles may be the temptation to allow an oil spill. In this case, the "other" is not just a few hundred customers but thousands, perhaps millions who live along the shoreline, both human beings and animals. If the captain's "new person," the person who through baptism "comes forth and rises up each day," is victorious, then life along the coast continues as it always has. Life continuing as it always has is a miracle, which is dependent on

the Creator making something new each day, and taking victory over destruction.[11]

While we may smile at the somewhat comical comparisons and examples in this extract, it is impossible to miss the importance of the point Wingren seeks to make, or the ingenious simplicity with which he underscores the radical nature of his dynamic interpretation of Luther. In this example, Wingren takes the Lutheran ethics of vocation and transfers it to a modern, urban industrial milieu in a complex society. This is significant and advanced reasoning about the local character of vocation and practical attention to the need of fellow human beings, ideas which Wingren had examined in comprehensive historical investigations in his doctoral dissertation. Here, he uses the seemingly trivial work of running a hot dog stand to illustrate these ideas. Yet, even in this concrete situation, baptism serves as a model for the interpretation of the Christian faith, along with an emphasis on the fact that the place for faith and vocation is the world, and not the church. The Lutheran concept of creation interprets the work of God as a sort of miracle, which he carries out from behind a mask in everyday life, without our being conscious of it. This idea is strengthened in the second example in the above excerpt, in which millions of people, who remain unknown to us, are able to continue living their lives thanks to the "new person" who is victorious over destruction through the professional decisions made by the captain aboard his oil tanker.

The hermeneutical model of argumentation that Wingren uses again and again in order to maintain theological continuity through variation, is based upon theological analogies over time. He thus often returns to the fact that Martin Luther was unable to find any references in the Bible that touched upon life in the monastery, enforced celibacy or the selling of indulgences. So what did this biblical theology have to say about his own era? What Luther does is that he *re-interprets*, *re-directs*, and *re-addresses* what Paul wrote about the Sabbath, unclean food or the requirement of circumcision, so that it struck the contemporary idea of justification through acts that prevailed in the concrete situation in Europe during the early 1500s. Therefore, in a fundamental way, this also means that one cannot remain Lutheran by simply repeating the positions that Luther held then. Instead, Wingren posited that individuals living in the late twentieth century must read Luther based on the contemporary issues that weigh upon people. The freedom that the early church found

11. Wingren, "Reformationens och lutherdomens ethos" (1971), 140.

from the requirement of circumcision, as articulated by Paul, and the break from enforced celibacy which was made through Luther, had for Wingren their equivalents in the liberating effects of creation theology from the monastery of pietism (the pious community), and the many requirements for personal achievement that modern society places on the individual, as well as the conservative view of church office which prevented women from being ordained. Given Wingren's sometimes strong identification with Luther, it is not difficult to see a modern Luther in the course of his own life, as when he broke with the isolation of the monastery, first from the free-church framework of his childhood, and later from the research cell of the university, in order that he might direct his work toward a social public sphere.

In the classic two-front war against Pietism and orthodoxy within the Lutheran tradition of interpretation to which Wingren adhered, Pietism was no longer the major problem, at least not for the later Wingren. Instead, it was orthodoxy that increasingly was becoming problematic, due to the changing social context of the times. However, Pietism and orthodoxy risk generating a confessionalism that locks itself within the church so that creation and the law in its first, earthly use tend to disappear. Yet, the *folk church* (territorial church, *folkkyrka*)[12] does not seem to take seriously the landslide that had occurred as a result of the separation of the civil and ecclesiastical municipality in Swedish society. Wingren maintains that, if the folk church in this situation, when the church once again has to be founded on voluntary work, merely attempts to maintain its position, the law may be the only thing that is heard. The churches continue to carry on an inheritance from the orthodoxy of the 1600s, when the churches in the Nordic countries re-created large portions of the medieval parochial system. According to Wingren, this was something completely foreign to the reformer in Wittenberg: "If he were to return to these Nordic churches, which refer to themselves as 'Lutheran,' Martin Luther himself would probably be surprised about many of the

---

12. In this book, the Swedish concept *folkkyrka* is translated as "folk church" (sometimes also adding "territorial church")—and not "national church," which has been a common translation previously. Due to the theological contents of this concept in Wingren's work, a folk church is by essence different from, even if it might in particular circumstances be, a state church. Wingren advocated a theologically—and not politically (democratically)—motivated idea of the folk church, whose strong biblical influence also differs from the ethnic components associated with "nation" and "folk."

religious phenomena in their present-day lives. He would think that he had returned to the 'monastery.'"[13]

Another factor deepening the need for a recontextualization of Luther and a new type of reformation within current Lutheranism is, for Wingren, the theological consequences of urbanization. If we do not consider seriously the problems and limited relevance inherent in the ethics of proximity in a complex society, the consequences may be that the current use of Luther will take on a strongly preservative function:

> The natural environment of the Lutheran idea of vocation is thus the countryside and small towns: in large cities, it becomes paralyzed. Since the recent history of Europe has to a large degree brought with it urbanization and continued depopulation of rural areas, Lutheran Pietism has, by inner necessity, been driven into political conservatism.[14]

As a result of the dissolution of the ties between state and church brought about by secularization, Lutheran theology finds itself in an entirely new situation, in which the church must find new and different ways to interpret general human life as a life created by God. Only through such a recontextualization can secularization be of benefit to the tradition of the Reformation. If we continue to relegate creation and the law to the sphere of the state, and allow the church to stand only for the gospel, the result will be devastating, according to Wingren. An affirmation of secularization without a theology anchored in creation theology runs the risk of the connection between the gospel and the body being weakened, and in the worst case, being severed entirely: "A church which cannot interpret the first article of faith from within itself, from within its own proclamation, education and the care it provides for souls, is not ripe for secularization."[15] The worldliness of society and culture is fully legitimate. It can even be legitimated theologically, but the church must anchor the worldliness of the world through creation theology—and at the same time not be consumed by contemporary society. Here, as an expression of the inescapable internal tension within eschatological thinking between "already now" and "not yet," Wingren stresses the importance not to un-

13. Wingren, "Protestantisk arbetsetik och europeisk vardag" (1985), 10.
14. Wingren, *Creation and Gospel* (1979/1979), 50.
15. Wingren, "Reformationens och lutherdomens ethos" (1971), 136. Cf. "No part of the credo during the 1900s ought to have been so neglected or outrightly resisted as the first article of faith." Ibid.

derscore the fact that Jesus did not himself create or leave behind after any culture, not even a single text.

The recontextualization of Luther, which Wingren carries out in his later authorship, had its roots in the pronounced dynamic character of his interpretation of Luther which he sketched out in his dissertation in 1942. Wingren likens this recontextualization to a liberation, and in keeping with this idea, he published a booklet titled *Luther Liberated* (*Luther frigiven*, 1970). In his later authorship, the changeable character of the concept of *Stundelein* ("the time"), as found in Luther's works, interacted with secularization, within a common theological framework. Yet, although the church itself must articulate and materialize the theological contents of creation and the law, Wingren still does not recognize the church as the primary place for ethics and politics. It is, instead, the individual person's commitment, present in a disguised way in many places in the community, which gives the individual a sort of mediating role between the church and the world: "the route from baptism out into the world runs via each individual's relation to the other."[16] In contrast to his earlier positions, the "late" Wingren is willing to support that in certain situations—i.e., when the general public opinion is unresponsive—the church should take the lead in collective action, outcries, demonstrations and so forth. Yet, even if the church reacts in a political way, as a church, it has no monopoly on political action or any sole right to relevant action. The basic model is that the law drives acts forward in order to meet the needs of the other, when such actions do not occur spontaneously. This occurs in conjunction with a judgment in the human consciousness that eliminates self-righteousness. For this to occur, no sermons are necessary. In situations in which created life is openly attacked, however, preachers must speak out, even if it means speaking out against general human occurrences in the world.[17]

In his book *The Modernization of Lutheranism . . . ? The New Correction of the Lutheran Doctrine of Calling by Gustaf Wingren's Theology of Creation in Comparative Perspective*, Norwegian theologian Roger Jensen seeks to show how the functional political democracy in Sweden—in sharp contrast to the never-realized dreams of the Weimar

---

16. Wingren, "Reformationens och lutherdomens ethos" (1971), 139.

17. Cf. "What the church cannot, is not allowed to do, is to leave the created life totally undefended when it is openly attacked, in front of the eyes of all, by destruction. Here the proclamation must speak, and speak of worldly things." Wingren, "Teologins kyrkokritiska funktion i Norden under 1980-talet" (1980), 65.

Republic—created the social conditions for the interpretation of Luther that Wingren developed. Jensen maintains that the contextual and flexible character of Wingren's concept of vocation was a prerequisite for the horizontal democratic social structure and belief in rationality in Sweden during the prosperous postwar years: "It is nonetheless an expression for a view of humanity that is extremely modern in its emphasis upon the human being as reason and capacity."[18] Jensen points out Wingren as one of the foremost contemporary critics of Luther's idea of vocation, and whose criticism is in part directed against the weak links between the gospel and the body in Luther's theology, and in part directed against Luther's tendency to remove royalty and authority from the church's proclamation of the law, so that spiritual government becomes entirely limited to the proclamation of the gospel.[19]

It is no coincidence that the above-mentioned study is from Norway, a country that Wingren was invited to visit many times during the 1980s. Although Wingren had a good, long-term working relationship with Professor Jacob Jervell of Norway, his breakthrough in that country came as a result of his radical and sharp criticism of the society of late capitalism in the wake of the social-ethical awakening in the years after 1968.[20] Svein Aage Christoffersen, a professor at the Faculty of Theology at the University of Oslo and a leading figure in the organization Forum for Christians Socialists, became Wingren's bridge to Norwegian networks. Christoffersen emphasizes that Wingren's critique was in and of itself not original; what was original, and deeply so, was the theological basis that Wingren provided for this type of critique. In his presentation, Christoffersen trains his focus on a special point in Løgstrup's ethics

18. Jensen, *Modernisering av lutherdomen*, 70. Cf. "Wingren's positive and optimistic adaption of reason, and on the other hand, his accompanying egalitarian adaptation of ethics, that is, his emphasis of ethics as something common [to all humanity]. On both of these points, Wingren differs from the mainstream of the reception of Luther in Sweden and Germany, and also in Holland. I maintain that the context in which Wingren lived and worked made it possible for Wingren to see sides of Luther that would not have been easy to identify in other contexts." Ibid., 90. It is interesting that Jensen so clearly points out the emphasis on rationality and reason in Wingren's interpretation of Luther, since precisely these aspects of Wingren's work have been so regularly questioned. Yet for Jensen's own part, this is not a positive thing; rather, he maintains that this is problematic in a postindustrial and postmodern era, when confidence in reason and its superior function is flagging.

19. Ibid., 74.

20. Christoffersen, "Gustaf Wingrens teologiske etikk i spenningen mellom lov og evangelium," 40.

which spoke to him; specifically, that Løgstrup never identifies the ethical demand with the prevailing social norms of a society at a specific time. The ethical requirement is radical precisely in that its focus is upon doing what is best for the other, and nothing else. The radicalness associated with the ethical demand means that it cannot have a conservational function, but rather just the opposite. It functions critically in the direction of change. However, according to Wingren, what Løgstrup overlooks is that the gospel, too, can serve in this creative and re-creative function in society.[21] Another original aspect we find in Wingren is the perspective he takes from underneath, in other words, from the view of the oppressed toward their oppressors, from the powerless toward those who hold power. Løgstrup could not imagine that new creation might also emanate from the gospel and the church, primarily because earlier, the church had held a monopoly on new creation by claiming monopoly on ethics and morality. But according to Wingren, new creation may also come from the gospel. Furthermore, the gospel may contribute to let the expression of the law be disclosed in all its radicalness. However, it must be noted that the choice of political position always occurs according to the conditions of the law; it can never be generated from the gospel. Wingren rejects all kinds of instrumentalization of the Christian faith, all attempts to reduce the faith to just a weapon in the political struggle.[22]

Critique of the Ideology of Growth

What is the content of Gustaf Wingren's social criticism? What is its primary focus? Considering these questions, I believe that we once again must remind ourselves of the importance of Greta Hofsten. Not only had she prompted a new political consciousness in Wingren, Hofsten also had her own professional background as a leading figure in Swedish labor market policy and politics. There is an intriguing connection between their two respective spheres of knowledge, which established a complimentary relationship between Hofsten's labor market policy experience and the research Wingren had carried out since the early 1940s on Luther's teachings on vocation and the concept of work. Hofsten discovered a radical social critique in Wingren's work, of which the author himself

---

21. Ibid., 42. Gustaf Wingren developed this critique of Løgstrup in writings such as his article "Skapelse och evangelium: Ett problem i modern dansk teologi" (1977).

22. Cf. also Wingren's discussion with Helge Hognestad in chapter 8 of this book.

was unaware, but which he later embraced and further developed. His inspiration thus came from Hofsten. She disclosed new aspects of Wingren's work, which she encouraged and which they elaborated together. However, this was never developed as a kind of intellectual symbiosis. Even in their jointly written texts, it is still possible to identify two distinct voices. The concrete division of labor that they employed becomes evident in the books that they published together. Here, we can see that they never wrote joint texts (with one single exception, the articles on Sara Lidman); instead, they alternated their respective contributions concerning various themes. Wingren's contributions were written from his basis in biblical, historical and contemporary theology; Hofsten wrote from a political perspective, including a more elaborated attentiveness to the general human experience.[23]

How can we comprehend the connection between Wingren's focus on the concept of work, which found its early manifestation in his 1942 doctoral dissertation on Luther's teachings on vocation, and the skills in labor-market politics that Hofsten had gained from working for more than a decade in various capacities in the Swedish Labor Market Administration? First and foremost, we may state that, in the post–World War II years, when the effort to create a social-democratic welfare state in Sweden was in full swing, labor-market policy was an area of strategic importance for the entire social-political sphere, since its purpose was to balance the main goals of Sweden's economic policy: full employment, stable prices, economic growth and balance in Sweden's payments to other countries. Quite simply, the vision was that Swedish labor-market policy would work in conjunction with the country's economic policies to fine tune the development of Swedish society by stimulating the labor force to mobility, both geographically as well as socially. In the beginning, Hofsten was enthusiastic about her work, but over time she felt an increasing sense of discomfort over the cost of the human suffering that these efforts brought about. In reality, labor-market policy resulted in the marginalization and elimination of workers. In addition, the new order of things in post–World War II Sweden meant that socialism was forsaken, and in its place a new market-adapted social democracy was developed.[24]

23. Wingren and Hofsten, *Tro och främlingskap* (1979), *De levandes mod* (1981), and *En liten katekes* (1983).

24. In her article "Fyrtio år med rösträtt," Hofsten disagreed with what Gunnar Myrdal had claimed immediately after World War II: "In our strivings, we are directed solely by the goal of achieving the higher efficiency in production that will make

At the same time, the fact that full employment was being replaced by the supreme goal of rapid economic growth was being hidden from view by various ideological disguises.[25]

Parallel to this development, Swedish social democracy was changed from within. Greta Hofsten had witnessed this herself by her intense political party involvement, in particular during her time in Kalmar in the 1950s. With the optimistic modernization and rationalization of Swedish society, new career possibilities opened up, and with them appeared the new social-democratic tycoon. The number of elected public officials dropped as the number of bureaucrats rose. The responsible citizen became a "customer." Democracy became "social-service democracy," resulting in a radical de-politicization of the Swedish citizenry: "Ask people what they want, and in which order and at what pace, and then carry out their wishes."[26] As a result, dissatisfaction became the driving political force of the Swedish people, and thus the primary task assigned to politicians was to eliminate the shortcomings that still existed in the system. It was at this particular point that labor-market policy entered the picture.

Many people, however, had to pay the price for the successful structural rationalization in Sweden during the 1960s, especially those who could not keep abreast of the development. Hofsten seemed to see how the dignity of working people, and even their very value as human beings, was threatened in the early 1970s, when Sweden moved to program budgeting, and systematically developed the tactic of describing unemployment as a result of the characteristics of the individual rather than the mechanisms of the labor market. In an attempt to manipulate the statistics to make them look better than they were, increased efforts were introduced to remove people from the workforce through archive work, protected workshops, and early retirement "due to labor market conditions."[27] Through this focus on the individual, the issues of the Swedish labor market were de-politicized, so that all questions regarding

---

possible more secure employment and better incomes for employees, and lower prices for consumers. The results that the corporation produces, and not the form of the corporation, are what interest us." Ibid., 22.

25. Cf. "My theory is that the government, the leadership of the party and the workers unions have completed the plan to create an ideological disguise for the difficulties that the current phase of capitalistic development puts a social democratic administration into." Hofsten, "Socialdemokratins dilemma," 183.

26. Hofsten, "Fyrtio år med rösträtt," 23.

27. Hofsten, "Socialdemokratins dilemma," 191.

economic power and the overarching direction of the development of Swedish society were removed from public debate.

Hofsten's objections to what was happening began when the term "labor market" was first coined, that is, when Sweden's market-adapted social democracy developed "a pronounced labor market-focused economic view of the relationship between capital and labor."[28] In the long run, the resultant de-politicization created a deep crisis for Swedish democracy itself. For Hofsten, what she considered as a political manipulation in association with Sweden's nuclear power referendum of 1980 became a major political loss, and she took it personally. Hofsten and Wingren had been personally engaged in the "No to Nuclear Power" campaign of 1976–80, and she had a difficult time accepting what she saw as a farce surrounding the "yes-no-yes explosions" in the referendum: "Never before have so many politically responsible persons in Sweden been deceived in such a smart way."[29]

Hofsten regarded the 1980s as a period of rapid de-politicization, and the democratic shortfall concerned her deeply. She watched how a kind of "economism" spread in the early 1990s, as a systemic shift in terms of a new, ideological politics that developed, which made women, the unemployed and those facing unemployment, and retirees the greatest losers. In the face of this situation, she sought to keep hope alive and her frustration under control, but she realized that the current development was moving in a direction different from the one she would have wished. In an article she wrote in 1992, we may recognize in her choice of words evidence of a sadness bordering on desperation:

> And the question is whether we have sufficient time to rebuild our political system from the ground up again, when we have not even completed drawing up the blueprints. We are forced into a race against time. In a few more years, the space for political involvement, which has already shrunken drastically, may be reduced to a one-room apartment with a galley kitchen. Not

---

28. Ibid., 191.

29. Hofsten, "Fyrtio år med rösträtt," 25. For many years, Gustaf Wingren showed his engagement in the antinuclear movement by wearing a pin with the words "Nuclear power? No thanks!" ("Atomkraft—nej tack!"). He also took part in the protest marches at the Barsebäck nuclear power station in southern Sweden. His opposition to nuclear power had an interesting parallel in K. E. Løgstrup, who strongly opposed the plans to develop Danish nuclear power. Ole Jensen tells of how as a retiree, Løgstrup participated in citizen's initiatives and increasingly became a sort of eco-activist. Jensen, *Historien om K. E. Løgstrup*, 253.

everyone will be happy that our citizenry will only be allowed the right to choose when it comes to their wallpaper, or so I hope.[30]

Later, in an article from 1995, the year before Greta Hofsten died of leukemia, she sought to establish a political position not only beyond optimism but also beyond cynicism. However, for her, it was not Sweden's faith in development that was the problem, but rather its cynicism, which made her write, "Cynicism feels no sorrow."[31] In a period of time when a cynical and nihilistic view of human life was spreading, Hofsten maintained that this view simply did not agree with reality; that is, it did not express the entire truth about the human condition:

> Each person who thinks about this without reservation has experiences that contradict this view of human life; experiences of people who act in a "self-forgetting" way, who set aside their own interests before the needs of others, who even risk their lives when others are in danger. These are not odd, saint-like figures, but "normal" people. Love exists, and it does not keep score. Mercy exists, and it empowers the person who witnesses and can empathize with the vulnerability of an unknown fellow human being. Trust, beyond all calculation, comes into being among people.[32]

In the same context, she presents a view of the human condition clearly inspired by Løgstrup, as she speaks of the necessity of "a double interpretation of what it means to be human." This is about an ambivalent view of humanity that can correct the unilateral interpretation of human life which characterizes both the optimism that dominated society earlier on, and the cynicism that she saw as the prevailing view of her own time. Would a more robust attitude be able to survive the winter of her current day and eventually win over her discouragement? The question remains and is still open, for Hofsten's engagement continued unflaggingly onward, even during her illness and until the day of her death. We can only speculate as to how well this analysis holds up today, and how Hofsten would have viewed today's social developments. It is nonetheless this political analysis that flows into Wingren's theology from the 1970s onward, and as we have seen already in chapter 5, influenced his later authorship.

30. Hofsten, "Fyrtio år med rösträtt," 26.
31. Hofsten, "Tidsspegel," 4.
32. Ibid., 6.

What were the organizational contexts of Hofsten and Wingren's sociopolitical involvement?

The organization that provided the most important institutional forum for Wingren and Hofsten once they had become a couple was without a doubt Christians for Socialism (*Kristna för socialism*). This movement, which never had more than about three hundred members in Sweden, took its inspiration from Norway, where the group Forum for Christian Socialists had burst upon the scene with thousands of members in the late 1970s and early 1980s. In 1977, during the last months before he retired, Wingren traveled with Hofsten to Rättvik, Dalarna, to take part in planning discussions for the establishment of Christians for Socialism in Sweden. The entries he made in his personal journal for these days show that his foremost contribution to the new organization was not political analysis: "GW presented a scripture lesson on Isaiah 43:25, Greta served communion." The newly established movement had several local chapters, organized well-attended summer meetings every other summer, and for a number of years published an ambitious journal, *The Eye of the Needle* (*Nålsögat*). Despite its brief life, it was a periodical of high quality, not least because both Hofsten and Wingren frequently contributed articles to it.

The important role that the Christians for Socialism group played in their shared life raises the question of Wingren's own political stance. From the outset, it must be remembered that Christians for Socialism never represented doctrinal socialism, and did not in any way give support to or encourage closer ties with the totalitarian states of the time which flew socialist or communist flags. Earlier, we saw how radical leftist language and certain references to Marxism appear in Wingren's books from the middle of the 1970s. In his autobiography from 1991, he declares outright that socialism is "the only reasonable position for the future, at least, for people directed by the gospel."[33] In the turbulent time around the turn of the decade in 1990, when the Soviet Union and an entire series of communist states began to fall apart, he stated that socialism is "more necessary than ever since the beginning of this century." In the same context, he speaks of the market as a "rock-hard killing force" and warns of "ruthless market forces."[34]

---

33. Wingren, *Mina fem universitet* (1991), 190.
34. Ibid., 190-91.

Against the background of his newly awakened interest in politics, we may bring the matter to a head and ask the question, was Gustaf Wingren a socialist? And if so, when did he become a socialist? Clearly, all the evidence shows that his basic stance up to and at the beginning of the 1970s was one of strong political disinterest. We have already stated how remarkable it was that he did not seem to have thought about the political implications of his having studied at Berlin University in 1938 when Nazi Germany was preparing for war. Later, we have seen his disinterest in the events of 1968. Perhaps we may only comprehend this disinterest as the reverse, a personality who showed an extraordinary focus on his research work, which, so to speak, he carried out in another world, a world of theology. Whatever political sympathies he did show, his position seemed to point toward a generally non-socialist political stance, and not a liberal one. In any case, the idea of taking part in the labor movement's First of May demonstrations or other manifestations of a socialist nature was foreign to the early Wingren. His theology was deeply anchored in an organic view of society, one that sought, in an almost communitarian way, to protect the cohesion of organic human community. In this sense, he was not the only person in modern Sweden who, in his criticism of the rationalizations brought on by industrialized society, in which "everything permanent is put into flux,"[35] made the transition to political radicalism, although he did so from a mainly conservative point of departure. Such a position could be called socialistic, but only if it were to undergo significant modifications.[36] If we speak about Wingren as a radical in a political aspect, we must remember that the concepts of "radical" and "conservative" are relative and variable over time; the content of these words are strongly dependent upon the context in which they are used. In any case, Wingren never thought of socialism as statification, but rather, spoke of socialism in terms of "allowing one's own existence to join with a community that benefits our fellow human beings."[37]

It is quite clear that Wingren's socialism came from Hofsten. At times his socialism may seem somewhat contrived, as in an article from 1976, where he considered the human condition in terms of a tension between evil and good, as he had done earlier, but here he speaks of

35. Cf. Berman, *All That Is Solid Melts into Air*.

36. On this point, Jensen has obviously (and falsely) been led to believe that Wingren had been a socialist his entire life. Cf. Jensen, *Modernisering av lutherdomen*, 45 n. 79.

37. Sollerman, "Hemma hos Greta och Gustaf."

the individual human being as an "election place," and the issue of the standard of living in industrialized countries as the strategic location for "voter observation." Suddenly, he even adds, "and, as I remember it, Mao expresses it . . ."[38]

Thus if the primary focus of Wingren's great recontextualization and political metamorphosis was not first and foremost about socialism, how then should we determine his identity? It would be most reasonable to say that Wingren developed a critique of civilization that was directed against the general ideology of development, nihilistic values, the breakdown of everyday life, degradation of working conditions, and so on. These were characteristics that he shared with many other conservative communitarians who had become radical in their criticism of the threats against organic communities and traditional values. I have chosen to describe the core of his radical political profile as a critique against the ideology of growth and the social pressure for individual achievement. In this context, Luther's concept of "justification by faith alone" comes into heavy use, since in light of Luther's model of interpretation, the ideology of growth, the social obsession with the maximization of profit, the increased demand for personal achievement and the pursuit of career and status, may all be considered as huge efforts to achieve justification through acts. The pressure for individual achievement results from the idea that the individual is considered the creating factor in his or her existence. According to Wingren's interpretation of Luther, this idea, that the individual is to be viewed as a product of him- or herself, is to be considered as a kind of idolatry. In the same way that Luther transfers Paul's criticism of circumcision and Jewish law to a critique of monastic life and the institution of indulgences, Wingren transfers Luther's critique of justifications through acts to modern systems of production, which from this perspective stand out as a false teaching that negates an understanding of life as creation, a gift to be received. This means that both the concept of creation and the teaching of justification collide with the modern ideology of production. Against this interpretation of human life, which is based on constant comparisons, he juxtaposes a sound indifference, which he is able to illustrate in the following way:

> A young woman in everyday clothing who attends the opening night of a theater production will naturally read the program and look up at the stage. But this young woman will not notice

38. Wingren, "En kristen människosyn," 15.

some grand female figure of society who makes a spectacular entry while finding her seat. A person like this young woman, indifferent, with an interest only in the play and not in status, is a stronger moral force than are indignant protests about elegant clothing and extravagance. Her indifference may bring forth in another theater attendee that which admonitions cannot, a longing for freedom from fetishes: "Oh, to be free like her!" A Christian who eagerly climbs the ladder of status may, through his mere industriousness, adopt what is perhaps the greatest fiend of our time. The destruction of our environment on a global scale, stupid reverence for annual increases in production, and the grotesque space race of the superpowers: all of these are simply magnifications of the competitiveness that begins when two individuals compare their own latest victories in increasing their standard of living.[39]

Once again we are dealing with a text by Wingren, which is as insightful as it is comical, in this case because of the author's seeming lack of experience with theater halls. Yet, not even the gigantic leap that he makes, from the high society lady in fine clothes to the space race between the super powers, can hide the ingenious way of presenting Luther's idea of justification by faith alone. The central theme of Wingren's social criticism is aimed at the degradation of and reduction in the value of human labor, which results in demands for increases in the pace of work. In the end, the fanatical ideology of growth and development, with its fixation on constant increases in production, results in people being pushed out of the workforce. Not only is this ideology of growth part of a nationalistic egoism that does not shy away from making money on the export of weapons, but it also creates environmental destruction that in the long run threatens all life on earth. Wingren claimed, for example, that the polluting of the Baltic Sea would have been a major theme for Martin Luther had he been alive today. The dogma of constant increases in production has become the overarching life view of contemporary society. People become the victims of the avalanche of economic growth as political parties urge one another on with increasingly unreasonable promises, in campaign after campaign: "Our present nations are in full swing with an abuse which today appears quite respectable: the destruction of the natural environment in the service of economic growth."[40]

---

39. Wingren, "Reformationens och lutherdomens ethos" (1971), 141.
40. Wingren, *Gamla vägar framåt* (1986), 45. Cf. ibid., 92.

In the same way as modern advertising tends to create needs that do not exist, national striving for economic growth *at any cost* risks leading to the indiscriminate production of *anything and everything*. To combat this, Wingren emphasized the need for international solidarity, which he sometimes expressed through fair-trade shopping, in his case at the fair trade store in Lund called The Globe *(Klotet)*, regularly taking part in public demonstrations, and making deliberate choices in one's personal lifestyle. Wingren believed strongly in the power of example. He often mentioned how liberating it could be to develop a sense of indifference to all of the competition in society, and that such indifference could provide inspiration for voluntary reductions in consumption. He placed community before competitiveness, and warned that the ideologies of unending progress and growth characterizing the current day would seriously weaken people's capacity to survive hardships and loss of prestige in society. The ideology of growth results not only in the exploitation of the world's poor, but it also negates Luther's classic teaching of justification by faith. Wingren did not hesitate to point out that "to evaluate a person according to what he can achieve is deeply un-Christian."[41] Theological teachings suddenly became political issues, when he stated that modern society and systems of production could be considered as a great striving after justification through acts.

We cannot doubt that this involvement in social issues was anything other than genuine, but at the same time it is easy to recognize the nostalgia in his criticism. Wingren's social criticism bears the stamp of his own sense of being an outsider in society, as well as his strong tendency

---

41. Wingren, *Rättfärdiggörelse av tro* (1978), 23. Using the concept of justification to make an examination of the modern production system as an expression of a "false teaching" is rather ingenious, but it is also not entirely unproblematic. Christoffersen raises objections to using not only the concept of creation but also that of justification as an ideological critique of latter-day capitalism. He asks whether thinking of this sort does not by extension imply a mixing of the law and the gospel. Christoffersen, "Gustaf Wingrens teologiske etikk is penning mellom lov og evangelium," 44–45. He further questions how a critique of society based on the concept of justification can have validity outside the walls of the church—and if it does not have validity, then we must ask ourselves whether Wingren has not fabricated a theological ethics that is based upon "the third use of the law" that he combated so vehemently in other contexts. But Christoffersen himself also replies that things need not be this way, since Wingren maintains that the gospel is a message that people cannot tell themselves; rather, it is something that must come "from without," a fact that becomes clear not least of all in times of passage such as our meeting with death. Ibid., 45–46.

to romanticize the past. In a text where he writes about how work was in the past, Wingren states,

> Today, people have much higher wages than they had in the past. Yet today, we must get up a whole hour earlier than we did in the past, sit in a car, and wait for traffic lights. A person carries out a full work task or two before they have even begun their work. When the workday is over, and one ought to be able to lie down and relax or take a seat at the evening meal, you have the same, hour-long, unnerving car ride before you. It is not only the lost time, but the psychological pressure. You cannot relax as you would during a walk, quite the opposite, you become tense, you have to be careful of other vehicles, road signs, traffic signals—when rest is what you deserve.[42]

In this text, "quality of life" is a keyword for Wingren, who himself did not have a driver's license, as he criticizes the ideology of growth. In this context, he writes not only about the pursuit of increases in the standard of living, but also (and somewhat typically for that time in Sweden) about people's many material possessions. In his little book titled *Liberated to Quality of Life* (*Frigörelse till livskvalitet*, 1975), he provides four examples of what he recognizes as the major problems and challenges of the time: noise and pollution, traffic, living conditions, and the stressful pace of work.[43] More and more frequently he also mentions the international perspective. The world is larger than Sweden; Sweden is only one of the municipalities in the world.[44] Wingren not only mentions the tension between social questions and eternal questions as a false juxtaposition; he also speaks about salvation and liberation as matters of being saved from *external* oppression, freedom from bodily imprisonment and *external* shackles. His theology has clearly become political, yet without activism:

> The liberation movements gaining ground today, and which the churches support, also work for an outward political and economic freedom. We should not be blind to the fact that today's churches have a good biblical basis for promoting this kind of freedom, and for being happy about it, wherever it is now emerging. It is not unreasonable to make intercession for African, Asian, and Latin American liberation in our congregational prayers during our worship services. The general congregational

---

42. Wingren, *Frigörelse till livskvalitet* (1975), 10.
43. Ibid., 9ff.
44. Ibid., 13.

prayer has always been a prayer for outward good, political and economic good *in the world*.[45]

These lines bear witness that the retired Lundensian professor had radically changed his views. He had moved far beyond the disinterest and disengagement he had earlier shown, as during the Lund Cathedral protest of the late 1960s, and was now developing his theological thinking in new ways, based on the social contextualization that had come to claim his interest. In addition to his new political focus, Wingren also found a broadened interest in culture, and he even found an almost youthful enthusiasm for popular culture. Once, as he sat and listened to the LP record "Sympathy for the Devil" ("Sympati för djävulen") by the Swedish avant-garde rock band *De dummaste*, I asked him whether he really enjoyed what he was listening to. He replied, "I've learned to appreciate this, too." One of the members of this music group was Martin Rössel, the son of Greta Hofsten's twin sister, Karin Rössel. As a seventeen-year old, Martin had been the youngest guest at Greta and Gustaf's wedding in June 1976. Martin, who today is a musician, songwriter and radio producer, has no special memories of that occasion. However, from later meetings, he does remember Wingren's rather special aura: "He had a bright red face, as if he lived with some sort of inner pressure. He looked determined and stern, as if he was angry, even when he was not—and he made very funny comments. There was actually something, rock 'n roll, about Gustaf; he was able to climb out of his role as a theologian."[46]

When Gustaf Wingren entered Martin Rössel's life as his aunt's new husband, a dialogue emerged in which Greta and Gustaf also demonstrated an interest in Martin's musical creativity. There was one song in particular that Martin had recorded with his band, *De dummaste*, which really fueled the conversation between them: "Run Out of Gas" ("Soppan är slut"), with lyrics by Martin Rössel, and music by Martin Rössell and Lars Kleveman:

> Jesus was a Guy with a Chevy Truck
> He drove thousands of miles and then oh tough luck
> The old thing just stopped he had run out of gas
> Poor Jesus had to get up and haul his ass
> And all of the Angels just looked up and wept

45. Wingren, *En framtid och ett hopp* (1977), 11.
46. Interview with Martin Rössel, April 21, 2010.

As Jesus up to God's own Gas Station now stepped
God then came out in his overalls
He looked like a car mech who'd had a tough call
He said Jesus, my son, turn home to your den
Cause we've run out of gas in Jerusalem!
When Jesus got the news he just turned his ass
Facing a town that had run out of gas
He then heard a voice within him say,
"My son you must try in the USA"
But all of the Angels just bent down in shame
As Jesus to God's own land then waned
New York was desolate mile after mile
A fabulous city that had lost its style
And all the poor people he met had to say
Was we've run out of gas in the USA!
Run out of Gas
Run out of Gas
Run out of Gas
Run out of Gas in the USA
Run out of Gas in every home . . .
Run out of Gas

Given his love of burlesque and all things provocative, it is not difficult to understand why Wingren would appreciate this song. He also understood that these lyrics had both theological and political dimensions. At face value, they tell about the oil crisis and material need in modern society, and of how political capital had been used up in the United States. Yet on a deeper level, the song also tells of a spiritual need that ultimately points toward Christ as a figure who is "out of gas" after having "poured himself out."

During the 1970s and 1980s, Wingren increasingly developed theological thinking in a political direction that resulted in a radical critique of power: "It is altogether impossible to achieve power and remain completely uncorrupted by it."[47] What is interesting about this critique of power is that it stems from the very heart of the Christian faith. In

---

47. Wingren, *En framtid och ett hopp* (1977), 3.

addition, it can be expressed in both positive and negative ways, in that it can be articulated in terms of life and freedom, as well as destruction and death. In one and the same context, Wingren is thus able to state the following:

> What is remarkable about the events and people of the Bible is, firstly, that salvation is constantly being given to the oppressed, to those who are down in the depths (those who have been forced out are not on the periphery; rather, they are the central point in events, in Babel, or under Rome). Secondly, salvation is freedom: the present and the future are filled not with laws, not with commands, but a freedom that continually expands forward.[48]

After this, he presents the following difficult-to-digest statement: "We will never come to terms with our own death on our final day if we do not learn to gladly 'receive' and in faith accept death before the day of our death. We gain 'a future and a hope' when we cease our pursuit of profit, when we no longer resist death, but rather affirm it, for the sake of all."[49]

During the 1980s, the peace movement grew, and both Wingren and Hofsten became involved in the campaign against nuclear weapons. At that time, many groups of professionals in Sweden were forming their own organizations against nuclear weapons, with the goal of stopping plans to locate medium-range ballistic missiles in Europe. Greta Hofsten's older sister, the diplomat Inga Thorsson, became an international voice in the campaign against nuclear weapons. While Wingren was by no means a pacifist, he rejected any notion that the theory of *bellum justum* (the just war) could in any way be relevant in an age when all of humanity was threatened by global destruction. How a weapon of this type could be referred to as an instrument of peace was incomprehensible to him. He also found it impossible to underplay the threat posed by nuclear weapons:

> There is not the least bit of evidence to support the claim that nuclear weapons will never be used. On the contrary, there are two circumstances that point in the opposite direction. First, people have always used the weapons that they have had at their disposal (gas, biological weapons, etc.), and they have done so despite the fact that their use has been forbidden. Secondly, nuclear weapons have in fact already been used.[50]

48. Ibid., 9.
49. Ibid., 18.
50. Wingren, *Gamla vägar framåt* (1986), 108.

For most of his adult life, and long after he was a student, Wingren remained a member of LuKRISS, the local chapter of the Student Christian Movement (SCM) in Sweden. He was a frequent speaker at meetings of the Lund chapter of the SCM, and at other local chapters throughout Sweden. The later Wingren also regularly attended SCM meetings in Lund in order to listen to other speakers. From the mid-1980s onward, Greta Hofsten accompanied him at these meetings. The students more or less expected them to attend, and their presence was in no way seen as odd, even though there was at least a full generation between the students and "Gustaf 'n Greta." The couple identified with these young people who were critical of church and society, and who questioned the day and age in which they lived.

Yet for the Hofsten-Wingrens, the most important congregation of which they were members was probably the group that gathered for Sunday Evening in the Crypt, arranged each week at Lund Cathedral. These meetings had a longer tradition in the Crypt, but were given a sort of social and political turn in 1979 by student pastors Anna-Karin Hammar and Leif Nilsson. Inspired by the German Church Days and their own experiences from Rostock in the German Democratic Republic, they sought to introduce political-theological analysis in conjunction with a worship service where the prayers offered during the service were focused on current social problems. Here, the concrete challenges that members met in their lives and in society were allowed to set the agenda for a liturgy and theological reflection strongly inspired by theologians such as Gustaf Wingren, Dorothee Sölle, and Olov Hartman.

Over time, Greta Hofsten became the advisory chairperson for the Student Chaplains in Lund, the group responsible for these unique worship services, and in that role, she influenced these activities in profound ways. Hofsten, as an experienced and knowledgeable person, offered the work a legitimacy, and also helped guarantee the group the freedom to develop in a creative way. Because Hofsten was such a voracious reader of daily newspapers, magazines, and books, she became a peerless source of suggestions about new and often young authors and researchers who could be invited in as speakers. Sunday Evening in the Crypt was an experimental and liturgically conscious environment in which an open atmosphere was cultivated. The group invited almost anyone who had anything important to relate, regardless of their faith or creed, to speak at the beginning of the meetings, which then always transitioned into a worship service with Holy Communion. After the service, the group would move to the Student Pastors' office facility on Kraft Square for a time of more informal fellowship. This format suited both Hofsten and Wingren, especially since Wingren found it difficult to endure regular worship services. These were events to which he was drawn, but which also caused him such a feeling of discomfort that it often took him quite a while to recover. Hofsten, too, simultaneously felt like a foreigner in, but yet found herself attracted to, the church, a tension that early on was reflected in her view of the church. In her diary entries from the mid-1960s, we can already find clear evidence of a view of the church where the gospel is interpreted from a horizon of understanding based in creation theology and a marked political edge:

> It is not foolishness, these matters of church community, community of faith, baptismal community, partaking in communion, whatever I might choose to call all of it. But tell me "Within, within the walls of the church," and I will answer—answer at last with a snort—"Go outside!" Draw a circle, a little circle of piety, and I will reply rather brusquely, "Go outside!" Then generously draw a larger circle, so large that we can safely say that when we walk on the streets of downtown Stockholm, we are walking among "our people" (the baptized ones), and I will still answer, baptized though I may be, with growing desperation, "Go outside!"[51]

In the Sunday Evening in the Crypt gatherings, Wingren and Hofsten found a sort of liturgical home. It provided them a place in the church as a new couple, who had each left their respective former lives behind. In a remarkable way, the unique and open atmosphere of these meetings mirrored Wingren and Hofsten's theological stance. Although they had not created Sunday Evening in the Crypt, Wingren's theology seems to have strongly inspired the priests who led this work, such as Anna-Karin Hammar, Pelle Bengtsson, Barbro Gustafsson, Pelle Lidbeck, Lotta Miller and others, and these gatherings became their spiritual home port. There were aspects of the fundamental structure of these gatherings that reflected a Wingrenian theology, and that can be recognized in the dialectical dynamic between creation and gospel. It represents a basic theological outlook in which the unique and distinctive nature of faith stands out as something that only radicalizes its openness. In the opening portion of the service, real-life challenges from society were considered; this portion of the evening was something that stood on its own. On the other

51. Hofsten, *Samtalsvis*, 64.

hand, communion was celebrated every Sunday evening in the Lund Cathedral crypt, so that there, in the innermost part of the mystery, they encountered something tangible and material that had always already existed outside: wine and bread, blood and bodies. In this way, the communion elements became a liturgical reply to the challenges of society. The worship service thus became "a manifestation of the materiality of God's presence in the world, an expression of an incarnation theology in which God's presence was bound up with that which is most deeply human."[52]

Creation Theology Becomes Ecological Theology

Given the way in which we mostly use the word "creation" today, it may be misleading to think that creation theology would automatically mean ecological theology. The center of interest for the early Gustaf Wingren, as he expressed himself in his writings from the 1940s and 1950s, was primarily the law (and its earthly use), although even at that time, the concept of the law was presented in a way that implies a concept of creation. Today we probably underestimate the fact that his theological project was derived in an almost genetic way from a reflection on the law and his critique of how repressed the idea of the first or earthly use of the law was among the dominant theologians of his day. In addition, his creation theology, when it had been explicitly developed, still did not contain any theological reflection considering nature, environment or ecology. Instead, it was primarily elaborated within the framework of a theological anthropology.

Any Swedish theologian who has an interest in theological anthropology is probably also interested in Denmark. As Harry Aronson stated in the introduction to his 1960 monograph on Grundtvig: "Pondering what a 'human being' is, is a typically Danish phenomenon."[53] As far as Wingren is concerned, Denmark clearly meant the city of Aarhus, and in turn, Aarhus meant K. E. Løgstrup. As we have seen, Wingren had first met Løgstrup during the summer term that he spent in Basel in 1947. In a diary entry from 20 May of that year, he writes, "Met with Prof. K. E. Løgstrup of Aarhus, long discussion with him." Nonetheless, more than two decades would pass before Løgstrup would be of any decisive importance for Wingren's own theological project—but once he was, the

52. Ibid.
53. Aronson, *Mänskligt och kristet*, 11.

intellectual and personal contacts between the two grew the more rapidly and powerfully. The high level of mutual regard between the two professors of ethics was manifested by the fact that they were both awarded honorary doctorates from the respective colleague's university.

Denmark always had a special place in Wingren's theology. Sometimes, he even spoke of himself as a disciple of Danish theology.[54] However, as we have seen, this did not refer to all Danish theology, but rather to the particular kind of theology characterized by a few special criteria: first, it had to be theology from Aarhus and not Copenhagen; second, it had to be part of the tradition of Grundtvig and not Kierkegaard; which, third, for a long time primarily meant the theology of Løgstrup and not his colleague Johannes Sløk.

Aarhus University is a relatively new seat of academic learning, and its theological faculty was not established until 1942, a recent date in comparison with the more profound historical roots at the Universities of Lund and Copenhagen. In 1942, the then-thirty-two-year old P. G. Lindhardt (1910–88) was employed as a professor of church history and the history of doctrine. Yet, the other professors who contributed to establishing the new environment of theology at Aarhus were also relatively young. In 1943, K. E. Løgstrup was connected to Aarhus University as a professor of ethics and the philosophy of religion. He was thirty-seven years old at the time, and as a matter of fact he had received this appointment because K. E. Skydsgaard had turned the University down and taken a position in Copenhagen. In 1945, Aarhus University was granted authority to award undergraduate degrees, and the same year, 38-year old Regin Prenter was appointed professor of dogmatics. The following year, in 1948, the University gained authorization to award graduate degrees, and Johannes Sløk (1916–2001) defended his dissertation, becoming the first person to receive a doctorate from Aarhus University. Sløk was somewhat younger, and had not advanced as far in his career as the others, but once he embarked on his career he held no less than three different professorships at Aarhus: professor of systematic theology (beginning in 1959), professor in the history of ideas (beginning in 1975), and professor of ethics and philosophy of religion (beginning in 1980).

The Aarhus Faculty of Theology was established in occupied Denmark during World War II, and the first years came to be dramatic. The professors were sometimes forced to go underground for political

---

54. Wingren, *Creation and Gospel* (1979/1979), 34.

reasons, and a number of students lost their lives as members of the Danish resistance movement. Instruction ceased altogether for several extended periods. Despite these circumstances, the faculty succeeded in creating a unique theological milieu. At the time, during the 1940s, they were all young and unknown, but twenty years later, by the 1960s, they had matured into leading, internationally recognized theologians in their respective areas. All of them were ordained Lutheran priests in the Church of Denmark, and all of them had grown up with a revival of dialectical theology and its struggles with the problem of secularization. Yet each of them was so different in regard to their respective theological positions that in his biography of "the great Danish theological generation," Svend Bjerg avoids speaking of an Aarhus school of thought as such. This would be difficult, considering that the members of the Faculty of Theology developed such varied academic specialties as ontological philosophy of life, christologically focused *theologia crucis*, and existential theology. Instead, Bjerg refers to the Aarhus theologians, emphasizing that there was no common position that united them, although they did share a commonality of issues.[55] Viewed from today's perspective, despite its small size, the Faculty of Theology at Aarhus University during the postwar years, very much looks like a theological dream team.

In seeking to identify common traits among the Aarhus theologians, Svend Bjerg notes that they all came from respectable segments of the Danish middle class. While they were certainly without any great economic resources, they were industrious and culturally open. Their religious views were influenced by their own experience of the Pietistic revivalist movements and Danish Grundtvigianism. They saw Germany as the obvious center of theological study, but even though all of them had been followers of Barth during the 1930s, none of them would remain faithful to his teachings. In the end, they came to end up in a quasi-liberal position. However, it must be remembered that it was a highly modified position, since each of them had made the journey from some form of private Christianity to an emphasis on a greater, more comprehensive

---

55. Bjerg, *Århusteologerne*, 10, 35. The best-known standard works of the Århus school of theology are probably Lindhardt's *Vækkelse og kirkelige retninger* (1951); Prenter's book on doctrine, *Creation and Redemption* (1951–53/1967); Løgstrup's book on ethics, *The Ethical Demand* (1956/1997); and Sløk's *Det absurde teater og Jesu forkyndelse* (1968).

context for faith, regardless of whether it was a question of life itself or the proclamations of the church.[56]

With the passing of the years, young men become old, and those who were once radical suddenly find themselves the target of a new generation of radical provocateurs. The fact is that the student revolts of the late 1960s came as a shock for all of the Aarhus theologians. They were neither tolerant nor understanding. They expressed their disgust in 1970 when Denmark adopted its new form of university administration that rang a death knell for the traditional position of status held by professors. The Aarhus theologians felt as though they were being forced to give up their life's work to the vandals of a new era. Prenter resigned in protest against the changes that he could see as nothing more than a decline. As he departed, he is said to have uttered the following sarcastic words: "Now, my dear teaching assistants, there is no longer any difference between my responsibilities or yours. There is only one difference left between us—and that is that I am world famous!"[57] He then left the academic world to become a local parish priest in the Church of Denmark.

During the 1960s and 70s, Wingren's enthusiasm for Danish theology found its epicenter in Løgstrup, and then in the 1980s and 1990s shifted backward in time to a stronger focus on Grundtvig. In his connection to Løgstrup, Wingren gained ties to a central figure in current Danish theology and intellectual life. We have already seen how Wingren felt that he found an adequate philosophy for his creation theology in Løgstrup's phenomenological description of the ontological conditions of human existence, such that the relationship between spontaneous and confining expressions of life serve as a de-mythologized version of the struggle between God and the Devil.[58] This phenomenological de-

56. Bjerg, Århusteologerne, 67-9.

57. Interview with Carl-Axel Aurelius, 8 January 2010. Cf. Bjerg: "It is part of the irony of history that the Aarhus theologians were accused of being bragging provocateurs because they kept repeating a single piece of wisdom that had long been the convention in German theological circles, [that of] the distinction that dialectical theology makes between religion and gospel or Gogarten's theory on secularization versus secularism." Bjerg, Århusteologerne, 26. Also cf. "I believe that the four of them had something personal at stake; not that they themselves felt threatened, but that they were now to give up their lives' work, the common theological institution they had built up, to vandals—the lecturers and students who had no sense of 'objective factuality.'" Ibid., 34.

58. While Løgstrup himself certainly argued that this phenomenological description of the basic human condition is close to a religious interpretation, in that it deals with a total interpretation of existence that is based on something outside of humanity,

scription sets humanity in a more comprehensive ontological context, in which humanity is not the cause of its own existence. Instead, the basis of human existence always lies *outside* of human beings themselves, in something that demands human responsibility. As early as in Løgstrup's doctoral dissertation, *The Epistemological Conflict Between Transcendental Philosophical Idealism and Theology* (*Den erkendelseteoretiske konflikt mellem den transcendentalfilosofiske idealism og teologin*, 1942), this phenomenology had served as a corrective to the centered subject of the Enlightenment. Nevertheless, this ontological determination of the fundamental human condition, with its implicit critique of the Enlightenment tradition that makes the human subject the center of the world and the measure of everything, lacks an ecological perspective. It was thus no coincidence that the dissertation that Wingren researcher Lars-Olle Armgard wrote about K. E. Løgstrup was titled Anthropology (*Antropologi*, 1971).

Someone who played an extraordinarily important role for Wingren when his creation theology finally became an ecological theology was Løgstrup's protégé, Ole Jensen. After a period as a professor of dogmatics at the University of Copenhagen, Jensen became dean of the cathedral at Maribo, Denmark, and later, rector of Askov Højskole (community college), known as the center of Grundtvigianism. Jensen took the anti-Enlightenment ideas found in Løgstrup's critique of neo-Kantianism and further developed them in an ecological direction. How this in particular influenced Wingren's theology can be seen in the presentation he makes in his book *Creation and Gospel: The New Situation in European Theology* (1979/1979), in which he devotes several pages to Jensen's dissertation, *Theology between Ilusion and Restriction* (in German: *Theologie zwischen Illusion und Restriktion*, 1975).[59] Here the concept of "illusion" stands for a sort of premodern, pre-Kantian theology that views God as active in nature, without any intermediary. After Kant, God was relegated from theoretical reason to the area of ethics. However, by doing so, we risk finding ourselves in restriction, which certainly frees theology from pre-

---

in contrast to the illusion that we ourselves are the reason for our existence, the spontaneous expressions of life indicate that human life always already has form, that is, it is "created." However, as Armgard emphasizes in his article "Den senare Wingren," this connection between the basic concepts of phenomenological analysis and the mythological configurations of theology is not actually an interpretation that Løgstrup explicitly made, but rather is to be considered the work of Wingren. Ibid., 14–15.

59. Wingren, *Creation and Gospel* (1979/1979), 56–60.

scientific illusions, in that theology gains its own reserve or area: "But in this reserve, only *human beings* are considered."[60] However, the tendency in modern theology to radically separate God and nature comes at a very high price, as demonstrated by ecological crisis and environmental destruction.

In his book *Kept by the Violence of Growth: Ecology and Religion* (*I tillväxtens våld: Ekologi och religion*, 1976/1979), Jensen presents a radical break with the ethnocentric ideology of expansion that characterizes the Western view of development, something which he recounts that he soon noticed when he spent a year in India. This expansion without end consumes the lives of other cultures and makes nature poorer, with worldwide catastrophe as its ultimate result. While biologists sound the alarm, economists present a calming message, and it is no surprise which of these two messages the politicians choose to listen to.[61] Growth is, however, not the same as development. The expansionist existence is actually an expression of a form of poverty in which we have lost the ability to find rest in our existence, to *live in peace*. Human beings need to rediscover that existence is greater than just themselves, but also that the scientific viewpoint is only *one* of many possible ways to approach reality. Jensen's ideological criticism is directed against the interests that direct the scientific thirst for knowledge in which truth is simply something that humanity may use to gain mastery over existence: "*Truth implies knowledge that can be used in a technical way.*"[62] Here we may recognize a critique of the instrumental reason that serves as an obvious parallel to (and precursor of) the one that Georg Henrik von Wright developed in his later works.

An important consequence of Wingren's reception of Løgstrup in general, and Jensen in particular, is that it places the problems of the Enlightenment (or more correctly, a reflection that is critical of the Enlightenment) at the center of his reflections on contemporary theology. What we have referred to as science ever since the time of Kant is no innocent, impartial science, but rather something loaded with a set of values, specifically, an instrumental reason associated with exploitation. By accepting this, we have simultaneously denied other values that are connected to respect and reverence for nature, and gratitude and joy in

60. Ibid., 57.
61. Jensen, *I tillväxtens våld*, 33.
62. Ibid., 46.

existence. Wingren summarizes the conclusions of Jensen's work in the following way:

> It is *these* values that are unscientific, and that must be removed from scientific work. In contrast, the values of exploitation are completely scientific, and are easily and unquestioningly included in new fields of science, which at the universities are being added to the old sciences as new fields of study and new professorships are being created. What unites the old and the new is the exactness in the work, the measurable results.[63]

He takes the forest as an example. It may be described in widely varied ways: as a potential source of pulp for making paper, but also as a place that calms the mind and symbolizes basic human needs. These latter dimensions are best expressed in poetic form, but such language is banned from the domains of science. In a situation like this, in which poetry is rejected in favor of diagrams and tables, the language of science, according to Wingren, increasingly stands out as pure stupidity.[64] Jensen directs his focus toward problems associated with the fact that since the nineteenth century, theology has, in a neo-Kantian spirit, not only accepted but of its own accord promoted and become one of the foremost proponents of this route of restriction. Modern theology is thus guilty of helping to spread the ideas of exploitation and environmental destruction—and this has taken place in conflict with the contents of the biblical texts. Wingren summarizes Jensen's presentation of the problem as follows: "How should we as theologians today return to a pre-Kantian directness in our view of God and nature, and at the same time be free of 'the illusion' in, for example, the thinking of the 1600s, this thinking which placed the story of creation in the science books, and reckoned it in centuries?"[65]

We may also articulate the challenge as a question of how we might remove ourselves from the restriction that has limited theological reflection only to human beings—without ending up back in the illusion. In his later writings, when Wingren explicitly incorporates the problem of the Enlightenment as an area of controversy for his thinking, we can see how, when he strives to come "down behind the Enlightenment," he takes (although not always successfully) pains to avoid assuming a premodern

---

63. Wingren, *Creation and Gospel* (1979/1979), 57.
64. Ibid., 57-58.
65. Ibid., 59.

position.[66] Yet, it is clear that through his ties to Denmark and Ole Jensen, Wingren gained the intellectual resources needed to further develop a critique of civilization. Yet, he was able to do so without having to incorporate a concept of revelation, which by juxtaposing Christianity against general human life, would lead to a peculiar miserliness in its evaluation of humanity.

In this context, Jensen was of great importance for Wingren, in that he developed a creation theology reflection concerning environmental issues that also included a clear perspective on ecology and global justice. Jensen's personal experiences from the Third World are in many ways exemplary and typical of his generation and this era. As a result of almighty Progress, traditional cultures are being exterminated (for example, what in Jensen's presentation is referred to as "Eskimo culture," but which today would sooner be referred to as Inuit culture), while at the same time, biological diversity is being dramatically reduced. Entirely in keeping with Georg Henrik von Wright's diagnosis, worldwide catastrophes seem to loom on the horizon as a result of the attempts by human beings to control and exploit nature through the use of technology. The pilgrim and the consumer are terrifyingly similar in their mutual disdain for the world. In Jensen's wake, Wingren describes contemporary people as "Gnostic, consumerist Libertarians" who wallow in what they actually despise.[67]

If Wingren previously, starting from the point of view of theological anthropology, had directed his criticism toward theologians who denied the creation, then the ecological theology he now elaborated worked as a critique against the ideology which holds that economic growth is the meaning of life—an economic growth that attempts to reduce nature to a raw material for industrial production, whatever the cost. A creation theology that primarily directed its criticism against other theologians is now being transformed into an ecological theology that instead directs its criticism against the destruction of the environment and the exploitation of the poor. It is here that the "later" Wingren identifies the great *No* to the first article of faith, which states that the Creator is active in everything and everyone. His attempts to use systematic theology to present

---

66. Ibid., 50–55.

67. Cf. "I feel that we relate to the world as though it were a bordello: we roll ruthlessly in what we despise. If we loved the earth, we would relate to it with a completely different sort of care and gentleness. We are Gnostic consumer-libertines—as if we needed to exterminate the world by eating it. Our ideology of expansion with its power-hungry drive to dominate is full of contempt." Jensen, *I tillväxtens våld*, 56.

the Christian faith in its entirety have been transformed into a critique of society and civilization. That creation theology now also means ecological theology, and that theology must be reconfigured as critique, is something that Wingren learned first and foremost from Denmark.

Shifting Theological Metaphors

The book that initiated the great recontextualization in Gustaf Wingren's later theological project was his *Change and Continuity* (1972). In this work, he identifies three dominant pairings that may serve as models of interpretation for understanding the Christian faith:

Imprisonment—Freedom

Death—Life

Sin—Forgiveness

The logic common to these three models is that Christ gives back something that humanity has lost. According to the first model, the gospel provides freedom, where there would otherwise be enslavement; according to the second, Christ brings life and health, where death and sickness has prevailed; and according to the third model, forgiveness is offered, where sin prevails. Wingren emphasizes that each of these models is to be considered as legitimate expressions of Christian faith, in the sense that they are all supported by the Bible and by Christian tradition. However, through their respective differences, they take on a completely different topicality and meaning, depending on the concrete historical situation in which they are applied.[68] I consider these three models as expressions of three different theological metaphors. If we re-arrange the order in which they are presented, I claim that we may also distinguish an increasing degree of rationalization in their expression. First, at the most basic level, we find biological metaphors in terms of life and death; secondly, we may speak of freedom/imprisonment as metaphors of struggle; and thirdly and finally, we may identify a legal metaphoric based on the conceptual pair of forgiveness/sin.

If we consider the developing logic of Wingren's metaphorical theology, there is a clear shift from his earlier authorship, which was dominated by legal metaphors in combination with metaphors of battle, to his later authorship, where we find a radically increased usage of

68. Wingren, *Växling och kontinuitet* (1972), 91–93.

biological metaphors while the legal metaphors disappear. However, it is also equally clear that this shift is a result of the radically changing contextual conditions of Christianity over time. The Middle Ages are gone, and the theological models that worked in Luther's day in the sixteenth century seem, in the present situation, no longer meaningful. According to Wingren, the culture of guilt that characterized Martin Luther's time is no longer desirable or current.[69] In the same way as the movement from Luther to Irenaeus was connected with profound social changes, the current transformation of the world brings about a changed theological metaphor:

> People no longer ask, in any case, not as unilaterally as during Reformation times, for forgiveness of sin alone. They ask for health, for life and meaning, both for themselves and for the social contexts of which they are part. Need is the need of emptiness, more or less as in the late Antique times.[70]

When Wingren makes the case for the relevance and topicality of Irenaeus in today's society, he also elaborates the theological context that prevailed in the comprehensive process of formation of dogmas in the 300s and 400s AD. It is this pre-Constantinian situation that Wingren wants to pay attention to in a post-Constantinian era in today's Europe. The first time he elaborates this perspective extensively is in *Human and Christian: A Book on Irenaeus* (1983), which in many respects follows the lines of his earlier Irenaeus studies—but with the major difference that

---

69. Cf. "Martin Luther the man was plagued throughout his life by abnormally strong feelings of guilt. He probably would have died as a relatively unknown mentally ill man if he had not found the message of justification without one's own works, i.e., by faith alone." Wingren, *Gamla vägar framåt* (1986), 134.

70. Wingren, *Växling och kontinuitet* (1972), 54. Irenaeus worked in proximity to the New Testament writers and the early formation of the canon. We can see the beginnings of the shift from Luther to Irenaeus that took place in Wingren's later theological works in some of his early thinking, as for example in his dormitory room in Berlin in the summer of 1938, when he writes, "Our sociological situation is more like that of the New Testament than that of the Reformation. There is greater reason to suppose that the New Testament can provide guidance than Martin Luther can." Then, however, he states that Luther is always needed, because he is "the one who can best maintain the peculiarly biblical. However, Luther is not suited for use as a point of departure. Our point of departure must be the concrete ethical problems as they are presented by the present day." Wingren, "Johanneum Journal," 86. These thoughts from 1938 strengthen the impression that in the final part of his career, Wingren reconnected with sources, themes, and positions that were prevalent in his earliest theological reflections.

it is now pursued using a completely different social contextualization of the early church father's theology. The contents of the foundational idea of the Christian confession, that *salvation means becoming human again*, must be interpreted differently today, in a situation in which the conditions are more similar to the first century AD than they are to the sixteenth century. Similar to the time of the early church fathers, a sort of Gnosticism characterizes the current day. In addition, there are similarities with the first century in the current interest in the Devil and evil. For this reason, Wingren emphasizes the significance of the confrontation with Gnosticism: "The entire gospel is lost if belief in the creator is not the first article of our confession."[71]

Wingren uses Ireneaus to make the claim that we *all live the same life*. The ordinary, unreligious, human life is a life with God. One need not read the book of Genesis to understand what life is. Even today there are strong Monophysitic tendencies in contemporary theology that claim Christ's divinity at the cost of his humanity. But if salvation is equal to *recapitulatio*, then salvation must also mean becoming fully human again: "But he who lives and gives us eternal life is *a human being*, the only completely healthy human being in existence. He is not supernatural. Without him, however, we are unnatural and dead."[72]

By way of the later Wingren's focus on a biological metaphoric configured by death/life as found in Irenaeus, there is also a shift away from Luther's legal theological metaphoric, rooted in his wrestling with the complex of sin, guilt and forgiveness. In Irenaeus, anthropology and christology are being developed by the same terminologies, based on the simple fact that Jesus is human.[73] Here, the emphasis is placed on the corporeality of faith, of growth as a process through which both human beings and God *become* human. This is a reason why Irenaeus' reflections on edification were so important.

If we compare Wingren's presentation on Irenaeus in his book *Human and Christian* (1983) with his earlier presentations from 1939 and 1947/1959, a paradoxical image emerges. The later book is configured by a stronger contextualization, which is also manifested by its much stronger biographical focus. Thus, we learn that Irenaeus lived between the years 130 and 200, that he was part of a group who emigrated from

---

71. Wingren, *Människa och kristen* (1983), 18.
72. Ibid., 18.
73. Ibid., 40.

Asia Minor to Lyons, and that he developed his theology during a period of time in which the Bible acquired its two testaments (the Old and New Testaments) and the confession of the faith received its three articles (the Father, the Son and the Holy Spirit). However, although Wingren emphasizes the universal characteristics of the theology of Irenaeus—*Ireneaeus is the theologian of the undivided church*[74]—it is obvious that he makes this Eastern theologian far more Western than he really was. In Wingren's presentation, Irenaeus does not even seem to be a Catholic, but rather more of a Lutheran—and in fact, more like a Danish Grundtvigian. Despite his emphasis on the universal perspective, here Wingren completely ignores the Orthodox tradition, which historically was the one to which Irenaeus was closest.

Yet, Wingren's book, which is ostensibly about Irenaeus, a man who during the second century came from present-day Turkey to present-day Southern France, is equally as much a book about Denmark and Grundtvig—an original Lutheran theologian who lived seventeen hundred years later. Moreover, there is a direct link between these two theologians, because it was Grundtvig who first translated Irenaeus into Danish, long before there was any translation of his writings into Swedish. On the flyleaf of his 1983 book on Irenaeus, Wingren actually chose to place a quotation from Grundtvig: "Human first, then Christian, this is the sole order of life." But this is only the tip of the iceberg, so to speak, for in this book about Irenaeus, Grundtvig is far and away the most cited theologian after Irenaeus himself. Wingren later stated that his own path to Irenaeus and the early church had passed via Denmark.[75] This is of significance, but probably not entirely correct, and should be seen as an afterthought and later construction rooted in the strong identification that Wingren had found with Grundtvig, a phenomenon that occurred late in Wingren's life.

In his youth, Grundtvig had experienced Pietistic revivalist movements. The practitioners of these movements often sought to foster feelings of guilt in members of their congregations, intending to produce personal crises in the individual that would result in religious conversions. Because Grundtvig had thus lived through a childhood of degenerated Lutheranism full of guilt complexes, he was "vaccinated against all attempts to force people into the scheme of sin/forgiveness. Instead, the

---

74. Ibid., 105.

75. But Wingren also states that Danish theology served as a mentor to him when he sought to translate the ideas of Irenaeus to the modern day. *Creation and Gospel* (1979/1979), 34–35.

scheme of life/death came to dominate his authorship."[76] In other words, Grundtvig went from Paul to John. Thus, to him, the Christian faith was a matter of the victory of life over death. The texts of Grundtvig's hymns are teeming with earthly life, and his main source of inspiration was Irenaeus, who, because he understood salvation as *recapitulatio*, presupposed an articulation of the idea of creation. Grundtvig's theology is a genuine folk theology, a theology for the people, characterized by a strong identification between the human and the Christian. To be Christian, one need not cease being human (or Danish, or Swedish or anything else).

It is important to note that Wingren's shift from Luther to Irenaeus was also a shift in direction toward Grundtvig, a Lutheran. For Wingren, however, the route to Grundtvig seems to have gone via Løgstrup. In hindsight, the work of Harry Aronson during the 1950s and 1960s was precursor to many of the ideas that would later characterize Wingren's theological focus during the 1960s, and even more notably in the 1980s. First, it is a matter of a "social" turn in theology and an interest in a social contextualization of theological reflection, something which already interested Aronson during the early 1960s before he left the Faculty of Theology to become a national administrator for Sweden's upper-secondary schools. Secondly, however, it is a matter of Grundtvig. During the second half of the 1950s, Aronson was one of Wingren's doctoral students who managed to study in the USA and Denmark before defending his lengthy dissertation on the theology of Grundtvig in 1960. While Wingren valued Aronson as a doctoral student, the subjects Aronson was pursuing at the time were by no means elements that Wingren during this period sought to include in his own theological research. In regard to the later influence that Wingren found in Grundtvig, it seems that he was rather reluctant to give credit where credit was due. Not only did his Irenaeus book from 1983 bear a quote from Grundtvig on its flyleaf, yet its very title *Människa och kristen* (*Human and Christian*, using Christian as a noun) is extremely similar to that of Aronson's dissertation, *Mänskligt och kristet* (*Human and Christian*, using Christian as an adjective). In addition, Aronson disclosed strong connections between Grundtvig and Irenaeus in his dissertation. Beside Grundtvig, Irenaeus is the most often quoted theologian in the study, next to Martin Luther. Aronson's first chapter, titled "Life and Death," deals with the conditions of human existence from the perspective of battle against the scourges

---

76. Wingren, *Mina fem universitet* (1991), 155.

of death, theological anthropology in the drama of history, the restoration of creation (which Aronson spells *rekapitulatio*, with a *k*), and the concepts of healing and growth based on the ideas of Irenaeus. In his second chapter, titled "Divine and Human," Aronson deals with the connections between anthropology, soteriology, Christology, and salvation as a restoration of God's creation. The third and final chapter takes up themes such as school, church, and the prominent role of the mother tongue in Grundtvig's world. If it is true that Wingren's book about Irenaeus is almost equally as much about Grundtvig, then Aronson's book about Grundtvig is almost equally as much about Irenaeus.

Wingren's focus on Irenaeus in his later theology represented not only a return to the study he published in 1947, but also his return to the patristic and exegetic materials that captivated his interest in the 1930s, before Luther, for reasons beyond his control, suddenly rose to the top of his list of research projects. In an unusual way, it is as if Wingren returned to the place where his entire theological journey began. He did, of course, find similarities between the two, for example, neither Luther nor Irenaeus focused on the problem of the lack of knowledge. The differences between the two, however, were great. Luther saw the human condition as characterized by the fact that humanity is weighed down by sin and is doomed, which implies a view of salvation as the forgiveness of sin in accordance with a legalistic theological metaphor. Irenaeus saw humanity as afflicted by sickness, and thus dying, which implies that salvation is interpreted in terms of healing, health, restored and fulfilled healthy human nature. Aronson's insight of how crucial the choice of metaphor is for the interpretation of Christianity also shows the important shifts in thinking that were inherent in Wingren's own theological project. The gospel, as presented in his early theology, was about forgiveness for people weighed down by sin and guilt, or freedom for those who live under enslavement and oppression. Yet as time passed, Wingren's presentation of the gospel came instead to be more and more focused on the offer of life and health for people for whom the destruction had meant sickness and death.

But what are the consequences of this shift for Wingren's theological project in its entirety? We must remember the vital importance that the concept of the law had held for his theological thinking. We might say that he established and developed his understanding of the concept of the law in his doctoral dissertation in 1942, and then used it as his primary tool in his critique of Barth, Nygren, and Bultmann in his book on the problems of theological method from 1954. In the first part of his book on dogmatics from 1958, he examines the concept of the law more precisely, and incorporates it into the greater framework of an overall presentation of what Christian faith is: with a trinitarian grammar and a well thought out christology correlated by a theological anthropology. Yet, even if there could be said to have been a sort of parallel line in the form of his patristic studies from 1936, 1939, and 1947/1959, there are obvious complications that must be dealt with when Wingren pushes the concept of the law as part of a legal or battle metaphor to the side. What does it mean that Wingren, through his theological shift of metaphors, moved himself into a lawless land? And what sort of consequences did this shift have for his theological project in general, and the strategic importance of the concept of the law in his critique of other theologians in particular? The metaphorical pluralism which he promoted from the 1970s onward is associated with some very fundamental shifts in his basic theological views, and probably his basic view of life itself.

Wingren was convinced that he lived in a new era fraught with new challenges. This was the basis for the pronounced shift from Luther to Irenaeus as his dominant source of theological inspiration in his later books, and his shift from the use of legal metaphors to biological ones. In addition, it is in light of the connections he makes to Irenaeus that we may understand how and why Grundtvig increasingly not only seems to be the hero in Wingren's theological narrative, but also becomes someone with whom Wingren strongly identifies. Finally, Wingren pointed out Grundtvig's hymn, "O liv som blev tänt," found in the Church of Sweden hymnal as no. 258, as his all-time favorite. This hymn contains *not a single word* about sin, guilt, or debt; instead, it tells of the victory of life over death. It also teems with biological metaphors: "To live where death has met its master," "the warmth of the heart," "love that grows like the shining warmth of the sun," "Where roses die not, nor birds," "From the valley of the shadow of death to the land of the living," "A bubbling spring with life for all," "the drink of health," and so on—including the hymn's closing words, which Gustaf Wingren and Greta Hofsten used as the title of one of the books that they issued together: *The Courage of the Living* (1981).

8

"This Plague of Egocentricity"

DURING THE LAST CENTURY the importance, position, and conditions of the church in Swedish society have changed dramatically. At the time of Gustaf Wingren's birth in November 1910, Sweden was still largely a homogeneous Lutheran society, almost without any kind of freedom of religion, as we know the term today. Although the growing free church movement that had begun in the mid-1800s had given rise to the beginnings of religious pluralism in Sweden, it had done so within the framework of Christianity in general and Protestantism in particular. Wingren himself would be forty years old by the time blasphemy ceased to be a punishable crime, and obligatory membership in the Church of Sweden was no longer an obvious and necessary requirement for many careers, such as member of the Swedish parliament, and teacher of Christian theology and religious studies.

Ever since the Thirty Years' War in the seventeenth century, the Nordic countries had been bastions of Lutheranism, with strong national churches and lively and productive theological scenes. In more recent times, the Nordic countries, like the rest of northern Europe, had undergone a profound process of secularization. The changes that took place on the religious scene in Sweden closely resembled those that occurred in the other Nordic countries. However, the history of the church in modern Sweden differs significantly from the other Nordic countries in one particular respect: in Sweden, the Pietist revivalist movements that swept over the country in the later part of the nineteenth century developed in a separatist direction, giving rise to numerous free church denominations outside the state church. In the other Nordic countries, the revivalist movements were channeled back into the mainstream, so that they remained within the auspices of the Lutheran state churches of those countries. The more separatist tendency in the development of the Swedish free church movement has given Swedish religious geography its unique configuration among the Nordic countries, and has made for a different set of conditions and possibilities for the nation's overall theological orientation, as well as for individual life projects.

In the manufacturing town of Valdemarsvik, as in other small towns in Sweden at the time, spiritual life was characterized by the tension between the local parochial Church of Sweden, which was still a state church, and a number of free church congregations of various types.[1] The overarching tension inherent in the Swedish religious landscape was also part of the private life of the Wingren family. Both Gustaf Wingren's father and mother were deeply rooted in the free church movement, specifically The United Methodist Church of Sweden, and both had been shaped by the piety and sense of moral restriction characteristic of Methodist congregations. One event that set an indelible stamp on young Gustaf Wingren occurred on 21 March 1916, when his father, Gustaf Fabian, submitted a written request to withdraw his membership from the Methodist congregation of Valdemarsvik. Instead he turned toward the local Lutheran church and attended Sunday service in the parish church in Valdemarsvik for the rest of his life. In his autobiography, Wingren uses this confrontation with the free church's cloister of piety in order to paint the picture of his father as a Lutheran par excellence. In Wingren's depiction, his father had made the same personal journey as Martin Luther, who had left the exclusive spiritual community of the monastery, with all of its religious and moral restrictions, for an ordinary, worldly life involving family and children. It was a life that Luther came to see as the only true spiritual life, due to the conviction that being worn down by the cares of everyday life generated infinitely greater sanctification than was possible in the solitude of the monastery cell. In his memoirs, Wingren also interprets his father's move from free church to state church in

---

1. It is important here to avoid the potential confusion associated with speaking of the Swedish free church in the singular, which both historically and structurally obscures the fact that this term covers a broad spectrum of traditions and positions that sometimes differ markedly from one another. The flora of free churches in Sweden spans from the precursor of the neo-evangelical awakening (The United Methodist Church of Sweden) and its Lutheran heirs (The National Evangelical Foundation, The East Småland Missions Society, The Mission Covenant Church of Sweden, The Swedish Mission Alliance) to the precursors of the older Baptist movements (The Baptist Union of Sweden, The Örebro Mission, The Swedish Holiness Covenant) and The Swedish Pentecostal Movement.

political terms, making it a matter of social class. He portrays Fabian's departure from the Methodist congregation as a move away from a lot of free-church shopowners whom he neither measured up to socially nor fit in with:

> Being a tanner was, however, by harsh necessity a dirty job. The chemicals used to turn animal hides into colored leather also leave their indelible colors on the hands of the tannery workers, and no soap can help. My father was not a proper man, and he was well aware of it . . . Around 1918, he began attending services at the parish church in town. And there he remained for the rest of his life, as a faithful attendee.[2]

However, when Gustaf's mother, Engla Teresia, died suddenly in the early 1920s, and his father was unable to manage the situation, it was free church members who came in and took care of the household, saving the day for the Wingren family. Gustaf's pious Methodist aunts, one of who was even a council member in the local Methodist congregation, surrounded the sorrowing family with love. The attentions poured upon them by these free church ladies made it possible for the Wingren children to grow up in an orderly home. Despite Gustaf Fabian's move to the local Church of Sweden, free churches were never far away. On Sunday mornings, when young Gustaf sat next to his father in the parish church, they were both nonetheless surrounded by this free church atmosphere. The free church also remained very much a part of the family's personal history and social context, and in that day and age, the culture of free churches implied restrictive behaviors, such as total abstinence from alcohol. Gustaf's own relationship to the free church movement was further strengthened by the close relationship he had with his aunt Ellen. She was a soldier in the Salvation Army, and she played an important role in young Gustaf's life, and later in life, as an adult, he visited her frequently in Stockholm in associatation with his many job-related visits to the capital. In addition, Signhild, his wife-to-be, had grown up in a family strongly involved in the Seventh Day Adventist congregation in Valdemarsvik. All of these elements of Gustaf's background certainly further contributed to the feeling of being divided as he sat in the state church pew next to his father:

---

2. Wingren, *Mina fem universitet* (1991), 17. However, the author's timing (1918) does not coincide with the church records from the local Methodist congregation, which instead indicate the year 1916.

The lack of integration, the feeling of discord, was an essential part of adolescent distress. There was nothing to link together the facts of eating, singing hymns, playing football and going to the cinema. Sexuality and the sordid fact of women giving birth to children were forgotten pieces of reality when one played the violin or sang in the choir death was completely ignored ... Religiousness was included there, too. One was converted and shook off certain habits. But life was not integrated by piety. On the contrary, religiousness was still only a speciality, one among all the others.[3]

In order to understand the external landscape for Wingren's focus on theological integration and his ecclesiological orientations, it is also necessary to consider the secularization of Swedish society, and in particular the institutional dimensions of the secularization process. The standing of the Church of Sweden changed dramatically during the twentieth century. Major milestones in this process included the new law regarding religious freedom, which came into effect on 1 January 1952, and the new laws of 1 January 2000, that considerably weakened the ties between the Church of Sweden and the state. Along with the continuing secularization of Swedish society, these changes helped create a new religious landscape that today includes a growing number of other religions, thanks in particular to the immigration of increasing numbers of non-Europeans to Sweden. Wingren's reflections on the conditions of the church were determined by this rapidly changing religious landscape during a century in which the blueprints of Swedish society in general were being almost completely rewritten.

Nevertheless, Wingren's position as a leading Lutheran theologian in Sweden was not only affected by the Church of Sweden's complicated external relationship with the free churches, but also by the inflamed internal relationships within the Church of Sweden itself. An extra Church Assembly in 1958 passed a resolution to open up the ordained ministry of the church to women. It was a highly controversial decision. In the debate preceding the decision, the country's leading Bible scholars had submitted a statement in which they maintained that passing this resolution was in conflict with the words of the Bible. The decision remained in effect, although a conscience clause was added that provided some room for individual measures by those who resisted the ordination of women. The question of the ordination of women became one of the major

3. Wingren, "Creation: A Crucial Article of Faith," (1966/1971), 14.

conflicts in the Church of Sweden for the rest of the twentieth century. Today, a little more than a half a century after the issue was first raised, it certainly seems as though the high church movement has triumphed and won this battle in nearly all respects, primarily in the matter of liturgy, but also when it comes to ecclesiology and the theology of ordained ministry—but not, however, on the particular matter of the ordination of women.[4] Today, the Swedish high church movement seems to have lost all momentum, and ironically, the priesthood in the Church of Sweden is increasingly becoming a female profession.

This final chapter of my presentation departs from the timeline followed thus far in this book in order to examine the question of Wingren's views on the church in general. Clearly, Wingren's attempts to deal with the church were determined both by the church's external confrontation with Pietism and the free churches, and its internal confrontation with the high church movement and the question of ordination of women. However, Wingren's view of the church is even more than a marginal issue; in many ways it is of vital importance to the overall interpretation of his theology that this book seeks to present. At the same time, it is nothing more than just a closing chapter. Wingren's theology in its entirety cannot be encapsulated within the framework of a presentation of the church and, as we have seen several times, his theology cannot be exclusively labeled as a theology of the church.

Christian theology has always had an institutional relationship with the church, and this was especially the case during the period of time covered by this biographical investigation. Wingren was involved in the church, both as a pastor and as a university professor, although this involvement differed significantly, depending on in which of the two capacities he was acting. Without doubt, it was clearly his ambition to avoid any confusion between theology and preaching. To what extent he was successful with this in practice is, at least in part, another question. Nevertheless, it was not possible during Wingren's lifetime, nor is it possible today, to completely separate these two major fields from one another. The churches were, and are also today, the most important users and takers of academic theology in teaching and research. During

---

4. Cf. "For the high church people themselves, I would think it must feel odd when today they have achieved triumph on the superficial level. Their gestures and hand motions have spread, and are used even by those who do not embrace a single typical high church doctrine." Wingren, "Vad kan vi komma att få från svensk högkyrklighet i framtiden?" (1972), 431.

the twentieth century, the question of what sort of relationship theology should have with religious institutions in Swedish society became a controversial issue. During the course of this century, the exclusive relationship with a specific church denomination was dissolved, and Swedish theology came to encompass a broader variety of worldviews. At the same time, Swedish university politics in general have changed dramatically. Following the Hedenius debate of the 1950s, many in Sweden became afraid of being associated with theology and religion in any way. Today, the situation has changed dramatically and there seems to be almost a requirement from Swedish government authorities that the universities must have broad, well-developed relationships with society in accordance with the so-called third task of the universities, in addition to the traditional tasks of teaching and research. The increasing focus on economic benefit has further hastened developments, so that social benefits and examinations have become a rather crass necessity, to the point of their being the ultimate justification for the existence of the universities. This growing interaction between academia and the surrounding society has resulted in numerous challenges and complications. Today, as it had been for Wingren, it is not however a question of if, but rather of how, these relationships should be managed. As Niels-Henrik Gregersen has stated, hardly anyone would complain if a researcher in the life sciences promotes healthy food, nor is a musicologist less of a music expert if he also happens to play in an orchestra (although such involvement is no guarantee that he is a good researcher). In the same way, Wingren's interest and involvement in the church in no way disqualified him as a university professor. In accordance with Gregersen, systematic theology is contemporary theology and should be described as a cultural science in which descriptive and normative elements are part of a complicated dynamic, so that basic research and applied research also go hand in hand, as they do in the natural sciences, medicine, and the social sciences.[5]

Complicated Relationships with the Church

The church occupied a natural and yet problematic position in Gustaf Wingren's life and in his theology. He loved the church, yet he could also unleash his most derogatory criticism and wrath upon it. Wingren held a number of leading positions within the Church of Sweden, but over time

---

5. Gregersen, "Dogmatik som samtidsteologi," 293.

came to prefer a place on its margins. In later years, he often said that he entered the church through the cellar. He meant this not only figuratively, it was also true in a literal sense, given his faithful participation in the Sunday Evening in the Crypt gatherings at Lund Cathedral.

Wingren was an ordained minister in the Church of Sweden for three and a half decades. For several short periods, he was enrolled as a parish priest, and even later, he was sought after to officiate at baptisms, funerals, and weddings. However, above all else, to most people in the church he was known as an exceptionally gifted preacher. A number of his doctoral students went on to become bishops, and two became archbishops. Wingren himself could also have become a bishop had he only been prepared to give up his academic career, but that was something he did not want to do. He served lengthy terms on church policy boards and commissions, not only on the local level and the diocese, but also at the national level as well. In addition, he represented the Church of Sweden at national and international ecumenical committees and meetings. Even the humor that Wingren cultivated together with his interest in intrigues and conflict underscores his involvement in the church, because the stories he told very often dealt with pastors.

Nonetheless, Wingren was a fiery critic of the church, and at certain times in his life he found it difficult to endure the church at all. After he had participated in a Sunday worship service it could sometimes take hours before he was able to shake off his discomfort and agitation over what he had experienced. It was as if he was simultaneously drawn to the church and upset by it in a complicated love-hate relationship. For this reason, it is important that Wingren's personal and professional involvement and engagement in the church should not be misunderstood. In Sweden, an often-repeated perception has been that Wingren's theology was in fact only for use as encouraging instruction for pious groups in the church. While many have certainly held this idea with appreciation, the claim has also often been used as an attempt to marginalize Wingren and reduce his importance and thus eliminate him from the theological and academic scene altogether. Both of these groups overlook the fact that hardly any established professor of theology in Sweden during the twentieth century has expressed such harsh criticism of the church as Wingren. Thus, to the extent that he has made any contribution to the church (and that is definitely the case), this contribution must also include a great deal of criticism of the church. Furthermore, Wingren's criticisms must be conceived as an integral part of his academic work.

In addition, the passion for scientific progress and academic virtues were not only natural parts of Wingren's identity as a university professor; he always maintained that they should be taken in full earnestness in society and in the church, all the way to the pulpit:

> In general, the churches accept the historical examination of the Bible only in a half-hearted way. It is not allowed in the pulpit; from the pulpit, only voices from a previous period of time are employed. However, not until a historical view of the Bible makes its way into the proclamation of the gospel will our preaching be renewed.[6]

Wingren's criticism of the church was a fully integrated part of his theology, and this criticism in turn was founded upon his life-long interest in exegetics and biblical theology. He accepted and embraced scientific examination of the Bible without any reservation. Yet his criticism of the church also came from within: it gathered its nourishment from theology and it also had obvious theological points. Thus, he did not hesitate to emphasize, and in fact reveled in, how spiritual leaders are described as scoundrels in the Old as well as the New Testament:

> What we refer to as "Christianity" originated through treachery, betrayal and failure . . . The treachery against Christ exists at the heart of the church; it is an integral part of God's victory in Christ. No real renewal has taken place in the church without difficult-to-heal discord within the church. Almost all of those who have effectuated renewal in any social context have been more or less pushed to the periphery while their work of renewal was taking place.[7]

The form-historical exegetic research in particular opens up considerable possibilities for those who want to demonstrate what is worth noting in the scandalous tales of the authors of the *gospel*s, who show in detail how poorly their own leaders behaved. One example is the first Easter, when the disciples forsook and denied everything that they had come to believe. Moreover, these tales were told about individuals who had until recently been leaders of the early church. Wingren's generous openness about these things becomes understandable only when viewed from the background of his conviction that the life and work of the church should be directed by the gospel message of forgiveness and grace. In the same

6. Wingren, *Gamla vägar framåt* (1986), 47.
7. Wingren, *Växling och kontinuitet* (1972), 32.

way, Wingren emphasized the criticisms the prophets leveled against religion and the authorities, its institutions and leadership, as exemplified in a sermon from 1973, when he said, "Not one of these other people describe their king in such merciless words as King David is described in the Old Testament, he who deceived Uriah and took his wife Bathsheba, the king who was put in his place by a simple prophet: 'You are that man. You stole the poor man's only lamb.'"[8]

Even though Wingren's criticism of the church was already thoroughly established in his biblical theology, it reached its greatest triumph in his Luther studies. Using the Bible to criticize the church was one of Luther's favorite strategies, and Wingren therefore pointed out each facet of church criticism in Luther's theology. For example, in his doctoral dissertation, Wingren refers to the Commentary on the Book of Romans, where Luther describes the desire to "separate oneself from other people and recognize them as inferior to oneself in holiness" as "satanic seduction," and states that so much of what is called "holiness" is actually "the work of the devil." Wingren's exegesis of Luther seems to reach its culmination when he states that the church and religious life are to me considered as "the very center of the devil's activity."[9] In Wingren's studies on Luther, we also encounter the phrase in which he likened the church to a "plague of egocentricity" that I have used as the title of this chapter:

> The scale by which he measures himself is Christ's complete sacrifice of his own life for the salvation of others. The problem with me, says Luther, is that I "seek my own interests," for even in religion, a human being is concerned with himself, and with nothing else. This is Sin, and it is indelible. Sin rules the entire world, and it culminates in the church, this plague of egocentricity. There is only one single place in the world where this egocentricity is revoked, and that is in the sacrificed Christ.[10]

If Wingren's criticism of the church is focused on egocentricity, then its positive counterpart is the recognition of faith as an attitude that does not seek its own interests, but rather exists for others. In biblical terms, it is a matter of a tension between Adam, who represents those who seek to keep their lives for themselves, and Christ, the second Adam, who

---

8. Wingren in a sermon preached on 15 June 1973; quoted in Karlsson, *Predikans samtal*, 92.

9. Wingren, *Luther on Vocation* (1942/1957), 91. Cf. "The sect shuts its eyes to the fact that the Devil lives in us." Wingren, *The Living Word* (1949/1960), 186.

10. Wingren, "Luther i Sverige idag" (1988), 367.

instead pours himself out for the sake of others. This does not mean that Wingren thereby idealizes the world, as some have tended to do, and which he himself criticizes when he claims that he wants to avoid such moralistic claims as the world is superior to the church, or that the church is superior to the world. It is more a case of emphasizing the duplicity that runs throughout our entire existence. Stated positively, we could say that Wingren took his point of departure in the idea of the acting God, who is present in the world and who seeks everyone.[11]

This is yet another area where Wingren uses the same Lutheran reasoning as the author Lars Ahlin, who later became his friend, to elaborate on his criticisms of the church. In his novel *Night in the Market Tent*, Ahlin tells of Hog-Lasse (*Gris-Lasse*), a man who is alone and humbled, wandering around the town dump with a ragdoll that he has set on top of a little white plaster of Paris church. Ahlin gives the character a voice as follows:

> You know, it's both sad and true. This doll's situation is like our human situation. There's no room for people in the church... Don't you know that human beings cannot be accommodated in the church, and that no church can accommodate human beings? A human being is always too big, and the church is always too small.[12]

In the same way as Wingren, Ahlin finds that the primary place for the presence of God is to be found in spaces outside the church service, and it is in this place where Hog-Lasse is being addressed with the following scolding:

> You're too big to fit in here . . . Get out of here now! There's no room for you, don't you see? It's crowded enough here already . . . A lot of people have already left . . . I am the Man who went away to prepare a room, he replied. You have been baptized in my name. Your name has been written in the Book of Life, and there it will be alive.[13]

This story, with its criticism of the church, is inspired by the same Lutheran sources that Wingren used. Wingren's and Ahlin's interpretations of Luther incorporate a strong anti-Pietistic polemic, in the sense that they are both determined by a particular reading of Luther, in which the

11. Wingren, *Exodus Theology* (1968/1969), 101.
12. Ahlin, *Natt i marknadstältet*, 155–56.
13. Ibid., 156.

theological position is viewed against a dual background: on one hand, that of Pietism, and on the other, Lutheran orthodoxy (later succeeded by the high church movement). However, according to Wingren, both of these alternatives seem united in an ecclesiastical egocentricity in which the church is concerned with itself.[14] But when the church is thus considered the privileged place for the presence of God, it may often be difficult to imagine that God could be universally present in everyday life.

Wingren was, and always remained, a theologian who supported the concept of the *folk church* (territorial church, *folkkyrka*). However, the matters he assigned to this concept changed over time. In this ecclesiological context, he leans toward, and at the same time corrects, the ideas of Swedish theologian and bishop Einar Billing. We have seen previously how Wingren identified strongly with Billing, who in turn was affected by his own opposition to leading figures in the growing free church movements, such as Paul Peter Waldenström, according to whom the congregation primarily was based on the religious conversion of the individual. As we have seen, this view of the church was also a dominating element during Wingren's youth. He never tried to hide the fact that he was critical of many forms of free church piety, and his agreement with Billing is evident when he uses the following quote from him:

> There are those who regard it as a very enviable thing when a minister can speak to a congregation whose members have attached themselves to him personally without reference to any other reasons. They may have joined him because of the similarity between his and their spiritual life, or because of their appreciation of his religious personality. For myself I must confess that I cannot think of anything more terrifying.[15]

In order to articulate an alternative to this terrifying spiritual milieu, Billing developed his concept of the folk church. This means, according to Billing, that the church should be organized in a way so that it best can communicate grace to the people. His model for the folk church

---

14. Wingren, *Tro och främlingsskap* (1978), 68. In a later discussion of the challenges facing the Nordic national churches in a society where people fare badly, Wingren states, "While all of this is now going on, the church as an institution seems to be fixated upon itself in a hypnotic way, woeful over its losses, busy in its own self-defense, and occupied with keeping as much as possible of its time-honored position." Wingren, "Teologins kyrkokritiska funktion i Norden under 1980-talet" (1980), 64.

15. Billing, *Den svenska folkkyrkan*, 41, quoted by Wingren, *An Exodus Theology* (1968/1969), 100.

is Christ, who goes forth among the people (the folk, *folket*) and offers them forgiveness of sins. In the same way that the masses around him were heterogeneous, representing the most varied spiritual viewpoints, the church should also be just as frustratingly varied in its makeup: "It is typical that Billing conceived of the *parish church* itself as an *act*, a *divine act* directed to *all residents in the area*. It is directed to all these people irrespective of any religious qualifications they may possess."[16]

Here, the contrast with the ideals of the Swedish free church movements is obvious, when Wingren emphasizes that the delineation between the church and the people must be fluid at the least, or better yet, without borders.[17] In the spirit of Billing, Wingren made a virtue out of this vagueness. In *The Articles of Faith* (*Trons artiklar*, 1968), he writes the following, in his characteristically pointed way: "The devastated and damaged church has its sharp, clear borders. It can always give a report about who is 'inside' and who is 'outside,' because this church has been assembled to answer the question of who it is who 'has,' of who it is that owns."[18]

Wingren, however, emphasizes that Billing's concept of the folk church also implies a clear break with the old Swedish ideal of the state church. At the heart of the idea of the folk church, it is not the people who are the subject, but rather, the forgiveness of sins. The arguments for the religiously motivated concept of the folk church are theological and not political; it is a matter of quality rather than quantity. Even though Wingren argued that the democratization of the church was something that should be both affirmed and developed, it was not democratization of the church that motivated the idea of a folk church. Many free churches were in fact more democratically organized, but were still not considered

---

16. Ibid., 9.

17. Cf. Håkanson's reasoning on the difference between a borderless church and a church with moveable borders, in his *Vardagens kyrka*, 101.

18. Wingren, *Trons artiklar* (1968), 37. Cf. "We still live in the post-Pietist period in which almost all central Christian terms—gospel, salvation, conversion, faith—are loaded with notions of separation from common human society, or of breaking away from the requirement of solidarity that is placed on us by secular society, embodied for example by the labor union movement. The shyness of the modern national church ideology in the face of such centrally Christian terms may be precisely shyness. It is not a matter of hostility, but rather of a refusal to break out of an existing community, in the sense of a refusal to 'convert' oneself. In a way, the point of the spear is directed toward the religious group nourished by private spirituality, in other words, toward a great entity that from the beginning stood in opposition to the national church." Wingren, *Folkkyrkotanken* (1964), 60.

to be folk churches. Rather, the real motivating principle Wingren found in the gospel: "The way the gospel message reaches the people is through constant motion—it is the movement of the folk church."[19]

The concept of the the folk church may conjure an image of an immovable, rural, local parish idyll; but in his studies on Billing, Wingren instead emphasized the strong element of change inherent in the idea of a folk church. As a matter of fact, change is already part of this concept from the outset. In his argumentation, Billing had no ambition whatsoever of re-creating an organizational makeup similar to the early church congregations, since he considered their situation completely different from the conditions faced by the congregations of the folk church of Sweden. According to Billing, the church certainly has an eternal task, yet he emphasized strongly that this task could only be carried out through flexibility and changeableness. At all times the organizing principle emanates from the gospel and the forgiveness of sins, but with regard to the question of how this is best achieved in a specific period in history, there is freedom to act. Once again, we see how Wingren brings out the emphatically historical and changeable aspect of Billing's understanding of Christianity. As long as the overarching purpose of the gospel is supported, or at least not disturbed, by a connection with the state, then this relationship ought to be maintained for pragmatic reasons. Every aspect of the organization and activities of the church are subordinated to this changeableness, and are regulated only to the degree that they serve to convey the gospel to the people—the folk.

Here, it is important to remember Billing's great interest in religious freedom. This was manifested most clearly in the fact that it was Billing, as a representative of the state Church of Sweden (and not the state itself) and as the great polemicist against the free churches, who argued for expanded religious freedoms in Swedish legislation in order to safeguard the right of each individual to withdraw from the church of his or her own free will.[20] Billing was convinced that only when people had the right to freely leave the church, would it become clear that it is the gospel, and not the forces of the law, that directs and regulates the church: "In my

---

19. Ibid., 22. Cf. how earlier in the same text, he writes about "the idea of the church that is thought on the basis of the seeking gospel, continuously open to a changeable outward order." Ibid., 15.

20. Wingren, *An Exodus Theology* (1968/1969), 10–11.

view, the religious task of the church requires a consistent implementation of the principle of freedom."[21]

It is clear for purely biographical reasons, and as well in his research, that the early Wingren saw Pietism, the revivalist movements, the Swedish free church movements and the swarming interpretations of the Christian faith as the great threat. During that early period he expressed himself in terms such as the following: "The vital decisions in today's theology are not being made in Lutheranism's struggle against Rome—they are being made in the church's struggle against swarming, modern ideas."[22] However, I hold, at least in part in agreement with Ola Sigurdson, that it was in fact not the awakening movements that constituted Wingren's primary front of confrontation. Rather, his polemics were directed against the growing high church movement (with the reservation that this was a matter of a gradual shift that occurred over time).[23] Whatever the case may be, it is clear that the stance that is so obvious in his work from the 1930s, 1940s, and 1950s, and particularly in his interpretation of Luther, was determined mainly by an anti-Pietistic polemic. However, this started to change after 1958. At the Assembly of the Church of Sweden that year, the decision was taken to open the ministry of the church to women. In an almost overly explicit way, the high church resistance to the ordination of women that followed this decision would come to determine the way Wingren, during the decades to come, would frame his discussions regarding the politics of the church.

When poet and literary scholar Gunnar D. Hansson began work on his impressive dissertation on Lars Ahlin, *The Disorder of Grace: Studies on Lars Ahlin's Novel* Pious Murders (*Nådens oordning: Studier i Lars Ahlins roman* Fromma mord), he soon realized that there were strong ties between Ahlin and Wingren. Hansson decided to make a trip to Lund to interview Wingren. On 22 October 1976, Hansson found himself at Wingren and Hofsten's apartment at Warholmsväg 6B, seated before the professor and armed with a notebook and many questions. In the middle of the interview, the telephone rang. Greta answered the telephone, and Gustaf called out to her, "Who is it?" Greta replied across the apartment, "It's Sundby." At this time, I do not believe that Gunnar D. Hansson knew that the Archbishop of Sweden, Olof Sundby, had been one of Wingren's

---

21. Billing, *Den svenska folkkyrkan*, 121.
22. Wingren, "Utläggningens problematik" (1950), 249.
23. Sigurdson, *Karl Barth som den andre*, 95ff.

doctoral students, and he was probably not informed of the fact that the old academic adviser was deeply disappointed by his former doctoral student for not having defended the cause of women pastors strongly enough. Given his own personal background in the pious area on the Swedish West coast that was dominated by conservative church life, Hansson had a certain level of respect for bishops and theologians. Thus, it was with some surprise that he witnessed, first how Wingren's face became bright red, and how he then turned and shouted loudly, so that it most certainly would be heard over the telephone: "Tell that bastard to go to hell!"[24]

In order to appreciate this anecdote, we need to remind ourselves not only of Wingren's love of combat, and of the fact that the current archbishop was his one-time student, but also that in his later writings, Wingren became increasingly focused on the issue of the ordination of women. It became in fact a cardinal question in his theological thinking, one to which he constantly returned, regardless of the topic of the discussion at hand. There is hardly any issue that he prioritized more highly, and, moreover, there was hardly any issue that elicited more energy and wrath from him. As it transpired, the changes within Church of Sweden have largely gone the way he wanted. Nonetheless, considering the great efforts he invested in the question of the legitimacy of the ordination of women, it is in retrospect remarkable how little appreciation he seems to have gained for his efforts.[25] Instead, his efforts seem to have isolated him. Over time, they seem to have generated a sort of silence on the part of his allies and his opponents, which in the long run probably only made him even more fixated on the issue. The question is, however, whether the space he devoted to the issue of the ordination of women caused his theology to be considered as more church-oriented than it actually was. We may also wonder why other theologians did not join him in his fight for this cause.

24. Interview with Gunnar D. Hansson, 11 May 2010.

25. It is remarkable that Wingren was not granted a more prominent presentation in the book assembled in celebration of the fiftieth anniversary of the first women priests in Sweden, *Äntligen stod hon i predikstolen* (2009). His name is mentioned only once by Boel Hössjer Sundman in her article "Möta nutidens människa och ge ett svar på hennes livsfrågor," in a list of individuals who had worked to make it possible for women to be ordained (ibid., 152). The only contribution to the book in which he plays a more important role is Margareta Brandby-Cöster's "Dubbla budskap—vilket skall firas?" Ibid., 171–73. Brandby-Cöster quotes long sections of Wingren's article "Skamfläcken," from *Broderskap*, no. 9, 1984. Otherwise, he is surprisingly absent.

The entire story is rooted in the conflicts that preceded and followed the decision taken at the 1958 Church Assembly to open the office of ordained ministry to women in the Church of Sweden. In 1946, a resolution to make this change had progressed as far as the Second Chamber of the Swedish Parliament. In its findings, the committee formed that year stated: "The reliance of our church upon the Bible as the norm for Christian belief and Christian life does not from any standpoint prevent the entrance of women to the office of the priesthood." The theological discussion was, however, by no means brought to an end with this statement. Instead, this was the point at which the real battle began. In 1951, as a reply to the committee's conclusion, the so-called "Exegete's Declaration" was published in which all of the professors and assistant professors of biblical exegesis at the Universities of Lund and Uppsala (with the single exception of Gösta Lindeskog) declared with their full academic weight, that the ordination of women was incompatible with the words of the New Testament.[26] The text of the declaration was only a few lines long and contained no actual Bible references. But in the debate that ensued, it came to light that the places in the Bible at which the declaration hinted referred to the decisive role to be played by a Jewish father at mealtimes, and the Apostle Paul's words about how the women of a congregation should keep silent. When those who resisted the ordination of women lost the vote at the 1958 Church Assembly, the exegetes once again took action by submitting a written reservation against the decision. In addition, they were able to bring about the so-called conscience clause, which made it possible for those who opposed the ordination of women to avoid working with female priests.

These events etched themselves on Wingren's mind, and helped direct his life and work. He was convinced that the decision to allow the ordination of women was correct, based on the actual conditions for a Lutheran church. In his world, the actions and lack of real arguments by those who opposed the ordination of women were not only wrong and unacceptable; their behavior constituted the greatest treachery in post-World War II Swedish church history. He often stated that the exegetes had cultivated a conversation-killing stance, and maintained that the

---

26. Erik Sjöberg, who authored the chapter "Bedömning av frågan om kvinnan och prästämbetet med hänsyn till kyrkans trohet mot bibeln" in the committee's findings, was not indicated as one of the individuals who did not sign, because at the time he was a teacher at a public secondary school for boys in the Norrmalm district of Stockholm.

brief format and lack of concrete references to the Bible in their declaration were intended to make rebuttals impossible.[27] Again and again, like a disappointed dueler who could find no opponent, Wingren returned to how inconceivable he found it that those who resisted female ordination had been allowed to hide behind legal arguments and did not participate in a true debate. He asked and begged them for debate, but they would not or dared not respond.[28] Thus, there was never any proper public exchange of ideas in which the arguments of either side could be systematically evaluated, which frustrated Wingren greatly—for many reasons.

Even when viewed from a short-term historical perspective, the actions of the exegetes in this case were rather remarkable. In 1921, thirty years before the Exegete's Declaration, the two professors of exegetical theology at Lund University had officially declared that there were no biblical arguments against the ordination of women whatsoever. In the debate, Wingren stated ironically that research had obviously made unexpected progress in 1951.[29]

Over time, Wingren continually returned to the issue of the ordination of women. It seems as if there was no issue with which he dealt that did not offer him an opportunity to battle with those who opposed ordination of women as ministers. The issue even created a chasm between the two volumes of his first dogmatic work, *Creation and Law* (1958/1961)) and *Gospel and Church* (1960/1964). As I have stated earlier, the second volume is strongly colored by the fact that his disagreement with the opponents of ordination of women became acute following the church assembly of 1958. Without mentioning the ordination of women as ministers with a single word, the whole presentation is to be considered as an attack against the ministerial theology used by those who resisted the decision. For example, this can be seen in the strong demarcations he made against the idea of apostolic succession, comprehended as a channel of office in *Gospel and Church*. This stance also influenced the reception of the book. Here, as elsewhere, the biblical theology of Oscar Cullmann plays a significant role in that Cullmann identifies the principles of the formation of the canon by referring to the historical fact that the authority was founded by the Apostles themselves, and not in something that was transferred through any ceremony of consecration.

27. Wingren, *Tolken som tiger* (1981), 76.
28. Cf. for example Wingren, *Gamla vägar framåt* (1986), 40.
29. Ibid., 75.

This theme then recurs in one Wingren book after another. It is actually rather surprising that the question plays such an important role also in the book he later issued on theological methods, education and research, *The Silent Interpreter* (1981)—and equally as surprising that hardly any of those who took part in the voluminous debate that followed the publication of the book made note of it. In this context, it is interesting to note that for Wingren, this question was a matter of scholarliness. Over time, he grew increasingly frustrated over the lack of critical scientific examination of the issue by members of the Swedish academic community. Thus, the claims that there were convincing exegetical arguments against women in the priesthood were never really tested. In the late 1980s, he issued one of his many challenges to the academic community regarding the matter in the following way: "Today, after almost forty years, we urgently wait for a knowledgeable exeget to accept the task of making a critical examination of this New Testament research and its claimed validity. No such examination has been carried out thus far."[30] Even Wingren's last major book, his intellectual autobiography, *My Five Universities* (1991), contains arguments on the issue of female ordination. The polemics are unmistakable: "Now that the unity of Holy Communion in the Church of Sweden has been broken apart after 1958, it is quite clear that from the perspective of the Lutheran confessional meetings, an open split in the Church would have been the correct way to resolve the conflict."[31]

He then broadens the perspective by moving the focal point from the ordained women who had been excluded from serving communion, and who had thus been afflicted by what he calls crystal clear sexual discrimination, to the absurd fact that the bishops who stood for differing views on the matter (for or against women as ordained ministers) could themselves, in the company of their clergy brothers, easily celebrate communion together in undisturbed harmony.[32] After more than half a century, the retired Lundensian professor was still boiling with anger when reminding himself of the way in which the issue had been handled. The final words of his memoirs leave posterity with no doubt over his views on the matter:

> To claim the same wages, the same housing accommodations, the same sort of pension from the same treasury, but not be able

---

30. Ibid., 75–76.
31. Wingren, *Mina fem universitet* (1991), 87.
32. Ibid., 195.

to eat the bread and drink the cup together that Jesus established on the night he was betrayed, is a scandal that has occurred in Sweden only once, and it was one time too many. A repetition of this scandal is unimaginable.[33]

Before we devote ourselves to a more systematic examination of Wingren's argumentation on this matter, let us take a step backward to see how the issue of the ordination of women was a key element in his conflict with his predecessor, Anders Nygren. As a matter of fact, the issue of women as ordained ministers adds a few more pieces to the puzzle of the complicated relationship between the two men. Just after his retirement, Wingren looked back on his conflict with Nygren and stated that the issue of the ordination of women actually stood out as the decisive context for understanding the texts that he had authored during those years:

> The conflict with Lundensian theology was therefore unavoidable. It was a conflict that was rooted in my own existence, rooted in the factors that caused me as a fifteen-year-old in a small industrial community to hit upon the strange idea of devoting my life to theology. The situation was aggravated, however, by a development in the Swedish Church: a militant high church movement emerged during the years when I pursued my doctoral studies and wrote my first short essays. As it grew stronger, it became focused on the clergy, thus causing the church to be alienated from the people. An explosion had to occur—and it did—over the issue of female clergy.[34]

In conjunction with the Church Assembly of 1958, Anders Nygren had in effect taken the same conservative side as Bo Giertz, Gustaf Adolf Danell, and Bertil Gärtner by expressing a reservation against the church's decision to ordain women: "In my view, it is a tragedy that Nygren's theology should come to this on the practical level."[35] Here, Wingren does not hold back his opinion, and describes the practical application of Nygren's

---

33. Ibid., 197. Cf. how on his eighty-fifth birthday, toward the end of his thank you speech, even here he asked about the presence of women in theology and in the church: "What more can I ask—have not all of my wishes been wonderfully fulfilled? No, they are not! One wish is nowhere near being fulfilled, not at all here today, and only in the very beginning [of being fulfilled] outside this symposium and this auditorium. I had entirely different hopes of seeing women take their rightful place in theology (as well as in the church)!" Wingren, "Tal den 29 November 1995."

34. Wingren, *Creation and Gospel* (1979/1979), 10.

35. Ibid., 11.

theology as "a clearly reactionary position."[36] In other words, Nygren's stance in regard to women as ordained ministers is anything but a marginal question; it originates straight from the philosophical basis of his theology.

This relationship became even more evident in 1972, when Wingren reviewed Nygren's recent work, *Meaning and Method: Prolegomena to a Scientific Philosophy of Religion and a Scientific Theology*. Here, the now-retired bishop had resumed his academic ambitions by undertaking a rather impressive update of his philosophical system, now using Ludwig Wittgenstein's later philosophy of language games and life forms. However, Wingren was not at all impressed. In his review, titled "Old Philosophy Becomes Like New" ("Gammal filosofi blir som ny," 1972), he maintained that what Nygren had done, without admitting to his neo-Kantian works of the 1920s that Wingren claimed the author had hidden from his international readers, was to repeat the same old viewpoints, but this time using English-language philosophical terms. Wingren compares this to "a change of clothes: today English clothing, with the German ones hanging in the closet."[37] In contrast to Gustaf Aulén, who constantly changed his mind, Nygren always said the same thing he had already said before—this time, using Wittgenstein's theory of language games as "a springboard for returning to what he had previously claimed in his earlier works half a century before."[38] Wingren makes special note of Nygren's use of two separate spheres for his activities, so that science is never allowed to speak out against the Christian faith; thus every imaginable form of collision between science and religion may be avoided and explained away as misunderstandings and confused categories. What Nygren is careful not to reveal to his international audience, stated Wingren, is the theological agenda tied to this philosophy, and which exists mostly to induce conservative rural deans in the Church of Sweden to rejoice:

> What is not directly underscored here is the shielding and conservative effect for the church that such talk of entirely separate cohesions of meaning have, on a purely theological level. In regard to Swedish culture, Nygren has a peculiar dual nature. Philosophically, he is radical, but theologically, he is a pronounced conservative, applauded by the conservative Lutheran revivalist movement, with its stonghold on the west coast of

36. Ibid., 10–11.

37. Wingren, "Gammal filosofi blir som ny" (1972).

38. Ibid.

Sweden. This dual role is the result of the way in which his cohesions of meaning are shielded from one another.[39]

Behind Nygren's philosophical and ever-so-modern facade, Wingren presumes that he can discern a man who in fact seeks security by avoiding criticism and interpretation, someone who is fleeing from Rudolf Bultmann's program of de-mythologization and a critical scholarly examination of the Christian faith. What looks like academic method in Nygren's philosophy and theology is in fact only poorly disguised apologetics. Wingren claimed that Nygren had constructed an isolated and protected area, within which church and faith cannot be criticized. In this way, the opposition to the ordination of women as ministers made itself immune to scientific examination.

Wingren returned to the same theme in a 1988 article, "Anders Nygren and Swedish Theology Today" ("Anders Nygren och svensk teologi av idag"). Here, he posits that it was precisely the work of the exegetical theologians in the 1950s and onward that made the high church movement seem as though it had been approved by scholarly theological methods, and which created feelings of guilt in those who accepted the ordination of women. Wingren asks how this could have come to pass without any sort of scholarly examination of the issue.[40] However, a central element in Wingren's own argumentation is that the use of exegetical arguments as a major barricade against women as ordained ministers, as presented in this debate by Professor Anton Friedrichsen and his many followers, was from an international perspective something extraordinary and completely unique to Sweden.

Wingren presented his most systematic argumentation on the issue in his book *Going Forth on Ancient Roads: The Task of the Church in Sweden* (*Gamla vägar framåt: Kyrkans uppgift i Sverige*, 1986). Here he admits that one may question whether it was suitable from an ecumenical standpoint of a single church denomination to make such a radical decision as opening the priesthood to women precede all others, as the Church of Sweden did. Nevertheless, he made it absolutely clear that this decision was in no way associated with any biblical or theological problems for Lutherans, and for that matter, hardly any for Catholics or Anglicans either. For a Lutheran church, there is great freedom in regard to outward arrangements and, according to Wingren, all questions of

---

39. Ibid.
40. Wingren, "Anders Nygren och svensk teologi av idag" (1988), 17–18.

church office, including the issue of men and women as priests, are such outward questions. Different arrangements may be employed in different places and at different times, as long as they are suitable. Everything is subordinate to the gospel. Freedom and diversity will not break the church apart. What will create a direct split in the church, however, is the way in which the question of women as ordained ministers had been handled by the Church of Sweden:

> In Sweden, we are in disagreement on precisely the point on which, according to the confession, we must agree, namely, on the matter of the administration of the Sacraments . . . This is completely impossible according to the confession. The split in the church is a fact. According to the confession, two irreconcilable Churches of Sweden came into existence in the spring of 1960, that is, April 1960. When the leadership of the church expresses itself on what occurred from 1960 and onward, and when they happily claim that despite all of the problems, they have succeeded in maintaining "the unity of the church," the implication of such claims is that those who make them are denying the confession of their own church. This is true both for those bishops who ordain women and those who refuse to ordain women. All of them have fallen from the Augsburg Confession. Their fall occurs when they claim that the unity of the church has been preserved. What has actually been preserved is only the outward unity, in that the two churches use the same buildings, the same system of wages, and so on. According to the Augsburg Confession, these things have nothing to do with the unity of the church.[41]

Here, Wingren, the great polemicist, is completely serious when he claims that not only those bishops who use arguments from the New Testament to refuse to ordain women, regardless of whether the argument is about the laying on of hands or regulations of office, break with the Lutheran confession in a completely incomprehensible way, but that also those bishops who ordain women, and who at the same time accept this unsustainable arrangement in the church, are also directly breaking with the confession. Wingren thus claims that if we indeed follow the Lutheran Confessional Writings, then the Church of Sweden has already split, and in reality become two separate churches.[42]

---

41. Wingren, *Gamla vägar framåt* (1986), 39.

42. Ibid., 58-59. Cf. "They obtain congregational posts from the open church, they receive their retirement from it, and during that church's high holy days they demand

An important question in the debate dealt with the matter of apostolic succession. According to Wingren, the idea of apostolic succession is to be considered as a late Anglican invention; it is not Lutheran, nor was it important even in the context of the English Reformation in the sixteenth century. This concept does not appear until the ninteenth century, and at this time as one of the weapons in the Anglican Church's defense against aggressive and growing free church movements in England. In the late 1970s, Wingren himself described apostolic succession as "one of the most miserable theories in church history, poorly supported on nearly every point."[43] He pointed out that the Lutheran churches of Norway and Denmark had held their ground and seen the matter more clearly, when they quite simply refused to be included in the order of succession. In sixteenth century Denmark, there had been no bishops who wanted to change sides after the Reformation, the Danes had therefore called Johannes Bugenhagen, a professor of theology and a parish priest in Wittenberg, to Copenhagen to officiate at the installation of bishops in Denmark. In this way, Denmark was never included in the apostolic succession—nor did this church want to be included.[44] Here, as usual, Wingren is unable to conceal his delight with Denmark: "They refuse to give in to such superstition. Let us be free from this stupid idolatry!"[45] Furthermore, the letter sent by the conference of bishops of the Church of Sweden to the bishops of the Anglican Church on 21 April 1922, stated that while the Swedish bishops accept the shared communion suggested by the Anglicans, they cannot accept the Anglican motivation for it, since the Church of Sweden cannot in any way recognize apostolic succession as a basis for a common doctrine or full communion with any other church. In a Lutheran church, everything, even a position of office, is subordinate to the gospel, which cannot be disposed of at will.[46] When Wingren seemed to discern a political current within the international ecumenical movement, which continually placed the matter of apostolic succession on the agenda, he also decided to relinquish all of his duties with the World Council of Churches.[47]

---

special treatment. This is in complete disagreement with the Lutheran confession." Ibid., 58.

43. Wingren, *Tro och främlingsskap* (1978), 30.
44. Wingren, *Gamla vägar framåt* (1986), 67.
45. Wingren, "Människa först—kristen sedan" (1994), 11.
46. Wingren, *Svenska kyrkans ekumeniska ansvar* (1959), 17.
47. Wingren, "Mina sex universitet" (1983), 44.

Wingren was convinced that in an evangelical Lutheran church such as the Church of Sweden, no kind of argumentation supporting apostolic succession is possible. Because of this, the argumentation had to be pursued in another, more biblical, direction instead. Harald Riesenfeld, Bertil Gärtner and other Swedish high church exegetes soon realized that they themselves were going against the Lutheran confession in regard to the views they expressed on succession in church office. What could they do? They simply shifted their weight to the other foot, and claimed instead that the Bible was on their side. First, a priest must be a man because, according to Paul the Apostle, women should "keep silent in the congregation." Secondly, because the Jewish faith holds that the father of the family is the head of the table at mealtimes, Holy Communion must be administrated by a man. On this point, Wingren answered dryly that the subordination of women was understandable given the specific historical context; in the New Testament environment, it was obvious to all. In other words, according to Wingren, things could not have been otherwise. He then moves to the weak and sparse biblical material that the opponents of women as ordained ministers used to support their position, by pointing out the contradiction between speaking and eating. How could these opponents reach the conclusion that women could not administer communion—by using an argument based on texts that deal with something entirely different, namely, speaking? Allow me to include a lengthy quote from Wingren here:

> But Reisenfeld and Gärtner are totally focused on the places in Paul's letters where he declares that women should remain silent. From them, they draw the conclusion that a woman cannot administer communion. She may speak, hold a position at a diocesan chapter and direct a diocese, participate in church assemblies and craft church laws (women in Sweden already had these rights within the church, and no high church representatives objected). The exact thing that the Bible forbids a woman to do, she may freely do in the world of the Swedish high church—just as long as she does not administer communion! There is not a single Bible reference that supports this very specific prohibition. It is inconceivable that scholarly Bible researchers on the university level would lend their authority to support such an argument.[48]

---

48. Wingren, *Gamla vägar framåt* (1986), 50.

On the next page, the author states that the Swedish exegetes who attempt to continue the miserable tradition from the 1950s are doomed to fail in their argumentation, for the simple reason that the New Testament does not deal with the topic of ordained ministry at all. Wingren continues like this, driving a wedge into the weak spot that he believes he has identified in the opposition to women as priests. In his view, the interplay on this issue between high and low church people is not only artificial, but is also based on an unholy alliance. Obviously, the high church university theologians who argue against female ministers cannot share or feel any sympathy for the fundamentalist belief in a literal interpretation of the Bible and teachings of verbal inspiration that characterized the skepticism of low church opposition to the ordained ministry of women and toward historical-critical Bible research. Nor could the low church groups follow Riesenfeld and Gärtner, because of their stance that allowed a church office holder decide who could administer communion, based on the Anglican teaching of apostolic succession. Furthermore, it probably would have pushed low church opponents of the ordination of women into despair if they knew that Catholic tradition could in fact be changed, and that if the Pope would only make a decision to allow the ordination of women, there could be women priests in the Catholic church as well. While neither Anglicans nor Roman Catholics base their teachings on the Bible only, low church Protestants do, since for them, tradition has no normative meaning. Thus, although high and low church Lutherans are certainly united in their opposition to the ordination of women, they do not accept each other's specific arguments against it. On this point, Wingren cannot refrain from commenting that in the 1980s, Harald Riesenfeld, professor of New Testament studies at Uppsala University, left the Church of Sweden and the Lutheran confession, and became a Roman Catholic. Riesenfeld's declaration that in making this move, he had not changed his views on any major point, evoked the following comment from Wingren: "In other words, in regard to his opinions, he was thus [already] a Catholic back in the 1950s when he stated his views on ordination in the Church of Sweden."[49]

When Wingren wrote *Going Forth on Ancient Roads*, he perceived a risk in the late 1980s that the high church movement might take over the Church of Sweden if it were to be separated from the Swedish state. Wingren had advocated the separation of the church from the state since

49. Ibid.

he had changed his opinion on the matter in 1971; however, given the situation in the 1980s, he was threatened by the fact that the proponents of the high church movement were so well organized and powerful:

> If the state loosens the ties to our Lutheran church, there is, at least for now, only one group prepared to take over the spiritual leadership of the [new] free church that will be formed, and that is the narrow-minded, door-closing group. Under the direction of this group, a free-standing church would be going astray.[50]

The situation was further worsened by the fact that the direction in which the group representing the only visible alternative was heading was also considered a cul du sac. In Wingren's view, the movement that defended the folk church by focusing on democracy and quantitative argumentation lacked a clear foundation in the Bible, and seemed in general weak in theological argumentation. The paradoxical consequence of this was, according to Wingren, that the members at the decision-making level of church administration would have difficulty articulating the pure teachings they, in their practice, advocated.[51] Wingren's *Going Forth on Ancient Roads* (1986) never did become a great success, and the reason for this may be found in the text itself as well as in the context in which the book was launched. While this book was certainly the most systematic ecclesiological work that Wingren published, his obsession with the issue of the ordained ministry of women disturbed the clarity of the ideas he presented within it. It is impressive that he continued the discussion on the matter, but it is also a fact that whenever one takes part in a debate, one inevitably becomes colored by the views of the opposing side. But what was even worse, by sharply criticizing both the high church opponents of the ordination of women as well as the democratically minded proponents of the folk church, Wingren tended to be lost in the no-man's-land between the two warring factions. Thus, he had few allies, nor did he develop a feasible strategy. However, I believe that the causes were to be found more deeply imbedded within the context, and once again, text and context had drifted apart. However, in order to recognize what was actually happening, it is necessary to open up the question in a wider perspective.

50. Ibid.

51. Cf. how Sandahl states that Wingren's criticism of church life takes place on three fronts; in addition to Pietism and the high church movement, he mentions the social-ethical efforts in the spirit of Karl-Manfred Olsson, which lead to the political and democratic idea of the folk church. Sandahl, *Folk och kyrka*, 152.

In *Going Forth on Ancient Roads* Wingren advocates a low church view of ordained ministry that is so low that it would scarcely be attractive to anyone wishing to develop a theology of ordination. He based his views on the New Testament and the works of Luther, according to whom everyone who is baptized may also be recognized as a priest. According to Wingren, it is thus neither a shortcoming nor a coincidence that the Bible and the confessional writings do not say anything about the person who becomes a priest through ordination. Rather, a person becomes a priest when one receives a call: "I am called to be a priest the moment an actual congregation tells me that I am welcome to come and serve as their priest."[52] In a book he published together with Greta Hofsten, *Faith and Alienation* (1978), he summed up his position in the following way: "I felt then and feel now, that on no point does a priest perform any duty that could not be performed by any Christian."[53] Thus, Wingren's view on the ordained ministry stands in sharp contrast to the renaissance of the theology of ordained ministry that characterized the Church of Sweden during the latter half of the twentieth century. He strongly challenged those who advocated a three-fold ministry consisting of diaconate-priest-bishop, even when they attempted to tone down the hierarchical nature of this proposed ordination structure. Thanks to his basic Lutheran view, Wingren found it difficult to present good arguments for having a diaconate in the church because it raised suspicions of Pietism, and he never (with one single exception) argued for female bishops for the simple reason that he was skeptical of the office of bishop in general. Dag Sandahl, an angry and embittered opponent of ordination of women as ministers, stated laconically that when Wingren renounced his ordination in 1974, he was obviously not renouncing much—and thus it was not much to speak about.[54]

When looking for the reasons for Wingren's marginalization within the Church of Sweden from the 1970s onward, I believe that it was not only because Sandahl and others were occupied with the issue of the ordained ministry, but also because the question of ordination of women

---

52. Wingren, *Gamla vägar framåt* (1986), 37. Cf. how he emphasizes that the Bible makes no mention of church office holders, and that during the Reformation, people spoke of the general office of priest but never mentioned any person being employed full time—all such things are motivated by practical reasons. Wingren, *Växling och kontinuitet* (1972), 37.

53. Wingren, *Tro och främlingsskap* (1978), 11.

54. Sandahl, "Digra och ödesdigra kapitel," 66–67.

took on an increasingly central importance in the entire church. Wingren always spelled "church" with a small *c*, but at the same time he lived in an era when many people in the Church of Sweden felt the need to spell it with a capital *c*. In the context of the day, despite his strong defense of women priests, he still appeared as a far too inadequate defender of priests (and bishops and deacons) to be appreciated as provider of theological resources for argumentation at a time when the major issue on the agenda was the question of the ordination of women. The context of the debate had drifted away from Wingren's texts. Fewer and fewer people felt the need to be associated with him, and this was definitely the case with his book *Going Forth on Ancient Roads* (1986).

The very word "layman" made Wingren uneasy. It was a word he personally would have preferred to avoid altogether, because the frequent use of this word was the result of a church fixated on an ordained ministry; a church which in the wake of the battle over the ordination of women no longer had a positive term for its members: "The term seems to me to imply a devaluation of baptism. Calling a member of a congregation a layman labels him by what he lacks, rather than by what he has received. This erroneously places the ordination of the clergy at the center of the church."[55]

In Wingren, this polemic is justified by his radical horizontalization of the church, an idea he claimed was also supported in the New Testament, which speaks of "all Christians, the entire congregation" as "priests."[56] The fixation on an ordained ministry distanced people from the fact that ordination is so much less important than baptism. As a result, the church has also lost its focus on "the rather colorless members of the congregation, those who live their everyday life of death and resurrection."[57]

The gospel is always at the center of interest when Wingren talks about the church. There is no community of converted people, no ordained ministry, nor any confessional writings—nor any democratic order—that can be placed above the gospel. The church can exist without the office of bishops, as well as other elements of the ministerial and administrative structure of the church. In general, it is a misuse when the

55. Wingren, *Folkkyrkotanken* (1964), 7. Cf. his later published lecture "Begreppet lekman" (1982), which he originally delivered on the occasion of being made an honorary doctor at the University of Oslo in 1981.

56. Wingren, *Kyrkans ämbete* (1958), 8.

57. Wingren, "Begreppet lekman" (1982), 186.

Bible is used as a manual on how to regulate the organizational issues of the church. On this front, freedom prevails. What is important is to what degree the church's outward arrangements support the task that Christ has given the church. Wingren continually returns to this fact, and it seems as if he can scarcely find sufficient words to express how important this is in a Lutheran church such as the Church of Sweden:

> ... to say again something that has already been said. No matter how many times we may say it, it will still be forgotten. Thus, once again: Everything that serves the gospel is good and may as a matter of course be used by the church.[58]

"Turn Your Face towards the Storm and Sing Heave-Ho!"

Gustaf Wingren was ordained as a minister in Linköping Cathedral by Bishop Tor Andræ on Sunday, 15 December 1939, the year that World War II had dashed his plans to pursue research on the early church fathers. Wingren would serve as pastor in a local parish for only three short periods: from January to September 1940 in Gamleby, in October 1940 in Valdemarsvik, and from July 1943 to January 1944 in Motala. However, throughout this period, he preached nearly every Sunday. He had much less time for preaching as an associate professor during the second half of the 1940s and during his first decade as a full professor, but from the 1960s onward, he once again became a frequent and much sought-after preacher.[59] In addition, he delivered innumerable radio devotions, and published meditations on Bible texts in various periodicals.

Yet there were also other gifted preachers, such as Ludvig Jönsson (1923–85), who served as cathedral dean in Stockholm during the first half of the 1980s. In an article about Jönsson's preaching, originally published as a review of Jönsson's book *Homilies for Seekers* (*Postilla för sökare*), Wingren elaborated on a few ideas in a programmatic manner, thus also disclosing his own views on preaching. The article may even be interpreted as a pregnant homiletic sketch.[60]

---

58. Wingren, *Kyrkans ämbete* (1958), 34.

59. Karlsson, *Predikans samtal*, 67.

60. This article, titled "Människor lyssnar—varför?," was originally published in *Sydsvenska Dagbladet* on 10 December 1982, and later included in *Tyngd och nåd i svensk skönlitteratur* (1991).

Wingren begins by stating that even if we listen to a preacher attentively, it does not necessarily mean that we like what we hear. What is absolutely necessary for listening, however, is that we are "not able to discern in advance what the preacher is going to say."[61] In other words, the preacher's comments on the text are expected to disclose something new; they should provide something unexpected and surprising, yet based on something that is already known. Wingren wrote that Jönsson's preaching had a particular capacity to find its way into the everyday crises and challenges of the listeners, rather than simply remaining in the realm of generic spiritual problems. Through his successful, varied use of the "general concept" of "accepting our crisis as a necessary loss, as a death that is needed in order for resurrection to take place,"[62] his sermons found their way behind the well-kept facades that people and society maintain. For people to dare to relinquish their grip and "tell it like it is" requires trust. It is entirely a matter of a view of life based on a very specific interpretation of death:

> Death means giving up oneself, and no longer being able to control one's own existence. When we release our grip, when we no longer ask whether or not our life has been a failure, then we can die. Our entire life is an exercise in dying in this way. This death is always followed by resurrection, new creation, health and wholeness.[63]

Love, according to Wingren, implies death. It is a matter of dying a little, in the sense of no longer existing for oneself, but rather for the other. Wanting to preserve one's life at any price, means the same as not wanting or not daring to die, and thus not really being alive. If we follow this interpretation of the human condition, we are brought to a place outside of ourselves where we recognize that the sources of life and faith primarily exist outside ourselves. For this reason, the sermon should not begin in one's own existence; it is not the preacher's own life that the sermon should emphasize. Thus, according to Wingren's interpretation of Ludvig

---

61. *Tyngd och nåd i svensk skönlitteratur* (1991), 57. Cf. how in his foreword to *Texten talar: Trettio predikningar* (1989) Wingren expresses hopes that his collection of sermons might help preachers "in the most difficult aspect of their work, the continual struggle with those texts that keep cropping up again and again, and that do not seem to tell us anything." Ibid., 7.

62. Wingren, *Tyngd och nåd i svensk skönlitteratur* (1991), 58.

63. Ibid.

Jönsson, the gospel is, in general, nothing that we can give to ourselves, but rather, something that must be given to us from outside.

In many ways, there seems to be a discernable family resemblance between the works of Ludvig Jönsson and Gustaf Wingren, in theory as well as in practice, and in particular when it comes to preaching. There was a similar resemblance in Wingren's relationship to Henrik Ivarsson, who in the early 1950s was something like a favorite disciple among the doctoral students associated with Wingren, and involved in a research project on the sermon. In the beginning of his career as a professor, Wingren nourished plans of achieving a methodological break with Nygren based on the problematic of the sermon and founded on the program implied in his book from 1949/1960.

Henrik Ivarsson's dissertation, *The Task of the Sermon: A Typological Study with Special Regard to Reformational and Pietist Preaching* (*Predikans uppgift: En typologisk undersökning med särskild hänsyn till reformatorisk och pietistisk predikan*, 1956), consisted of a comparative study in which genuine reformational preaching (of Martin Luther) and Pietist preaching (of Anders Nohrborg, Johan Möller, Henric Schartau) were evaluated against one another. The final chapter of the dissertation also included an examination of how the sermon functions within Lutheran orthodoxy. The method of the study is typological and comparative in its approach, so that the different preachers stand as examples of certain pronounced types of preaching.[64] Against the sermon's main task of disseminating the forgiveness of sins through the proper use of law and gospel, the author places a Pietist conversion sermon, with the primary concern to disseminate knowledge. In the tradition of preaching within Lutheran orthodoxy, the forgiveness of sins is replaced by penance as the major concern. Ivarsson's dissertation lacks a section providing a summary of its findings, yet its very structure makes it easy to discern the two-front juxtaposition so typical of Swedish Luther research, in which the depiction of Luther takes its shape in confrontation with Pietism and orthodoxy. Other than a brief, introductory theoretical reflection, the dissertation consists mostly of typological reviews of the materials. However, the work gives a sense of a strong underlying inspiration from Ivarsson's adviser, Wingren, and his colleague, Sven Kjöllerström, as well as an international authority who at that time played a decisive role for Wingren: Gerhard Ebeling.

64. Ivarsson, *Predikans uppgift*, 14.

Late in 1956, the same year that Wingren was consumed by his bitter fight with Nygren, and issue after issue of *Swedish Theological Quarterly* (*STK*) was occupied by their agitated debate, Henrik Ivarsson was to defend his dissertation. At the defense on 1 December that year, Associate Professor Gunnar Hillerdal (later rector in Växjö) and Associate Professor Helge Brattgård (later bishop in Skara) served as opponents. Although they were both disciples of Wingren, they were not gracious, and delivered harsh criticism. Yet, the truly harsh treatment came three days later at the grading evaluation. Much to the surprise of Ivarsson and the anger of his advisor, the committee declined to award Ivarsson the competency of an associate professor. At that time, this was equivalent to the derailment of one's academic career: Ivarsson, the gifted student who had followed in Wingren's footsteps by employing his innovative methodological work, had no further future at Lund University. In his personal journal entry for 4 December 1956, Wingren commented briefly on the faculty's grading evaluation in a way that reveals his indignation: "No discussion took place. Prepared utterances were recited." Ivarsson left Lund and pursued a career on the Central Advisory Board of the Church of Sweden, and later became a pastor in the Stockholm suburb of Råsunda.[65] However, Wingren never stopped pointing out what a brilliant dissertation Ivarsson had written. After the defeat associated with Ivarsson's dissertation defense, Wingren methodically withdrew, and his doctoral students worked mostly with historical descriptions. It took a long time for Wingren to recover from this defeat. For decades, he continued to return to the topic of Ivarsson's dissertation with praises for its high quality. It was not by coincidence that Ivarsson's dissertation touched upon a subject that was central to Wingren's own theological project.

A little more than two decades later, Wingren found himself in a situation where he was confronted with a new opportunity to do something innovative concerning the task of preaching. By this time he was retired, and the drama was played out in a neighboring country, Norway. Wingren was invited to the University of Oslo to serve as the primary faculty opponent during the defense of a dissertation by thirty-eight-year-old Helge Hognestad. This task came to be part of the growing ties to Norway that Wingren cultivated during the 1970s and 1980s. A number of the professors from the Oslo theological faculty who were involved in the defense

---

65. Henrik Ivarsson's daughter, Malena Ivarsson, later published a novel with strong autobiographical elements, in which her father and his work played a significant role; see Ivarsson, *Time Out*.

had collaborated with Wingren for years. The doctoral student himself was a member of Norway's Forum for Christian Socialists, an organization in which Wingren and Hofsten were heavily involved. Yet, there were even more connections that would converge in what would come to be referred to as "the Hognestad case." The matter revolved around an examination of preaching as a practice, a topic of strategic importance for Wingren's theological project, and one which also might offer Wingren the possibility of a sort of revenge for the humiliating defeat he had suffered in connection with Henrik Ivarsson's dissertation. For Wingren, Hognestad also served as a Norwegian parallel to that kind of criticism of ideologies within theology that Ole Jensen had already developed in Denmark. In a way, Hognestad's dissertation thus brought together the two Norwegian networks that Wingren had cultivated: on the one hand, the academic, theological network of the Faculty of Theology at the University of Oslo, and on the other, the grass roots movement of Christian socialists that had become an increasingly important political forum and source of inspiration for Hofsten and Wingren. Furthermore, in "the Hognestad case," the issue of the relationship between theology and politics came to a head, and because of this controversial dissertation, it also became a necessity for Wingren to clarify his own position in this field.

Helge Hognestad's doctoral dissertation, *Preaching as Legitimization* (*Forkynnelse som legitimering*, 1978), is composed of four sections: an exegetical portion, which treats the Gospel according to Matthew based on a method of redaction-criticism; a portion based on sociology of knowledge inspired by Berger-Luckmann and Habermas, considering the church as an institution that legitimizes itself through its preaching; a homiletic portion, in which Hognestad analyzes concrete expositions of the texts of Matthew presented in Norwegian press and radio during the years 1974–76, based on the thesis that the "movement" of the texts does not move from the text to the listeners, but rather from institution to the listeners; and a concluding fourth section, where the author presents his own theory concerning preaching.[66]

Through inspiration from the form-historical school and redaction-criticism, Hognestad takes his point of departure in how, from the very

---

66. Hognestad's dissertation was later published as a two-volume work in 1978: *Preaching Toward a Breakaway. 1. The Gospel of Matthew and the Church's Use of It* (*Forkynnelse til oppbrudd. 1. Studier a Matteusevangeliet og kirkens bruk av av det*), and *Preaching—Defense of the Church? 2. The Gospel of Matthew and the Church's Use of It* (*Forkynnelsen—kirkens forsvar? 2. Studier i Matteusevangeliet og kirkens bruk av det*).

beginning, the gospel texts have served as sermons in specific situations. The original historical context of the Gospel according to Matthew is that of an early Christian congregation under hard pressure from its surroundings. After the catastrophic fall of Jerusalem in the year 70 AD, the people had been confronted by the necessity of taking sides and reevaluating their positions; in other words, they had been forced to reinterpret history. Yet, despite the fact that everything in this text thus seems to address the matter of breaking with the past and thinking along new lines, Hognestad shows in his dissertation that nineteen hundred years later, in Norway of the 1970s, the same texts were being used almost without exception to legitimize the status quo within the church. In other words, the sermons convey a message completely foreign to the very texts on which they are based. With few exceptions, the pattern is quite clear, and Hognestad comes to the conclusion that "[w]e can understand knowledge as a *mirroring* of the church-created reality, and at the same time, as a way of *legitimizing* it."[67] But the fact that the sermon serves as institutional legitimization and that it makes use of the texts to simply give biblical authority to what the preacher says, this also means that the church turns its back on society: "The crisis of the sermon is thus far deeper than the church normally admits, because it has failed to view this crisis in the context of the church's place in a society rife with crises and opposition."[68]

For several reasons, Hognestad's dissertation gave rise to a major debate. His investigation was not only an attack against the Lutheran state church in Norway, it was also part and parcel of a pointed political confrontation taking place in the country between Christianity and socialism. Later on, Hognestad's application for a job as parish priest in the Norwegian town of Høvik unleashed one of the most bitter church conflicts in postwar Norway—however, that is another story.[69] Hognestad's doctoral dissertation together with his defense awakened great

67. Hognestad, *Forkynnelsen—kirkens forsvar?*, 102.
68. Ibid., 115.
69. Hognestad later published a collection of his own sermons, *Gud på Høvik* (1981), and then a more programmatic, general theological book about the place of religion in a postreligious era, *En kirke for folket* (1982), which concludes with a challenge to establish a new religious orientation by taking common responsibility for discussion of God. The latter book contained great ambitions for achieving something parallel to the role that Paul took in the early church, but this did not come about. With the exception of a certain measure of media attention, Hognestad disappeared into the margins.

interest and brought about such a major public discussion considering basic theological problems that the journal *Norwegian Journal of Theology* (*Norsk Teologisk Tidsskrift*) even published an expanded thematic issue to document the debate.

One of the dissertation opponents, Guttorm Fløistad, at that time associate professor in the history of ideas, maintained that the dissertation was disjointed, and that its author had failed to show how its various parts fit together. Furthermore, the method, based on the sociology of knowledge renders the vital theological concepts as "remarkably insubstantial," leading him to posit the earnest question of whether this dissertation gives any room at all for a specific problematic of religion.[70] In his rebuttal to Hognestad, Professor of Exegetical Theology Jacob Jervell emphasized the dissertation's experimental and quite nontraditional structure, one that overrides the borders of its subject area, and he raises his objections to Hognestad's use of the Gospel of Matthew, which he claims "is not in any way acceptable."[71]

However, the discussion took on an especially sharp tone when Jervell's colleague, Per Lønning, made his entry into the debate. He began by praising Hognestad for breaking with the sort of preaching that is unconsciously characterized by a certain political stance, but then immediately noted that Hognestad's dissertation itself is unclear in regard to the issue of normativity, as it is based on a specific, normative understanding of reality (that of Marxism) in an unproblematic way, without asking whether it was a true absolute: "Hognestad makes no basic reservations in regard to the reality limitations of Marxism."[72] In Hognestad's investigation, theology is subordinated to the political debate in a way so that it never appears as anything more than just a phase within an exchange of political opinions. Hognestad reduces theology to politics, and his Marxist absolutism leads to nihilism. Based on this unconscious normativity, Per Lønning draws some overall conclusions, which are also revealing for the broader context of the debate. He maintains that in contrast to what had previously been common among Christian socialists in Norway, Hognestad breaks with every form of confessional anchoring and normative views of the Bible, which only shows "the impossible aspects

---

70. Fløistad, "Opposisjonsinlegg," 227, 236ff.
71. Jervell, "Matteusevangeliet?," 247.
72. Lønning, "Om ikke-bevisstgjort normativitet," 258.

of the agenda of his predecessor."[73] Lønning thus turned Hognestad's dissertation against the entire movement of the Forum for Christian Socialists, and stated that in Hognestad, he had found the final proof of the impossibility of uniting Marxism and Christianity.

Wingren had been asked to serve as the primary faculty opponent and when he took the podium on 30 September 1978 in the old ballroom at the University of Oslo to present his opposition, the air around him was charged with theological and political controversies. Wingren had positive comments about the dissertation, and praised the author as a constructive and gifted person with great capacity and skill. But he also leveled heavy criticism at Hognestad's shortcomings in his actual treatment of the subject of preaching. Wingren's method for walking the political minefield before him however differed from that of the other speakers. He pointed out that Hognestad combined a unilateral, christological determination of the concept of God with a tendency toward political activism—and reduced them both to the issue of changing society. In Wingren's opinion, the consequences were devastating. Through this approach, Hognestad risked losing all theological resources to an interpretation of social development in terms of general human values and norms that are not christologically determined. Simultaneously, there is no room left to speak about justification by faith rather than deeds. All this results in a reductionistic understanding of the eschatological future: "nor is there any new 'word' or new 'message' to a dying person, to someone who has been denied the possibility of undertaking a breaking-up in a social sense, but who is forced to view his own 'breakup' in terms of the fact that he will die now, today, tonight."[74] According to Wingren, Hognestad's interpretation of preaching simply did not contain any message by which people can live and die. Because Hognestad was so preoccupied with acts that can change society, and so uninterested in words that can be spoken to dying and condemned people, he would never move any closer to an answer to the question of what a sermon actually is. Wingren stated that it may be possible to establish a theory of social-ethics in the way that Hognestad had structured his investigation, but it would not be possible when it comes to homiletics.[75] To summarize, Wingren's critique

---

73. Ibid., 266.
74. Wingren, "Tre motforestillinger" (1978), 209.
75. Ibid., 213.

of Hognestad's dissertation was harsh, but it was less a matter of politics than of theology.

When Helge Hognestad got his chance to defend himself, he did so by attacking. He began by clarifying his view on historical materialism and the legitimizing function of the church in society. In addition, he put forward his only real conclusion, which was the remarkable distance separating text from preaching, showing that in practice, fidelity to the Bible lacks respect for historical texts when they are exposed in worship services and sermons. Hognestad maintained that Wingren's concentration on justification through faith alone and the death and resurrection of Jesus implied a concentration on life after death and a retreat into the personal sphere, shifting the perspective away from the social forces that determine the framework for life and death.[76] Further, he maintained that the doctrine of justification made preachers feel that they could offer people forgiveness for sins, which they have no right to administer. The entire idea of the forgiven person is an illusion, a dangerous illusion in which the church behaves as though God "went behind people's backs." In short, forgiveness is impossible if it does not take place through the people who suffer due to evil acts. Forgiveness requires action and yet more action, but the church has transformed this practice into a dogma. Hognestad continued in this way and also took a critical stance toward Wingren's unilateral focus on the death and resurrection of Jesus, when asking: Is it not God who creates all life? A narrow gauge theology, which is concerned only with historical events, will easily become blind to the new creation that is taking place right now.[77] In his defense, Hognestad repeatedly returned to the importance of practice and claimed that he did not want to hear about the dangerous division between law and gospel. Instead, he wanted to talk about the church's involvement in the system of capitalism.

A review of the pointed polemics surrounding Hognestad's doctoral dissertation and Wingren's involvement in them raises questions concerning how Wingren himself dealt with the relationship between theology and politics. In his reply to Hognestad's defense, Wingren was even more determined in his tone than before. He began by stating: "In all scientific writing, one must know what one is talking about." Then he stated that Hognestad had not even attempted to define what a sermon

---

76. Hognestad, "Troverdig forkynnelse—for hvem?," 276–77.
77. Ibid., 278.

is—how then could he study it?[78] Wingren further stated that Hognestad wanted to criticize the political and social practices in the Church of Norway, claiming that this task could be achieved without undertaking a homiletic study. Sermons are not even the most relevant material for a study of this sort, and Hognestad's investigation still lacked a concept defining what a sermon is, and how it differs from all other speaking forms and practices. Wingren underscored that a sermon is an "especially unique speech" that differs from political messages and analyses of the condition of society, but also from lectures about prayer, meditation, and psychological empowerment. A sermon is an exposition of a Bible text for contemporary people. Hognestad's failure to define the concept that was of central importance to his study was, according to Wingren, the root of all the problems that followed.

The way in which Wingren defined the importance of the repeated act of preaching was tied to his conviction that the basic human problems that are associated with the sermon are in fact permanent, regardless of whether the surrounding society is a dictatorship or a democracy: "There is no form of political system that can eliminate these problems. It is meaningful to preach only as long as these permanent problems persist. If these forms of human need did not exist, it would be sufficient to undertake political action and, as a basis for these actions, hold political speeches."[79]

Wingren proceeded by stating that there is nothing original in Hognestad's political stance, and if he continues to argue only in political terms, the church will not be changed at all; instead, it will only cleave even harder to a conservative position. Hognestad's dissertation could have been original if it had been an investigation in homiletics. He had, however, precluded this possibility through his failure to understand what a sermon is. The sermon must start from the occurrence of a "legalism of justification by deeds," exactly what this legalism is about cannot be discerned through a reading of the Bible. Here, Wingren returns to one of his favorite themes, emphasizing that Luther "is not in any case interested in the specific righteousness by law that Paul spoke of."[80] In the same way that Luther would not have been able to find any proponents of circumcision in his era, today we will not be able to find many people de-

78. Wingren, "Behovet av en klar definition" (1979), 110.
79. Ibid., 112.
80. Ibid., 113.

voted to the monastic life, confession, and prescribed penances. The task of the sermon is to crush this tyranny, and in order to complete this task, the preacher must say something new based on an old text, something that is not stated in the text, but that is implied by the text; only then will the listeners be able to hear the gospel in the gospel. According to Wingren, neither the acts that grow out of everyday ethical demands nor political projects can be found in the Bible. Instead they are *already there*, present in the form of "the needs of the other," in what our fellow human beings need at our workplaces or in what can be discussed reasonably in the public sphere. What the sermon provides is not found in people's everyday, creation-given lives but is something that is transmitted against all legal righteousness. No human being can forgive sins; only God can do that. According to Wingren, what the church does administer is the gospel. This gospel is something that no one can control or direct, and it cannot be reduced to a political activity. Nevertheless, preaching that serves as a liberating message for people, something that makes it easier to breathe, requires that the preacher identify what it is that is really afflicting people in a particular day and age. There is no doubt regarding this point, for Wingren:

> Today, in order to achieve a viable doctrine of justification in our sermon, we must first and foremost identify what form *legalism* is taking today. Legalism is not the requirement of circumcision (it was for Paul, but is not now!). Legalism is *not* life in the monastery (*it was for Luther, but is not now!*). We must go straight out into society and right into the souls, especially the souls of the outcasts of society, and ask: What is it in our time that motivates "deeds" day after day, fine, proper, beautiful, and praiseworthy acts? What is it in our time that is crushing people, creating neuroses, causing sleeplessness, social exclusion and despair? In my view, we will get exactly the same answer to both of these questions: the push for continual increases in production brought on by industrial society, the mentality of unending economic growth, the pursuit of status. We have thus identified today's legalism. Today, this is the enemy against which we must direct a real proclamation of justification by faith alone.[81]

There is an obvious connection between Wingren's views on preaching and his social criticism, but note that he brings these two components together in a completely different way than does Hognestad. Through

---

81. Ibid., 113–14.

his confrontation with Hognestad, the emancipated Lutheranism that Wingren cultivated was elicited even more clearly. This is a view of the gospel that does not tolerate any sort of formalization. It breaks all orders and demarcations, and yet requires contextually determined forms and limitations. Thus, Wingren identifies the gospel as a force beyond all logic and planning. It is a constantly living source of life that resists all kind of control. Nonetheless, it is also equally as clear that politics belongs to the sphere of the law, and as such, it is subordinate to a kind of reason that is potentially shared by all human beings. Both gospel and politics require movement and change in order to function at all.

Over the course of his life, Wingren preached and kept a few hundred sermons. Already in the early 1960s, Wingren was in conversation with the Swedish publishing house Gleerups regarding the publication of a collection of his sermons, but the book never materialized.[82] However, during his time as a professor, he did publish a long series of small booklets containing his sermons on Bible texts, often those he had presented in the form of radio meditations. However, in the 1980s things started to change. In his contribution to the anthology *Faith in a Time of Doubt* (*Tro i en tid av tvivel*, 1985), which he titled "Proclaiming the Gospel" ("Att förkunna evangelium"), he presented an outline for the structure of sermons for the major church holidays of the year. Later on, he developed this outline into a collection of sermons, issued in his book *The Text Is Speaking: Thirty Sermons* (*Texten talar: Trettio predikningar*, 1989). However, each of these publications was comprised of written sermons that Wingren had never preached in public. Posthumously, in 2010, the most comprehensive collection of "real" sermons by Wingren was published in one volume with the title *Homilies: Gustaf Wingren Preaches* (*Postilla: Gustaf Wingren predikar*, 2010), edited by Jonny Karlsson and Karin Larsdotter.[83]

Wingren's sermons have been made the object of research and scholarly examination in a doctoral dissertation defended by Jonny Karlsson in 2000: *The Conversation of the Sermon: A study on the Role of the Listener in the Sermon in the Work of Gustaf Wingren, Using Michail*

---

82. Cf. the long-term agreement that Wingren makes (as recorded in his journal) on 7 April 1962, which included several books, among them "a book of speeches and sermons to be published by Gleerups," but which never came to be.

83. This book contains a collection of sermons spanning a church year, preached by Wingren between 1938 and 1988, based on texts from the pertinent books of the Gospel. It was published in conjunction with Wingren's one hundredth birthday anniversary in November 2010 by the Swedish publishing house Artos, thus after the Swedish edition of this book was issued.

Bachtin's Theory of Dialogicity (*Predikans samtal: En studie av lyssnarens roll i predikan hos Gustaf Wingren utifrån Michail Bachtins teori om dialogicitet*). This study is one of the most important works that have been written about Wingren, in part because it is not predetermined in either a positive or a negative way by Wingren's own narrative, and in part because it examines materials that no previous researcher of Wingren has made use. By combining the perspectives of theology and communication theory, Karlsson is able to examine the connection to the listener in Wingren's sermons. Through this focus on the importance of the listener in the context of the sermon, Karlsson has succeeded in bringing together Wingren's theological hermeneutics with his sermons, and thus also in part his hermeneutical theology. In keeping with Wingren's theological project, Karlsson identifies a practice in which "the external nature of the word is preserved, without God and/or the listener becoming objectified," which enabled Karlsson to pursue his study independently of anthropocentric as well as theocentric homiletics.[84] Through his use of Michail Bachtin's dialogical understanding of language and humanity, he has succeeded formulating a general, human theory which, by showing that preaching follows the same rules as all other forms of speech, eliminates the risk of considering preaching as something mystical. In this way, Karlsson develops a theory of preaching that serves as a linguistic equivalent to Wingren's creation theology and theological hermeneutics.[85] What Karlsson has done, is to apply Wingren's theory of addressing to Wingren's own sermons by examining the nature of the connection with the listener. He does so by analyzing different sermons dealing with one and the same Bible text. In a remarkable way, this comparison also brings out the unique nature of Wingren's ideas on how continuity can only be maintained through change.[86] Karlsson's work succeeds in telling us something new about Wingren while managing to remain in close contact with Wingren's systematic theological authorship.

---

84. Karlsson, *Predikans samtal*, 27–41.

85. Ibid., 297.

86. Cf. the conclusion the author draws when he compares two sermons that Wingren preached on two completley different occasions eighteen years apart: "The differences to be found between the two sermons are due not to Wingren having changed theologically in any fundamental way, but rather to the fact that the sermons were presented in two different contexts. In part, they had different listeners, and in part, the world looked very different in 1973 than it had in 1956." Ibid., 11–12.

Let us focus on one special comparison in Karlsson's dissertation that in a particular way clarifies Wingren's theological position and provides many new perspectives, but also elaborates the ecclesiological problematic that is in particular being examined in this final chapter. Karlsson's comparison deals with two different sermons on the same text from Ezekiel 37:1–14, an aporetic and fascinating text written in a prophetic style about how God gives life to old bones and how tendons, flesh, and skin grow upon them and they are brought to life again due to the work of the Spirit. This is a text that certainly necessitates different interpretations. In the first place, Wingren preached on this text in Lund Cathedral on 15 September 1956, in conjunction with Theologians' Days. In his interpretation of the text in this specific context, he uses a series of analogies between "Israel then" and "the church today" in order to create a connection to the listeners intended for the exclusive group of priests-to-be who were listening to him, in other words, a context consisting of theologians who were active participants in the work of Church of Sweden. Wingren then individualized his analogy by making another analogy, this time between the prophet Ezekiel and the listener. By creating an opposing voice through the use of opposing pairs, Wingren enters into a dialogue with that which has yet to be said in the listeners. In this way, Wingren's sermon becomes "a speech about something that has taken place, but it is also a direct address, in the sense that these descriptive words about what has taken place are words that have importance for the people who are listening."[87]

In Jonny Karlsson's presentation, this sermon from 1956 is compared with a sermon about the same text that Wingren delivered at the Immanuel Church in Stockholm on 15 June 1973. This time, the context is not the Church of Sweden, but rather the Mission Covenant Church of Sweden, and more specifically, its annual General Assembly, a gathering of that denomination's highest-ranking representatives. This second sermon was also presented in a different era, in the aftermath of 1968, several years into the decade of the 1970s. During this period of time, Wingren himself was involved in a process of metamorphosis, a sort of "political" turn that brought him to view society as the most important context for his work as a theologian. This time, it seems as if Wingren himself is transformed into a prophet, and takes on the characteristics of a Pietist revivalist preacher. There is also a shift in the analogies he uses, for example when he now

---

87. Ibid., 89.

makes an analogy between the hard, straight and open language "in the demonstrations our youth are holding in the streets" and the prophetic language in the Old Testament. He continues, stating that "we need an analysis, a hard, basic analysis of the state of the Christian church groups in our country, one which speaks out about how things really are, by naming dead as 'dead.'"[88] But in the same way that faith in the future, as it is depicted in the book of Ezekiel, is based upon old bones that gain new life, Wingren ties contemporary challenges to the necessary movement from death to life as found in his grain-of-wheat eschatology. In his analysis of the sermon, Karlsson points out how Wingren in this specific context creates a connection to his listeners by comparing "our churches and chapels, where they are now located, disseminated throughout Sweden" to the dead bones that Ezekiel saw being given new life. Wingren even puts some strikingly modern statements in the Old Testament prophet's mouth: "We should be somewhat skeptical of these likeable denominational pedagogues."[89] Perhaps Wingren's polemics against advocates of the state church on one hand and against charismatics and Jesus-people on the other may be seen as a way of creating a connection with his contemporary listeners in the specific context in which he was speaking. His presentation was constructed by a series of opposites and polemic shifts. At one point in the sermon, he suddenly says:

> Yes, that which is old gains new life—but not when our gaze is turned backwards! On the contrary, what totally fills Ezekiel's view is *the future*. It is the future of resurrection on the third day, yes, in everything that the Bible tells us about. Turn your gaze today toward world starvation, toward the population explosion, toward the arms race, toward South Africa's silent buildup toward another catastrophe! "Turn your face towards the storm and sing Heave-Ho!"[90]

This passage of the sermon, which Karlsson describes as "stylistically planned, rich and rhetorically charged," contains a cluster of phrases and then an equally as drastic and abrupt turn.[91] The final words of this passage come from "Deckhand Jansson" ("Jungman Jansson"), the beloved traditional ballad by the Swedish poet Dan Andersson. In his sermon,

---

88. Ibid., 94.
89. Ibid., 101.
90. Wingren, quoted in ibid., 95, cf., 105.
91. Ibid., 105.

Wingren encourages the church to do as the sea-roving rascal in the song: "Turn your face towards the storm and sing Heave-Ho!"

Jonny Karlsson describes the subtle way in which Wingren enters into a dialog with "that which has yet to be said" by "a distancing and 'alienating' effect, or a sort of shock therapy intended to require his listeners to relinquish their anxious looking back, and to dare to look forward."[92] He describes the poetic figure of Deckhand Jansson, who taunts death in his blundering, yet honorable, way "among the sharks of the South Sea so blue," as a fitting image of the role that a prophet plays in his own day. Yet, we might wonder if Wingren is even more subtle than that. At this meeting of free church temperance folk, he may have been using this colorful and beloved figure from Swedish literature and the song as a Trojan horse. Although the character of Deckham Jansson may seem innocent, however, he is actually a hard-drinking ne'er-do-well who forsakes his true love. Given what we know about Wingren's strong tendency to think in profound strategic ways, and his own free church background, it is difficult to believe that his use of this image is a coincidence. While he may have sounded much like an old free church revivalist preacher as he spoke to this gathering of pious, orderly people, the church critic and provocateur in him was also present.

I am also led to wonder whether in this sermon from June 1973 Wingren was simultaneously sending a secret message to one of the people who he knew sat listening to him, but who in many ways was a foreigner at the General Assembly of the Mission Covenant Church, namely, Greta Hofsten. Towards the end of his sermon, he employs the old revivalist device of a personal address to the individual listener and states that there need not be many who speak the words that God commands: "If necessary, it will be sufficient if just one single human being does not remain silent—does not remain silent." History, Wingren said, provides many examples of the power of truth, even when it is spoken by only a few; he continues:

> For this reason, this evening's text from Ezekiel speaks to a single person, a single child of humanity here in the Immanuel Church tonight. We do not know where this person is sitting; we do not know whether this person is a man or a woman. Perhaps it is a young person, someone whose voice has yet to be heard in public, and who is afraid at the thought that "it might

---

92. Ibid., 106, 110.

be me!" Everything depends on obedience and patience and persistence.[93]

The fact that he offered a way out with the possibility that it might be a young person does little to weaken my personal suspicion that he was trying to address one specific person. Following Wingren's sermon, the mood of the group that evening was one of engagement, and many of the attendees wanted to speak with the famous professor from Lund University. Wingren, however, wanted only to speak with Greta Hofsten. She was the only person he wanted to see, and no one else.[94] This is of course only to be considered as speculation on my part. Perhaps his attempt to address the individual listener was merely part of his attempt to follow a revivalist sermon outline.

It is significant that Wingren was invited to preach at the assembly that marked the very epicenter of the Swedish Mission Covenant Church at the beginning of the 1970s. In parallel to his growing frustration with the Church of Sweden (the missed opportunity to uncouple the church from the Swedish state, the conflicts regarding the ordination of women as priests, the drawn-out battles over social ethics, and so on), the Swedish Mission Covenant Church started to become more open. Even though he found it difficult to endure the upper-middle class nature of the Mission Covenant, its moral observance, its splendor and the always threatening mentality of self-justification by deeds, he was nonetheless attracted to its folksy simplicity and the growing political radicalization that was evident among its members at that time. For the next two decades, Wingren would be a popular speaker at many gatherings within the Mission Covenant Church throughout Sweden.

Lennart Molin played an important role in Wingren's new relationship with the Swedish Mission Covenant Church. Not only was he the chairperson of the Mission Covenant Youth Movement (SMU), but he was also one of Wingren's doctoral students at Lund. In time, he became a faculty member at the Theological Seminary at Lidingö (the present-day Stockholm School of Theology), where Wingren was frequently invited to speak as a guest lecturer. In 1986, when Molin was asked to take on the editorship of the theological periodical *Faith & Life* (*Tro & Liv*), he first made sure that his old professor would be willing to be a regular

93. Wingren, quoted in ibid., 98–99.
94. I have gathered the context of the sermon from an interview with Lennart Molin on 6 October 2009.

contributor to its pages. It is telling that although Wingren published many of his major early articles in the "official" *Swedish Theological Quarterly* (STK), once Lennart Molin became editor of *Faith & Life*, he published his articles in that periodical instead. Between 1986 and 1996, a dozen major articles by him were published in this journal.[95]

A Church without the Middle Ages?

In January 1971, Gustaf Wingren changed his mind on the issue of the relationship between church and state in Sweden. In an article in the daily newspaper *Svenska Dagbladet* on 14 February 1971, he declared that while he had never seen any reason why the church should not accept state funding for a good cause, it was now clear to him that the church could not be renewed from within its existing organization. A radical change of the external structural relationships was required. In the little book in which he declared his change of heart, *The Answer Is Yes: A Word about Church and State* (*Svaret är ja: Ett ord om kyrka och stat*, 1972), Wingren presented his views using a series of theses. The first of these theses went as follows:

> If we are to speak of church and state in Sweden in the 1970s, we must keep in mind everything we know about the development of the church in Europe during the fourth century, the

---

95. The articles that Wingren published in the journal *Tro & Liv* (*Faith & Life*) in a little more than a decade provide a good picture of his theological interests during that time (article titles translated to English here, for the purpose of illustration): "Sweden's Only Barthian" (1985, issue 5), "The Theology of Olov Hartmann" (1987, issue 3), "The Resurrection of Christ: The Victory of the Gospel Over the Law" (1987, issue 6), "What is Law and What is the Gospel Today?" (1988, issue 5), "Anders Nygren and Swedish Theology Today" (1988, issue 6), "God's People Live by Baptism: Christian Considerations on the Term 'Layman'" (1989, issue 2), "Implications of 'Education' [Bildung]: The Christian Roots of a Secular Concept" (1989, issue 5), "Faith and Theology" (1990, issue 2), "The State and the Gospel" (1990, issue 5), "For the sake of the Humanity: Humanity and Creation" (1991, issue 3), "Religion and Gospel" (1991, issue 6), "The Creator Spirit and the Holy Spirit" (1992, issue 4), "God's Love in the Straightjacket of the Law" (1995, issue 1), "Grundtvig and His Message to Us Today" (1995, issue 3), "The Trinity" (1996, issue 1), and "Christian or Natural Ethics?" (1996, issue 3). The fourth issue in 1996 was a thematic issue on the theology of Gustaf Wingren, with material from the Gustaf Wingren Society's first conference, held in Linköping. That same year, Wingren concluded his contributions to *Tro & Liv*, and Lennart Molin stepped down from his post as editor.

development of the church in Europe during the sixteenth century, and the development of the church during the twentieth century.[96]

In fact, another thirty years would pass before the relationship between church and state in Sweden would be redefined in any significant way. Nonetheless, Wingren was clear about the general tendency: the church in Sweden was approaching the situation that had prevailed prior to the fourth century AD, when Emperor Constantine made Christianity the state religion of the Roman Empire. The Middle Ages, a period when church and state were closely linked, were over. Moreover, the extended Middle Ages brought about by the state church system of Lutheran orthodoxy was over. Thus, according to Wingren, the church found itself back at the point where it all began.

We have already seen how Irenaeus played a key role in the writings of Wingren. Early in his career, through his research on Gnosticism, Wingren became interested in this prominent theologian of the early church, who became an important source for his own theological reflections. From the 1940s through the 1980s, Irenaeus was also important for the shift that took place in the dominant metaphorical theology that Wingren used, from judicial to biological. Over time, the historical context of Irenaeus became of growing importance to Wingren when he came to realize the theological significance of the fact that Irenaeus lived in an era that in many ways resembles our own. Irenaeus lived before the Constantinian era, and specifically before the church became part of the power structure of the state. In modern-day Sweden, it seems that we in a similar way live *after* this era, as we are approaching a post-Christian age when the church is no longer a factor of power, and Christians more often find themselves to be in minority. Wingren saw this post-Constantinian challenge early and recognized it as a great opportunity. In addition, he argued that given this situation, Irenaeus would have a growing importance and relevance for our time. Through this historical contextualization, it also becomes clear that the situation of the church and theology has changed dramatically:

> When Luther came onto the scene, all of the kings in Europe were Christian, all legislation was full of biblical terminologies, and all the inhabitants of Europe were baptized. Irenaeus wrote five books against the Gnostics in a period of time when there

96. Wingren, *Svaret är ja* (1972), 7.

was not a single Christian government, no laws were written using the Bible as their basis, an era when only a few people in Europe had been baptized.[97]

Seen from this perspective, the European parochial system, in which an entire continent was organized according to religious dictates and divided into parishes, seems more like an intermediary stage in European history. In other words, our situation today resembles that of Martin Luther less and less—and looks more and more like the situation in which Irenaeus lived. In the early 1970s, Wingren stated, "The situation of the 1500s is over, and the day of the early church is our day."[98] However, he immediately added the statement that faith in creation can be at least as strong in a situation in which the authorities do not consider themselves to be Christians and the world does not care about the church. In the first centuries AD, Christians lived as a minority in the midst of a heathen society, and yet they recognized those in positions of authority, regardless of their faith, as tools in the service of God. In effect, the confession of faith that placed creation first was formulated during a time when the church found itself in a martyr situation. It was also in this context that the church created a theology in which the death and resurrection of Jesus was presented as something that was for all humanity. One of the challenges in our post-Constantinian era is that the church must rediscover and reinvent ways to bring together everyday life and the worship service, creation and gospel, society and church.

In his later writings, Wingren could not resist describing this changed situation in political terms. In his autobiography, *My Five Universities* (1991), he states that "if we as Christians in Sweden are already a minority, if Sweden is governed by a fanaticism for economic growth, then let us be a consciously *fighting* minority that places *the good of humanity* as our goal, and not our own profit!"[99] In his dissertation on Wingren's concept of the church, Bo Håkansson has demonstrated this shift from the early Wingren's focus on the folk church in the midst of society to the later Wingren's concept of a church that has become a small, contrasting group of oddballs who eagerly resist the mainstream developments of society.[100] Here, however, it is important to remember

---

97. Wingren, *Människa och kristen* (1983), 10.
98. Wingren, *Växling och kontinuitet* (1972), 115.
99. Wingren, *Mina fem universitet* (1991), 179.
100. Håkansson, *Vardagens kyrka*, 230–32. Cf. Sjödin, "Kufarna skall bygga

that his affirmation of the minority situation had primarily a political dimension. In this sense as well, the church seems to find itself back in a situation resembling its early days:

> Originally, the gospel was the liberating words of an outcast king to the powerless and downtrodden. It functioned best when the church that carried it forth had not yet been truly accepted by any worldly authority. It is not unimaginable that the church might once again become a similar fringe phenomenon. The idea that this would be an irreplaceable loss is not supported by any thorough studies on the subject.[101]

The last sentence of this quotation indicates that Wingren recognized mostly opportunities in a post-Medieval situation for the church. Early on, Wingren had become aware that the post-Constantinian situation opened new ecumenical possibilities for the Church of Sweden. In his book, *Gospel and Church* (1960/1964), he had already noted how the new patterns of housing and employment tended to challenge the logic of the traditional, territorial congregation. In the 1960s, but especially after his change of mind in 1971 regarding the issue of church and state, Wingren cultivated great ecumenical hopes at the national level. As Sweden's state church and free churches were increasingly becoming more alike, approaching one another through their internal transformations, he foresaw with enthusiasm the possibility of their future convergence. Here, it is important to remember that in 1929 it was the bishops of the Church of Sweden, led by Einar Billing, who demanded that the politicians adopt a policy of voluntary withdrawal from the church, entirely in keeping with Martin Luther's (and Billing's own) thesis that the church should be governed by the gospel, and not by law. This was an idea that Wingren wholeheartedly embraced. He thus saw the inner logic of social change pointing toward a concept that he felt the church ought to affirm: *"free choice by free individuals in Swedish society."*[102]

It is easy to talk about freedom, but difficult to put it into practice, and both the state church and the free churches faced complications in doing so. Before the law of religious freedom came into effect in 1952, the free churches had actually been categorized as "foreign confessions of faith" in Sweden. Over time the free churches had increasingly come to

---

framtidens kyrka," interview with Wingren.
   101. Wingren, *Växling och kontinuitet* (1972), 187.
   102. Wingren, *Fram emot en enad kyrka* (1971), 25.

take on responsibilities and an active role in the broader Swedish society, far beyond the smaller circles of their own congregational members. According to Wingren, this trend toward taking responsibility for the entire Swedish population meant that the free churches were approaching a view of the people that the folk church had always held. Wingren made a note of what he saw as evidence of significant change among Sweden's free churches such as youth camps, chaplaincy work in hospitals and prisons, as well as the fact that free church buildings and congregations were now increasingly being given geographical names; he saw all of this as evidence of significant transformations. The most significant change, however, was that the free churches had gained the right to perform marriages. This act, which is not mentioned at all in the New Testament, has direct civil and legal ramifications in Swedish society, since it may determine rights of inheritance, familial obligations, and child support: "This is an important role, which makes free church pastors into servants of Swedish society."[103] From this, Wingren draws the conclusion that while the law regarding freedom of religion is *distancing* the folk church from Swedish society, it will simultaneously bring the free churches *closer* to society. In a way, it could be said that the free churches had gained some of the characteristics of a folk church: "In the new openness of the free churches toward society, there is an element of 'the forgiveness of sins for the people of Sweden.'"[104] This also provides a foundation for what he mentions in terms of "a new form of ecumenical coexistence within the framework of freedom of religion."[105] From this background, Wingren is also able to speak of ecumenism as a task of the people and a task of the folk church.

In the mid-1960s, Wingren thought that he could identify a series of changes that were headed in the right direction: the law on religious freedom, laypeople's increased responsibility for church administration within the Church of Sweden, a new vitality in the volunteer work carried out by state church congregations, and more. Yet, he saw glaring shortcoming on one critical point: "Nothing new is happening [in the relationship] between the national church and the free churches in Sweden."[106] Among the explanations he heard as to why no ecumenical initiatives had been pursued, he flatly denounced the formulaic opposition between

---

103. Ibid., 27. Cf. Wingren, *Folkkyrkotanken* (1964), 37ff.
104. Ibid., 73.
105. Ibid., 39.
106. Ibid., 70.

the "offered grace" of the folk church and the "received grace" of the free churches. Wingren felt that both sides had changed so much that this way of stating the problem was overplayed and outdated. On the one hand, the folk church had changed through increased volunteer work, so that the folk church concept of a pure messenger of grace without any requirements has, as a result of Sweden's law on religious freedom, become an outdated idea.[107] But on the other hand, segments of the free churches had begun to show ambitions toward taking social responsibility that stretched far beyond their own pious circles. Their new practice of open communion in free churches also played an important role in this process of change. Thus, states Wingren, gift and task, word and deed, must be correlated to find a new balancing point in a new era.

In that period of time, Wingren perceived clear tendencies toward a future convergence of these churches, one that would unite the neo-evangelical (or at least the non-Baptist) free church denominations rooted in Lutheran Pietism with the Church of Sweden. Twentieth century patterns of geographic mobility and new communications had created a new social infrastructure, which in turn had opened up new ecumenical opportunities: "*In this sort of situation, ecumenism becomes a task of the folk church.*"[108] In the mid-1960s he spoke of the importance of "keeping two windows open": a window "of the people" toward society, and an "ecumenical window" toward the (non-Baptist) free churches.[109] Nevertheless, he had no illusions that the free churches would ever completely let go of their focus on a congregation of individuals, and considered that the Church of Sweden could not relinquish its focus on the entire territory.[110] For this reason, in the writings he authored in the 1960s, he opens the way for surprisingly bold ecumenical experiments linked to the contemporary social developments:

---

107. Ibid., 33.
108. Ibid., 76.
109. Ibid., 15.

110. Wingren emphasizes that even if the church's relationship to the state were to change, such that the Church of Sweden and the free churches soon found themselves in similar situations, there would still be a fundamental difference: "On the matter of openness, the absence of permanent borderlines among the population, the Church of Sweden would still be an offense from the viewpoint of the free churches." Wingren, *Kyrkans isolering* (1958), 16. In the same context, however, he raises the question of whether some Christian denominations in Sweden ought to openly begin negotiations with one another and discuss the possibility of mergers and unions.

> At present, the territorial congregation is undergoing so many other changes that a congregation of individuals inside the limits of the parish "territory" is imaginable, even a congregation of individuals that has its own administration of the sacraments. News of that sort might not be the most earth-shaking among the changes that the territorial congregation will have to face in the new social structure.[111]

The last sentence of this quotation indicates that Wingren had become increasingly aware of the fact that the new communications of the 1960s had begun seriously to undermine Einar Billing's parish idyll of communities in the Swedish countryside, where housing, work, and worship were organically intertwined in a specific geographic locality. In the new emerging society, people live in one place but work in another, and furthermore often spend their weekends in a different place than where they are during their workweek, with the following consequence: "Today, it is difficult to identify where a person's *place* is, or where their true *home* lies."[112] What does it mean to be a folk church (territorial church) in this new emerging society?

In his search for natural patterns of living that might be used to support the concept of the folk church, in the seventies Wingren began to lean toward the new sense of belonging that now could be recognized in the larger cities. For example, individuals in the city of Stockholm no longer refer to themselves as residents of a particular inner-city parish, such as Gustav Vasa or Katarina, but as Stockholmers. Wingren also elaborated on how the automobile and television might usher a renaissance in family life that ought to be taken advantage of and fostered.[113] Wingren's ideas may at this stage be to some extent naive and not fully developed, and he would later abandon some of them; nonetheless, his search for natural patterns of life demonstrates the strong degree of change that he associated with Billing's concept of the folk church. He was also open to unconventional solutions to the outward arrangements or organization of the church. For, according to Wingren, if we "monotonously repeat Billing's old formulas,"[114] we are not being faithful to the classical idea of the folk church, because the idea of a folk church requires first and foremost that we consider *change* seriously.

111. Wingren, *Folkkyrkotanken* (1964), 78.
112. Ibid., 82.
113. Ibid., 83ff.
114. Ibid., 33.

Yet, even Wingren's ecumenical theology has a strong foundation in biblical theology: "This unique phenomenon of the early church is the four gospels, and we ought to be mature enough to draw the obvious ecumenical conclusion from this fact."[115] Thus, plurality and diversity in modern Christianity have direct correspondence in the plurality that characterizes the four gospels. In this context, Wingren refers to Ernst Käsemann, a student of Bultmann, and Käsemann's arguments that the gospels do not sing the praises of uniformity. Instead, they are in fact the most important reasons for rifts between church groups:

> The New Testament does not provide support for the unity of the church, but rather its variety of different confessions. Matthew, Luke, Paul, John, the pastoral letters to the early congregations, and so on: all of this looks like a broad array of various confessions of faith, present already in the canon itself.[116]

Wingren asks, why on earth we would expect to find fewer varieties of Christianity today than there were at the beginning? Instead, the variations of possible interpretations ought to increase as Christianity grows across time and space. In the early church there were different christologies in different places: "Lutheran, Reformed and Anglican are no more different from one another than were Antioch, Alexandria, Rome, or Asia Minor in the third century AD. The latter were all able to co-exist within the same, undivided church, while the former cannot."[117] In other words, according to Wingren, it is not uniformity that is biblical, but rather diversity. The early church could tolerate, withstand, and even celebrate the existence of four different versions of the gospel story about the same series of events: "When the church is radical and open it is exactly when it is radically biblical."[118] To be biblical is to safeguard diversity, multiplicity of interpretation, and openness.

This basis in biblical theology is in no way in opposition to a critical stance or the development of scientific methodologies. On the contrary, a necessary requirement for taking benefit from this diversity is to let go of literal faith and inspirational teachings, and instead take the Bible seriously as a historical human document:

---

115. Wingren, *Gamal vägar framåt* (1986), 31.

116. Wingren, *Växling och kontinuitet* (1972), 42.

117. Ibid., 105. Cf. "The great ecumenical variety of the present day is like a new version of the rich variation found in the early church." Ibid., 129.

118. Ibid., 165.

In the twentieth century, the authority of our faith is quite simply *the book of the Bible in all its diversity, as it is disclosed by historical biblical criticism.* Precisely as a human document, influenced by its environment and varied, is the way in which the Bible is the authority in a church in which diversity and personal freedom prevail.[119]

Here we see Wingren's view of a biblical faith that requires peaceful coexistence between different types of faith. In this situation, it is in fact the legislation of society, together with the development of modern communications and transportation systems, that have opened up possibilities for developing and living with the plurality that is a matter of course in the Bible texts.[120]

Nonetheless, Wingren's attitude toward ecumenism is not entirely straightforward. On the one hand, he may sound like an apostle of diversity and tolerance; but on the other hand, it is difficult to escape from the fact that he was a polemicist who more than once discharged his anathemas both within Church of Sweden and against other churches, primarily Catholics and Anglicans.[121] We should also keep in mind that his idea of the post-Constantinian context of Christianity, understood as a church without the Middle Ages, may also be considered as part of an anti-Catholic polemic that Wingren cultivated from the beginning to the end of his theological career. Even the way in which the Faculty of Theology at Lund University focused on the two specific epochs of the first and sixteenth centuries implied that it had in practice chosen to skip over the entire "Catholic Middle Ages." We have already seen Wingren's journal entries from his summer in Berlin in 1938, in which he reasoned that we ought to allow the high church movement, because it can offer an alternative that might keep people from becoming Catholic by conversion.[122] More than half a century later, he made the choice to conclude his memoirs by pointing out two cities where organized tyranny, directed against the individual, reigns, namely Moscow and Rome.[123] This is a

119. Ibid., 129.

120. Ibid., 105.

121. Håkansson, *Vardagens kyrka*, 125.

122. Cf. "In some ways, it is a good thing that the high church movement is gaining ground. In this way, the church is protected from Catholicizing tendencies." Wingren, "Johanneum Journal," 136. And further: "Thus Rome moves off into the distance again. Crypto-Catholicism is . . . practically extinct." Ibid., 137.

123. Wingren, *Mina fem universitet* (1991), 188–89.

remarkable parallel to draw, and not only for ecumenical reasons. As he wrote these lines in the early 1990s, just after the fall of the Berlin Wall, Wingren seemed to expect that the same sort of sudden revolution that had taken place in Moscow would also happen in Rome. He was full of expectation that the power structure in Rome would change, and that the papacy would alter its stance on celibacy and the administration of the sacraments by women. Such a change would also alter the situation for the opponents of the ordination of women within the Church of Sweden.

Among the primary challenges that Wingren identified in a post-Constantinian theological situation was the question of how creation faith could be maintained after the formal ties between the church and the state were broken:

> This second act begins in earnest when every existing church is a free church, when no Christian parish any longer has geographical boundaries, and when membership in the church depends entirely on personal decision. I am a Christian, I choose to become a member. *Thus we begin to discover what was lost when the territorial parish was dissolved* ... It is only the church building itself that understands what the gospel proposes to do with men ... They bear witness to *the God who acts*; they speak about him who seeks *all*.[124]

The idea of the church building, and not a religious person, being the carrier of faith and theology, as the only one that understands what the gospel proposes to do for men, is an intriguing one. We can understand its potential to create controversy even better if we consider the Pietistic tendency to identify the location of faith within the inner being of each individual human. Here, too, the relationship between creation and body is sundered for the benefit of an inner spirituality. In times when the territorial parish congregation is no longer intact, the question of how to maintain the idea of the active, acting God who seeks all people could also be articulated in the following way: How can we preserve what creation theology teaches us about the general human condition in a situation where the organizational structure in and of itself does not express

---

124. Wingren, *Exodus Theology* (1968/1969), 99–101. If we may on one hand note that Wingren in fact precedes the discussion of the church's post-Constantinian context that would later be pursued by (among others) postliberal theologians and proponents of radical orthodoxy, we may also on the other hand note that Wingren moved in a diametrically opposite direction by directing the focus for the work of theology in this concrete situation to the concept of creation and the generally human.

this, and when Christianity may even find itself in a minority position? When facing this challenge, Wingren argues that we gain no help from Billing, because he never developed a theological anthropology that has anything to tell us about creation as such. Despite his openness and broad views, Billing seems paradoxically to have created an ecclesio-centrism that is unprepared to interpret theologically the individual as a human being, and the world as world. Billing, the great theologian and originator of the concept of the folk church, seemed to move in a direction opposed to that of creation theology, in that he tended to make all of society into a church. Moreover, Billing's basis in the forgiveness of sins eliminates God's continual and natural connection with general human existence, since according to Billing's way of thinking, God does not make his first contact with the individual until infant baptism.[125]

Considering this background, we may wonder about the possibilities for Wingren to instead develop an ecclesiology based on creation theology, which from the very outset implies a certain distance from the church and the risk of an eventual church-centrism. What remains of the church in the works of Wingren? In one instance, he emphasized the importance of a broadening of God's interface with the world. In cheerful and even humorous terms, he sketches out the following action program for the church:

> Presumably, and especially among Christian people, we will need to arrange long-term linguistic training in which, for example, people are taught to use the word "God" solely in terms of workplaces, solidarity, helpfulness, sunshine and rain, and so on, but *never* name the word "church" during the entire conversation. After years of training courses of this type, it might then be possible for us to cleanse our language, which today is swamped with an egocentric interest in the church and its possibilities of survival. Among all the fronts that have been opened

---

125. Cf. "Einar Billing is the first person in Sweden whose theology issued in ecclesiology; he had no interpretation of creation and law, no anthropological theology. Furthermore, he was the first one who gave fundamental significance to the external form of organization for the fulfillment of the function of the church in proclaiming the gospel." Wingren, *Exodus Theology* (1968/1969), 131. Compared with Grundtvig's ecclesiology, Billing's concept of the territorial, folk church is characterized by the fact that "the movement is frozen, the journey comes to a rest in the local church parishes" in a static way. Wingren, *Människa och kristen* (1993), 99. Cf. the context conveyed in ibid., 98–99, where the author compares Billing's view of the church with that which is found in Grundtvig.

up by the confrontation between the gospel and the twentieth century, this is the most important one.[126]

In order to understand the unique nature of Wingren's attempts to integrate that which is human with that which is Christian, world with church, and weekday with worship service, we must examine how he recognized the relationship between the individual and the church. In a small booklet from the mid-1950s, originally conceived as two radio lectures and then later published in various formats, Wingren discusses the issue of the isolation of the church, the nature of this isolation, and its causes. He denies the idea that the isolation of the church is a matter of low numbers—and furthermore that it could be solved by increased attendance. According to him, it will not help if there would be twenty people sitting in the church instead of three: "you will be just as isolated after those seventeen more people have entered."[127] Once again, egocentricity is the antagonist in Wingren's drama. The entire self-obsessed ecclesiocentrism, which is temptingly close at hand whenever people express concern over the isolation of the church, leads in a theologically faulty direction: "A worship space may be filled to capacity, but isolation will still be there . . . if the members of the congregation are concentrated upon themselves."[128] Thus, in order to understand the nature of the isolation of the church, we must instead direct our attention toward the fact that the connections between Christian life and human life have been broken in our everyday situations. According to Wingren, the question of "How may the church reach out?" has only one reasonable answer, and that is that "the church is already out there."[129] The baptized individual is thus at the center of the dynamic that Wingren perceives as the basis for the presence of the church in the world:

> In the meantime, the week between Sunday and Saturday is filled with hours and meetings with people. It is to these hours and meetings that the positive power of Sunday's worship service should flow. If this does not occur in those of us who visit the Sunday worship service, if our lives from Monday morning to Saturday are an area entirely to themselves, then it is this shortcoming from which the isolation of the church arises. If

---

126. Wingren, *Växling och kontinuitet* (1972), 174.
127. Wingren, *Kyrkans isolering* (1958), 11.
128. Ibid., 18.
129. Ibid., 14.

Sunday worshippers are this way, then the church in its entirety necessarily becomes turned inward upon itself and concerned with itself without interruption, expecting that the world will at last allow it to have everything that has to do with the church to itself, in peace.[130]

As an alternative to church-centrism, Wingren imagines a church of the everyday, in which each Christian represents the church, and thus has full authority and responsibility for the task of the church for the people. If isolation has gained a foothold in everyday life, then the congregation is living a false life, which no congregational activity can correct. Furthermore, if the people who participate in the worship service do not bring their everyday lives with them into the worship service, it will remain only an isolated event. When church members are isolated from common human life in their everyday lives, then the church is isolated. The reason this is so is because Christianity has far too often been associated with saying No, No, No and refraining from involvement. In this kind of situation, the gospel about Jesus who went straight into human emergency situations cannot function. Human life in everyday situations does not need to be spiritualized in order to become theologically interesting. By digging through the sources from ancient Christianity and from the Reformation, Wingren seeks to re-establish a *No* that is "embedded in a roar of Yes."[131] Only in this way can we once again see the connection between a true human church and the circumstance that the head of this church is also human.

How should we then view Wingren's understanding of the church? At a symposium held in conjunction with Wingren's eighty-fifth birthday, I presented the following question as a task worthy of examination:

> In this situation, it would be a fruitful undertaking to develop an ecclesiology based on the ideas of the theologian who continually warned of "the churchification of God," and who stood out as one of the most vocal of Sweden's church critics. What would a potential ecclesiology look like, if we view creation as the "horizon of understanding" of the gospel, and in keeping with Wingren, suppose that it is not possible to describe the relationship between Christ and the church without simultaneously qualifying the positive relationship between the church and the world and the inner connection between everyday life and the

---

130. Ibid., 12.
131. Ibid., 5.

worship service? It is a matter of moving toward an ecclesiology that is not centered on the church, in which the church can only be "for others," just as Christ did not live for himself but always lived "for others," and in which the unique nature of the church can only function precisely as a radicalization of its openness. In short, if we could develop an ecclesiology that was focused on *recapitulatio* and "the healing of human life," what would it look like?[132]

Portions of the answers to these questions can be found in Bo Håkansson's doctoral dissertation, which in its very title accurately characterizes the ecclesiology of Wingren as a *church of the everyday*. It would probably be difficult to articulate a more reasonable description of Wingren's view of the church than this short formula. Håkansson summarizes Wingren's integrating view of the church using two dialectically related characteristics: *the church in the everyday life of the people*, and *the humanity of Christ in the church*.[133] In this dialectical conception of the church, we may recognize how Wingren's criticisms against low church Pietism and his criticism against the Anglican-influenced high church movement coincide in a devastating way, because both of these movements tend to remove the presence of God and theology from everyday life, relegating them instead to a church that risks becoming precisely a plague of egocentricity. Yet, the aim of the church can never be to "churchify" human beings or the world. The little congregations of Pietist believers, the office-oriented high church, and the folk church as envisioned by Einar Billing using the forgiveness of sins as a way to include everyone—all risk undermining our recognition of the world as God's world. According to Wingren's theology of creation, the aim of the church must instead be the healing of human life (*recapitulatio*), which implies *a non-church-centered ecclesiology*. It is not possible to specifically describe the relationship between Christ and the church without simultaneously qualifying the positive relationship between the church and the world, and thus the inner connection between everyday life and the worship service. A church that takes the humanity of Christ seriously truly becomes part of God's *recapitulatio*: "The community of the church is the community of natural life; we could say that it is the healing of human life."[134] If we

---

132. Kristensson Uggla, "Möjligheter i Gustaf Wingrens teologi," 87–88.
133. Håkansson, *Vardagens kyrka*, 29–53.
134. Wingren, *Living Word* (1949/1960), 176.

understand the church in this way, then the church must continually be self-critical in order to be a church.

When Håkansson attempts to determine the nature of the church as seen in the basic ideas of Wingren, he points out a theme that we have seen earlier in this book: the church must be directed and ruled by the gospel. This presumes that the church is based on something that exists *outside* the church itself, something that the church cannot control or direct, but which nonetheless provides great freedom in regard to the concrete forms for the realization of the gospel. When he emphasizes baptism as that which constitutes the church, it is important to examine its integrating role in the relationship to the Christian faith and to human life in general. Baptism is the first sacrament, and denotes openness, while communion, "the repeated giving of life," tends to take on a more exclusive or closed character.[135] For Wingren it is quite simply the case that everything can be summarized in baptism: it is an act that is identified with Christ's death and resurrection, and each and every person's daily death and resurrection. In connection with Per Erik Persson, Bo Håkansson speaks of a hermeneutics of the interpretation of life in order to make the point that this basic approach to the church also serves as an interpretation of life in its entirety.[136] Wingren was able to express it in the following way:

> In general, it is the case in each era of church history that the true meaning of baptism during the period in question is best disclosed in the texts that deal with something *other* than baptism. If baptism has a real meaning for life, then it will come to the fore and be at the heart of how we deal with all problems.[137]

One point where Håkansson raises serious questions concerning Wingren's views on the church has to do with the community dimension. Here, Håkansson continues a criticism that Ola Sigurdson and others had directed against Wingren from the perspective of a *communio-ecclesiology*, which makes membership in the body of Christ the central requirement for understanding the church, and warns that the folk church only increases the current tendencies toward individualism and privatization.[138]

---

135. Håkansson, *Vardagens kyrka*, 39–40.

136. Ibid., 38. Cf. the book that Per Erik Persson published together with Lars Eckerdal, *Dopet som livstydning*.

137. Wingren "Begreppet lekman" (1982), 178.

138. Cf. for example Sigurdson, "Kyrkan som de heligas samfund."

Throughout his presentation, Håkansson pursues a recurring reasoning about the role of the community in an ecclesiology like Wingren's, which does not in any way include an ambition to create any sort of exclusive *communio*. The church, according to Wingren, is constituted not by confessional texts, church office (in apostolic succession), or by the fact that people come together and form a group—everything stands and falls with the gospel. Wingren expressed his point in a provocative way:

> The religious professionals, who are all around us, have often built up for themselves a field of activity delimited from normal human community life, and made "churchliness" a sphere of its own on earth—or we ourselves tempt them into such a sphere in order to continue all our forms of activity. If the dual externalities would come into acceptance, then all that might remain of everything would be nothing else than prayer and everyday work! What purpose should "congregational life" then serve? To these people, Luther's words bring a slight feeling of fear.[139]

However, community is not entirely absent from Wingren's equation, but it is never considered as a foundation. Instead, it is seen as a fruit that results from people being reached by the gospel. Nonetheless, Håkansson states that Wingren seems so completely influenced by the sharp polemics against the ideal of a pious community as presented by Pietism, and fixated on church office as seen in a self-absorbed church organization, that there is little space left over for speaking of the church as community. He admits that Wingren tends "to underappreciate the possibility of creating a nonexclusive community, based on the conditions presented in his own theology."[140] In the conclusion to his voluminous dissertation, Håkansson returns once again to this lingering problem in Wingren, stating that "the individual must bear the entire responsibility for being a church without the supporting community of *koinonia*."[141] This critique comes not from the position of the Pietist congregation, but rather, from the opposite direction: Håkansson criticizes Wingren because in his later writings, he seems to retire to the Pietist side, and thus neglects the possibilities that might exist in the broad concept of the folk church. Similar to his campaign against the opponents of the ordained ministry of women,

---

139. Wingren, "Vad betyder Luther idag?" (1967), 18.
140. Håkansson, *Vardagens kyrka*, 319.
141. Ibid., 359.

Wingren's campaign against legalism and moralism has rendered church office and the institution of the church nearly invisible.[142]

Here, we enter into another area where Håkansson raises questions. He asks whether *the everyday church* risks becoming too "everyday-like." Håkansson specifically feels that there is a risk of a collision between Wingren's critique against fixation on the church and "humanity's longing for separateness, holiness and respect for the mystery":

> Everyday life must occasionally give way to the religious holidays, to the mystery, the celebration, liturgy and play. The low viewpoint, the "frog's perspective," the dry, plain everyday nature that Wingren speaks of so often, is perhaps not sufficient for gaining an overview of life and putting it into context.[143]

In an article that was (rather remarkably) published in a *Festschrift* dedicated to one of the primary figures of Sweden's high church movement, Gunnar Rosendal (known as "Father Gunnar"), Wingren takes up this theme in a way that we might not expect. In other contexts, he had previously stated that the low church movement, in contrast to the high church movement, had a tendency to disregard the worship service.[144] Here, he emphasized that we must overlook the high church movement's naïve liturgical inventions, and the misleading dogmatic theses about the offices of priest and bishop, respectively, as something that lend validity to the sacraments, in order to recognize what is the true task of the high church movement: the renewal of the worship service.[145] Yet, he recognizes it as a tragic turn in the later history of the Church of Sweden that renewal of the celebration of Holy Communion had to be realized with the help of the high church movement, for that movement had brought a strongly hierarchical view of church office. He puts most of the blame for this on the exegetes and the Luther scholars, who did not dig into their mines soon enough—and for this reason, the renewal had to come from outside, by way of the Anglican Church.[146]

---

142. Ibid., 360.

143. Ibid., 314.

144. This is a corrective against a form of national church thinking that according to Wingren is characterized by "fear of any distance from the general populace— people feel plagued by the many confessional moments within the worship service, and tend to want to obscure them somewhat." Wingren, "Vad kan vi komma att få från svensk högkyrkligheten i framtiden?" (1972), 429.

145. Wingren, *Folkkyrkotanken* (1964), 63.

146. Ibid., 64.

In his article honoring Father Gunnar, titled "What Can We Expect from the Swedish High Church Movement in the Future?" ("Vad kan vi komma att få från svensk högkyrklighet i framtiden?," 1972), Wingren seems rather like an outsider, since all of the other contributors to the Festschrift were purely high church theologians. In the *Festschrift*, Wingren became encapsulated in a foreign body, in the same way that the high church movement tended to become a sect, or foreign body, within the folk church.[147] Although Wingren takes pains to emphasize that the ideas of Father Gunnar are not as foreign to him as to many others, and that for his part, he has at times been "not unopposed to breaking away."[148] He claims to affirm the confessionally faithful as well as the sacramental and liturgical characteristics that Rosendahl presents in his book *The Renewal of the Church* (*Kyrklig förnyelse*, 1936). Yet, when he reached the third chapter of Rosendal's book, which deals with the hierarchical nature of the renewal of the church, he finds himself in complete disagreement. Wingren found it impossible to accept this characteristic, and for this reason: he emphasized that the "we" in the title of his article should be understood as "we who stand on the outside," in other words, we who are not part of the Swedish high church movement and who will never be part of it.[149]

However, even if we others must remain outside the high church community because of its hierarchical nature, Wingren asks himself what we others may, nonetheless, expect to gain from the fact that the high church movement exists within the Church of Sweden. Part of the answer to this question relates to the need for clarity regarding the worship service and the confession of faith in a specific historical situation at a time when the church's relationship to the state is changing in Sweden, and when the convictions of the church are no longer the convictions of the general Swedish population: "To be able to see this, to see it without blinkers on, and nonetheless be *happy*, is what is needed from the church in the future."[150] In this regard, the experiences of the high church movement as a minority will prove useful in the future, when the Church of Sweden will need to see itself as a minority. However, the theological profile of the high church movement means that it will not have much to offer for the confrontation with the most important challenge in the post-

147. Ibid.
148. Wingren, "Vad kan vi komma att få från svensk högkyrkligheten i framtiden?" (1972), 427.
149. Ibid., 428.
150. Ibid.

Constantinian context: the need to rehabilitate and restore the concept of creation, making it possible to interpret those people who are outside the church as tools in the hand of God.

Nevertheless, even if the little clique of the high church movement has developed a capacity for separating itself, for being peculiar in its taste in clothing, actions and tone, it is inescapably true that this group has an important contribution to make, and that it will be in the area of the worship service and its renewal. In this context, Wingren emphasizes the necessity of a combination of liturgical multitude and simplicity. A folk church that recognizes baptism as the basis of the church, and for which communion serves as a recurring act that follows baptism and that develops the message and implications of baptism, ought not to have any clear borders among the general population. Yet, if this equation is to function at all, a few people must probably be a little more profiled, and it is here that the high church movement has its place. But toward the conclusion of his remarkable essay, instead of focusing on the tendencies toward isolation and sectarianism that he recognizes as characteristics of the high church movement, Wingren brings out the importance of *happily* being a minority. There are, in other words, different ways to be a minority: "One may in fact be a minority and know oneself to be so *for* the others, *for* the many."[151]

Being for Others

Throughout his entire life, Gustaf Wingren was a fanatical football fan. However, even in regard to sports, he remained faithful to his home diocese: he was a lifelong follower of the two most famous football teams from his home area, IFK Norrköping and Åtvidabergs FF. With equal measures of pride and self-irony in relation to the Swedish football icon Nisse Liedholm, he could state: "There are only two people of any real importance originating from Valdemarsvik—and the other one is Nisse Liedholm." The football field as an arena for strategic and tactical operations held a drama that corresponded directly to Wingren's "inner arena" and his great theological interest in stories and conflicts.

Gustaf loved to watch TV, especially when he could watch a football match. However, Greta had firmly decided that they would not have a television in their home. Perhaps she saw TV as a waste of time. Perhaps

---

151. Ibid., 433.

this decision was part of the kenotic process of self-proletarianization that they were pursuing together. In any event, it did not help that I, with my family background, told her time and time again that a TV was in fact the most important piece of furniture in a working-class home. Yet, there was no real discord between the pair regarding whether or not to have a television, and the dispute came to an abrupt end in 1993 when Lund University made Gustaf a Jubilee Doctor. To help mark the occasion, several other students and I took up a collection to give him—a television.

Before the television arrived in the Wingren home at Warholms väg 6B, Gustaf would often make his way to our student collective in the bishop's residence at Nicolovius väg 12 to watch major football games. The five of us rented the house, which stood on the outskirts of the university district, from the then-Bishop of Lund, Per-Olov Ahrén. The bishop himself lived in the stylish old Bishop's Mansion located further along Sandgatan, close to the University Library. On one occasion in the middle of the 1980s, our living room was packed to capacity with students who had come to watch a game that I believe was a match with the national team, or perhaps a game featuring the IFK Gothenburg team in an international cup match. We had given Gustaf a place of honor in a leather easy chair, directly in front of the television. There were students from many different fields of study watching the game that day, and not many of them knew who this elderly man in the knitted sweater was.

At a decisive moment toward the end of the match, the star of the team, Torbjörn Nilsson, suddenly had an open goal, but did something inconceivable: he passed the ball to a teammate, who then shot the ball into the undefended goal. The room erupted into a deafening roar. It was a thrilling moment, and we all shouted like madmen. In the middle of this chaos, Gustaf rose up from his easy chair, raised his hands in the air like an Old Testament prophet, and shouted in a loud voice: "He is acting like Jesus! Torbjörn Nilsson is acting like Jesus! He gives to others!"

The room fell into complete and utter silence. People stared at the old man, and did not understand a thing. The game went on, and after a while, everyone began talking again. But a few of us who were present will never forget that moment, which in many ways illustrated who Gustaf was. He was and always would be a *homo theologicus*, who seemed to peer out at society from the isolated position of his chair of learning. His language and his frame of reference were those of theology. In many contexts, this posed yet another disability for him, but the other side of the coin was that he had a unique ability to interpret the most common everyday occurrences in theological terms. On that day, in Torbjörn Nilsson's unselfish act, Gustaf recognized the basic story that had characterized all of his thinking and that he had developed theologically in innumerable variations throughout his entire life. He saw someone who let go of the most important thing in his life, or, to express it in a more theological way, someone who "poured himself out."[152]

The meaning of life is to be *for others*. What is most important in life exists outside ourselves. This is the key element in Wingren's interpretation of the human condition. The ability to put oneself in the other person's shoes is entirely necessary for living a complete life. At its utmost, love is a matter of having one's center outside of one's own self. This is also the image of Christ that emerges from the theology of Gustaf Wingren. Christ is the one who from beginning to end is only for others—and this is precisely what makes him so genuinely human. But if this is true, then the identity and actions of the church must also be characterized by being for others. The church's center of gravity does not exist inside the church itself; the church must instead be open toward what exists outside the church, because the church is quite simply centered outside of itself. Around 1960, Wingren expressed this idea in the following provocative terms:

> The Church exists for the sake of the unredeemed who are outside it. This is its *raison d'être*. If instead it exists only for the sake of its members it will be in continual conflict with its indwelling Lord.[153]

What is a person who lives *for others* like? How could we organize a church that has as its goal to place those who are not members of the organization at the center of its organization? How can and should we cope with the gospel, something that no one can control or direct? In order to answer these questions, we must look toward a *practice of transformation*, configured by the capacity to meet the basic paradoxes of existence with a dialectical approach. How to achieve this is a life-long challenge for which there is no purely theoretical solution.

Throughout his entire theological career, Wingren criticized theoretical attempts to determine the nature of the phenomenon of

---

152. Football player Torbjörn Nilsson actually seems to have gone along with the personal reconfiguration that Gustaf Wingren outlined for him, because for the life of him, Nilsson proved to be unable to remember during which match this event took place. His good deeds seem to have left him to make room for others, in an almost Lutheran sense. Interview with Torbjörn Nilsson, 27 May 2010.

153. Wingren, *Gospel and Church* (1960/1964), 10–11.

Christianity by isolating and identifying something distinctly Christian, something that definitely *separates* Christians from all others. According to Wingren, however, it is not possible to articulate what Christianity is, without simultaneously articulating something that this faith shares and has in common with all other people. An understanding of the actions of God as a link in a restoration and completion of creation (*recapitulatio*) assigns human nature a normative role when defining this faith. This does not mean that there is nothing that is distinctly Christian, but it does mean that the uniqueness of the Christian faith only allows itself to be articulated and preserved through a positive connection to general human existence. The task to develop such an interpretation of Christianity, an ecclesiology and a theological anthropology that are characterized by such a basic pattern, will of course be a truly difficult undertaking if we limit ourselves to purely theoretical perspective.

Wingren's biting criticism of a church formed by a plague of egocentricity is based on the conviction that the church cannot be a church if it is solely focused upon itself. Only by being *for others* can the church follow Christ, the one who was only *for others*. The church is not based on foundations, structures, channels of office or religious experiences, nor does the church control its own center; rather, the church's center of gravity lies outside the church itself, in a life lived *for others*. In the works of Wingren, the metaphor of the grain of wheat, applied within an eschatological perspective, served as a paradigmatic model for understanding church practices and programs of action. The grain of wheat achieves nothing for itself when it falls onto the ground and dies. But later on, it provides new life—*for others*. In the same way as the theology of Wingren has its origin in something that is not theology, so does theology have its continuation in something that is not theology. To borrow an ingenious formulation from Victoria Fareld, a Swedish scholar in the history of ideas, it is a matter of *being outside oneself within oneself*.[154]

In 1967, on the four hundred-fiftieth anniversary of the Protestant Reformation, Wingren published an essay titled "What Does Luther Mean for Us Today?" ("Vad betyder Luther idag?"). Here, he highlights how differently people thought in Luther's day in the sixteenth century; however, in regard to our understanding of life, Luther the reformer is unendingly contemporary. Wingren maintains that "Luther's great contribution to the cleansing of our life" begins with "the point on which

---

154. Fareld, *Att vara utom sig inom sig*.

Martin Luther himself begins to speak to us today . . . his favorite theme: the difficulty of believing."[155] However, the positive side of *impossible est credere* deals with the fact that through the Lutheran idea of having one's righteousness outside of oneself, we can come to terms with egocentricity and self-absorption. True humanity is understood based upon how we in two directions live outside ourselves: in part, in relation to God, and in part, in relation to our fellow human beings.[156] If we choose to see God's forgiveness as something that exists outside ourselves, we avoid a Christianity that is pasted on, with the positive result that human nature can simply remain human. In this context, Wingren claims that "we all need a Savior in order to simply become fully human."[157]

"In this dual 'outside myself,' there is a sort of humility that is not at all modern," writes Wingren.[158] Moreover, it is this dual externality in which we live outside ourselves in a double sense, by which we realize our full humanity. No relationship, writes Wingren, is as personal as this one, in which we live outside ourselves in a double sense. He continues: "If we were able to be "outside ourselves" and simply listen to the word, we would thus be able to be within a much greater Human Being than we are ourselves, one who lived for nothing other than to give himself for us."[159]

At this point in the works of Gustaf Wingren, the image of Christ and the image of the human being meld together. This is what happens not only when we are touched by the message of the Bible texts, but also in our everyday life: "Through our common, everyday work, we exist *in* each other's lives."[160] Christ is the true human being in that he is outside himself—in the same way that we become truly human when we dare to be outside ourselves.

* * *

When Gustaf Wingren telephoned friends and their families, he had a quirky habit of introducing himself with the following words: "It is I." This grammatical absurdity was a play on language, something in which he sometimes indulged with delight. Yet in a way, he was also placing

---

155. Wingren, "Vad betyder Luther idag?" (1967), 17, 19.
156. Ibid., 17.
157. Ibid., 19.
158. Ibid., 16.
159. Ibid., 21.
160. Ibid.

himself "outside himself within himself." But who was Gustaf Wingren, really? What can we finally know about a person? The more I have worked on this book, the more enigmatic Gustaf Wingren has become to me. I have become increasingly uncertain about who he really was. It seems that just as I begin to discern the silhouette of his identity, new perspectives open up, others disappear, and behind his character, surprising new characters emerge in seemingly endless succession.

Writing an intellectual biography is a very special task, one that requires that the writer constantly remind himself that in the end, there will always remain a chasm between living a life and telling a story. This is one of several reasons why I have chosen not to attempt a strict chronological presentation. A human being *is certainly not* a story. Life becomes truly human when being narrated; yet, the life of a human being can nonetheless never be fully captured in a story. It is thus no coincidence that Paul Ricoeur chose to conclude his monumental work *Memory, History, Forgetting* with a poem, which already by its very form serves to mark the limits of knowledge:

> Under history, memory and forgetting.
>
> Under memory and forgetting, life.
>
> But writing a life is another story.
>
> Incompletion.[161]

---

161. Ricoeur, *Memory, History, Forgetting*, 506.

Acknowledgments

IN THE FOREWORD TO his biography of Professor Johannes Sløk, *Man Is a Misconception: My Friendship with Johannes Sløk* (2007), Kjeld Holm, bishop of Aarhus, Denmark, writes of the difficulties inherent in writing about persons whom you knew well while they were alive. When Sløk passed away in 2001, many people asked Holm if he intended to write a book about his mentor. He said no, for the following reason: "He was too close to me at the time, both in life and in death. The distance needed to be able to write a book about a man and his ideas did not exist."[1] Eventually, Holm did write his book about Sløk—and near the end of Sløk's life, Bishop Holm had mentioned to him that he hoped to write a book about him someday. To which the old professor replied, "Well, who the hell else would do it otherwise?"[2]

In the same way, I felt that someone should write a book about Gustaf Wingren. In the first chapter of this book, I give some good reasons for doing so. Something I did not do, however, was to mention the special challenges associated with the writing of an intellectual biography. The biography as genre has long been questioned, particularly in academic contexts. This has changed over time, and today we recognize a dramatic increase of interest in biographical investigations as research method. We have thus been able to read a great number of outstanding biographies of philosophers, written by authors such as Ray Monk and François Dosse. I have taken a great deal of inspiration from these two authors as I have pursued the task of writing a sort of theological biography, a presentation that weaves together the story of a life with quite a lot of theological and

1. Holm, *Mennesket er en misforståelse*, 9.
2. Ibid., 15.

philosophical reflections—not to mention the many historical contextualizations that must be undertaken during the course of the journey.

Many people have contributed with "living material" to my study. However, as I have pointed out a number of times, writing history is first and foremost a process of selecting what to leave out. There is no end to what could be told, and an endless number of persons who could tell it. While some individuals may be upset about what I have written about them, there are probably even more people who (for good reason) are disappointed that I neither interviewed nor mentioned them in this book. The selective process of writing history is as inexorable as it is painful.

I wish to extend warm thanks to all (see the list of sources) who were willing to tell about their encounters with Gustaf Wingren—and with Greta Hofsten, too. Thanks go to the personnel at the Lund University Library and to Fredrik Tersmeden at the national Arkivcentrum Syd in Lund; thanks also to Kjetil Hafstad for his time and for providing contacts in Oslo, Claes Hollander for providing an inventory and access to materials in the archives of Radio Sweden, Jan-Olav Henriksen for insights into the Norwegian scene, Ralph Engstrand for archival work with the church records of the United Methodist Church of Sweden, and Lennart Bernhardtson for research in Revhaken.

I want to extend thanks to the Stockholm School of Theology and its president, Owe Kennerberg, and other colleagues there. During the year when I wrote this book, I was, in addition to my regular duties, engaged part-time as a professor of philosophy and culture at that institution, and had opportunity to lecture and give a course on the theology of Gustaf Wingren. This provided great stimulus to my writing process. Thanks to the students who participated. Monica Helles also deserves thanks for all her support on practical matters.

I want to extend hearty thanks to the large group of people who devoted considerable time to reading, proofing, and providing comments on the manuscript at various phases and in various capacities: Pelle Bengtsson, Anne-Louise Eriksson, Eskil Franck, Pierre Guillet de Monthoux, David Karlsson, Mikael Lindfeldt, Merete Mazzarella, Lennart Molin, Finn Petrén, Jayne Svennungson, Per Wirtén, and Ulrika Wolf-Knuts. Thank you, Martin Lind, for your help with photo captions.

There is a group of individuals who not only read the manuscript in one version after another but also helped gather material, becoming a sort of virtual research group for me, and who thus deserve a very special thank you: Harry Aronson, who during his year as a "Jubileum Doctor" graciously received me during many visits in Lund and Båstad, and who as an older colleague and friend supported me through the entire process; Jonny Karlsson, who shared both sources and intimate knowledge of the ideas of Wingren that he had built up through writing his doctoral dissertation; Per Erik Persson, who nearly returned to his old role as my academic adviser and read my texts with blinding speed, attention to detail and area knowledge, and often at short notice; Rune Romhed, who at times was almost a research colleague, copied piles of texts, again and again read and provided written feedback on my texts as the most qualified doctor. A special thanks goes to Anna Wingren Kedidjan for conversations, materials, photos, and contacts with the family, and also to Finn Petrén for conversations and photos. Thank you also to the editors of this book: Christina Sejte, who despite a tight schedule agreed to work with my text, and David Karlson, who made a final review of the text onboard his sailboat between Bohus-Björkö and Havstenssund.

Finally, my warmest thanks go to Föreningen Konstsamfundet (The Society of Arts), which finances the Amos Anderson Professorship at the Swedish-speaking university in Finland, Åbo Akademi University. I have come to see this seat of learning as a fortress of cultivation and Bildung, charged with the double task of being a university and safeguarding the Swedish cultural heritage of Finland.

Postscript to the English Edition

IN ASSOCIATION WITH THE English edition of this book, I have resisted the temptation to rewrite the text, thus transforming it into a new book. Of course, some few corrections and explanations have been necessary to add in order to make the presentation accessible for non-Swedish readers. Besides the fact that I have included information about the posthumously published *Homilies: Gustaf Wingren Preaches* (*Postilla: Gustaf Wingren predikar*, 2010), I have refrained from investigating the English-speaking reception of Wingren's theology—and limited myself to the intention to further contribute to a broader picture of this work in future research. In general, English translations have been used, when available, but original titles and dates of issue have been added, in order to maintain the chronological dimension of Wingren's work. In this edition, pictures have been removed and the number of foot notes reduced.

I would like to express my gratitude to the translator, Daniel M. Olson, who worked hard in order to make the Swedish text available for an English-speaking audience—despite the difficult times he experienced. After Dan delivered his manuscript, I was gifted with a number of people who supported me in different ways in my efforts to cultivate the text further: Elizabeth Nyman has supported me with language check; Johnny Jonsson, Martin Lind, and Lennart Molin have read through and corrected the manuscript; Mattias Martinsson, Lars Trägårdh, Sven-Erik Brodd, and Nancy Mace have helped with references, technical language issues, and references. Thanks also to KG Hammar, who gave me the initial impetus for this project.

Above all and in particular, I would like to express my gratitude to Carol Adamson, who did the final copyediting of the book. Without our cooperation this English edition would never have been concluded.

Finally, I would like to thank Birgit och Sven Håkan Ohlssons stiftelse for generous financial support to the translation.

Literature and Other Sources

Books, selected articles, and booklets by Gustaf Wingren, arranged chronologically by the publication date of the original Swedish version. If there is an earlier English translation than the one cited, the date is given in brackets after the Swedish version.

1930s and 1940s

"Marcions kristendomstolkning." *Svensk Teologisk Kvartalskrift* 12 (1936) 318–38.
"Frälsningens Gud såsom skapare och domare" *Svensk Teologisk Kvartalskrift* 16 (1940) 322–39.
"Skapelsen, lagen och inkarnationen enligt Irenaeus." *Svensk Teologisk Kvartalskrift* 16 (1940) 133–55.
Luthers lära om kallelsen. Lund: Gleerup, 1942. Translated by Carl C. Rasmussen as *Luther on Vocation* (Philadelphia: Muhlenberg Press, 1957). Reprint, Eugene, OR: Wipf & Stock, 2004.
"The Christian's Calling according to Luther." *The Augustana Quarterly* 21 (1942) 3–16.
"Einar Billings teologi." *Svensk Teologisk Kvartalskrift* 16 (1944) 271–301.
Människan och inkarnationen enligt Irenaeus. Lund: Gleerup, 1947. Translated by Ross Mackenzie as *Man and the Incarnation: A Study in the Biblical Theology of Irenaeus* (Philadelphia: Muhlenberg Press, 1959). Reprint, Eugene, OR: Wipf & Stock, 2004.
"'Ordet' hos Barth." *Svensk Teologisk Kvartalskrift* 24 (1948) 240–67.
"Arbetets mening." *Svensk Teologisk Kvartalskrift* 25 (1949) 278–86.
Predikan: En principiell studie. Lund: Gleerup, 1949. Translated by Victor C. Pogue as *The Living Word: A Theological Study of Preaching and the Church* (Philadelphia: Muhlenberg Press, 1960). Reprint, Eugene, OR: Wipf & Stock, 2002.

1950s

"Tro och sanning." *Svensk Teologisk Kvartalskrift* 26 (1950) 7–23.
"Utläggningens problematik." *Svensk Teologisk Kvartalskrift* 34 (1950) 403–12.

"Några karaktäristiska drag i modern teologi." Inaugural lecture of 3 November 1951. *Svensk Teologisk Kvartalskrift* 4 (1951) 241–47.
Teologiens metodfråga. Lund: Gleerup, 1954. Translated by Eric H. Wahlstrom as *Theology in Conflict: Nygren, Barth, Bultmann* (Philadelphia: Muhlenberg, 1958).
"Einar Billings teologiska metod." In *Nordisk teologi: Idéer och män. Festskrift till Ragnar Bring den 10 juli 1955*, 279–92. Lund:Gleerups, 1955.
"Teologiens metodfråga." *Svensk Teologisk Kvartalskrift* 1 (1956) 36–41.
"Nomos och Agape hos biskop Nygren." *Svensk Teologisk Kvartalskrift* 2 (1956) 122–32.
"Filosofi och teologi hos biskop Nygren." *Svensk Teologisk Kvartalskrift* 4 (1956) 284–312.
Skapelsen och lagen. Lund: Gleerup, 1958. Translated by Ross Mackenzie as *Creation and Law* (Philadelphia: Muhlenberg Press, 1961). Reprint, Eugene, OR: Wipf & Stock, 2003.
Kyrkans ämbete. Lund: Gleerup, 1958.
Kyrkan och samhället. Stockholm: Sveriges kyrkliga studieförbund, 1958.
Kyrkans isolering. Stockholm: Sveriges kristliga studentrörelse, 1958.
Svensk teologi efter 1900. Stockholm: Sveriges kristliga studentrörelse, 1958.
Svenska kyrkans ekumeniska ansvar. Lund: Gleerup, 1959.

1960s

Evangeliet och kyrkan. Lund: Gleerup, 1960. Translated by Ross Mackenzie as *Gospel and Church* (Philadelphia: Fortress, 1964). Reprint, Eugene, OR: Wipf & Stock, 2006.
Folkkyrkotanken: Kyrkan i 60-talet. Stockholm: Diakonistyrelsens förlag, 1964.
"Mina ämnesval. Apologia pro vita mea. Teologiskt självporträtt." *Vår Lösen* 57 (1966) 494–500. / "Creation: A Crucial Article of Faith; My Selection of Topics." In *The Flight from Creation*, 13–30. Minneapolis: Augsburg, 1971.
"Vi och Vietnam." *Kristet Forum* 13 (1966) 42–44.
"Vad betyder Luther idag?" In *Luther idag: Svenska kyrkans reformationsjubileum 1967*, 5–26. Lund: Håkan Ohlssons, 1967.
"*Trons artiklar: Tre radioföredrag.*" Lund: Gleerup, 1968.
Einar Billing: En studie i svensk teologi före 1920. Lund: Gleerup, 1968. Translated by Eric Wahlstrom as *An Exodus Theology: Einar Billing and the Development of Modern Swedish Theology* (Philadelphia: Fortress, 1969).

1970s

Luther frigiven: Tema med sex variationer. Lund: Gleerup, 1970.
Socialetik i Stockholm: Dokument från 1950-talets svenska kyrkoliv. Uppsala: Pro Veritate, 1970.
"Reformationens och lutherdomens ethos." In *Etik och Kristen tro*, edited by Gustaf Wingren, 112–47. Lund: Liber, 1971.
"Klipp av, bygg upp!" *Svenska Dagbladet*, 2 February 1971.
Fram emot en enad kyrka: Variationer över Matt. 28:18-20. Stockholm: Gummesson, 1971.

The Flight from Creation. Minneapolis: Augsburg, 1971.
Växling och kontinuitet: Teologiska kriterier. Lund: Gleerup, 1972.
"Gammal filosofi blir som ny." *Sydsvenska Dagbladet*, 12 August 1972.
"Vad kan vi komma att få från svensk högkyrklighet i framtiden?" In *Opuscula Ecclesiastica: Studier tillägnade Gunnar Rosendal den 4 april 1972*, edited by Oloph Bexell, 426-33. Uppsala: Pro veritate, 1972.
Svaret är ja: Ett ord om kyrka och stat. Lund: Gleerup, 1972.
Credo: Den kristna tros- och livsåskådningen. Lund: Gleerup, 1974. Translated by Edgar M. Carlson as *Credo: The Christian View of Faith and Life* (Minneapolis: Augsburg, 1981).
"Den springande punkten: Påminnelser om en överhoppad bok." *Svensk Teologisk Kvartalskrift* 50 (1974) 101-7.
Frigörelse till livskvalitet. Stockhom: Gummesson, 1975.
"Lars Ahlin = evangelium = obegriplighet." *Sydsvenska Dagbladet*, 5 January 1975.
"En kristen människosyn." In *Årsbok för kristen humanism 1976*, edited by Carl-Henric Grenholm, 11-23. Stockholm: Gummesson, 1976.
Två testamenten och tre artiklar. Stockholm: Gummesson, 1976.
"Livets mening." *Sydsvenska Dagbladet*, 27 April 1976.
En framtid och ett hopp: Fyra morgonandakter. Stockholm: Verbum, 1977.
"Livsåskådningarna och frågan om kristendomens egenart." In *Livsåskådningsforskning*, edited by Ragnar Holte, 183-203. Acta Universitatis Upsaliensis: Symposia Universitatis Upsaliensis annum quingentesimum celebrantis 4. Stockholm: Almqvist & Wiksell, 1977.
"Skapelse och evangelium: Ett problem i modern dansk teologi." *Svensk Teologisk Kvartalskrift* 1 (1977) 1-11.
Rättfärdiggörelse av tro: Fem lutherska morgonböner. Stockholm: Gummesson, 1978.
"Tre motforestillinger." *Norsk Teologisk Tidsskrift* 1 (1978) 203-14.
"Behovet av en klar definition. Metodiska synpunkter på Helge Hognestads doktorsavhandling." *Norsk Teologisk Tidsskrift* (1979) 109-14.
Tro och främlingsskap. Åtta brev. Lund: Skeab, 1979. Coauthored with Greta Hofsten.
Öppenhet och egenart. Evangeliet i världen. Lund: Liber, 1979. / *Creation and Gospel: The New Situation in European Theology*. Introduction and bibliography by Henry Vander Goot. 1979. Reprint, Eugene, OR: Wipf & Stock, 2004.

1980s

"Teologins kyrkokritiska funktion i Norden under 1980-talet." *Svensk Teologisk Kvartalskrift* 56 (1980) 61-68.
Tolken som tiger: Vad teologin är och vad den borde vara. Stockholm: Gummesson, 1981.
De levandes mod: Tolv morgonandakter om tro och vardag. Stockholm: Bonnier, 1981. Coauthored with Greta Hofsten.
"Begreppet lekman." *Norsk Teologisk Tidsskrift* (1982) 177-87.
"Pensionärer och avlidna: En liten hjälpreda vid innanläsning." *Tro & Liv* 1 (1982) 2-23.
Människa och kristen: En bok om Irenaeus. Stockholm: Verbum 1983.
En liten katekes. Stockholm: Verbum, 1983. Coauthored with Greta Hofsten.
"Mina sex universitet." In *Tro & Tanke: Teologi och kyrka*, 42-51. Uppsala: Svenska kyrkans forskningsråd, 1983.

"Kärnan i Luther katekes." *Nålsögat* 4 (1983) 10–1.
"Luther idag: Människans ansvar i skapelsen." In *Luther idag: Åtta lundaföreläsningar*, 81–90. Lund: Religio, 1983.
"Skamfläcken." *Tidningen Broderskap* (1984) 9.
"Folkkyrkotanken i Sverige under 1900-talet." *Kirke og Kultur* (1984) 514–29.
"Att förkunna evangelium." In *Tro i en tid av tvivel*, edited by Margareta Brandby-Cöster et al., 82–109. Stockholm: Verbum, 1985.
"Mänskligt och kristet: Om kyrkans identitet." *Tro & Liv* 2 (1985) 2–8.
"Protestantisk arbetsetik och europeisk vardag." *Kirke og Kultur* (1985) 2–12.
"Kerygmatisk och positivistisk exegetik." *Tro och liv* 6 (1985) 3–14.
"Sveriges ende barthian." *Tro & Liv* 5 (1986) 16–23.
Gamla vägar framåt: Kyrkans uppgift i Sverige. Stockholm: Verbum, 1986.
Vinst eller förlust? Åtta andakter i radio. Stockholm: Verbum, 1988.
"Anders Nygren och svensk teologi idag." *Tro & Liv* 6 (1988) 11–19.
"Luther i Sverige idag." *Vår Lösen* 6 (1988) 366–69.
Texten talar: Trettio predikningar. Stockholm: Verbum, 1989.

1990s

"Tro och teologi." *Tro & Liv* 2 (1990) 9–15.
Tyngd och nåd i svensk skönlitteratur. Edited by and coauthored with Greta Hofsten. Lund: Religio, 1991.
Mina fem universitet: Minnen. Stockholm: Proprius, 1991.
"För människans skull: folklighet och skapelse." *Tro & Liv* 3 (1991) 2–10.
"Religion och evangelium." *Tro & Liv* 5–6 (1991) 2–9.
"Bredden gick förlorad." In *Under Lundagårds kronor. Femte samlingen*, vol. 1, edited by Gunvor Blomquist, 122–30. Lund: Lund University Press, 1991.
"Nygren, Anders (1890–1978)." *Theologische Realenzyklopädie*, 24: 711–15. Berlin: de Gruyter, 1994.
"Människa först—kristen sedan: Grundtvig och hans budskap till oss i dag." *Nålsögat* 4 (1994) 10–14.
"Förord." In *Predikan: En principiell studie*. Skellefteå: Artos, 1996.

Published Works about Gustaf Wingren

Almén, Edgar. "Gustaf Wingren: Växling och kontinuitet." *Svensk Teologisk Kvartalskrift* 1 (1974) 31–36.
———. "Wingrens teologiska argument." *Tro & Liv* 4 (1996) 15–24.
Anderson, Mary Elizabeth. *Gustaf Wingren and the Swedish Lutheran Renaissance*. New York: Peter Lang, 2006.
Andersson, Lars. "Kväll i maj." In *Tolkning och konfrontation: Ett symposium om Gustaf Wingrens teologi med anledning av hans 85-årsdag den 29 november 1995*, edited by Göran Bexell, 53–59. Lund: Religio 47: Skrifter utgivna av Teologiska Institutionen i Lund, 1996.
Armgard, Lars-Olle. "Gustaf Wingrens senare författarskap—några gamla vägar framåt." *Svensk Teologisk Kvartalskrift* 1 (1987) 11–16.

Aronson, Harry. "Minnesbilder." In *Tolkning och konfrontation: Ett symposium om Gustaf Wingrens teologi med anledning av hans 85-årsdag den 29 november 1995*, edited by Göran Bexell, 95-100. Lund: Religio 47: Skrifter utgivna av Teologiska Institutionen i Lund 1996.

Bexell, Göran. "Wingrens teologi—en karakteristik och utblick." In *Tolkning och konfrontation: Ett symposium om Gustaf Wingrens teologi med anledning av hans 85-årsdag den 29 november 1995*, edited by Göran Bexell, 13-29. Lund: Religio 47: Skrifter utgivna av Teologiska Institutionen i Lund, 1996.

Christoffersen, Svein-Aage. "Gustaf Wingrens teologiske etikk i spenningen mellom lov og evangelium." In *Tolkning och konfrontation: Ett symposium om Gustaf Wingrens teologi med anledning av hans 85-årsdag den 29 november 1995*, edited by Göran Bexell, 39-51. Lund: Religio 47: Skrifter utgivna av Teologiska Institutionen i Lund, 1996.

Eckerdal, Lars. "Kampen mot den konstruerade draken." *Tro & Liv* 6 (1981) 24-28.

Gerhardsson, Birger. "Tiger gör jag inte, sa exegeten." *Tro & Liv* 6 (1981) 15-23.

Gierdi, Per Arne. "Tolken som ikke tiet." *Korsvei* 1 (2001).

Hallgren, Bengt. "Käre Gustaf!" In *Tolkning och konfrontation: Ett symposium om Gustaf Wingrens teologi med anledning av hans 85-årsdag den 29 november 1995*, edited by Göran Bexell, 100-102. Lund: Religio 47: Skrifter utgivna av Teologiska Institutionen i Lund, 1996.

Hallonsten, Gösta. "En lundateolog minns." *Signum* 4 (1992) 118-23.

Hemrin, Sven. "Redaktionellt." *Tro & Liv* 6 (1981) 1-8.

Hillerdal, Gunnar. "Det teologiska klimatet i Lund omkring 1950." In *Tolkning och konfrontation: Ett symposium om Gustaf Wingrens teologi med anledning av hans 85-årsdag den 29 november 1995*, edited by Göran Bexell, 31-38. Lund: Religio 47: Skrifter utgivna av Teologiska Institutionen i Lund, 1996.

Holte, Ragnar. "Tolken som röt eller pensionärernas gräl." *Tro & Liv* 6 (1981) 32-38.

Håkansson, Bo. *Vardagens kyrka: Gustaf Wingrens kyrkosyn och folkkyrkans framtid*. Lund: Arcus, 2001.

Jeffner, Anders. "Några reaktioner på Wingrens senaste stridsskrift." *Tro & Liv* 6 (1981) 29-31.

Jensen, Roger. *Moderniseringen av lutherdomen . . . ? Gustaf Wingrens nue skapelsetologiske tilretteleggelse av den lutherske kallslære*. Oslo: Det praktisk-teologiske seminar, 2003.

Karlsson, Jonny. *Predikans samtal: En studie av lyssnarens roll i predikan hos Gustaf Wingren utifrån Michael Bachtins teori om dialogicitet*. Skellefteå: Artos, 2000.

Kristensson Uggla, Bengt. "Möjligheter i Gustaf Wingrens teologi." In *Tolkning och konfrontation: Ett symposium om Gustaf Wingrens teologi med anledning av hans 85-årsdag den 29 november 1995*, edited by Göran Bexell, 80-88. Lund: Religio 47, Skrifter utgivna av Teologiska Institutionen i Lund, 1996.

Ledin, Leif, et al. "Gustaf Wingrens tryckta skrifter 1933-1995." In *Tolkning och konfrontation: Ett symposium om Gustaf Wingrens teologi med anledning av hans 85-årsdag den 29 november 1995*, edited by Göran Bexell, 109-47. Lund: Religio 47, Skrifter utgivna av Teologiska Institutionen i Lund, 1996.

Lundstedt, Vilhelm. "Vetenskap eller trosförkunnelse som merit för professur?" *Stockholmstidningen*, 1 May 1951.

Øjestad, Audun. *Studie i Gustaf Wingrens teologi med særlig henblikk på hans forståelse av evangeliet og socialetikken*. Bergen: Hovedoppgave i kristendomskunnskap ved Universitetet i Bergen, våren 1975. Stencil.

Olivecrona, Karl. *Vetenskap eller trosförkunnelse som merit för professur?* Lund: Ph. Lindstedts Universitetsbokhandel, 1950.

Reilly, Francis J. *Law and Gospel in the Theology of Gustaf Wingren: A Study of His Methodology and Ecclesiology*. Washington, DC: Catholic University of America Press, 1974.

Sandahl, Dag. *Folk och kyrka: Debatten i Svenska Kyrkan kring Socialetiska delegationen och dess evangelisationsmodell 1952–1972*. Stockholm: Verbum 1986.

———. "Digra och ödesdigra kapitel—Wingren och högkyrkligheten i växelverkan." In *Tolkning och konfrontation: Ett symposium om Gustaf Wingrens teologi med anledning av hans 85-årsdag den 29 november 1995*, edited by Göran Bexell, 61–72. Lund: Religio 47, Skrifter utgivna av Teologiska Institutionen i Lund, 1996.

Sigurdson, Ola. *Karl Barth som den andre: En studie i den svenska teologins Barth-reception*. Stockholm/Stehag: Symposion, 1996.

Sollerman, Bruno. "Hemma hos Greta och Gustaf." *Tidningen Broderskap*, 10 January 1992.

Stefánsson, Torfi. *Tigern som tolkar: Konfrontationer i Gustaf Wingrens teologi med särskild hänsyn till teologins uppgift inom universitet, samhälle och kyrka*. Lund: Lunds Universitet, 2004.

Vander Goot, Henry. "The Fundamentality of Creation in the Theology of Gustaf Wingren: Illustrated from the Controversy with Anders Nygren." PhD diss., University of St. Michael's College, 1976.

Werkström, Bertil. "Minnesbilder." In *Tolkning och konfrontation: Ett symposium om Gustaf Wingrens teologi med anledning av hans 85-årsdag den 29 november 1995*, edited by Göran Bexell, 105–6. Lund: Religio 47: Skrifter utgivna av Teologiska Institutionen i Lund, 1996.

Unpublished Sources in Libraries and Archives

Lund University Archive

The papers of Gustaf Wingren, deposited by Anna Wingren Kedidjan. These include diaries, letters, newspaper clippings, and notebooks, including Wingren's notebooks from his time at the Johanneum in Berlin during the summer semester of 1938, and some notes from the following years through 1945. The author refers to the latter as "The Johanneum Journal."

Arkivcentrum Syd in Lund

Records from the meetings on 24 October 1950 of the Faculty of Theology (also 1949/50–1950/51), together with extensive appendices.

Records from the meeting of the Greater Academic Council in Lund on 16 December 1950.

Lund Cathedral Archives

Dossier C23. Register number 41/74.

Private Collections

Wingren, Gustaf. *Marcion och Irenaeus—studier över skapelsetanken* (1939) (*Marcion and Irenaeus: Studies on the Idea of Creation*). Unpublished copies of Wingren's licentiate dissertation owned by the author.

Gustaf Wingren. "Tal 29 november 1995." Copy of manuscript owned by the author.

Universitetskanslerns för rikets universitet utlåtande till Konungen ang. återbesättande av professuren i systematisk teologi med undervisnings- och examinationsskyldighet i teologisk etik vid universitetet i Lund, den 13 mars 1951, 207/49. Copy owned by Anna Wingren Kedidjan.

The author has also gained access to private correspondence to and from Gustaf Wingren. The following letters have been referenced in the book: Jan Bengtsson (20 September 1986), Gösta Hallonsten (25 June 1992), and Per Erik Persson (28 September 1981). These letters are found in the recipient's possession. I also refer to letters sent to Gustaf Wingren from Ragnar Bring (4 April 1985) and Olof Sundby (16 October 1974). These letters are in Gustaf Wingren's personal papers in the Lund University Library. Letters from Gustaf Aulén (12 November 1949) and Yngve Brilioth (22 December 1954) are owned by Anna Wingren Kedidjan, as is Niclas Kedidjan's eulogy, "Griftetal vid Gustaf Wingrens jordfästning 10 november 2000 i Allhelgonakyrkan i Lund."

Interviews

The following persons generously agreed to be interviewed for this book:

Carl-Gustaf Andrén (21 January 2010), Lars-Olle Armgard (18 January 2010), Harry Aronsson (20 and 21 January 2010, 8 April 2010), Carl-Axel Aurelius (8 January 2010), Göran Bexell (21 April 2010), Bengt Hallgren (20 January 2010), Anna-Karin Hammar (12 May 2010), Gunnar D. Hansson (11 May 2010), Anders Jeffner (25 Janauary 2010), Niclas Kedidjan (7 April 2010), Inge Lønning (26 February 2010), Lotta Miller (30 April 2010) Lennart Molin (6 October 2009), Nils-Gunnar Nilsson (26 May 2010), Torbjörn Nilsson (27 May 2010), Per Erik Persson (20 January 2010, 7 April 2010), Kåre Petrén (9 April 2010), Rune Romhed (20 April 2010), Martin Rössel (22 April 2010), Bertil Werkström (23 Janary 2010) samt Anna Wingren Kedidjan (7 April 2010).

Digital Sources

The most comprehensive bibliography of Wingren's publications is on the homepage of The Gustaf Wingren Society (hosted by the Linköping diocese of the Church of Sweden), where it is possible to download more than one hundred of Wingren's articles: http://www.svenskakyrkan.se/default.aspx?di=376133&ptid=0.

A video interview of Gustaf Wingren conducted by Göran Bexell in 1997 has been recorded by Lund University Museum (*Lundaprofiler*): "Lundateologin och världen."

Other Literature

In order to conform with the nature of the text, the following sources have been arranged alphabetically. When there are multiple titles by the same author, these have been arranged chronologically according to the date of the first edition.

Adams, Tim. *On Being John McEnroe*. New York: Crown, 2005.
Adorno, Theodor, and Max Horkheimer. *Dialectic of Enlightenment*. Translated by John Cumming. New ed. London: Verso, 1979.
Ahlin, Lars. *Fromma mord*. Stockholm: Tidens, 1952.
———. *Natt i marknadstältet*. Stockholm: Bonniers, 1957.
Andrén, Carl-Gustaf. "1900-talet: Fakultet, universitet och samhälle." In *Theologicum i Lund. Undervisning och forskning i tusen år*, edited by Birger Olsson et al., 38–56. Lund: Arcus, 2001.
Armgard, Lars-Olle. *Antropologi: Problem i K.E. Løgstrups författarskap*. Lund: Gleerup, 1971.

Aronson, Harry. *Mänskligt och kristet: En studie i Grundtvigs teologi.* Stockholm: Scandinavian University Books/Bonniers, 1960.

———. "Från industrialism till postindustriellt samhälle: Analys av en socialetisk, ideologisk och existentiell problematik." In *Etik och kristen tro,* edited by Gustaf Wingren, 162–203. Lund: Liber, 1971.

Arvidsson, Håkan. *Vi som visste allt: Minnesbilder från 1960-talets vänsterrörelse.* Stockholm: Atlantis, 2008.

Aulén, Gustaf. *Dogmhistoria: Den kristna lärobildningens utvecklingsgång från den efterapostoliska tiden till våra dagar.* Stockholm: Norstedt, 1917.

———. *Christus Victor: An Historical Study of the Three Main Types of the Idea of the Atonement.* Translated by A. G. Hebert. London: SPCK, 1931.

———. *Den allmänneliga kristna tron.* Stockholm: Diakonistyrelsens förlag, 1965.

———. *Kristen gudstro i förändringens värld: En studie.* Stockholm: Sveriges kyrkliga studieförbund, 1967.

———. *Dramat och symbolerna: En bok om gudsbildens problematik.* Stockholm: Diakonistyrelsens förlag, 1967.

———. *Från mina nittiosex år: Hänt och tänkt.* Stockholm: Verbum, 1975.

Aurelius, Carl-Axel. *Luther i Sverige: Svenska Lutherbilder under tre sekler.* Skellefteå: Artos, 1994.

Aurelius, Erik. *Du är den mannen! En bok om att förstå och förmedla bibeltexter.* Skellefteå: Artos 1997.

Barth, Karl. *The Epistle to the Romans.* Translated by Edwyn C. Hoskyns. London: Oxford University Press, 1933.

Bengtsson, Jan. *Den fenomenologiska rörelsen i Sverige: Mottagande och inflytande 1900–1968.* Göteborg: Daidalos, 1991.

Berman, Marshall. *All That Is Solid Melts into Air: The Experience of Modernity.* New York: Simon and Schuster, 1982.

Bexell, Göran. *Teologisk etik i Sverige sedan 1920-talet.* Stockholm: Skeab, 1981.

———. "Etik." In *Theologicum i Lund: Undervisning och forskning i tusen år,* edited by Birger Olsson et al., 168–79. Lund: Arcus 2001.

Billing, Einar. *Luthers lära om staten i dess samband med hans reformatoriska grundtankar och med tidigare läror.* Edited by Gösta Wrede. Stockholm: Verbum, 1900/1971.

———. *De etiska tankarna i urkristendomen—i deras samband med dess religiösa tro.* Stockholm: Sveriges Kristliga Studentrörelses Bokförlag, 1907/1936.

———. *Den svenska folkkyrkan.* Stockholm: Sveriges Kristliga studentförbund, 1930.

Bjerg, Svend. *Århusteologerne: P. G. Lindhardt, K. E: Løgstrup, Regin Prenter, Johannes Sløk. Den store generation i det 20. århundrades danske teologi.* Viborg: Lindhardt og Ringhof, 1994.

Brandby-Cöster, Margareta. "Dubbla budskap—vilket skall firas?" In *Äntligen stod hon i predikstolen! Historiskt vägval 1958,* edited by Boel Hössjer Sundman, 162–80. Stockholm: Verbum, 2008.

Bring, Ragnar. *Dualismen hos Luther.* Stockholm: Diakonistyrelsens förlag, 1929.

Castells, Manuel. *The Information Age.* 3 vols. Oxford: Blackwell, 1996–2000.

Cullmann, Oscar. *Die Christologie des Neuen Testaments.* Tübingen: Mohr, 1957.

Eckerdal, Lars, and Per Erik Persson. *Dopet—en livstydning: Om dopets innebörd och liturgi.* Stockholm: Verbum, 1981.

Ehnmark, Anders. *Avskifte: 5 politiska memoarer.* Stockholm: Nordstedts, 1983.

Eklund, Jan. "Bokkrönikan." *Dagens Nyheter*, 16 January 2010.
Ekstrand, Thomas, and Matttias Martinsson. *Tro och tvivel: Systematiska reflektioner över kristen tro*. Lund: Studentlitteratur, 2004.
Fareld, Victoria. *Att vara utom sig inom sig: Charles Taylor, erkännandet och Hegels aktualitet*. Göteborg: Glänta Produktion, 2008.
Fløistad, Guttorm. "Opposisjonsinnlegg," *Norsk Teologisk Tidsskrift* 1 (1978) 215–40.
Furberg, Mats. *Allting en trusu? En bok om livets mening*. Lund: Doxa, 1976.
―――. "Filosofiskt 50-tal i Göteborg." In *Kvantifikator för en Dag: Essays Dedicated to Dag Westerståhl on His Sixtieth Birthday*, 95–108. Göteborg: Philosophical Communications, Web Series, No. 35, 2006.
Gadamer, Hans-Georg. *Truth and Method*. Translation revised by Joel Weinsheimer and Donald G. Marshall. 2nd ed. London: Continuum, 2004.
Guillou, Jan. *Ordets makt och vanmakt: Mitt skrivande liv*. Stockholm: Piratförlaget, 2009.
Gyllenkrok, Axel. *Systematisk teologi och vetenskaplig metod med särskild hänsyn till etiken*. Uppsala: Uppsala universitets årsskrift, 1959.
Grane, Leif. *Vision och verklighet: En bok om Martin Luther*. Translated by Margarta Brandby-Cöster. Skellefteå: Artos, 1994.
Gregersen, Niels-Henrik. "Dogmatik som samtidsteologi." *Dansk Teologisk Tidsskrift* 71 (2008) 290–310.
Habermas, Jürgen. *Between Naturalism and Religion: Philosophical Essays*. Translated by Ciaran Cronin. Cambridge: Polity, 2008.
Hammar, K. G. *Det som hörs: Ett predikoteoretiskt perspektiv*. Älvsjö: Verbum, 1985.
Hansen, Knud. *Den kristna tron*. Translated by Margareta Brandby-Cöster. Stockholm: Bonniers, 1984.
Hansson, Gunnar D. *Nådens oordning: Studier i Lars Ahlins roman Fromma mord*. Stockholm: Bonniers, 1988.
Harnack, Adolf von. *Lehrbuch der Dogmengeschichte*. 3 vols. Darmstadt: Wissenschaftliche Buchgesellschaft, 1886–90.
―――. *Das Wesen des Christentums. Sechzehn Vorlesungen von Studierendenaller Fakultäten im Wintersemester 1899/1900 an der Universität Berlin*. Leipzig: Akademische Ausgabe, 1902.
―――. *Marcion. Das Evangelium vom fremden Gott. Eine Monographie zur Geschichte der Grundlegung der katholischen Kirche*. Leipzig: J. C. Hinrichs, 1924.
Harvey, David. *The Conditions of Postmodernity: An Enquiry into the Origins of Cultural Change*. Oxford: Blackwell, 1990.
Hedenius, Ingemar. *Tro och vetande*. Stockholm: Bonniers, 1949.
―――. "Det teologiska fakulteternas framtid." In Ingemar Hedenius and Harald Eklund, *Om teologien och kyrkan*, 7–51. Uppsala: J. A. Lindblad, 1958.
Hofsten, Greta. *Samtalsvis*. Stockholm: Bonniers, 1969.
―――. "Socialdemokratins dilemma—speglat i några arbetsmarknadspolitiska texter." In *Planeringens gränser: Om framtidsplanering, framtidsstudier och social förändring i avancerade kapitalistiska samhällen*, edited by Torsten Björkman et al., 179–93. Stockholm: Forum, 1976.
―――. "Kristna i kamp för socialismen." In Greta Hofsten et.al., *Kristne i politisk kamp*, 4–11. Oslo: Forum for kristne sosialister, 1978.
―――. "Kristet språk och vänsterns språk." *Nålsögat: Forum för socialism och kristendom* 1–2 (1986) 3–5.

———. "Klyvnad och trolöshet: Om gnosticism och nihilism i dag." *Zenit* 92 (1986) 74–80.
———. "Åttiotalets ickemotstånd." *Nålsögat: Forum för socialism och kristendom* 3 (1986) 6–7.
———. "Fyrtio år med rösträtt." *Ord & Bild* 2 (1992) 21–26.
———. "Tidsspegel: '... och låter det regna över onda och goda'—funderingar om människosyner." *Ord & Bild* 2 (1995) 4–6.
Hofsten, Greta, and Gustaf Wingren. *Tro och främlingskap: Åtta brev.* Lund: Skeab, 1979.
———. *De levandes mod: Tolv morgonandakter om tro och vardag.* Stockholm: Bonnier, 1981.
———. *En liten katekes.* Stockholm: Verbum, 1983.
Hognestad, Helge. *Forkynnelse til oppbrudd. 1. Studier i Matteusevangeliet og kirkens bruk av det.* Oslo: Universitetsforlag, 1978.
———. *Forkynnelsen—kirkens forsvar? 2. Studier i Matteusevangeliet og kirkens bruk av det.* Oslo: Universitetsforlag, 1978.
———. "Troverdig forkynnelse—for hvem? Svar til Wingren, Jervell og Lønning." *Norsk Teologisk Tidsskrift* 79 (1978) 267–84.
———. *Gud på Høvik: Prekener fra Høvik menighet.* Oslo: Pax forlag, 1981.
———. *En kirke for folket.* Oslo: J. W. Cappelen, 1982.
Holm, Kjeld. *Mennesket er en misforståelse: Mit venskab med Johannes Sløk.* Copenhagen: Rosinante, 2007.
Holte, Ragnar. *Luther och lutherbilden: En kritisk granskning.* Stockholm: Proprius, 1984.
Hössjer Sundman, Boel, ed. *Äntligen stod hon i predikstolen! Historiskt vägval 1958.* Stockholm: Verbum, 2008.
———. "Möta nutidsmänniskan och ge ett svar på hennes livsfrågor." In *Äntligen stod hon i predikstolen! Historiskt vägval 1958*, edited by Boel Hössjer Sundman, 150–61. Stockholm: Verbum, 2008.
Ivarsson, Henrik. *Predikans uppgift: En typologisk undersökning med särskild hänsyn till reformatorisk och pietistisk predikan.* Lund: Gleerup, 1956.
Ivarsson, Malena. *Time Out.* Stockholm: Bokförlaget A, 1991.
Jeanrond, Werner. *Theological Hermeneutics: Development and Significance.* London: Macmillan, 1991.
Jeffner, Anders. *Kriterier i kristen troslära: En principiell undersökning av nutida protestantisk dogmatik inom tyskt språkområde.* Uppsala: Uppsala Universitet, Teologiska institutionen, 1976.
———. "Livsåskådningsforskning—material och metoder." In *Livsåskådningsforskning*, 17–39. Stockholm: Acta Universitatis Upsaliensis: Symposia Universitatis Upsaliensis Annum Quingentesimum Celebrantis 4 (1977).
———. *Vägar till teologi.* Stockholm: Skeab, 1981.
———. "Dogmatik in den nordischen Ländern." In *Theologische Realenzyklopädie*, 9:77–92. Berlin: de Gruyter, 1982.
Jensen, Ole. *Theologie zwischen Illusion und Restriktion: Analyse und Kritik der existnzkritischen Theologie bei dem jungen Wilhelm Herrmann und bei Rudolf Bultmann.* Munich: Kaiser, 1975.
———. *I tillväxtens våld: Ekologi och religion.* Translated by Barbro Hallén. Stockholm: Verbum, 1976/1979.

―――. "Teologisk ideologikritik som opgave for de dogmatiske prologomena." *Fønix* 1 (1977) 39-54.

―――. *Historien om K. E. Løgstrup*. Copenhagen: Anis, 2007.

Jervell, Jakob. "Matteusevangleiet?" *Norsk Teologisk Tidsskrift* 1 (1978) 241-48.

Jönsson, Ludvig. *Postilla för sökare*. Stockholm: Bonniers, 1979.

Kemp, Peter. "Den religiøse lidenskab: Sløk mellem Kierkegaard og Løgstrup." In *Mig og evigheden: Johannes Sløks religionsfilosofi*, edited by Lars Sandbeck, 23-47. Copenhagen: Anis, 2007.

Kristensson Uggla, Bengt. *När kartan inte stämmer: Teologiska och filosofiska orienteringsförsök*. Stockholm: Verbum, 1993.

―――. *Kommunikation på bristningsgränsen: En studie i Paul Ricoeurs projekt*. Stockholm: Symposion, 1994.

―――. *Slaget om verkligheten: Filosofi, omvärldsanalys, tolkning*. Stockholm/Stehag: Symposion 2002/2012.

―――. "Tolkningens metamorfoser i hermeneutikens tidsålder." In *Text and Existens: Hermeneutiken möter samhällsvetenskapen*, edited by Staffan Selander and Per-Johan Ödman, 23-42. Göteborg: Daidalos, 2005.

―――. *Ricoeur, Hermeneutics, and Globalization*. London: Continuum, 2010.

Lévinas, Emmanuel. *Humanism of the Other*. Translated by Nidra Poller. Urbana: University of Illinois Press, 2003.

Lidman, Sara. *Din tjänare hör*. Stockholm: Bonnier, 1977.

―――. *Vredens barn*. Stockholm: Bonnier, 1979.

―――. *Nabots sten*. Stockholm: Bonnier, 1981.

―――. *Den underbare mannen*. Stockholm: Bonnier, 1983.

―――. *Järnkronan*. Stockholm: Bonnier, 1985.

Liedman, Sven-Eric. "Humanistiska forskningstraditioner i Sverige: Kritiska och historiska perspektiv." In *Humaniora på undantag: Humanistiska forskningstraditioner i Sverige, en antologi av Tomas Forser*, 9-78. Stockholm: Norstedts, 1978.

Lindfelt, Mikael. *Teologi och kristen humanism: Ett perspektiv på Torsten Bohlins teologiska tänkande*. Åbo: Åbo Akademis förlag, 1996.

―――. *Att förstå livsåskådningar—en metateoretisk analys av teologisk livsåskådningsforskning med anknytning till Anders Jeffners ansatser*. Uppsala: Acta Universitatis Upsaliensis, 2003.

Lindgren, Astrid. *Nils Karlsson pyssling*. Stockholm: Wahlström & Widstrand, 1949.

Lindhardt, P. G. *Vækkelse og kirklige retninger*. Copenhagen: Reitzel, 1951/1959.

Lundborg, Johan. *När ateismen erövrade Sverige: Ingemar Hedenius och debatten kring tro och vetande*. Nora: Nya Doxa, 2002.

Løgstrup, K. E. *Den transcendentalfilosofiske konflikt mellem den transcendentalfilosofiske idealisme og teologien*. Copenhagen: Samlerens forlag, 1942.

―――. "Etiske begreb og problemer." In *Etik och kristen tro*, edited by Gustaf Wingren, 207-86. Lund: Liber 1971.

―――. *The Ethical Demand*. Notre Dame: University of Notre Dame Press, 1997.

Lønning, Per. "Om ikke-bevisstgjort normativitet." *Norsk Teologisk Tidsskrift* 1 (1978) 249-66.

Moberg, Vilhelm. *Utvandrarna*. Stockholm: Bonnier, 1949.

Molander, Bengt. *Kunskap i handling*. Göteborg: Daidalos, 1993.

Møllehave, Johannes. *Där kärleken bor: Predikningar.* Translated by Margareta Brandby-Cöster. Lund: Arcus, 1999.
Nietzsche, Friedrich. *Will to Power.* Edited and translated by Walter Kaufman and R. J. Hollingdale. New York: Vintage, 1968.
Nordin, Svante. *Från Hägerström till Hedenius: Den moderna svenska teologin.* Lund: Doxa, 1984.
———. *Ingemar Hedenius: en filosof och hans tid.* Stockholm: Natur & Kultur, 2004.
Nowotny, Helga, et al. *Re-thinking Science: Knowledge and the Public in an Age of Uncertainty.* Cambridge: Polity, 2001.
Nygren, Anders. *Religiöst apriori.* Lund: Gleerup, 1921.
———. *Dogmatikens vetenskapliga grundläggning: med särskild hänsyn till den Kant-Schleiermacherska frågeställningen.* Lund: Gleerup, 1922.
———. *Filosofisk och kristen etik.* Lund: Gleerup, 1923.
———. *Agape and Eros.* Translated by A. G. Hebert and Philip S. Watson. London: SPCK, 1932-39.
———. "Till teologiens metodfråga." *Svensk Teologisk Kvartalskrift* 1 (1956) 20-35.
———. "Ytterligare till teologiens metodfråga." *Svensk Teologisk Kvartalskrift* 2 (1956) 133-60.
———. "Slutreplik angående teologiens metodfråga." *Svensk Teologisk Kvartalskrift* 4 (1956) 313-22.
———. *Meaning and Method: Prologomena to a Scientific Philosophy of Religion and a Scientific Theology.* Translated by Philip S. Watson. Philadelphia: Fortress, 1972.
Olsson, Herbert. *Grundproblemet i Luthers socialetik* 1. Lund: Lindstedts, 1934.
———. *Calvin och reformationens teologi.* Lund: Lunds universitets årsskrift, 1943.
Persson, Per-Erik. *Att tolka Gud i dag: Debattlinjer i aktuell teologi.* Lund: Gleerup, 1971.
———. *Att dela Guds hållning mot djävulskapet.* Stockholm: Gummesson, 1972.
———. "Att måla i svart och vitt," *Tro and Liv* 6 (1981) 9-14.
———. "1900-talet: Utbildning, ämnesområden och examina." In *Theologicum i Lund: Undervisning och forskning i tusen år,* edited by Birger Olsson et al., 57-75. Lund: Arcus, 2001.
Petrén, Per. *Skapelse och frihet: En bok om Gustaf Wingrens teologi.* Grimsås: Grathia, 1995.
Polanyi, Michael. *The Tacit Dimension.* Chicago: University of Chicago Press, 1966.
Prenter, Regin. *Skabelse og Genløsning: Dogmatik.* Copenhagen: Gads, 1951-53.
Ricoeur, Paul. *Time and Narrative.* Vol. 1. Translated by Kathleen McLaughlin and David Pellauer. Chicago: University of Chicago Press, 1984.
———. *From Text to Action.* Translated by Kathleen Blamey and John B. Thompson. Essays in Hermeneutics 2. Evanston: Northwestern University Press, 1991.
———. *Oneself as Another.* Translated by Kathleen Blamey. Chicago: University of Chicago Press, 1992.
———. *Memory, History, Forgetting.* Translated by Kathleen Blamey and David Pellauer. Chicago: University of Chicago Press, 2004.
Rosendal, Gunnar. *Kyrklig förnyelse.* Osby: Pro ecclesia, 1935.
Ruin, Hans. "Filosofen som hade rätt men fel." *Dagens Nyheter,* 23 January 2010.
Sandbeck, Lars, ed. *Mig og evigheden: Johannes Sløks religionsfilosofi.* Copenhagen: Anis, 2007.
Sigurdson, Ola. *Karl Barth som den andre: En studie i den svenska teologins Barth-reception.* Eslöv: Symposion, 1996.

———. "Kyrkan som de heligas samfund: På väg mot en evangelisk communio-ecklesiologi." In *På spaning efter framtidens kyrka*, edited by Sune Fahlgren, 49–72. Örebro: Libris, 1998.

———. *Den lyckliga filosofin: Etik och filosofi hos Hägerström, Tingsten, makarna Myrdal och Hedenius*. Stockholm: Symposion, 2000.

———. *Det postsekulära tillståndet: Religion, modernitet, politik*. Göteborg: Glänta, 2009.

Sjödin, Tomas. "Kufarna skall bygga framtidens kyrka." *Trots allt* 10 (1993) 25–27.

Skogar, Björn. *Viva vox och den akademiska religionen: Ett bidrag till tidiga 1900-talets svenska teologihistoria*. Stockholm: Symposion graduale, 1993.

Sløk, Johannes. *Det absurde teater og Jesu forkyndelse*. Copenhagen: Gyllendahl, 1968.

Stolpe, Jan. "Greta Hofsten, 1927–1996." *Svenska Dagbladet*, 19 July 1996, and *Dagens Nyheter*, 31 July 1996.

Swedenmark, John. "Bortom bortträngningen: Kristendomen och dialektiken oidipus-identifikation." *Divan: Tidskrift för psykoanalys och kultur* 1–2 (2004) 64–73.

Toulmin, Stephen. *Cosmopolis: The Hidden Agenda of Modernity*. Chicago: University of Chicago Press, 1990.

Tracy, David. *The Analogical Imagination: Christian Theology and the Culture of Pluralism*. London: SCM, 1981.

Tyberg, Anders. *Anrop och ansvar: Berättarkonst och etik hos Lars Ahlin, Göran Tunström, Birgitta Trotzig, Torgny Lindgren*. Stockholm: Carlsson, 2002.

Wermlund, Sven. *Det religiösa språket*. Stockholm: Almquist & Wiksell, 1955.

Westerberg, Anders, et al., eds. *Världsproblem och kyrkofrid: Domkyrkoaktionen i Lund november 1968. Dokument och kommentarer till en rättegång*. Lund: Faxböckerna, 1970.

Wittgenstein, Ludwig. *Philosophical Investigations*. Translated by G. E. M. Anscombe. Oxford: Blackwell, 1953.

Wright, G. H. von. *Explanation and Understanding*. London: Routledge and Kegan Paul, 1971.

———. *Vetenskapen och förnuftet: Ett försök till en orientering*. Stockholm: Bonniers, 1986.

———. *Myten om framsteget: Tankar 1987–1992 med en intellektuell självbiografi*. Stockholm: Bonniers, 1993.

Index

Adam, 197, 305
Adams, Tim, 16, 380
Adamson, Carol, 371
Adorno, Theodor W, 257–58, 380
Ahlin, Gunnel, 206
Ahlin, Lars, 187, 204–7, 306, 310, 375, 380, 382, 386
Ahrén, Per-Olov, 361
Almén, Edgar, 14, 124, 376
Anderson, Amos, 369
Anderson, Mary Elizabeth, 32, 89, 376
Andersson, Dan, 339
Andersson, Lars, 14, 376
Andrén, Carl-Gustaf, 15, 380
Andrén, Åke, 14
Andræ, Tor, 325
Anscombe, G E M, 386
Aristotle, 116, 133–34, 226
Armgard, Lars-Olle, 15, 200, 249, 286, 376, 380
Aronson, Harry, 23, 24, 98, 169, 175, 179, 235, 282, 294, 295, 368, 377, 380, 381
Arvidsson, Håkan, 381
Aspelin, Gunnar, 45, 46, 121, 221
Augustine, 77, 78
Aulén, Gustaf, 12, 22, 29, 48, 68, 72–76, 92, 105, 110, 111, 118, 146, 197, 215, 219, 237, 316, 379, 381
Aurelius, Carl-Axel, 380, 381
Aurelius, Erik, 381

Bach, Johan Sebastian, 48

Bachtin, Michail, 336, 337, 377
Bagger-Sjöbäck, Bertil, 182
Bagger-Sjöbäck, Edith, 181, 182, 212
Bagger-Sjöbäck, Eduard, 181, 182
Bagger-Sjöbäck, Hans, 182
Bagger-Sjöbäck, Lennart, 182
Barth, Karl, 8, 24, 25, 32, 37, 39, 42, 49, 52, 54–60, 71, 86, 87, 99, 100, 101, 102, 104, 106, 113, 114, 119, 123, 144, 145, 147, 153, 202, 214, 259, 284, 295, 342, 374, 374, 376, 378, 381, 385
Bathsheba, 305
Bellman, Carl-Michael, 206
Bengtsson (married Lilliehöök), Ingrid, 12, 13
Bengtsson, Jan, 54, 221–23, 379, 381
Bengtsson, Pelle, 281, 368
Bergendahl, Ragnar, 48
Berger, Peter, 329
Bergman, Ingmar, 212
Bergsten, Torsten, 237, 246
Berman, Marshall, 272, 381
Bernhardtson, Lennart, 368
Bexell, Göran, 12, 28, 32, 48, 107, 173, 376–78, 380, 381
Bexell, Oloph, 375
Billing, Einar, 12, 17, 26, 72, 73, 76, 79, 89, 90, 104, 108, 110–14, 124–26, 128–30, 137, 138, 140, 141, 146, 174, 196, 197, 227, 307–9, 345, 348, 352, 355, 373, 374
Bjerg, Svend, 284, 285, 381

Björkman, Torsten, 382
Blamey (née McLaughlin), Kathleen, 385
Blomquist, Gunvor, 376
Bohlin, Torsten, 12, 55 384
Borg, Björn, 16
Brandby-Coster, Margareta, 251, 311, 376, 381, 382, 385
Bratt, Peter, 183
Brattgård, Helge, 328
Brilioth, Yngve, 105, 108, 110, 123, 234, 379
Bring, Ragnar, 22, 34, 36–40, 42, 43, 46, 55, 65, 68, 72, 76, 92, 100, 103, 106, 107, 109, 110, 112, 114, 123–26, 128, 136, 219, 237, 374, 379, 381
Brodd, Sven-Erik, 371

Buber, Martin, 222
Buchman, Frank, 235
Bugenhagen, Johannes, 319
Bultmann, Rudolf, 25, 49, 52, 55–60, 145, 214, 295, 317, 349, 374, 383

Calvin, John, 34, 35, 385
Camus, Albert, 11
Carlson, Edgar M, 375
Carlsson, Johan, 97
Carlsson, Sten, 46, 121
Castells, Manuel, 167, 381
Christoffersen, Svein-Aage, 265, 275, 377
Constantine, 343, 344, 345, 350, 360
Cullberg, John, 111, 221, 251
Cullmann, Oscar, 99, 101, 103, 141, 160, 235, 313, 381
Cumming, John, 380
Cronin, Ciaran, 382
Cöster, Henry, 251

Danell, Gustaf Adolf, 143, 315
Darwin, Charles, 10
David, 305
Descartes, René, 59, 116
Dibelius, Martin, 103
Dosse, François, 367
Düben, Anders von, 51

Dutschke, Rudi, 193
Dylan, Bob, 167

Ebeling, Gerhard, 10, 327
Eckerdal, Lars, 237, 239, 242, 246, 356, 377, 381
Ehnevid, Tord, 249
Ehnmark, Anders, 184, 185, 381
Ehnmark, Erland, 42–44
Eidem, Erling, 217
Eklund, Harald, 40, 41, 44–46, 125–27, 382
Eklund, Jan, 11, 382
Ekstrand, Thomas, 382
Engeström, Sigfrid von, 36, 111
Engstrand, Ralph, 368
Engström, Thore, 46
Eriksson, Anne-Louise, 368
Ezekiel, 338, 339

Fagerberg, Holsten, 237
Fahlgren, Sune, 386
Fareld, Victoria, 363, 382
Fløistad, Guttorm, 331, 382
Forser, Tomas, 384
Franck, Eskil, 368
Frei, Hans, 59
Friedrichsen, Anton, 29, 239, 317
Frostin, Per, 173
Fröding, Gustaf, 204
Furberg, Mats, 128, 158, 159, 382

Gadamer, Hans-Georg, 5, 122, 133–35, 382
Gärtner, Bertil, 10, 14, 143, 231, 315, 320, 321
Geijer, Erik Gustaf, 166
Gerhardsson, Birger, 179, 237, 239, 242, 377
Gerleman, Gillis, 42–44
Gierdi, Per Arne, 25, 377
Giertz, Bo, 143, 315
Gogarten, Friedrich, 285
Gorkij, Maxim, 209
Guillet de Monthoux, Pierre, 368
Guillou, Jan, 183, 185, 186, 382
Gustafsson, Berndt, 61
Gustavsson, Barbro, 61

INDEX

Gyllenberg, Rafael, 98
Gyllenkrok, Axel, 234, 235, 237, 239, 240, 244, 251,382
Grane, Leif, 298, 251, 382
Gregersen, Niels-Henrik, 302, 382
Grenholm, Carl-Henrik, 375
Grundtvig, Nicolai Fredrik Severin, 10, 199, 231, 250, 252, 282–85, 293–96, 342, 352, 376, 381

Habermas, Jürgen, 20, 21, 329, 382
Hägerström, Axel, 44, 72, 73, 132, 385, 386
Hägglund, Bengt, 48
Hafstad, Kjetil, 368
Haikola, Lars, 10
Håkansson, Bo, 32, 259, 308, 344, 350, 355–58, 377
Hallén, Barbro, 383
Hallgren, Bengt, 4, 235, 377, 380
Hallonsten, Gösta, 111, 113, 223, 377, 379
Hammar, Anna-Karin, 280, 281, 380
Hammar, KG, 231, 382
Hansen, Knud, 251, 382
Hansson, Gunnar D, 187, 207, 310, 311, 380, 382
Harnack, Adolf von, 60, 75, 77, 80, 82, 107, 108, 382
Harrie, Ivar, 223
Hartman, Lars, 14
Hartman, Olov, 180, 204, 280, 342
Harvey, David, 256, 382
Hebert, A G, 381, 385
Hedenius, Ingemar, 132, 215–29, 302, 382, 384–86
Hegel, Friedrich, 162, 255, 382
Heidegger, Martin, 54, 56, 117, 199, 215, 222
Heidenstam, Verner von, 204
Hellborg, Clas, 173
Helles, Monica, 368
Hemrin, Sven, 237, 241, 377
Henmark, Kai, 183
Henriksen, Jan-Olav, 368
Hermerén, Göran, 222
Herrmann, Wilhelm, 383
Hillerdal, Gunnar, 17, 18, 328, 377

Hitler, Adolf, 107
Hofsten, Erland von, 182
Hofsten, Greta (née Bagger-Sjöbäck) 2–4, 6, 13, 24, 26, 28, 30, 178– 96, 198, 204–10, 212–14, 231, 232, 251, 266–72, 277, 279–81, 296, 310, 323, 329, 340, 341, 360, 361, 368, 375, 376, 378, 382, 383, 386
Hognestad, Helge, 328–36, 375, 383
Hök, Gösta, 36
Hollander, Claes, 368
Hollingdale, R J, 385
Holm, Kjeld, 367, 383
Holmström, Folke, 111
Holte, Ragnar, 237, 240–44, 375, 377, 383
Hooft, Visser't, 248
Horkheimer, Max, 257, 258
Hoskyns, Edwyn C, 381
Husserl, Edmund, 221
Hössjer Sundman, Boel, 311, 381, 383

Irenaeus, 22, 25, 26, 28, 35, 37, 42, 51, 53, 63, 74, 75, 77,78, 80, 81, 84– 88, 95, 96, 98–100, 124–26, 129, 145, 146, 162, 201, 291, 292–95, 343, 344, 373, 375, 379
Isaksson, Håkan, 183
Ivarsson, Henrik, 327, 328, 383
Ivarsson, Malena, 328, 282

Jacob, 186, 197
Jarl, Stefan, 171
Jaspers, Karl, 56, 222
Jeanrond, Werner, 6, 383
Jeffner, Anders, 14, 15, 228–30, 237, 239, 240, 242, 245–47, 377, 380, 383, 384
Jensen, Ole, 10, 200, 249, 269, 286–89, 329, 383
Jensen, Roger, 264, 265, 272, 377
Jervell, Jacob, 265, 331, 383, 384
John, 294, 349
Jonsson, Johnny, 371
Jönsson, Ludvig, 325–27, 384
Josefsson, Ruben, 36, 44, 111

Kant, Immanuel, 59, 73, 132, 286–88, 316, 385
Karlfelt, Erik Axel, 204
Karlsson, David, 368, 369
Karlsson, Jonny, 8, 32, 119, 124, 130, 158, 180, 217, 325–40, 369, 377
Käsemann, Ernst, 349
Kaufman, Walter, 385
Kedidjan, Niclas, 16, 379, 380
Kemp, Peter, 250, 384
Kennedy, Robert, 171
Kennerberg, Owe, 368
Kierkegaard, Søren, 59, 186, 199, 249, 250, 252, 283, 384
King, Martin Luther, 171
Kjellin, Bo Fredrik, 172
Kjöllerström, Sven, 39, 40, 43, 44, 121, 234, 235, 239, 327
Kleveman, Anders, 277

Lagercrantz, Olof, 183
Larsdotter, Karin, 336
Ledin, Leif, 25, 377
Lévinas, Emmanuel, 60, 384
Lidbeck, Pelle, 281
Lidman, Sara, 205, 207–9, 267, 384
Liedholm, Nils, 360
Liedman, Sven-Eric, 137, 384
Lietzmann, Hans, 107
Lilliehöök (née Bengtsson), Ingrid, 12, 13
Lind, Martin, 172, 173, 368, 371
Lindbeck, George, 59
Lindegård, Sven, 177, 178
Lindeskog, Gösta, 312
Lindfelt, Mikael, 229, 368, 384
Lindgren, Astrid, 215, 384
Lindgren, Torgny, 386
Lindhardt, P G, 250, 283, 284, 381, 384
Lindroth, Hjalmar, 37, 38, 42, 43, 45, 46, 110, 120, 122, 124, 125
Lindström, Henning, 36, 111
Lindström, Martin, 172
Lindquist, Jan, 171
Løgstrup, K E, 199, 200, 203, 227, 249–51, 259, 265, 266, 269, 282–87, 380, 381, 384
Lønning, Inge, 380
Lønning, Per, 331, 332, 383, 384

Luckmann, Thomas, 329
Luke, 349
Lundberg, Karl, 20
Lundborg, Johan, 217, 384
Lundstedt, Vilhelm, 216, 377
Luther, Martin, 16, 21, 22, 25–28, 32, 34, 37, 38, 51, 53, 60, 62, 63, 66, 68, 73, 75, 78–80, 86, 88–96, 99, 108–11, 114, 115, 121, 124, 125, 129–31, 144–46, 149, 150, 155, 174, 175, 178, 193, 194, 196, 197, 199, 201, 207, 208, 211, 220, 227, 235, 243, 244, 251, 261–63, 207, 208, 211, 220, 227, 235, 243, 244, 251, 261–65, 273–75, 291–98, 300, 305–7, 310, 316–20, 322, 323, 327, 330, 334, 336, 343–47, 349, 357, 358, 362–64, 373–76, 381–83, 385

Mace, Nancy, 371
Mackenzie, Ross, 373, 374
Marc-Wogau, Konrad, 221
Marcion, 22, 53, 54, 62–66, 74, 77, 78, 80–83, 86–89, 107, 108, 114, 115, 146, 147, 151, 156, 202, 373, 379, 382
Marshall, Donald G, 382
Martinsson, Mattias, 371, 382
Marx, Karl, 198, 199, 201, 221, 271, 331, 332
Matthew, 329–31, 349, 383
Mazzarella, Merete, 368
McEnroe, John, 16, 380
McLaughlin (married Blamey), Kathleen, 385
Miller, Ann-Charlotte, 281, 380
Moberg, Vilhelm, 215, 384
Molander, Bengt, 117, 384
Molin, Lennart, 237, 341, 342, 368, 371
Møllehave, Johannes, 251, 385
Möller, Johan, 327
Møller, Otto, 249
Monk, Ray, 367
Montaigne, Michel de, 116
Myrdal, Alva, 386
Myrdal, Gunnar, 267, 386
Myrdal, Jan, 183

INDEX

Naess, Arne, 222
Niemöller, Martin, 193, 248
Nietzsche, Friedrich, 59, 100, 119, 256, 257, 385
Nilsson, Gert, 249
Nilsson, Kjell-Ove, 237
Nilsson, Leif, 280
Nilsson, Nils-Gunnar, 23, 380
Nilsson, Torbjörn, 361, 362, 380
Nohrborg, Anders, 327
Nordenstam, Tore, 128
Nordin, Svante, 220, 221, 385
Norman, Birger, 183
Norman, Ragnar, 48
Norrman, Ylva, 12
Nowotny, Helga, 176, 385
Nygren, Anders, 17, 25, 29, 34, 35, 47–69, 71–87, 91, 95, 96, 100–102, 105, 106, 108–14, 123, 124, 132, 137, 138, 142, 143, 145, 146, 176, 182, 212, 214–16, 218, 223, 227–28, 230, 234, 235, 246, 249, 252, 295, 315–17, 328, 342, 374, 376, 378, 385
Nygren, Gotthard, 68
Nygren, Hildur, 47
Nygren, Irmgard, 68
Nyman, Elizabeth, 371

Odeberg, Hugo, 21, 22, 41, 43, 44, 106, 108, 111, 115, 124, 125, 136, 243
Ödman, Per-Johan, 384
Ofstad, Harald, 221, 222
Ohlsson, Birgit, 372
Ohlsson, Sven Håkan, 372
Øjestad, Audun, 32, 378
Olivecrona, Karl, 44, 45, 111, 121,124, 126, 127, 378
Olson, Daniel M, 371
Olsson, Birger, 380, 381, 385
Olsson, Herbert, 34–48, 89, 108–12, 121, 240 ,244, 385
Olsson, Karl-Manfred, 322
Origen, 77. 78. 85
Østergaard-Nielsen, Harald, 249
Ottesen-Jensen, Elise, 183
Overton, Charles Ernest, 10

Palme, Olof, 170
Paul, 77, 82, 88, 108, 114, 161, 261, 262, 273,294, 312, 320, 334, 349
Pellauer, David, 385
Persson, Per-Erik, 15, 76, 173, 176, 179, 231, 232, 237–39, 242, 249, 253, 256, 369, 379–81, 385
Persson i Skabersjö, Ivar, 47
Petrén, Finn, 182, 209, 368, 369
Petrén, Henrik, 182, 209
Petrén, Kåre, 182, 209, 380
Petrén, Per, 32, 154, 385
Phalén, Adolph, 73
Plato, 116, 226
Pogue, Victor C, 373
Polanyi, Michael, 117, 385
Poller, Nidra, 384
Pontoppidan, Morten, 249
Pleijel, Hilding, 41, 44, 234
Prenter, Regin, 39, 40, 99, 125, 283–85, 381, 385

Rasmussen, Carl C, 373
Reilly, Francis J, 32, 378
Riesenfeld, Harald, 29, 320, 321
Ricoeur, Paul, 7, 8, 127, 134, 135, 365, 384, 385
Ritschl, Albrecht, 115
Robinson, John A T, 8
Rodhe, Edvard, 48
Romhed, Rune, 369, 380
Rosendal, Gunnar, 258, 359, 375, 385
Rössel, Karin, 180, 182
Rössel, Martin, 277, 278, 380
Ruin, Hans, 215, 385
Runestam, Arvid, 12

Sahlin, Margit, 204
Sandahl, Dag, 32, 173, 179, 231, 322, 323, 378
Sandbeck, Lars, 384, 385
Sartre, Jean-Paul, 215, 222
Schartau, Henric, 327
Schleiermacher, Friedrich, 73, 75, 218, 385
Schmid, Herman, 173
Schmidt, Karl-Ludwig, 11, 49, 50, 101, 103, 235

Sejte, Christina, 369
Selander, Staffan, 384
Sigurdson, Ola, 32, 55, 58, 144, 166, 217, 310, 356, 378, 385
Sjöberg, Erik, 312
Sjödin, Tomas, 344, 386
Sjöman, Vilgot, 171, 183
Skogar, Björn, 386
Skydsgaard, K E, 36, 249, 283
Sløk, Johannes, 250, 283, 284, 367, 381, 383–86
Söderblom, Nathan, 29, 72, 73, 79, 126, 130, 227
Søe, Niels Hansen, 38, 39
Sölle, Dorothee, 280
Sollerman, Bruno, 272, 378
Stefánsson, Torfi, 32, 378
Stendahl, Krister, 29
Stolpe, Jan, 186, 386
Strindberg, August, 169, 248
Sundby, Olof, 177, 178, 310, 311, 379
Sundman, Hilda, 19
Sundman, Signe, 19
Svennungson, Jayne, 368
Swedenmark, John, 166, 386

Taylor, Charles, 382
Tersmeden, Fredrik, 368
Tertullian, 77
Thomas Aquinas, 34
Thompson, John B, 385
Thorsson, Inga (née Bagger-Sjöbäck) 182, 279
Thurneysen, Eduard, 235
Tingsten, Herbert, 218, 220
Törnvall, Gustaf, 89
Toulmin, Stephen, 116, 117, 386
Tracy, David, 7, 135, 386
Trägårdh, Lars, 371
Trillhaas, Wolfgang, 10
Trotzig, Birgitta, 386
Tunström, Göran, 386
Tyberg, Anders, 207, 386

Uriah, 305

Vallquist, Gunnel, 180
Vander Goot, Henry, 32, 375, 378
Vennberg, Karl, 207

Wagndal, Per, 249
Wahlstrom, Eric H, 374
Waldenström, Paul Peter, 307
Wallin, Johan Olof, 231
Watson, Philip S, 385
Wedberg, Anders, 221, 222
Weibull, Lauritz, 179
Weijne, Josef, 47
Weinsheimer, Joel, 382
Werkström, Bertil, 4, 235, 378, 380
Wermlund, Sven, 128, 386
Wernant, Karin, 12
Westerberg, Anders, 173, 386
Westerståhl, Dag, 382
Wetterberg, Gunnar, 173
Wingren, Anders, 23, 68
Wingren, Anna Kedidjan, 11, 23, 68, 99, 369, 378–80
Wingren, Ellen, 299
Wingren, Engla Teresia (née Sundman) 19, 165, 298, 299
Wingren, Gustaf Fabian, 19, 20, 30, 48, 61, 211, 212, 298, 299
Wingren, Harry, 30
Wingren, Lage, 30
Wingren, Maj, 30
Wingren, Signhild (née Carlsson) 3, 12, 23, 24, 68, 97, 178, 179, 299
Wingren, Valborg, 30
Wirtén, Per, 368
Wittgenstein, Ludwig, 117, 118, 225, 227, 257, 316, 386
Wrede, Gösta, 381
Wright, Georg Henrik von, 227, 257–59, 287, 289, 386
Wolf-Knuts, Ulrika, 368

Yogi, Maharishi Mahesh, 183

Zedong, Mao, 273

www.ingramcontent.com/pod-product-compliance
Lightning Source LLC
Chambersburg PA
CBHW022227010526
44113CB00033B/515